IN THE MASTER'S EYE

In the Master's Eye

REPRESENTATIONS OF WOMEN, BLACKS, AND POOR WHITES IN ANTEBELLUM SOUTHERN LITERATURE

SUSAN J. TRACY

University of Massachusetts Press • Amherst

Copyright © 1995 by The University of Massachusetts Press
All rights reserved
LC 94-49536
ISBN 0-87023-968-6
Designed by Susan Bishop
Set in Poppl-Pontifex by Keystone Typesetting, Inc.
Printed and bound by Braun-Brumfield, Inc.

Library of Congress Cataloging-in-Publication Data
Tracy, Susan Jean, 1947–
In the master's eye : representations of women, Blacks, and poor
whites in antebellum Southern literature / Susan J. Tracy.
p.   cm.
Includes bibliographical references (p.   ) and index.
ISBN 0-87023-968-6
1. American literature—Southern States—History and criticism.
2. Literature and society—Southern States—History—19th century.
3. Women and literature—Southern States—History—19th century.
4. American literature—19th century—History and criticism.
5. American literature—Men authors—History and criticism.
6. Working class whites in literature. 7. Southern States—In literature.
8. Afro-Americans in literature. 9. Social classes in literature.
10. Patriarchy in literature. 11. Poor in literature. I. Title.
PS261.T73   1995
810.9'975—dc20   94-49536

British Library Cataloguing in Publication data are available.

Contents

Acknowledgments

THIS BOOK would not have been written without the encouragement and support of a number of people. Primary are those who kept me employed during the dismal decade of the eighties, when so many of my comrades were forced out of academia. My thanks to the members of the Schools of Social Sciences and Humanities and Arts at Hampshire College, and to the faculty in the Women's studies department at the University of Massachusetts, Amherst, for their continued support. My gratitude as well to Adele Simmons, former president, and Penina Glazer, former dean of faculty of Hampshire College. My gratitude extends to Joseph Duffey former chancellor at the University of Massachusetts, whose generosity and kindness I will always treasure.

The ideas in this book developed over more than a decade as I approached the study of gender, race, and class in American culture—first as a student and then as a professor. Listing those people who have had an intellectual influence on me hardly seems an adequate tribute, but it will have to suffice. Robert Stanfield, Mason Lowance, Sidney Kaplan, Milton Cantor, Leonard Richards, and Stephen B. Oates of the University of Massachusetts, Amherst, originally inspired my interest in American studies, the nineteenth century, and African American history; Paul Boyer and Henry Steele Commager sharpened my sense of history as an imaginative and critical discipline; Paul Worthman, Alexander Saxton, Gary Nash, and Temma Kaplan directed my initial studies in social, women's, and labor history and Marxist theory at the University of California at Los Angeles; Robert Padgug, Phillip Greven, Judith Walkowitz, Daniel Walkowitz, Tilden Edelstein, Paul Clemens, and the late Warren Susman of Rutgers University, trained me as a historian. Many of these people are recognized as distinguished scholars; they are also exceptional teachers whose enthusiasm and dedication to their students have been an inspiration.

Hampshire College has provided me with an extraordinary laboratory in which to test my ideas. The individualized curriculum for the students and team teaching for the faculty offered a particularly stimulating atmosphere in which to carry on research. Many thanks to those people I have taught with over the years whose own distinguished scholarship demanded I do my very best: Nancy Fitch, Joan Landes, L. Brown Kennedy, Reinhard Sander, Laurie Nisonoff, Robert Coles, and Miriam Slater. I thank as well those colleagues I have encountered at Hampshire and in the Five Colleges on whom I can always depend for a stimulating discussion or to whom I turn when I get stuck: Arlene Avakian, Amrita Basu, Joyce Berkman, Aaron Berman, Myrna Breitbart, Jules Chametzky, Margo Culley, Susan Douglas, Lee Edwards, Ann Ferguson, Leonard Glick, Alan Goodman, Lee Heller, Allen Kaufman, Bruce Laurie, Debra Martin, Cynthia Packard, Kathy Peiss, Mary Russo, David Smith, Doris Sommers, Carrie Mae Weems, and E. Frances White. Catherine Clinton of Harvard University has been most generous in her support of me and my work.

Clark Dougan and the University of Massachusetts Press should be commended for their willingness to take a chance on an unorthodox project. My sincere appreciation and gratitude to Milton Cantor who as a dear friend and colleague helped me edit a lengthy manuscript down to its bare bones. Over the last five years, I have joked with friends that my epitaph should read, "Done in by WordPerfect." Many thanks to those who have dragged this skeptic into the computer age and have bailed me out of major computer disasters: Liz Aaronsohn, Harriet Boyden, Mimi Katz, and Deborah Tomasi.

I get by with a lot of help from my friends and family. I would like to thank those friends who have never stinted in supplying love, laughter, and ice cream: Liz Aaronsohn, P. Roberts Bailey, Sarah Boy, Marcia Carlisle, Alice Dembner, Julia Demmin, Deborah Gaines, Pat Griffen, Mary Ann Jennings, Deirdre Scott, Eileen Stewart, Peggy Anderson and Andrea Wright, Merle Bruno and Peter Vincent, Dick Lipez and Joe Wheaton, Leslie Mason and David Kerr, Betty Mitchell and Mark Gerstein, Philip and Carol Rosen, Leighton Whitaker, the Common Womon Softball Team. I would like to recognize those people who have helped me get through this last and most difficult year: Douglas Anderson, Bev Cowdrick, Susan Craig, Katja Hahn D'Errico, James Gemmell, Mary Hocken, Janice Jorgenson, Ann Kearns, Ann Kerrey, Lisa Leukhardt, Hedy Lipez, Nancy and Tom Lowry, Judith Mann, Paula Murphy, Gregory and Toni Prince, Magdalia Rivera, and my Hospice bereavement group.

Just before I sent off this manuscript, I joked with my sister-in-law that whole families have been started and completed in the time it has taken me to finish this project. My love and gratitude to those families: my brother, Peter, and his wife, Phyllis, and their sons, Taylor and Christopher; my cousin Barry Kingston, his wife, Deborah, and their children, Nathaniel and Emily; and my best friends, Marie and Frederic Hartwell and their children, Jennifer, Adam, Toby, and Emily, who have helped me remember what was important during my trials in academe and who always help me chase the blues away.

To my sorrow, many family and friends who I would have like to read this book have died. This project might have been dedicated to any one of them. I remember first my parents, Carlton B. Tracy (1915–59) and Marjorie Mac-Naught Tracy (1919–65); my aunt, Dorothie Kingston (1925–76); my grandfather, Jay Tracy (1887–1976). Warren I. Susman (1927–85), a pioneer in cultural history, was an impassioned teacher and mentor whose lessons I take with me daily into the classroom and library. In January 1994, as this manuscript was being completed, my partner, Madilyn J. Engvall, died suddenly of brain cancer. Her steady calmness, patience, intellectual curiosity, and sense of humor sustained me and brightened my life. It will be difficult to go on without her.

Sidney Kaplan (1913–93), noted scholar in African American studies and my mentor and friend for more than twenty years, originally suggested this study. This book is dedicated to Sidney and Emma Kaplan. I have treasured their friendship and their example of political commitment and distinguished scholarship.

IN THE MASTER'S EYE

Introduction

IN CHOOSING to study the work of those Southern white males who have been credited with creating "Southern literature," I decided to concentrate on an elite group who expressed the worldview of the planter class at the moment when it took the offensive against antislavery Southerners and Northerners. My argument is simply that the proslavery argument concerns gender and class relations as well as race relations. Embedded in the proslavery argument are assumptions about the nature of women and non-planter-class males that shaped how social and political life evolved in the antebellum South. It isn't merely that these texts are sexist, racist, or class-biased, but the ways in which they codify these prejudices leads us to a clearer understanding of planter-class worldview.

I started where everyone starts who undertakes a study of Southern literature and culture, with Jay B. Hubbell's critical *The South in American Literature*; I then returned to Wilbur J. Cash's *The Mind of the South* and William Rogers Taylor's *Cavalier and Yankee*. Hubbell pointed the way to the authors I eventually chose: George Tucker, John Pendleton Kennedy, William Alexander Caruthers, Nathaniel Beverley Tucker, and William Gilmore Simms. Much later, Richard Beale Davis led me to James Ewell Heath, the only true liberal of the group.[1] Cash reminded me that regardless of what apologia I found in planter sources and those of their sympathizers, frontier violence and sadism lay just under the surface in the antebellum South. And Taylor confirmed my instinct that if I considered the images of women, blacks, and poor whites both in relation to the planter hero and in relation to each other, I would not only understand the proslavery argument in a new way; I would begin to understand why this literature is forgotten.

Although in the end, I would disagree with Vernon L. Parrington's assessment of William Gilmore Simms as a democrat and a realist ruined by aristocratic romanticism, his initial suggestion that the North had changed after 1812 while the South remained true to its eighteenth-century roots and his method of analyzing the political and economic foundations of literary production served as critical principles for my own thinking and practice.[2]

My primary theoretical assumption is that the lived material conditions under which people exist create social structure and social power, and that people in power institutionalize their ideas in a variety of ways. I found Karl Marx's following observation particularly applicable to the antebellum

1

South: "the ideas of the ruling class are in every epoch the ruling ideas: i.e., the class, which is the ruling material force of society, is at the same time its ruling intellectual force. . . . The ruling ideas are nothing more than the ideal expression of the dominant material relationships grasped as ideas; hence of the relationships which make the one class the ruling one, therefore the ideas of its dominance."[3] My reading of Antonio Gramsci led me to expect an alternate hegemony to the dominant one and my reading of Raymond Williams led me to expect that neither the material base nor the ideological superstructure was rigid and fixed, but rather fluid and contradictory.[4] Although I thought I would start with Marx's premise and assume that the Southern ruling class functioned in the way that Marx described, I expected that the evidence I would uncover about the authors' lives and about Southern society would lead me to rethink his proposition along the lines that Williams had suggested. Because I was studying literature, I expected these authors to engage with the complexity and contradiction in the human condition. Similarly, and perhaps a bit naively, I speculated that some yeomen would emerge as heroes in the new democracy, that there would be portraits of rebellious and free blacks as minor but significant characters, and that I would find a range of female characters in a variety of relationships with one another. What I didn't expect was that Marx's thesis would hold and the historical romance as a man's story would dominate the literature, thus precluding substantial descriptions of the plantation household or daily plantation life.

Since I started this study, a diverse group of scholars has created "cultural studies," an interdisciplinary and multicultural field that describes not only *what* ideas and images are produced in a given society by a given group, but explores *how* and *why* they are produced. Because this particular interdisciplinary study moves within the fields of social, political, and intellectual history as well as women's, African American, and labor history, it should be understood as part of this new endeavor.[5] I think of it as a Marxist feminist project that follows Lucien Goldmann's injunction to consider the parts of a literary text in relation to the whole.[6] The questions discussed in Part I are concerned with the economic, social, and political setting of these novels; the relation of these authors to the planter class; and the material and intellectual setting in which these novels were produced. Parts II through IV deal with the fictional world created by these authors. My discussion of George Tucker and James Ewell Heath in Chapter 4 argues that one can discern a range of opinion on slavery until 1831–32, when in the wake of the Nat Turner rebellion and the Virginia Slave debates the planter class began its policy of crushing antislavery opinion in the South. In Parts II through IV, I break with customary literary practice by decentering the authors and their texts and examining directly the images of women, blacks, and poor whites. This approach has the distinct advantage of revealing the similarities among these authors in spite of their seeming political differences as they create and re-create certain types of characters in their fiction. It allows the reader to ascertain the social vision that permeates this fiction. The primary disadvantage of this approach is that it also decenters the reader accustomed to approaching literary analysis author by author and text by text. The reader's momentary discomfort, I hope, will be assuaged by a convincing argument.

In discussing the images of women, blacks, and poor whites in this literature, I relied heavily on the Southern social history and literary criticism being published literally between the chapter drafts of this manuscript. Still, there are some social historians whose work proved critical for this study. Anne Firor Scott and Catherine Clinton provided valuable studies that enhanced my understanding of plantation mistresses; Robert Shallhope, Angela Davis, John Blassingame, George Rawick, Herbert Gutman, Lawrence Levine, Bertram Wyatt-Brown, Deborah Gray White, and Sterling Stuckey provided the critical information on planter violence, slave culture, and the slave's experience of slavery, so I could reliably critique the representations of plantation people in this literature.[7] Although the study of nonplantation whites continues to need contemporary revisionist scholarship, Steven Hahn was generous in sharing early chapters of his admirable dissertation, which later emerged as the award-winning *The Roots of Southern Populism.* And James Oakes's controversial *The Ruling Race* provided a critique of my initial position that allowed me to tighten my analysis. Finally, although I disagree with Eugene Genovese's construction of the master-slave relationship, I have been influenced by his early argument that a society with precapitalist labor relations and without fundamental capitalist institutions is not a capitalist society. I amend that proposition to make a distinction between mercantile capitalism and industrial capitalism, but his initial formulation helped me to understand the political economy of the antebellum South.[8]

Although I have now read widely in literary theory and criticism during what will surely be remembered as one of the more confusing decades of literary discourse, in the end only a handful of studies influenced my thinking. In the beginning, there was Simone de Beauvoir. She showed me before Sander Gilman how within Western patriarchal literary convention men created themselves in poetry, novels, and drama as Subject through their creation of "woman" as the Other against whom they measured their "humanness." I surmised that that principle of projection might be applicable to the planter creation of blacks and poor whites as well as women.[9] Other feminists who influenced my analysis were Sheila Rowbotham, Adrienne Rich, and Cynthia Griffen Wolff, who in a critical essay pointed to the inherent sexism in the literary construction of the romantic hero and heroine.[10]

Although Jean Fagan Yellin and William R. Taylor had taken up the authors I consider in this study, Yellin concentrated on the authors' biographies and their images of African Americans and Taylor argued mistakenly that the plantation was a "matriarchy."[11] Prior to the 1970s, previous analyses of images of African Americans were encyclopedic treatments like Sterling Brown's *The Negro in American Fiction,* which only skimmed the texts I was considering. With the exception of Minrose Gwin's fine analysis and an early chapter of Hazel Carby's 1987 study, many of the most intriguing literary analyses of African Americans and women in the mid-1970s and 1980s have been those that have resurrected and analyzed the work of black and women writers and that argue for an African American and women's literary tradition.[12] Much of this criticism treats texts written after the Civil War and assumes a capitalist base for literary production. Finally, with a couple of exceptions, it seems few scholars since the 1930s have been interested in the issues of class in Southern literature except those people interested in the Southern humorists.[13] In the end, I leapt from the base which the forementioned scholars provided.

From the comments I have received on this manuscript, I should make a statement about what this manuscript is not. It doesn't treat the nostalgic mythmaking of post–Civil War authors like Thomas Nelson Page or Thomas R. Dixon. Although recent studies on the sentimental novelists of the 1850s suggested E.D.E.N. Southworth and Carolyn Lee Hentz as possible subjects, I decided that these and other Southern women novelists of the period deserved a volume in itself, one that would necessarily incorporate several chapters on the Southern response to Harriet Beecher Stowe's *Uncle Tom's Cabin.*[14] Similarly, I was persuaded that my concern with the African American literary response to slavery should be treated in another volume. Instead, I have concentrated on the leading Southern authors who had as their primary concern furthering the antebellum proslavery argument and who developed the first stereotypes of the plantation.

When one considers the literacy rate in the South, the size of the reading public, and the class alliances and politics of the authors themselves in conjunction with the form and content of their work, one reaches two conclusions. First, with the exception of James Ewell Heath who paid the price of intellectual oblivion for his liberalism, this literature was intended to be and succeeded as a proslavery literature that did not speak to post–Civil War Americans except as nostalgia; second, it demonstrates that the proslavery argument was as much about gender and class as it was about race relations.

When I started this study, I knew I was going to reverse William Rogers Taylor's proposition. Instead of centering on the white, male hero in his Southern manifestation, the "Cavalier"–an idealization of the historical planter–I decided to focus on the female, black, and poor white characters as a way of decoding exactly how these authors created planter heroes who realized their heroism through domination and defeat of the Other. In order for the "hero" to emerge as "moral man," a woman, always of his race and class, must be victimized and rescued by him in his symbolic defeat of an "inferior" man. I have concluded that the romantic heroic mode is the most reactionary form in our literary tradition and reinforces the most conservative and antidemocratic gender, race, and class impulses. Said another way, there is only room for one hero in the romance. Although momentary short-term gain may be realized in having the avenging hero be a woman, a person of color, or a working-class person, the fact that someone is victimized and someone else is symbolically defeated means there have been role reversals, but no real challenge to the conservative legitimation of violence to restore "law and order."

While the antebellum Southern fiction considered in this study may be considered "a literature" because of its thematic integrity and its shared vision of a Southern past and present, there is not a single novel that does justice to the complexity of the human spirit. Instead, the historical romance in the hands of these authors, especially Simms, has the staying power of a "thriller." Because they offer caricatures of human beings and are virtually interchangeable with one another the specifics of each novel can be forgotten quite easily. Each character in these novels has a "place" based on his or her gender, race, and class, and with one or two exceptions, the characters act within the prescribed boundaries for their respective stations in life. While this literature shares some of the characteristics of popular fiction, then, the authors' unbridled hostility to the hopes and dreams of average people precludes their work from being acceptable to the middle-class reader. Every line and every scene in this literature was written to assure the reader of the natural superiority of men to women, of whites to blacks and Native Americans, and of the planter class to all other classes. These novels are more valuable then as the cultural artifacts of a defeated planter class than as works of art. They stand as a testament to the failure of an earlier conservatism and dramatically demonstrate the inherent weakness of the elitist fallacies upon which conservatism is based.

I

THE ANTEBELLUM SOUTH AND THE PRODUCTION OF SOUTHERN LITERATURE

INGLEHARDT looked at Bertha. His purpose was to compel her in terrors especial. She stood with clasped hands, in an indescribable torture, incapable of speech. Her eyes were vacant, glassy, fixed, yet intelligible. She gave no other sign. . . .

The features and movement of Travis, looks and gestures, on the instant seemed to undergo a sudden change. His form was bent forward, as if crouching and creeping up. The movement was stealthy, like that of a cat. His braceleted hands were lifted up before his breast, and slightly thrust forward. The fists were doubled. There was a mixture of ferocity and cunning in his eyes, as he approached, which suddenly arrested the attention of Inglehardt. At that moment a pistol-shot was heard without. Both Inglehardt and the Trailer started, the former catching up his sword. . . .

That momentary withdrawal of his eye lost him the natural influence with which he might have controlled the growing insanity of his captive. In that one moment, Travis—his soul freed from its master—made a single, tiger-like bound—threw down the table between them—threw himself directly, fully, fairly, upon Inglehardt—and the two went down together to the floor, crushing the chair beneath them, and shaking the very house in their fall.

The cut and thrust of Inglehardt, meanwhile passed clean through the body of his assailant—passed through a vital region—inflicting a mortal wound, which left him but a few moments of life. . . .

Henry Travis soon found himself in the grasp of Willie Sinclair—safe—while in a moment after, the Trailer went down lifeless beneath a single stroke from the powerful claymore of the dragoon.

A few moments sufficed for the rescue of Bertha. She was borne way by her lover from the horrid spectacle. . . .

—William Gilmore Simms, *Eutaw*

1. The Antebellum South

THE EPIGRAPH introducing this section offers the standard climax for an antebellum Southern historical romance; namely, the planter-class hero's daring rescue of the passive and virginal planter-class heroine from the rapacious grasp of a middle-class or poor-white villain. The historical romance was the form Southern writers adapted from Samuel Richardson's sentimental novel and from Sir Walter Scott's historical novel. Southern writers borrowed from and modified each of these forms to create in the Southern historical romance a hybrid form of the new genre, one that envisioned the men of the planter class engaged during the American War of Independence in a heroic world-historical struggle for their race, class, section, and country.

The melodramatic scene takes on new meaning when one realizes that "Travis" is a nouveau riche planter whose daughter, Bertha, and son, Henry, have been held captive by the son of Travis's former overseer, Richard Inglehardt, a Tory. "The Trailer" was one of the poor white men in Inglehardt's gang of criminals who guarded Henry. In rescuing the heroine and defeating the enemies of his class and country, William Sinclair, the son of an established South Carolinian family and a patriot officer, establishes at once his gender, class, and national superiority.

In its most self-conscious and highly developed form—realized most consistently in the work of William Gilmore Simms—the antebellum historical romance operates on at least two levels in depicting a particular conservative vision of Southern society and in offering a Southern nationalist interpretation of the American Revolution. It not only salutes the triumph of the United States in the American Revolution and glorifies the Southern role in that victory, but argues for a postwar society in which the "naturally superior" leaders of that heroic victory—the members of the planter class—will govern.

The period from 1828 to 1832 marked a turning point in Southern history and culture as the nullification controversy, the Nat Turner rebellion, and the ensuing Virginia Slave debates coupled with an organized Northern antislavery movement forced members of the planter elite to defend their "peculiar institution." Increasingly, in political speeches, editorials, newspaper articles, pamphlets, court decisions, Sunday sermons, and novels, members of the planter class and their intellectuals articulated a worldview

9

that justified their gender, racial, and class domination of Southern society and linked their rule to the progress of "Western Civilization." In articulating the worldview of the planter class, especially after 1831–32, a small group of antebellum Southern writers not only increasingly isolated themselves from their fellow Northern authors, but created a proslavery literature that now seems as anachronistic as the planter class in whose defense it was written. This study examines the work of six antebellum Southern writers and traces a shift in their work from George Tucker's and James Ewell Heath's work of the 1820s to a militantly conservative defense of slavery in the proslavery fiction of William Alexander Caruthers, John Pendleton Kennedy, Nathaniel Beverley Tucker, and William Gilmore Simms.

The Southern planter class stood atop a highly stratified society, one in which land and slaves were understood to be the basis of social status and wealth. In round figures, of twelve million people in the South, roughly eight million were white, four million were black slaves, and 250,000 were free blacks. Of the white population, roughly 46,000 (less than 5 percent) owned twenty slaves or more and were designated "planters," a "middle-size" plantation having one thousand to fifteen hundred acres.[1] Three-fourths of the white Southern population didn't own slaves, while the "typical slaveholder" owned five slaves or fewer and lived on a farm of two hundred acres or less.[2] These small slaveholders often had supplementary occupations as artisans and tradesmen, businessmen, merchants, civil servants, doctors, lawyers, teachers, and other professionals. James Oakes has noted that the "typical" slaveholder didn't own the "typical" slave who was found on the large plantations.[3] Being a slaveholder, however, had an enormous impact on a man's vision of himself and his relation to his community. One historian has argued that a man who owned "two slaves and nothing else was as rich as the average man in the North," and "the average slaveowner was more than five times as rich as the nonslaveholding Southern farmer."[4] The percentage of white families owning slaves also differed as one traveled through different parts of the South. For instance, in South Carolina and Mississippi 50 percent of the white families owned slaves; in Alabama, Louisiana, and Florida the figure was 33 percent; and in Virginia, North Carolina, Kentucky, Tennessee, and Texas, it was 25 percent. Although in some counties of the "black belt" (Alabama, Georgia, Mississippi, and Louisiana) one of every two people was a slave, slaveholders moved in and out of the slaveholding class, often hiring out the slaves of their neighbors at harvest time.[5]

Most scholars agree now that the antebellum period witnessed the shift of Northern society from a traditional, deferential, pre-industrialist society to a more democratic, capitalist society with its corresponding development of middle-class liberalism as the dominant ideology.[6] In the South, given the new value of cotton due to the invention of the cotton gin, Southern planters, the sons and grandsons of the revolutionaries, shifted from arguing that slavery was a "necessary evil" to asserting it was a "positive good." Additionally, until the Civil War, this generation of Southern planters successfully resisted attempts from inside and outside the South to industrialize on a large-scale basis. Instead, they clung tenaciously to their slavery-based economy with its paradoxical notion of a "free" society based on traditional patriarchal relationships that institutionalized those distinctions between alleged "natural superiors" and "natural inferiors."

By the mid-nineteenth century, the history of the South had become the history of the interaction among men and women of three races; that is, the story of European expropriation of Native American land and of land development under British institutions, most notably the institution of slavery. Because this antebellum literature seeks to convince the reader that Southern society was orderly and "civilized" and to justify and explain Southern political economy, society, and culture, it is important to form a sense of which European institutions were transported to the New World and how they were transformed. Even if one could ignore the fact that proslavery writers often described slavery as a "patriarchal" or "domestic" institution, the contributions of scholars like Catherine Clinton make it necessary for the serious student of Southern history and culture to understand both the reality of the social relations within the white patriarchal family and planters' ideas about their families.[7]

The eighteenth century witnessed a major political-economic revolution in the West. The free-market economy advocated by Adam Smith and the French physiocrats replaced mercantile capitalism as the dominant Western economy. Nationalistic democratic revolutions defeated monarchy and installed republics first in the United States and France and then in other countries. While the aristocracy was decisively overthrown in France, persistent colonial ruling elites continued to hold power in the United States. They justified their dominance by appealing to pre-industrial concepts of society. Even though the North would shed this social vision in a generation, the Southern planter class continued to appeal to the vision of a stable and harmonious society, based on government by traditional elites. As one historian of the period has noted, the Federalists, who argued for the Constitution in the wake of the Daniel Shays–inspired uprisings, thought that "men could rise, but only within the social roles in which they were born. Their aim in life must be to learn to perform their inherited position with 'industry, economy, and good conduct.' "[8] In the new republic, freedom would be based on property ownership. True Lockeans, they believed that labor converted nature to property, and industry and frugality converted property to wealth. The ideal virtuous republican citizen, then, was an energetic, rational, self-controlled public spirited man who cared for his dependents and business and participated in local and state government. Government in the new republic was entrusted to the best man, not just to anyone who could win election. Although they recognized the danger of amassing large fortunes, they presumed their virtue and piety would protect them from the temptations of wealth: avarice, licentiousness, and corruption.[9]

Implicit in this vision of the virtuous citizen was a shared understanding of patriarchy. The patriarchal family—that which "protected" women, children, apprentices, servants, and slaves—was understood as the bedrock of society. The head of the household, the patriarchal "master," was invested with gender, generational, and class power as he represented his household in the public sphere. Women, as Mary Beth Norton and Linda Kerber have noted, were expected to find fulfillment as "republican mothers." That is, they were supposed to raise children, especially sons, to be industrious providers and virtuous citizens. Because of their temperament and primary loyalty to the family, women were supposed "naturally" to shun the rough and violent world of politics. In times of crisis, like the Revolution, they might emerge from their private households to organize product boycotts or knit socks for the troops or even to petition Congress for a redress of grievances, but they of course could not vote or, worse, stand for political office.

Kerber and Norton note the fear with which eighteenth- and early nineteenth-century men greeted the specter of political women who "might tend to destroy these degrees of subordination which nature seemed to point out." One periodical intoned, "however flattering the path of glory and ambition may be, a woman will have more commendation in being the mother of heroes, than setting up, Amazon-like, for a heroine herself."[10] Societal chaos would result were women to be political. Neither was it insignificant that when republican men, like John Adams, wanted to describe the moral failings of aristocracy or the "rabble," they argued that they were irrational and controlled by habits of vice: "vicious and luxurious and *effeminate* Appetites, Passions, and Habits" (my emphasis).[11] Dominating their fears, at one end of the spectrum stood the intellectual Amazon, the woman who competed with men in the classroom, in the marketplace, and in the political arena, allegedly against her nature and to the detriment of her family. At the other were the promiscuous aristocratic women who engaged in "liaisons" and the common prostitute, a woman without self-control or self-respect.

Similarly, in the wake of the Daniel Shays rebellions, Federalists North and South wanted to check the leveling tendencies of the Revolution. They created the idea of the "natural aristocracy," men who through their education, experience, and wealth were recognized by their communities as outstanding citizens, the natural leaders of society. As Gordon Wood has so ably argued, the political battle between the Federalists and Antifederalists was a disagreement about class rule and the promise of democracy. He notes that the Antifederalists essentially pitted themselves against that vision of the organic, deferential society that the Northern and Southern ruling elites promulgated as fostering harmony and order in society. Federalists like Robert Livingston of New York charged that the Antifederalists were debtors, schemers, and undereducated demagogues who were subverting societal order; they were the "licentious," while the natural aristocracy of the Federalist cause were "the worthy."[12]

In the 1830s when the antebellum Southern planter class sought to defend slavery, they turned to the social and political vision of this earlier period. Significantly, they used the patriarchal metaphor as the cornerstone of their defense of white supremacy and slavery. For instance, although he thought that slavery was economically inefficient, George Tucker noted that "on a well regulated estate," a slave is modestly disciplined and well cared for, like "a member of a sort of patriarchal family."[13] In considering the social relations and political rights among the members of the society, Tucker again turns to the patriarchal family to delineate the social order. In order to "best promote the public welfare and safety," he argues the heads of households should have the most liberty, followed by "a less portion to the females—and still less to the children—and the least of all (only perhaps, the protection of life) to the slave."[14] What Tucker is describing here is the hierarchal patriarchal family in which the male as husband and father is held accountable for the support and protection of his subordinates, who defer to his authority. In fact, under the practice of "coverture," until the mid-nineteenth century married women were subsumed into the patriarchal family under the authority of their husbands and were presumed to have "neither independent minds nor independent power."[15] In this context, then, rape was an injury to the father's interest in his daughter as "servant" and as vehicle to wealth through marriage. Rape was not a crime against a woman as an individual. While the male has value in himself, an "individual" with civil rights as a property-owner and citizen, women are only valuable in their social relations within the family. They are not "individuals" in any social, legal, or political sense of the term. It was not difficult then for planter-class males to argue that their slaves, allegedly members of the planter-class family, were similarly legally or politically dependent.

Perhaps George Fitzhugh is the most forthright in this regard. In making a case for both the superiority of a society based on slavery and against the claims of liberal Northern values, Fitzhugh argues that even women and children are essentially slaves due to their dependent natures and their natural incapacity for self-government. He argues: "It is contrary to all human customs and legal analogies that those who are dependent, or are likely to become so, should not be controlled. The duty of protecting the weak involves the necessity of enslaving them—hence, in all countries women and children, wards and apprentices, have been essentially slaves, controlled, not by law, but by the will of a superior."[16] On the Southern plantation, he argues, unlike in Northern capitalist society, Christian morality pervades the family so that "in the various familial relations of husband, wife, parent, child, master and slave, the observance of these Christian precepts is often practiced, and almost always promotes the temporal well being of those who observe it" (124). Fitzhugh argues that unlike the capitalist system, which alienates laborers from their work and turns the worker against his superior, the familial nature of the Christian plantation family promotes kindness, harmony, and order as long as irrational inferiors don't challenge the authority of the master. The selling of slave children, the rape of their mothers, and domestic violence within the plantation household are denied by Fitzhugh and others who seek in the patriarchal family, as did their eighteenth-century forebears, a metaphor for their authority and domination.

Of the authors considered in this study, George Tucker, Nathaniel Beverley Tucker, and William Gilmore Simms produced political essays on Southern society and slavery that supported the narratives they spun in their fiction. For instance, in describing the character of men and women, N. B. Tucker urges us

> to observe the multiplied diversities between the male and the female character, contrived with a view to the happiness and to the moral and intellectual excellence of both. Is it by chance, or by any necessary consequence of his sex, that *man* is bold, hardy, enterprising, contentious, delighting to struggle with difficulty, delighting in contests with his fellows, and eager to bear away the prize of every strife? Woman, on the contrary, timid, feeble, helpless, shrinks within the domestic sanctuary, and feels the great want of her nature is security for herself and her offspring.[17]

Like his conservative antecedents, Tucker thinks these differences between men and women are a result of God's plan of nature and are embedded in natural law.

Similarly, William Gilmore Simms assails women's claims to equal education and political rights with men simply because they are in the majority of the population. He assails government by majorities as government by "brute force," and inimical to freedom.[18] Significantly, the discussion of women's incapacity for independence and self-government appeared in essays these men wrote defending slavery. Simms was taking on Harriet Martineau, "a woman of the bold, free, masculine nature . . . impatient of the restraints of her sex, and compelled to seek her distinction in fields which women are rarely permitted to penetrate" (247). His essay was intended not only to defend the master-slave relation, but to put the intellectual and democratic Miss Martineau in her place. Just as the second part of N. B. Tucker's essays posits the superiority of slave labor to "free" labor for the society as a whole, Simms's essay makes a case for white supremacy in defeating Native Americans and enslaving Africans. Together these essays make a case for male supremacy, white superiority, and planter-class rule.[19]

Since the Southeastern tribes played a critical role in Southern social and political life until they were forcibly removed by federal government edict in the 1830s, Simms's discussion of Native Americans is not merely philosophical posturing. The existence of a viable Native American population, not only on the frontier, but within the Southern states as an assimilated and slaveholding population, posed grave social, economic, and political problems for elite and poorer Southerners alike. The achievements of the Cherokee especially belied the white contention that Native Americans were incapable of civilization.[20]

Simms added his voice to the national cry for expropriation of the land of Native American and for their extermination or removal to the Far West. Again, Simms turns to patriarchal metaphors to explain the nature both of the Native American and of the slave. He notes: "Savages are children in all but physical respects . . . you must teach them obedience. They must be made to know, at the outset, that they know nothing, and they must implicitly defer to the superior."[21] Again echoing Locke, the great failure of the Native American according to Simms is that he allegedly refused to labor and so was indistinguishable from "the hog which burrows along its borders" looking for food. "He must first *labor,*" intones Simms, "this is the destiny from which he is forever seeking to escape" (261). Simms further argues that had he, like the "savage" African, been brought to civilization through slavery, he would have proved the Africans' superior.

Simms, like other antebellum Americans, refused to recognize Native American assimilation (as occurred among the Cherokees) and then seems puzzled and saddened by Native Americans' apparent refusal to assimilate. Rejecting civilization, he argues, Native Americans are resisting progress. If they succumbed to "the full control of an already civilized people" like the Hebrews and Saxons before them, over time they would become civilized. Given Native American resistance to civilization, however, civilized men have only limited options: removal or genocide.[22]

What emerges from both Simms's and N. B. Tucker's essays, then, is a defense of slavery as a method of bringing uncivilized Africans to civilization in allegedly the gentlest way possible, through patriarchal government. The "civilized"/"uncivilized" dichotomy is ever present in their work. Civilized man is self-controlled, industrious, God-fearing, and respectful toward women, as witnessed in the institution of patriarchal Christian marriage. While the uncivilized man isn't licentious and corrupt in the manner of the European aristocracy, who have slipped into a state of dissipation, he has never known civilization. Simms describes the "free" African as irrational, improvident, and incapable of self-government. "A wandering savage," like the Native American, he allegedly refuses to labor. According to Simms, Africans brought to civilization through slavery live under conditions "which make the American slave so superior an animal to the African freemen."[23]

Similarly, Nathaniel Beverley Tucker notes that the white man found the African "a *naked* savage, prone to the unrestrained indulgence of sensual appetite," unclean, and a born thief and liar.[24] Tucker argues, however, that after two centuries of slavery, under patriarchal control that balances attention and benevolence with discipline and control, "the great body of slaves have become more attached, more content with their condition, less licentious and more honest" (337). Most significant, the master-slave relationship unlike that of capitalist and wageworker transcends a mere cash value. Instead, its character encourages mutual devotion, enduring familial connection, and reciprocal duties and responsibilities (338 and 339).

Lest we argue that enslavement of another is an act of aggression, Simms assures us in "The Morals of Slavery" that "it is his mental and moral inferiority which has enslaved, or subjected him to a superior" (269). Only when African Americans demonstrate they have improved morally and intellectually can they be free. But Simms doesn't expect that ever to happen. He notes that as the Anglo-Saxon seems to have his mission to conquer the continent and bring Native Americans and Africans to civilization the best he can, "the African seems to have his mission," as well: "He does *not* disappear" like the Native American, "but he still remains a slave or a savage!" Simms notes somewhat ruefully, "I do not believe that he ever will be other than a slave, or that he was made otherwise; but that he is designed as an implement in the hands of civilization always," as the lowest class of laborer and as a reminder to whites of their superiority and hence responsibility to an inferior race (270–72).

All of the authors except Heath argue that African American chattel slavery is essentially "patriarchal" in character. The slave, even adult men and women, are envisioned as children. For instance, Nathaniel Beverley Tucker notes that the same God who "blackened the Negro's skin and wisped his hair into wool" arranged for white Europeans to bring him to civilization in a particular patriarchal institution in which "the master's reciprocal feeling of parental attachment to his humble dependent" is reflected in the slave's loyal devotion to the master and his family.[25] That both blacks and whites accept the essence of this relationship as familial, Tucker argues, is reflected in their use of "my" to describe their relations. "My slave, Scipio" and "my mistress," Tucker contends, "is a term of endearment" not possession and servitude.[26]

In using the patriarchal family as their model for African American chattel slavery, proslavery Southerners like Simms and Tucker appealed to Northerners' own sense of their patriarchal rights and responsibilities. The oppression of women and children within the patriarchal family emerged as an accepted pre-industrial model for slavery and provided the planter class with moral justification for their oppression of African Americans. Although women and blacks were joined through planter sexism and racism under the government of one master, their different and unequal social relations of production and reproduction belied that planter misconception. In reality, paternalism masked the brute force that white male planters exerted unequally over women, blacks, and poor whites. While there is considerable evidence that the majority of white women accepted the inevitability of their bondage to white men of their class through racial, class, and psychological imperatives, the evidence of total African American submission to planter paternalism derives mainly from planter sources and thus must be viewed with suspicion.

The location of plantation mistresses within the institution of marriage and blacks within the institution of slavery provided the planter and his intellectual allies with the material basis for their justification of these groups' subordination to the planter. Seen in this light, "paternalism" is at once a code of manners and a prescribed set of behaviors that explicitly denies, but implicitly recognizes, the patriarch's right to violence toward his "dependents." Additionally, paternalism was a set of ideas articulated by the antebellum planter class and its intellectual allies to explain and justify their social relations of production and reproduction. Paternalism blunts the sharp edge of patriarchal oppression and lets the master feel morally justified in his oppression of his dependents. In fact, as a young man he is socialized to assume these social relations as a "sacred duty." The point of paternalism is to ensure that neither the master nor his dependents perceive these relationships as oppressive. The patriarch's inherent power remains hidden until his authority is questioned and then the full weight of his wrath crashes down on the offending party.[27]

In contrast, planter relations with poor whites were very different. Because the poor white male implicitly shared the planter's racial and gender power, planters had a more difficult time rationalizing their domination of him. Thus, on some level the poor white male was more threatening to the planter male than women and blacks, contained as they were on the plantation. Before and after the Revolution, poor and yeoman Southern white men had fashioned their own understanding of what it meant to be "free." Paradoxically, as Edmund Morgan has noted, it was based on the existence of slavery. A freeman was someone who didn't work for any other man. He set his own daily work rhythms, "free" from the scrutiny of the artisanal master, the planter, or later, the factory boss. When he married, supported his children, and cleared a small tract of land for them to subsist on, he demonstrated that critical self-mastery which made him eligible to claim his civil rights as a "citizen."[28]

It is highly significant that the planter class's assault on African-Americans took the form of a persistent and concerted attack on the traditional power and authority of the black male by denying him his "patriarchal rights." In denying the black male the right to protect his woman from rape and abuse, his right to live with and raise his children, and his right to his own labor, the members of the planter class sought to crush his will and to dominate his spirit. The attempted "emasculation" of the black male in slavery ritualistically played out the "cult of masculinity" as white males visited on black males their own worst fears.

In the plantation South, the black male thus prevented from assuming his adult role was designated a nonadult; that is, a childlike dependent, by members of the planter class. It should not be surprising, then, that the very class which effected such violence should describe their two chief victims, the black man and black woman, as "childlike" and "promiscuous" respectively. Fortunately, contemporary social historians have uncovered evidence which indicates that planters were largely unsuccessful in their goal of infantilizing African Americans. Black men and women formed viable communities that managed to shield the majority of their members from the worst forms of psychological abuse the planter class meted out, even if they couldn't protect them physically from planter violence.[29] In a continuing motif in Southern history, all classes of white males had a stake in planter control of black men. While poor and yeoman farmers might scoff at planter pretensions to superiority over them, they accepted completely the tenets of white supremacy promulgated to defend slavery.

Since many of these novels are set during the American Revolution, ideal masculinity celebrates conservative, martial virtues. The patriot planter is a proud and courageous soldier who exhibits intelligence, poise, and grace under fire, which distinguish him as a leader of men. He displays a noticeable absence of blood lust and even at times betrays some compassion for his enemy, especially those who are officers and therefore gentlemen. He is morally superior to his troops whose vicious passions he must restrain. He is obedient to the lawful commands of his superior officers; yet he is resourceful and ingenious in finding his own way if circumstances thwart the original plans. His primary mission in taking up arms is to defend his family, country, and honor. He is genial and articulate and can converse easily with his superiors and inferiors. In his relationship with women, he is polite, but not obsequious; self-confident, but not egotistical; attentive, but not vulgar. Like a medieval knight, he would risk his life to save a lady's life and honor. The fictional planter is gregarious, hospitable, charming, thoughtful, intelligent, and self-disciplined. Written as it is by nineteenth-century Southerners, this literature engages in a kind of ancestor worship suggesting that although the prototypical "gentleman" has passed from the scene, his heirs live on as masters of the great plantations. Although both the lives of William Gilmore Simms and his friend James Henry Hammond would seem to belie this contention, these men saw themselves as "natural aristocrats" who rose by their own merit and recognized superiority. As will become apparent, this myth is especially serviceable in establishing and maintaining the class position of planters.

Not surprisingly, these authors are noticeably silent about planter sexuality within or outside marriage, between whites, between blacks, and between whites and blacks. There are a number of low life characters who have suspicious parentage and there are five "fallen women" in the literature. But any discussion of male sexuality or male lust is represented as loss of self-control and is thus depicted as being more characteristic of poor whites than of planters. Interestingly, the post–Civil War stereotype of black men as uncontrollably lustful notwithstanding, most black men are portrayed in this literature as asexual family retainers and servants who barely have family relationships, much less sexual or love relationships with women of either race. So if the social historians are correct, and Southern men boasted to one another of their sexual prowess, that was one aspect of Southern male culture that didn't make its way into this literature.[30]

This proslavery literature leaves no doubt that the intent of planter paternalism was to control women and blacks, convince them to submit to planter authority, and to unite them with him against allegedly degenerate poor-white males. At the same time, it encouraged the planter to assume his allegedly God-given place as their "natural" patriarchal master. In the antebellum historical romance, which was the dominant form in this literature, we always come back to the same triptych: the helpless planter-class heroine flanked on one side by her would-be poor-white or middle-class seducer, and on the other side by the planter hero, who, assisted by his faithful black servant, is about to free her from her abductor and claim her as his wife.

Bertha Travis, Richard Inglehardt, and William Sinclair portrayed in the introductory epigraph to this part are not merely any characters in a novel. They are the cultural symbols that embody the ideals, fantasies, and values of the white males of the Southern ruling class, who sought to extend their hegemony into all aspect of social experience, including the area of cultural production.

2. The Production of Southern Literature

SOUTHERN antebellum writers faced enormous obstacles in their attempt to create a Southern literature. Like most of American society, the South was dedicated to materialism, but realized it in the production of cotton based on slave labor. The yeoman class and wealthy slaveholders who might have supported the arts instead directed their activities toward maximizing cotton production and profits. Similarly, they directed their intellectual energy toward reading articles and books about plantation management, agricultural improvements, and politics. As a consequence, the South failed to develop and foster those institutions critical to the education and intellectual development of the yeoman classes and the poor.[1]

INSTITUTIONS OF INTELLECTUAL PRODUCTION

During the antebellum period, the publishing base in the United States shifted from Philadelphia and Boston to New York. By 1840, New York was already the country's largest port city blessed with an extensive river network providing an efficient and economical conduit to the West. Such geographical advantage would make New York the country's mercantile and cultural center by 1860, a position it held until well into the twentieth century. Geography was the first obstacle that Southerners had to surmount.

Certainly the critical factor in selling books is connecting with readers. Again, Southern writers were extremely handicapped compared with Northern writers. Planters and poor whites collaborated in refusing to support a public school system in the South, thus ensuring that large numbers of the poor white and yeoman-class populations would remain illiterate.[2] In 1850, *DeBow's Review* reported the Southern illiteracy rate as 20 percent compared with 3 percent for the Middle States, and .42 percent for New England.[3] Additionally, Southern colleges failed to uphold even the most minimal standards, so they seemed more like elite high schools designed to discipline rowdy students than bastions of scholarly reflection and achievement.[4] With the possible exception of New Orleans, Richmond, and Charleston, Southern cities failed to provide the large and diverse population that has traditionally supported a variety of cultural institutions.

An obstacle that Southern authors shared with all American writers was the disorganization of the publishing houses themselves. The processes of soliciting and editing manuscripts, preparing them for the printer, printing them, and distributing them, was chaotic by today's standards. Communications and transportation within cities as well as between cities and towns were so primitive that there were long delays in the publishing process and manuscripts were easily lost and damaged. Additionally, there were many different kinds of business relationships that authors and publishers established with one another.

In one common kind of arrangement, the author paid for the stereotype plates and retained ownership of them, leasing them to the publisher for a period of time for a high royalty.[5] The problem with this method was that no one made any money until the costs of production were covered. Popular authors like Cooper and Irving were able to work out an arrangement with Matthew Carey of Carey and Lea in Philadelphia, who bought the rights to their work and sold it over a period of years. The authors were paid whether their work sold or not; or sometimes they worked out a simple royalty agreement. However, these kinds of arrangements were made only with the best-selling authors—none of them Southerners.[6]

Finding the market for literature was as elusive in the nineteenth century as it is today. Publishers like Carey would try to pinpoint where books were read and set up distribution outlets there. Sometimes he would take mail-order subscriptions before he printed texts. Publishers like Carey and the Harper brothers relied on "jobbers," men who traveled to the small towns and hamlets selling books. Obviously, they would concentrate on those communities where they had had success. Again, the South was at an extreme disadvantage since it offered few cities, a small reading public, and overwhelming geographical barriers for jobbers to contend with. Finding a Southern audience proved to be the most difficult task for these writers.[7]

One of the primary problems for the authors interested in developing an American literature was that their work was comparatively expensive to publish, especially when the publishers could steal popular and esteemed European authors at little or no cost. A novel in London might cost $7.50, but in the United States it would sell for $2.00. Because they had to pay their countrymen, publishers would bring out an American book at $3.00 with no guarantee of an audience.[8]

Between 1848 and 1880, a central shift occurred between American authors and publishers. Writers increasingly allowed publishers to take over the mechanics of publication and distribution in exchange for a flat fee or a percentage of the profits. Although authors were relieved to be absolved of much of the practical side of publishing and were grateful to be free to concentrate on their work, publishers made a new, and for some writers an impossible, demand: that they cater to the tastes and values of the emerging middle-class audiences in the North and West.[9]

Starting in the mid-nineteenth century in the United States, authors were required to be more conscious of the audience than they had ever been before. Some of them did better with this task than others. For instance, while Hawthorne assumed a single homogenous audience had been lured by a "d—d mob of scribbling women" who produced "sentimental trash," Melville assumed that there were at least two audiences, the indiscriminate masses ("middlebrows") and the intellectual elite ("highbrows").[10] The "American audience" they are referring to is the Northern urban middle-class audience whose primary readers were women. This segment of the population not only included the elusive middle-class novel readers; by the 1850s it had produced many best-selling novelists from among its ranks.[11] Although Kennedy's and Simms's works sold as well as Hawthorne's and Melville's, none of them tapped this voracious reading segment. In addition, Southerners carried their own disabilities, which became increasingly important as the sectional conflict heated up.

First, that part of the South which would be the most sympathetic to the characters and themes of this antebellum Southern literature was minuscule. The lack of public schools, a high illiteracy rate, a diminished city life, and the rural and agricultural character of Southern life conspired against the development of a Southern reading public. Moreover, with their more heralded Northern counterparts, antebellum Southern writers took as their primary subjects male lives and male life problems and appealed to "more substantial" concerns in their treatment of racial, class, and national issues; that is, to the conflicts among men. Additionally, like their Northern counterparts, Southern writers both courted and despised this new reading public. More than even Hawthorne and Melville, writers like Kennedy, N. B. Tucker, and Simms declared their refusal to debase their "art" by appealing to popular character types and themes.[12] Finally, their antidemocratic bias coupled with their persistent defense of slavery set them outside and against the values of the emerging bourgeois society that prevailed after the Civil War.

As affluent men who were born into or married into the planter class, they were allied with the ruling planter elite. However, as intellectuals in a profoundly anti-intellectual nation and section, they were deeply alienated from those they sought to serve. It is clear that they were valued by the planter class chiefly as articulate spokesmen for slavery. This same planter class, however, was completely indifferent to their cherished project of establishing and fostering the development of a Southern literature and contributing in that way to the development of an American literature. As individuals these authors solved this problem in different ways.

THE PRODUCERS OF SOUTHERN LITERATURE

With the exception of William Gilmore Simms, the authors treated in this study did not consider themselves "professional writers"; that is, as writers who produced a commodity, a novel, that they sold for money in the literary marketplace to support themselves and their families. Instead, they considered themselves "gentlemen" who pursued literature as an avocation. In this respect, they differed from both their Northern counterparts and their model, Sir Walter Scott. Their lives not only illustrate the difficulties and contradictions of being a fiction writer in the antebellum South, but underscore the importance of marriage to a planter's daughter as a sure path to wealth and social mobility. In spite of their dissimilar backgrounds and differing stands on specific political events and issues, these writers adhered to a conservative vision of society that legitimated the power of the planter class.

For example, John Pendleton Kennedy is the only writer who pursued a business career and who freed the slaves he owned as soon as he could. Nevertheless, his mother's family, the Pendletons, were a prominent Tidewater Virginia family whose lives Kennedy depicted in *Swallow Barn* (1832), one of the most enduring proslavery novels.[13] In contrast, George Tucker, a Bermudian by birth, married into the Byrd and Carter families, two of the most influential families in Virginia. The money that came to him from his slave property made it possible for him to take a low-paying job, as a professor at the University of Virginia, and to devote himself to literature and political economy.[14]

Similarly, William Alexander Caruthers was born into a West Virginian frontier business family where his father was a comparatively wealthy man. Although Caruthers was a serious student of medicine, earning his degree at the University of Pennsylvania in 1823, he had always maintained an interest in literature. His marriage to Louise Catherine Gibson, the daughter of a low-country Georgia planter, who inherited slaves and land valued at more than $40,000, allowed Caruthers to pursue his medical and literary interests free from economic worry.[15]

William Gilmore Simms, like Caruthers, was born into a Charleston business family and was raised by his maternal grandmother when his mother died and his father migrated to the frontier. His mother's family was the prominent low-country Singleton family whose patriarch, John Singleton, distinguished himself in the Revolution. Both the support from his father and the social connections of his mother's family opened doors for him that might have been closed otherwise.[16] In 1836, he married Chevellette Eliza Roach, the heir to the magnificent 2,500-acre "Woodlands" plantation that supported them their whole lives.[17]

Even James Ewell Heath, about whom very little is known and who produced the most radical novel under consideration, was the son of a prominent Virginia planter and politician. His family connections enabled him to be state auditor for more than thirty years. Heath, too, married into plantation wealth.[18] Finally, of all the authors considered in this study, only Nathaniel Beverley Tucker fits the prototype of the gentleman planter who was born into and married into a plantation family and used his fiction to support dogmatically slavery and "Southern nationalism."[19] With the exception of Kennedy, who was a successful Maryland lawyer and politician, these authors lived off the profits of slavery either directly or indirectly and thus enjoyed the luxury of disdaining allegedly crass Northern materialists who wrote for money.

Most studies of these writers overlook James Ewell Heath and emphasize the differences among the five other authors. George Tucker, John Pendleton Kennedy, and William Alexander Caruthers are categorized as "liberals" and Nathaniel Beverley Tucker and William Gilmore Simms are characterized as "conservative."[20] Drew Gilpin Faust has argued convincingly that N. B. Tucker and Simms perceived themselves and three other men as scorned geniuses who were ignored by the powerful planter elite. They formed a "'sacred circle'—a network of mutual and intellectual support" from which they "defined a common purpose: to reform the South to make a place for their particular talents."[21] Although Faust has made an valuable contribution to our understanding of these people, her use of Clifford Geertz and Victor Turner to analyze their position as intellectuals in Southern society obscures more than it explains. The work of Antonio Gramsci suggests a more helpful way to understand the fiction these authors produced in relation to their class and political affiliations.

In elaborating how a working-class revolutionary party might come to power, twentieth-century intellectual and revolutionary Antonio Gramsci, an early victim of Italian fascism, delineated the relationship of the intellectual to society in both pre-industrial and industrial society. Gramsci argues in *Prison Notebooks:* "Every social group, coming into existence on the original terrain of an essential function in the world of economic production, creates together with itself, organically, one or more strata of intellectuals which give it homogeneity and an awareness of its own function not only in the economic but also in the social and political fields."[22]

Gramsci divides intellectuals into "traditional" and "organic" intellectuals. He describes traditional intellectuals as those people "linked to the social mass of country people and the town (particularly small town) petit bourgeoisie" (14, also 6 and 7). They are lawyers or minor officials who bring country people into contact with the state administration, or who as priests, doctors, and teachers mediate between the people and the state. They have a different educational background and standard of living from that of the peasants and act as "social models" for them. In some situations, the peasant admires and respects the intellectual for his knowledge and sees him as a "gentleman"; at other times he expresses anger and resentment at him for not really working, that is, working with his hands (16). In Europe, traditional intellectuals, then, are connected to the aristocracy and defend traditional social and economic relationships. Their power derives not only from their own talents, but from their relationship with the ruling classes.

According to Gramsci, an intellectual is a person whose "specific professional activity is weighted . . . towards intellectual elaboration" rather than physical labor (9). Gramsci notes further that every ruling class that comes to power has as its task the problem of creating a new strata of intellectuals that articulates the values, ideas, myths, and social relations of the particular socioeconomic order in such a way as to give it coherence and preclude the perception by the dominated classes that ruling-class power is a result of conflict.[23] Instead, the ruling class will seek to prove that they rule by virtue of their own innate superiority and by God-given and/or "natural" circumstances. Therefore, whenever conflict occurs, as it must, it should appear illegitimate, against God's will or nature's plan.

Although Gramsci was obviously concerned with European history and politics and the creation of working-class intellectuals—"organic intellectuals" who would forge a revolutionary working-class party in Italy—his model is instructive in its connections between the formation of social classes, politics, and intellectual life. In the antebellum South, these writers were not only connected to the planter class, but started writing in defense of slavery at a point when the Southern planter elite felt threatened by democratic forces in the South and antislavery forces in the North. The education of these writers, their social relations within Southern society, the subjects and themes of their fiction and their politics, constitute them in the American context as "traditional intellectuals" who saw themselves as the inheritors and preservers of eighteenth-century republicanism and the social and political prerogatives of the planter elite.

As the life of William Gilmore Simms makes abundantly clear, the "traditional" intellectual in the South did not live by his intellectual work though he might live for it. The man who could afford to devote himself to literature, reform, or politics in the South was the slaveholder whose human capital provided him with the leisure to think. Journalists, lawyers, doctors, and ministers often held slaves who provided leisure and economic security, so they would be free to produce articles, essays, speeches, pamphlets, and sermons. Some of these "professionals" lived off the earnings of slaves from distant plantations or on that money provided by slaves who were hired out. All of the authors but Kennedy fit one of these patterns, and all but Simms would agree with Kennedy that "the composition of imaginative literature was the avocation of a gentleman and not a full-time pursuit."[24] Kennedy's biographer, Charles H. Bohner, notes "the literary life, in the eyes of Americans was suspect, an effeminate business as best."[25] In the South, the introspective and imaginative writer seemed oddly out of place unless he could be drafted into the war against abolitionism.

Since industrial capitalism triumphed as the dominant mode of production in the United States, the organic intellectuals were those who both spoke for and sought to reform bourgeois values and life. They realized that there was money to be made from their intellectual labor and were motivated by the prospect of creating an "American" literature. What made writers like Melville and Hawthorne furious was that their affluent middle-class audience would pay only to be entertained and uplifted, but not chastised and intellectually challenged.[26] William Gilmore Simms existed between these two worlds at a point of economic, social, and political transition. A literary nationalist, psychologically, he possessed the vision, the ambition, and the attitude of the Northern "professional" writer. However, like the other traditional intellectuals of his region, his slaves and his devoted wife made it possible for him to have a library of his own and he was valued by his fellow planters only as long as he produced proslavery essays and literature.[27]

It makes perfect sense then that the planter and professional elite would support and recognize the proslavery efforts of intellectuals like Simms and N. B. Tucker while being largely indifferent to their dreams for a Southern literature. Again Gramsci, in his *Prison Notebooks,* sheds considerable light on this situation and gives us a way to understand the difficult position in which these writers found themselves. Gramsci notes that "it happens that many intellectuals think they *are* the State, a belief which, given the magnitude of the category, occasionally has important consequences and leads to unpleasant complications for the fundamental economic group which *really* is the State" (16). Simms and Tucker resented the fact that their work was viewed as only a means to an end—the preservation and extension of slavery—and not valued in itself. That they were alienated by that fact and felt themselves to be marginalized outsiders and misunderstood geniuses did not make them outsiders or misunderstood. In fact there is considerable evidence to indicate that both men were respected and honored. They simply forgot that they were the footsoldiers and not the generals in the crusade for slavery, and they never quite understood that a predominantly Northern, urban, middle-class reading public would be neither entertained nor uplifted by their celebration of Southern nationalism and their depiction of the yeoman farmer as the natural inferior of the planter.

These authors with the most conservative elements of the planter class articulated a traditional vision of society contending that social harmony was maintained only when "natural inferiors" deferred to "natural superiors." They would agree with Lord Bolingbroke's 1738 assertion that "the image of a free people . . . is that of a patriarchal family, where the head and all the members are united in one common interest, and animated by one common spirit: and where, if any are perverse enough to have another, they will be soon borne down by the superiority of those who have the same." As Michael Wallace notes, the emerging consensus about the value of oppositional parties in a democracy quickly displaced this earlier vision of social and political order much to the distress of Northern and Southern conservatives alike.[28]

JACKSONIAN POLITICS AND SOUTHERN LITERATURE

The period from 1824 to 1840 witnessed the birth of the second American party system and a new form of democratic politics. Since political debate centered on the nature of republicanism and the form that republican institutions should take, issues of race, ethnicity, and class were central concerns of these new democrats. The Revolution had ushered in an era pregnant with hope that all men would be considered politically equal in the new republic. For most men, that translated into having equal rights of citizenship, especially the vote.

The old Federalist conception of republicanism still haunted these nineteenth-century Americans. Federalists thought that societal and government order was maintained only if "the respected and the worthy lent their natural intellectual abilities and their natural social influence to political authority."[29] In both the North and the South, it was permissible for a "man of merit" to rise from his humble birth and govern as long as he had accepted and assimilated the experiences and attitudes, education and wealth, refinements and style of the ruling elite. In their "revolutionary" break with European politics, the Federalists would ensure governance by this "natural aristocracy" by basing the franchise on property holding instead of aristocratic lineage. They assumed that anyone who had accumulated the required amount of property had demonstrated the requisite personal qualities to vote and govern. They set up different property requirements for voting and for officeholding to ensure that only the most "worthy" members of society would hold office.

In this worldview, republican rights were indissolubly linked with republican virtue. Conservative eighteenth-century republicans argued for a politics governed by the "manly" republican virtues: "restraint, temperance, fortitude, dignity and independence" and "frugality, industry . . . and simplicity." Theoretically, people having these virtues would put aside their own personal interests to promote the public welfare.[30] What good republicans feared was unbridled wealth, which fostered "vicious and luxurious and effeminate Appetites, Passions and Habits" and made men crave "dull animal enjoyment."[31] They also feared the violence and anarchy of the masses, which they assumed was caused by lack of self-control. The true Federalist never had any doubt that the "common man"—the debtor class, the improvident, the unskilled, and uneducated—was unqualified to vote much less hold office.

Although in class terms this was a highly elitist political vision, in practice it meant giving men with property the vote regardless of ethnic or racial considerations. In Pennsylvania and Massachusetts that meant that respected black merchants like Robert Allen and Paul Cuffe voted right along with Quaker and Yankee merchants.[32] Few frontier farmers or urban mechanics had the opportunity to attend school or acquire enough property to run for office, so they were left to exercise their newly won democratic rights by voting for their "superiors." When Martin Van Buren's "Barnburners" in New York challenged that conservative vision of democracy in 1821, thus ushering in a new political era, the planters of the Southeastern states still clung to the old republican ideals, while yeoman farmers and small slave-holders in the western parts of their states and in the Southwest embraced the new vision of republicanism.[33]

What the Jacksonian Democrats accomplished between 1824 and 1840 was to bring those excluded groups into the democratic process and into the Democratic Party by reestablishing the party system, but they founded their new democratic revolution on the backs of African Americans. Indeed, Ed-mund Morgan's paradox holds for the nineteenth as well as the seventeenth and eighteenth centuries as white manhood suffrage was won by scapegoat-ing African Americans as an "unworthy" and "licentious" race unfit to vote or hold office.[34]

By 1840, after Jacksonian "democracy" had run its course, 93 percent of the free black males in the North lived in states that virtually or absolutely excluded them from voting. New Jersey, Pennsylvania, and Connecticut dis-franchised blacks from voting in long and bitter struggles that pitted first the old Federalists and then the Whigs against the feisty Democrats. Only New England (except Connecticut), with 6 percent of the black population, kept black suffrage; even in New England, however, black voters reported being harassed going to the polls.[35]

It is no exaggeration to argue, then, that the Democratic Party joined Northern workingmen and Southern planters as a white supremacist party, while the Whigs emerged as the party of class and eighteenth-century re-publican virtue. For the purposes of this study, that also explains the appar-ent political distinction between "conservative" William Gilmore Simms, a lifelong Democrat, and "liberal" John Pendleton Kennedy, a Whig. During the nullification crisis in South Carolina, Simms, a unionist, remained true to his social base in Charleston of "high toned Charleston aristocrats." Like them, he couldn't force himself to mix with the "rabble" as the Calhounites had done and form their own political organization to oppose Jackson. In-deed, in the South Carolinian context, it was consistent for Simms to be a fervent Jacksonian, as C. Hugh Holman has claimed for him, and also be an elitist and white supremist.[36] Similarly, allegedly "liberal" John P. Kennedy, a man who sold his slaves and fought against slavery extension, recoiled at having to give up his seat to a black woman on a Northern train. He was horrified by what he considered the excesses of Jacksonian democracy, which he claimed had brought to political power "the profoundly ignorant, the vicious and dissolute, the fraudulent and debtors, the decayed and bro-ken down workingmen, the outlawed and cast out members of society."[37]

In spite of their disagreements with each other on antebellum political issues like the national bank, the protective tariff, or internal improvements, the antebellum Southern authors' social vision remains strikingly similar with its resounding gender, race, and class biases. Their social vision is that of eighteenth-century republicans who thought that the patriarchal family provided the metaphor for all social relations and who preferred a society and government where "natural inferiors" deferred to "natural superiors." Although the new middle classes in the North and the frontier slaveholders in the Southwest were increasingly rejecting this social vision, these writers consistently employed this conservative political vision to defend plantation slavery and planter government.[38]

ANTEBELLUM SOUTHERN WRITERS AND THE PROSLAVERY ARGUMENT

The people who took a proslavery stand in the antebellum period were convinced that African-Americans were inherently biologically, intellectually, and morally inferior to whites and that slavery based on that fact promoted social harmony since it recognized the immutable differences among people. Embedded within the proslavery defense lay a conservative, patriarchal vision of "civilized society" as organically and hierarchically established on gender, generational, racial, and class lines. The most important institution for these people and the one that they claimed provided the basis of government was the allegedly God-given patriarchal family, which sanctified male rule. In turn, slavery, a patriarchal institution, recognized this alleged black inferiority and gave blacks meaningful work and "protected" them from having to compete with "superior" whites.

Starting in the 1820s with the slavery debates over the Missouri Compromise and continuing through the Civil War, Southern planters and intellectuals turned to the patriarchal metaphor again and again as they asserted that they governed their slaves "in the same form of government to which abolitionists subject their wives and children."[39] That black slaves treated paternalism as a game and a wedge to manipulate their way to better treatment is evident from their own fiction and nonfiction accounts of slavery.[40]

Slave government like family government, then, was contained within the "private" realm of the family. Although there were laws against unusual cruelty to slaves, most Southerners didn't interfere with the planter's government of his slaves as they didn't interfere with his government of his wife and children. Planters enjoyed virtual unimpeded dominion over their slaves. When antislavery activists attacked the institution of slavery as un-American, un-Christian, immoral, and degrading to whites as well as blacks, they were not just attacking a labor system. Rather, they were assailing the character and integrity of the planter, who like the pre-industrial artisan master understood his place in the world as the skilled manager of a diverse workforce, a kind and benevolent husband and father, and a moral leader in the larger society. Not only were the antislavery activists impugning the integrity of the planter class as a whole, but in Southern planter eyes they were threatening to bring the state into an arena where it had never been before: the private relations of the patriarchal family.

The most articulate defenders of slavery—Thomas Cooper, Edmund Ruffin, Thomas R. Dew, Nathaniel Beverley Tucker, James Henry Hammond, George Fitzhugh, and William Gilmore Simms—presented a logically consistent conservative defense of the "domestic institution" that argued the inherent superiority of the white, male planter elite and their right to govern. They defended slavery, and they argued against Northern industrial capitalism and its new liberal bourgeois vision, which they contended would make political equals of inherently unequal people. While these conservatives admitted that unlike women and blacks, middle-class Northerners and Southern yeoman farmers and artisans were capable of sustaining themselves in a competitive economy and of exercising a measure of self-government, they argued that the poor white man's inferior intelligence and education, temperament, and breeding, made him unfit to assume the responsibility and duty of governing other men.[41]

The proslavery defenders were not uncritical supporters of slavery; they were also reformers who felt that a basically sound system could be improved. For instance, Edmund Ruffin was dedicated to halting soil erosion through "scientific agriculture." Similarly, William Gilmore Simms upbraided his fellow South Carolinian planters for their snobbery, hedonism, and profligacy, but saw those as individual failings rather than inherently systemic problems. James D. B. DeBow, in turn, urged the South to use some of its black labor as industrial labor and to convert to industrial production to make the South less dependent on Northern manufactured goods and Northern capital.[42]

When one speaks of "planter hegemony" in the antebellum South, then, one is describing the successful promulgation of a worldview that was accepted by a broad cross-section of the white Southern population, but that operated primarily in the interest of the ruling planter class. The proslavery defense comprised such a set of ideas and beliefs, so that to challenge one aspect of the ideology (say, white supremacy) was to undermine white, male planter power in its other spheres.[43] The proslavery theorists, like the great majority of intellectuals in any society at any given time, not only benefited from society as it existed, but chose to defend and reform the society they lived in rather than to overthrow it.[44]

One of the questions that has puzzled scholars about the proslavery defense was the "underlying motivation" of the proslavery writers. Some historians have argued that the proslavery defense was designed to defend the South as a "white man's country."[45] Another group of historians, opting for a modern psychological explanation, thinks that hyperbolic proslavery rhetoric in the 1850s was sparked by the abolitionists touching the raw nerve of planter guilt over slavery.[46] A third group, led by William Hesseltine, have asserted that proslavery men used arguments of racial superiority to stem the rising class conflicts; that is, "to convince non-slaveholding whites of the superiority of white over negro blood," and thus give to poor whites a racial connection to the powerful planter class, dulling their resistance to planter domination of the South.[47] Some of the most thoughtful and provocative studies like Robert Shallhope's have argued that issues of class and race cannot be compartmentalized into hierarchies of oppression since "the same men often in the same breath, manifest both class consciousness and racism" in their quest to maintain a "prebourgeois, structured, paternalistic, gentry society."[48]

Larry Tise argues in his provocative study of proslavery clergy that the proslavery writers are conservatives with ideals that may be traced to the eighteenth-century Federalists, but he asserts that dozens of conservative Northern clergymen and educators (especially from Princeton and Yale), who constituted an anti-abolitionist vanguard "infiltrated the South and unleashed among them the same set of notions, the same body of rhetoric and the same mechanisms that had enabled proslavery to be embraced by the growing American conservative tradition" a full decade before proslavery Southerners took up their pens.[49] Tise contends this conservative conspiracy slowly worked their ideas into Southern society to establish a regenerate conservative empire that challenged and undermined the more radical and democratic tendencies of the American Revolution. Because they lived in the North, they were among the first to witness the growth and success of the abolitionists whom they regarded as radical subversives of the Union. Tise argues that although they opposed slavery, they thought the Negro too inferior for full assimilation into U.S. society. Instead, they advocated that the slaves be Christianized, educated for freedom, and deported to Africa where they would serve as agents of Western civilization (67–73, 134–37, 183–362).

Arguing against established scholarship, Tise's formulation leads him to deny that there were important proslavery defenses before the summer of 1835 (the season of the abolitionist mail campaign); to assert that the nullification crisis in South Carolina was "insignificant" as a precedent for the development of the proslavery defense; and to claim that the proslavery argument was exclusively Northern in origin (261–302, 308–12).

The problem with Tise's argument is also its strength. On the one hand, he has offered a compelling sociological portrait of the anti-abolitionist clergy. On the other, in focusing so exclusively on the clergy to the exclusion of politicians and other intellectuals, as the narrative progresses he backs himself into a questionable conspiracy thesis whose assumptions are not borne out by this study. For example, he asks the reader to believe that Jeffersonian liberalism held such sway that a conservative defense of slavery was unthinkable before 1835. The work of George Tucker, Nathaniel Beverley Tucker, John Pendleton Kennedy, and William Gilmore Simms, all of

whom were familiar with Burke and the Federalist worldview and who before 1835 articulated proslavery views as did many of their peers, belies that
contention.[50]

The overwhelming evidence from this study of antebellum Southern literature supports Robert Shallhope's position as well as the early arguments
of Eugene D. Genovese and Eric Foner that the proslavery defense constituted a self-conscious assertion of the racial and class consciousness of
the planter class that was implacably opposed to the bourgeois vision of
American society articulated by the Republican Party in the 1856 and 1860
presidential campaigns.[51] Furthermore, these writers were unmistakably allied with the planter class. Their disagreements with each other arose in
intraclass debates. They never questioned the alleged inherent right of the
planter class to govern, just as they never questioned their own innate gender, race, and class superiority. As traditional intellectuals, they wrote essays
and novels that contributed significantly to the establishment of planter
hegemony and provided a literary proslavery legacy.

3. The Form of Southern Literature

IN AUGUST 1837, at a gathering of the Massachusetts Phi Beta Kappa society, young Ralph Waldo Emerson startled his audience by charging that Americans "have listened too long to the courtly muses of Europe" and argued that the future of American letters lay in the study of nature and in the examination of the truths of American experience.[1] Emerson's message came at a time when American letters were considered a provincial branch of English culture. British critics often charged that American arts and letters would never amount to much because the United States lacked the cultural requisites for greatness: a glorious past, a heroic aristocracy, and a singular racial and religious identity.

However, the key to American cultural identity would lie not in the past, but in the future; not in the celebration of aristocratic heroes, but in the recognition of the heroic in each individual; not on religious and political conformity, but in religious and political freedom. These are bourgeois, democratic values that celebrated the self-reliant, honest, industrious, and pietistic "freeman": the "individual" freed from the restraints of the past and from aristocracy. American literary nationalism of this period, then, envisioned white Americans as part of a divinely sanctioned plan to establish a virtuous, democratic republic on the North American continent populated by an Anglo-Saxon people who were "blessedly different" from both the "degraded and corrupt" Europeans and the "bestial and savage" Native Americans. Although Southern writers shared the latter vision, they dissented from the former and denied that men could ever be free from the past or their social inheritance. This Southern antebellum literature not only honors aristocratic Southern heroes of the American Revolution; it offers a vision of social harmony based on an allegedly natural and immutable gender, race, and class hierarchy, and is anti-individualistic to the core.[2]

The Southern writers considered in this study were influenced by Western European writers, especially English writers and literature whose forms they adopted. Their chief purpose in writing was to capture faithfully the spirit of Southern history as it influenced and was influenced by the main currents of American history and to make a literary proslavery defense of Southern society. As a consequence, these authors produced two kinds of novels: the plantation or "Virginia" novel, which was derived from the sentimental tradition established by Richardson; and the "historical romance,"

33

established by Sir Walter Scott.[3] Because they thought that the planter class should provide continual leadership in the South, they recorded and re-wrote the history of the South from a planter perspective in their novels; in so doing they subverted the literary forms and conventions they adopted. In the end, and in contrast to Scott, the historical romance in Southern hands emerges as a distinctly conservative form in its defense of traditional, pre-industrial capitalist society based on planter-class rule.

It is most likely that women like Margaret Cavendish (1624–74), Aphra Behn (1640–89), and Eliza Haywood (1673–1756) not only created the major characters and storylines of the novel, but had their work pirated by Daniel Defoe, Samuel Richardson, and Henry Fielding, who extended and modified the form and received credit for its invention. Nevertheless, these South-ern writers read Richardson's *Pamela* (1740), *Clarissa* (1748), and *Sir Charles Grandison* (1754) and credited Richardson with the invention of the new literary form. These novels reflected the new bourgeois consciousness that expressed itself in significant gender and class relations.[4] In Richardson's hands, the sentimental plot turned on a sexual theme: the seduction and/or rape of the innocent middle-class woman by a rakish, aristocratic villain. For instance, Ian Watt argues that with *Pamela* and *Clarissa,* bourgeois novelist Samuel Richardson makes a case for the bourgeoisie in its struggle against the older, corrupted European aristocracy, and articulates a new middle-class Protestant vision of female sexuality. The new chaste Protestant hero-ine not only actively resists her would-be seducer, but she is "innocent" of any sexual desire. In short, she is as "pure" in spirit as she is in body and she is sexually passive.[5] The only way she can be "taken" is legally through marriage (for example, Mr. B's proposal to Pamela) or through rape (for exam-ple, Lovelace's rape of Clarissa). On a gender level, then, feminine virtue and sexual purity is poised against masculine force and aggression.

Watt and Leslie Fiedler argue that this vision of human sexuality re-forms heterosexuality as innately sadomasochistic where sexual intercourse means punishment or death for the woman and conquest for the man.[6] In this view, Clarissa is not only the "New Woman," she is the representative of the new middle class: "the heroic representative of all that is free and posi-tive in the new individualism."[7] She is caught in a paradox; her sexual pas-sivity is the cause and precondition for her active and heroic defense of herself. Watt argues, then, that the sentimental heroine emerges as the an-tagonist of both a corrupted European aristocracy and the tyranny of the patriarchal family.[8]

In the United States in the late eighteenth and early nineteenth centuries, writers like Charles Brockden Brown, Susannah Rowson, and William Hill Brown not only tried to reconcile the private and public demands of the emerging bourgeois world with the private lives of citizens, but tried to ad-dress the class and gender implications of the American Revolution. Cathy

Davidson and Jane Tompkins convincingly argue that "a small body of Americans used the novel as a political and cultural forum, a means to express their own vision of a developing nation."[9] In the 1850s, Tompkins argues, the best-selling writers Susan Warner, Sarah J. Hale, Augusta Evans, and Elizabeth Stuart Phelps not only concentrated on the middle-class woman in the home, but created in novel form the "women's jeremiad." She asserts that these most abused writers were producing important "cultural work" in grappling with the fundamental contradictions of antebellum society, and that novelists like Stowe and Warner made "their bid for power by positing the kingdom of heaven on earth as a world over which women exercise ultimate control." The sentimental novelists in this view saw as their "world historical mission" to "educate their readers on Christian perfection and to move the nation as a whole closer to God."[10]

The sentimental novel's central focus is the heroine's world and the heroine's life problems, while the historical romance shifts the focus to the world of men and men's life problems. In the sentimental novel, the woman stands for the highest virtues of her class and of "civilization," and the threat to her—unbridled male sexuality—constitutes a threat to civilization itself.[11] In their adoption of this sentimental convention, these Southern authors leave intact the heroine's sentimental character, but transform her to an "aristocratic" planter's daughter and remake her into the more passive romantic heroine whose helplessness provides the romantic hero the pretext for heroic moral action.

The authors considered in this study maintain the Victorian sentimental vision of "woman" as a pure and sexually passive maiden, and as representative of Southern civilization, but they re-create her as the pure representative of the planter class. Unlike Pamela and Clarissa, who represent the working class and the middle class respectively and who are left on their own to resist the advances of the debased aristocratic villain, the Southern romantic heroine survives only through heroic male intervention. Except for an occasional upper-class British officer who admires her and tries to defeat the planter hero, the symbol of "Southern Civilization" always has a poor-white or middle-class abductor.[12]

As a character, the romantic heroine's stature is diminished when compared with the sentimental heroine since she has lost the capacity to act for herself. These Southern writers offer a worldview directly opposite to the bourgeois worldview offered by Samuel Richardson. The patriarchally conservative worldview—the vision of immutable difference between natural superiors and natural inferiors—thus asserts itself in the key scene in this fiction. The aristocratic planter hero not only rescues the naturally passive and dependent plantation heroine from danger; in the process he defeats his class enemy. Southern writers adopt literary conventions from the sentimental novel to assert their contention that in "civilized society" men protect their "natural dependents" from harm: children and slaves, from their own lack of responsibility and judgment; women from criminal men of the lower classes.

The intellectual world these Southern male authors inhabited was as complex as their social world. Primarily, they saw themselves as the inheritors of English intellectual traditions; yet they also saw themselves connected with and to the Romantic movement. As literary nationalists, they sought to create a uniquely American literature; yet, as Southerners, they also sought to celebrate and defend their section and its institutions, namely slavery. The new romanticism emphasized originality, uniqueness, emotion, and imagination compared with eighteenth-century formalism and its concern with symmetry, imitation, reason, and the quest for universal truths.[13] Indeed, the bourgeois democratic revolutions of the eighteenth century led to romantic concepts of the hero, the highest expression of individuality, where political figures like George Washington or Napoleon were envisioned as leading their people to a greater realization of "national spirit." The emergence of industrial capitalism and the defeat of the structures of absolutism opened up a new world order for nineteenth-century Europeans and Americans.

Writers and other artists of the period responded to this new world by inventing new forms of poetry (for example, the 1798 "Lyrical Ballads" offered by Wordsworth and Coleridge) and the novel. From roughly 1820 to 1880, the "novel" captured the imagination of the new bourgeois reading public and continued to develop as a form.

The original "romances" were originally Old French and involved tales of military exploits, exaggerated and fantastic to ensure the interest of the listening audience. Tending toward "the thrilling and the marvelous" and "the melodramatic," they dramatized the hero's quest, his arduous trials, and the magnificent victory that made him worthy to marry the king's daughter.[14] Sir Walter Scott returned to this tradition as he searched for an appropriate form to describe Scotland's transition from feudalism to capitalism, or modernism.

Although Scott chose to call his novel the "historical romance," ironically in his hands, its themes and characterizations were distinctly antiromantic. Like most English-speaking writers of the period, Scott drew the distinction between the "novel" and the "romance." The English novel, as it originated with Richardson and was developed by people like Fielding and Smollet, Austen and Dickens, was supposed to describe and depict real people, actual places, and probable events. Focusing on individuals and often on domestic affairs, the individual's problems, his or her thoughts, dreams, and psychology were able to be explored for the first time. In contrast, the "romance," like its medieval predecessor, was set in remote and exotic settings including the past, focused on the adventures of unusual people, and recorded remarkable or logically inexplicable events. In his historical romance, Scott took ordinary people and placed them in unusual settings and subjected them to extraordinary events that tested their character and their capacity to find and establish justice in the midst of social chaos.

In the United States, Northern and Southern writers were influenced by the nineteenth-century revolt against eighteenth-century classicism; however, only those writers who considered the individual to be their primary subject fully realized the romantic vision, which stressed individualism, originality, subjectivity, intuition, and sentimentality. Literary romanticism represented the protest of "free men" against a world dedicated to making money. The more optimistic and liberal strains of romanticism rejoiced in the individual's connection to God through nature, emotional spontaneity, individual uniqueness, and the glorious destiny of a people in tune with "progress." In contrast, the more pessimistic and conservative strains of romanticism betrayed a similar egocentric self-absorption, but reflected a brooding melancholia that focused on the "homelessness and loneliness" of the individual cast into the uncertainty of industrial society from the security of a simpler, rural life. What both strains of romanticism shared was their focus on the "truth" of the unique and irreplaceable individual experience in the author's quest to discover (in Hawthorne's words) the "truth of the human heart."[15]

In Northern writing, then, the "individual" might be a sea captain or a seventeenth-century Puritan woman—ordinary people in extraordinary circumstances. They had to balance the realities of their society with their passions and their personal sense of morality. As the individual works out his or her destiny, one is always uncertain whether or how he or she will prevail. Furthermore, the reader is asked to consider the psychology of these individuals, not only their social class.

In Southern literature, however, there are no "individuals" free from the limitations of their gender, race, or class; and nature is desirable only in its domesticated plantation version. The terrifying wilderness of the Native American and the alleged semibarbaric frontier of the poor white are repudiated by the planter hero. Consequently, in comparison to canonical Northern literature, the Southern novel is highly structured. Little is left to chance or to individual choice, and the conservative values of loyalty, duty, honor, self-sacrifice to family obligations, and responsibility for one's dependents are contrasted to the tyranny of uncontrolled passion, the recklessness of selfish individualism, and the foolish delusions of misguided "leveling impulses."

One of the reasons, then, that Southern writers were particularly attracted to Sir Walter Scott, was their impression that he shared their aversion to all aspects of modern, bourgeois society because his novels, in their recognition of the value of organic society, seemed to share their antiromantic affirmation of conservative values. However, closer examination of both Scott and these writers will reveal that to some degree all of them, but especially

Caruthers, N. B. Tucker, and Simms rejected the primary insight of Scott's work, which was that societies evolve; in particular the evolution of societies in Britain indicated that aristocratic, patriarchal, pre-industrial capitalist societies were doomed to extinction by the more progressive industrial countries.[16]

Scott's life and family connections serve as a guide to his social philosophy. He was born into a Scottish gentry family; his mother was the daughter of a prominent country physician and his father was a prominent Edinburgh lawyer. His father's family, the Scotts of Buccleagh, had been Borderers and young Scott spent most of his boyhood summers and several of his long convalescent periods at his paternal grandfather's farm, Sandyknowe. Although Scott had aspirations to be a painter and was first known for his translations of traditional Scottish ballads and poetry, he was a lawyer for most of his life. Politically, he was a peculiar kind of Tory conservative. Although he didn't care for the changes that industrial capitalism had brought England and Scotland, and sympathized with the poorer country people whose lives had been completely disrupted by the transition from feudalism to capitalism, he accepted that change as inevitable and put his faith in the promise of economic progress, which he thought would eventually benefit all strata of society. In many ways, then, Scott himself was a man of conflicting class loyalties, which, one critic has argued, give his work its unique balance and vision.[17]

Starting with *Waverley* (1814), Scott chose to portray the average man and woman who get caught in transhistorical events and who must respond to the political and social crises of their time. Scott's fiction as a whole traces the ethnic and class conflict that set Scottish Highlanders against Lowlanders, Jacobites against Hanoverians, Royalists against Roundheads, and the aristocracy against the bourgeoisie. Though they are average men and women, Scott's characters represent "social trends and historical forces" as Scott seeks a "middle way" through the economic and political crises of English history.[18] Most important, Scott defends economic progress that nevertheless leaves "an endless field of ruin, wrecked existences, wrecked or wasted heroic, human endeavor (and) broken social formations" in its wake.[19]

Scott offers a tragic vision of progress in which patriarchal, pre-industrial capitalist aristocratic culture with its values of "loyalty, honor, military skill, and heroic heritage of aristocratic family lines" was defeated by democratic, competitive, individualistic capitalism.[20] Both Scott's politics and his choice of literary form provide a striking contrast with these Southern antebellum authors, who strove to imitate his financial success and literary achievement more than they sought to reproduce his worldview.

For instance, Scott's hero is typically a mediocre English country gentleman of "practical intelligence" and "moral fortitude and decency" whose personality is complete when he is introduced and remains unchanged by his experiences. Like most people of his particular period, the hero is drawn into political turmoil or civil war, even though he isn't a particular passionate partisan of either side. One critic has called him a "symbolic observer" who embodies the tension of historical change.[21] Ultimately, however, he must choose between the two sides. The Scott hero like Edward Waverley (*Waverley*) or Frank Osbaldistone (*Rob Roy*), after some pained reflection, usually choose the side of the "progressive" capitalist forces. The actions of the hero bring the representatives of the two opposing sides together and the hero's rescue of, or marriage to the daughter of the defeated aristocratic chieftain serves to heal the wounds incurred by the civil strife, gives the hero and heroine a pretext for returning to "normal" life, and points to the future when their children and grandchildren will have forgotten the original cause for strife.

Duncan Forbes and Peter Garside have convincingly argued that Scott has been mislabeled a "romantic" novelist. Garside asserts that Scott's education and his extracurricular activities at Edinburgh University, and his later contributions to the *Edinburgh Review,* place him with the rationalist philosophers of the Scottish Enlightenment. Noting that Scott acknowledged Dugald Stewart as one of his mentors, Garside reveals that the themes of Stewart's history lectures were "the inevitability of progress, the importance of property in development, the power struggle between classes, [and] the effect of social environment on 'manners'"—all themes in Scott's work.[22]

Similarly, Georg Lukács has argued that Scott's genius lay in his ability to perceive that social change was historically significant when it had the capacity to change the lives and perceptions of everyday people.[23] The historical romance is "romantic" or unrealistic, when the author imagines adventures and coincidental intrigues for his characters that defy probability. It is supposed to be "realistic" in its descriptions of the economic and political transitions taking place over time and in its characterizations of different kinds of people. While Scott's work is a "romance," then, his use of and attention to ordinary people and especially his depiction of realistic "lowlife" characters, his limitations of his characters by their ethnicity and class, and consequently his denial of their uniqueness and spontaneity, make him an antiromantic producer of historical romances.

While the antebellum plantation novel strove to depict everyday life and everyday people (albeit from the planter's point of view), the Southern historical romance offered two primary plots: (1) it traced the tragic, but necessary Euro-American conquest of "uncivilized" Native Americans, led by the planter class; and (2) it depicted the planter-class's leading role in the historical defeat of the British and their middle-class and poor-white "tory" allies during the American Revolution.[24]

Although most of the authors followed Scott's lead in using nonhistorical figures as their heroes, their heroes were the antithesis of Scott's uncommitted average man who gets trapped in transhistorical events beyond his control. Especially in the work of Caruthers, Kennedy, N. B. Tucker, and Simms, the Southern hero is always morally and intellectually superior to the men he leads, and he always has an influence in shaping historical events.

For instance, Simms's and Kennedy's versions of the American Revolution describe and explain how planter-class men leading all other classes of Southern white men against the tyranny of British imperialism have earned the right to govern Southern society in peacetime. In their version, the American Revolution was a conservative revolution that was fought to preserve the social order rather than to transform it. Planters are envisioned as the defenders of the traditional, aristocratic, patriarchal order from outside invasion and from the chaos of civil war caused by ambitious and criminal middle-class and poor-white men. Planter authority creates order out of chaos and brings poor-white criminals to justice. The hero of this literature is not Scott's uncommitted average man, but the medieval epic hero who molds history and founds civilization.

Furthermore, in his preface to *The Yemassee* and again in a letter to Evert A. Duyckinck, editor of the *Literary World* and the Library of American Books and leader of the "Young America" group based in New York City, Simms asserts his preference for the "romance," which he compares to the "novel."[25] He acknowledges that he strives to combine the forms of the epic with the historical romance to create a uniquely Southern version of the historical romance. As a result, Simms's planter heroes dominate the action of the novel and emerge as the ideal of human perfection. Only John Pendleton Kennedy comes close to matching Scott's original vision of the inherent worthiness of the average man, but even Kennedy's plebeian hero, Horse-Shoe Robinson, constantly defers to the superior intelligence and graciousness of the gentleman planter Arthur Butler. It is understood that at the end of the Revolution, Robinson will resume his life as a farmer and a blacksmith and Butler and his children will govern the South. While Scott bows to the inevitability of industrial capitalism, these Southern writers argue that "American Civilization" will be best served by the triumph of an aristocratic, antibourgeois planter class in the South. Although these authors imitated Scott, they adapted the form of the historical romance to their own political purposes.

In spite of their personal and political differences, these authors were united in their feeling that they were creating a sectional, but essentially American literature that would survive long after they died. However, in defending the interests of a historically defeated class, they created an anachronistic literature that asserted in every characterization, every nuance, and every twist of the plot, the natural and immutable inferiority of women to men, of blacks to whites, and of all classes North and South to the planter class.

Rather than being a visionary who challenged the prevailing standards and turning his sight to the future, the Southern hero is a backward-looking conservative who seeks to preserve traditional society and his place in it.

Rather than seeking to escape "civilization," he strives to take his patriarchal institutions with him to the frontier where he dreams of extending plantation society and culture to the Pacific Ocean and into Mexico. Rather than seeing in the planter's defense of slavery the exact historical tragedy that Scott was describing for Britain, these authors defended the society that pitted itself against "progress."

Most literature offers one of two interpretive approaches: (1) the literature masks the ideological intent, which must then be discovered through careful analysis of its central myths and symbols; or (2) the literature itself challenges the prevailing assumptions of its time or extends their meaning to new levels. One thinks of Melville's work, which is both embedded in nineteenth-century America and challenges its most cherished beliefs (for example, white supremacy). In contrast, Southern antebellum literature offers sociological mythmaking not psychological depth and thus is transparent to any attentive student of Southern history. The didactic purpose of this literature is exposed in its form and content, which argue too persuasively against what scholars have over time established as the major character types, images, and themes of classic American literature.

For instance, A. N. Kaul argues, and most American literature scholars have agreed, that the theme of "American literature" is the individual's attempt to find moral regeneration in his reconciliation of his ideal of society and the reality of society. He notes that the pre–Civil War hero is an "individual" unfettered by social restriction and pressure; that he realizes his individuality and recognizes his need for community by establishing ideal communities in the wilderness; and that the exclusively male community he creates reflects his striving for "universal brotherhood" and "perfect fellowship." One does not have to agree with the myth of the lonely, white male hero who realizes both his masculinity and humanity in "conquering" the untameable wilderness and in taming allegedly inferior races of men to recognize that it reflects the worldview of the Northern and Western middle classes.[26] Even though Southern writers and politicians joined their Northern peers in creating a racist national policy of manifest destiny, they could neither envision leaving women behind nor imagine any kind of "brotherhood" with men they considered racially inferior to them with or without women.

In its popular form, Northern and Western fiction celebrates the heroic struggle of white men of all classes in their victory over nature and the "savagery" of Native Americans. In classic American literature—and specifically in Cooper's Leatherstocking tales—Natty Bumppo, the average man, abandons what he perceives as the corruption of civilization to realize spiritual innocence and moral purity in his marriage with nature and in his friendship with an Indian, Chingachgook, whom he calls "brother." It is hard to imagine Southern writers of this period emerging with Cooper's racial or class attitudes. Instead, they create stories in which planters lead men of the lower classes on their joint quest to search out and destroy Native Americans. Unlike Natty Bumppo, the Southern hero doesn't seek to abandon "civilization," but rather carries it with him to the wilderness where he reestablishes plantation society based on allegedly natural and immutable gender, racial, and class hierarchies.[27]

While the Northern vision of the American hero in this period is the unfettered, "free" man who competes with other free and equal individuals at sea, on the farm, or in the West, the Southern vision of the American hero is the "natural aristocrat," the planter's son who realizes his heroism through his acceptance of his social responsibilities and in his defense of the honor of his family and his country. In its celebration of the organic, hierarchical, and deferential society that the North was rapidly leaving behind, this Southern literature seems "un-American" in its rejection of romantic bourgeois individualism.[28] The historical romance, then, emerges on both sides of the Atlantic as the masculine redemption of the novel, elevating this previously "feminine" form to the level of "serious Art" by shifting its focus from the domestic sphere to the public and national sphere. Although Southern novelists of this period don't offer us "individuals" as heroes, they nevertheless depict superior heroic males who are self-assured and guiltless in their exercise of power.

Such "projection" by a dominant group expresses itself artistically in stereotypes, most often derogatory images originally rendered in art and literature; the images characterize members of an allegedly inferior and feared group by asserting their reputed unchanging essential traits. Originating as a term first in ceramics and then in printing, by the early nineteenth century "stereotype" began to take on its now familiar figurative use.[29] Although its origins are difficult to trace, certainly one of the first uses of the term in the United States must have been Samuel Cornish's explanation that he had chosen "The Colored American" as the title for his newspaper, since "Negroes, Africans, and blacks, all of which have been *sterotyped,* as names of reproach . . . are unacceptable." He contends, " 'Colored American' is the true term which is above reproach." Cornish's paper became one of the crusading abolitionist papers which advocated African American freedom from slavery and civil rights for African Americans in the North.[30]

A similar early use of the term emerges from nineteenth- and twentieth-century African American art history as blacks and their white allies took up the challenge of fighting racist stereotypes in painting and photography. In a letter written to the Reverend Theodore Tilton, abolitionist Lydia Maria Child comments on his March 1852 review in *The Independent* of Thomas LeClear's painting, "The Itinerants." LeClear painted a group of children gathered in front of an old woman's apple-stand, watching street musicians, a boy and a girl, play their instruments. Tilton admires the painting, but criticizes LeClear who "went out of his way to draw a black boy in the act of committing a theft, while all the children are drawn with honest faces."

Tilton then employs a "positive stereotype" in arguing "a real African, while such music was playing, would have stood absorbed with the music, and would never have thought of stealing an apple." He castigates LeClear for using art "for making a despised people still more despised . . . pressing them still lower down under ridicule and obloquy."[31] Child praises both Tilton's criticism and his characterization of the "real African." She relates in her letter that she always confronts children who use derisive ethnic slurs against the Irish, Jews, and blacks because although the "terms are harmless enough in themselves . . . they have become *stereotyped* forms of contempt, and therefore ought to be suppressed."[32]

The Tilton review and Child letter are valuable indicators that the term "stereotype" had passed into common use at this point and demonstrate what Sander Gilman calls the "positive" or ideal stereotype, which also evades individuality to project the supposed positive essential characteristics of a group. According to Tilton and Child, in this case the "real African" would be enthralled by the music, because it is implied "as an African" he would be musically inclined. Since the stereotypes of women tend toward both the positive and negative, it is important to note that positive stereotyping is also a distorting practice of writers and artists. One should note as well that conservatives are not the only people who strive to suppress from public expression those images and words they deem offensive. Here, Child would suppress what is now called "hate speech."

Historically, then, it seems that the first discussion of and opposition to stereotypes is found among those people specifically concerned with challenging ethnic and/or racial stereotypes. Given the early women's rights movement, it seems odd that there doesn't seem to be a similar drive against stereotypes of women, but perhaps that is a testament to women's enforced silence and the fact that nineteenth-century "domestic feminists" embraced the dominant positive stereotypes of women to carve out a place for themselves as the moral superiors of men; these women would "clean up" society and rid it of male vice.[33]

In the twentieth century, the literature on stereotyping has largely been developed by those scholars and social critics concerned with ameliorating prejudice and racism in American society. For example, in *Public Opinion* (1922), Walter Lippmann, concerned with the effect of mass media on public opinion and politics ("the world outside and the pictures in our heads"), devotes a section to stereotypes. He argues that people in modern and urban multiethnic society "define first and then see." He contends that "we pick out what our culture has already defined for us, and we tend to perceive that which we have picked out in the form *stereotyped* for us by our culture."[34] Stereotypes that emerge from art and literature, he notes, give shape to our "moral codes and our social philosophies, and our political agitations as well" (56). Stereotyping brings order to the chaos of modern life by reducing complex personalities to recognizable types. The problem arises, he asserts, not in the impulse to order, but in "the character of the stereotypes, and the gullibility with which we employ them," especially those that purport to represent ethnic and racial groups (60 and 61). Finally, Lippmann notes that stereotypes are created by a dominant group afraid of or seeking to control a subordinate group that confirms their inferiority. Any attack on such dominant stereotypes is thus perceived as "an attack upon the foundations of the universe" because it represents an assault on the social image of the dominant group and challenges that group's authority. Thus, Lippmann argues stereotyping is "the guarantee of our self-respect; it is the projection upon the world of our own sense of value, our own position and our own rights" (64).

Gordon Allport, an eminent social psychologist, also sees projection at the core of prejudice and notes that one maintains stereotypes through "selective perception and selective forgetting."[35] Like Lippmann, Allport is concerned with the role of the mass media in furthering stereotypes and contends that stereotypes of some groups change over time because they are "primarily rationalizers" that "adapt to the prevailing temper of prejudice or needs of the situation" (198 and 199). Allport's more psychodynamic theory postulates that in order to feel more than good about one's self but also superior to others, people project unwanted traits onto others that they fear or dislike in themselves—laziness, lust, dishonesty—thereby legitimating the mistreatment of the despised group. In this dichotomous worldview, the "good" projector creates a caricature of people who are allegedly so totally different from himself that he cannot be suspected of having any of the unwanted traits. He literally casts the unwanted attributes and the hated and feared group away from himself. Psychologically, the stereotyper creates extreme images to maintain his sense of self-respect and power. Clearly, when his fears are shared by others, they have more resonance in society and the stereotype is more powerful and thus more damaging to the stereotyped group (364–66).

Sander Gilman's *Pathology and Difference,* a contemporary study of stereotypical images of women, blacks, and Jews in fin de siècle France, builds on these observations and theories. His observations, like those of Lippmann and Allport, are helpful in our understanding of antebellum Southern literature. Like his predecessors, Gilman employs projection theory to explain stereotyping. He notes that stereotyping systems are "inherently bipolar, generating pairs of antithetical signifiers" (for example, the virgin and the whore, the Southern lady and the Jezebel) and that stereotyping indicates a subtext for a specific work that provides a key to cultural structures and ideologies. Through stereotypes, one can perceive directly the anxieties that haunt the "self" in its attempt to bring order out of chaos and to distinguish between the self and "the Other."[36] The potential for the "deep structuring" of stereotyping occurs for the individual in infancy at the moment when the child begins to develop a separate sense of self.

Gilman argues that initially the child demands and receives "food, warmth, and comfort" from "the world." As the child distinguishes more between the world and the self, however, anxiety arises from a "perceived loss of control over the world." Soon, the "child's sense of self" splits in two. The "good" self is secure and in control of the world; the "bad" self is insecure, out of control, and anxious. This split is "a single stage in the development of the normal personality," Gilman notes, but in it "lies the root of all stereotypical perceptions."[37]

Stereotypes are "a crude set of mental representations of the world," Gilman contends, through which individuals try to order the world as they seek to establish "a needed sense of difference" between the self and the "object," or the Other. "Stereotypes arise when self-integration is threatened." The individual perceives difference in others; his or her sense of the order of the world is thus challenged. One way to hold on to that primitive sense of control and order, then, is to "project" one's deepest anxieties and fears onto the source of difference. Accordingly the Other

> is invested with all the qualities of the "bad" or the "good." The "bad" self, with its repressed sadistic impulses, becomes the "bad" Other; the "good" self/object with its infallible correctness, becomes the antithesis to the flawed image of the self, the self out of control. The "bad" Other becomes the negative stereotype; the "good" Other becomes the positive stereotype. The former is that which we fear to become; the latter, that which we fear we cannot achieve.[38]

Both instances result in smoldering anger and resentment toward the perceived Other. In Gilman's view, then, the cultural stereotype that might be found in all forms of cultural production are more revealing of the producer's anxieties and fears than of the lived experience and essence of the targeted group. Stereotyping blurs individuality as members of the targeted group are reduced to their most common denominator of difference: gender, in the case of women; race, in the case of blacks; class, in the case of poor whites.

Embedded in Gilman's definition is the concept of "representation," a critical term for contemporary literary analysis. George Levine notes that representation often "assumes a foundational self as agent. The self employs language to represent a foundational reality that exists outside of language; representation (language) becomes a 'third thing.' Representation, moreover, implies that some correspondence between language and non-verbal reality can be established."[39] In literary works, one must assume that both the ideal and "realistic" characters are figments of the author's imagination and do not imitate "real life." They represent the author's vision of social, economic, and political relations and convey his or her understanding of moral society. For instance, the Southern belle and the childlike, faithful male slave stand as the two extremes in the 'crude set of mental representations' in the planter's world. On the one hand, he projects onto the belle his vision of all that he seeks to attain, but fears he cannot; in the other, he projects his greatest fear, the "emasculated male," the man who is a thing. Most significant, he believes his representations of these people who inhabit particular social positions in antebellum society to be true images of their essence. These particular Southern authors articulated the worldview of the planter class at the moment when it was attacked by Western bourgeois thinkers generally and abolitionists in particular. The "cultural work" realized in these novels defended the plantation from outside attack and internal subversion. It not only justified planter domination of his "natural inferiors," but enhanced the class's sense of its world-historical mission.[40]

4. The Genesis of the "Plantation Novel"

Whilst we entirely concur with him [Nathaniel Beverley Tucker] that slavery as a political or social institution is a matter exclusively of our own concern as much so as the laws which govern the distribution of property, we must be permitted to dissent from the opinion that it is either a moral or a political benefit. We regard it, on the contrary, as a great evil, which society sooner or later will find it not only to its interest to remove or mitigate, but will seek its general abolition, or amelioration, under the influence of those high obligations imposed by an enlightened Christian morality.

James Ewell Heath, *Southern Literary Messenger* (1835)

THE WORK of the authors considered in this study divides into two groups: that which was written during the 1820s, which takes a reformist position on slavery or which advocates its gradual abolition; and that which was written during the 1830s and after, which is a proslavery literature. George Tucker and James Ewell Heath belong to the former group while Kennedy, Caruthers, N. B. Tucker, and Simms belong to the latter. Although the authors are divided by their differing positions on slavery, they all (with the exception of Heath) express elitist class prejudices, and thus, in the "Age of the Common Man," must be considered conservatives. In fact, what links these Southern writers together (again with the exception of Heath) was their belief that the naturally superior men of the planter class should govern Southern society and should represent the South politically at the national level. Their position was not a concession to the pragmatic reality that planters had the most leisure time and were thus the most available for service, but resulted from their conviction that the Southern white planter was innately superior to the men of all the other classes in Southern society, and thus was the most fit to govern. In an egalitarian age, this became an increasingly untenable position.[1]

The lives of George Tucker and James Ewell Heath provide the reader with insight into the politics of their fiction. George Tucker was born into a prominent Bermuda shipping family that prospered during the American Revolution by trading with both the British and the Americans. When he was twenty, his cousins, Thomas Tudor Tucker (1744–1828) and St. George Tucker (1752–1827), helped him settle in Williamsburg, Virginia, to study law at William and Mary College. As a prosperous relative of distinguished Virginians, Tucker traveled in the most socially prominent circles, and in 1797 he married Mary Byrd Farley, the wealthy but sickly great-granddaughter of the legendary William Byrd II of Virginia. When Mary Byrd died in 1799, Tucker traveled abroad for a period and then married again, in 1802, to Maria Ball Carter, the seventeen-year-old daughter of Charles Carter and the great-niece of George Washington. Tucker, who was an inveterate gambler, soon lost his own and his wife's fortunes speculating in land. Fortunately, his wife's family was able to give them a "small farm" in Frederick County in the western section of Virginia, so that they were not destitute.

By 1808, Tucker had recovered enough by living economically to purchase another smaller farm, "Woodbridge." Although both Tucker and his wife hated living in "poverty" in the western part of the state and resented their friendly but uncultivated country neighbors, they prospered there. Tucker sold essays on economics and politics to local papers, continued to speculate in land, and of necessity became a competent if not accomplished lawyer. In 1818, Tucker enjoyed his first of three terms as a U.S. Congressman from Lynchburg, Virginia, their new home. Suddenly, at the height of his new success and their newfound prosperity, Maria Ball died with her fifth child in pregnancy.[2]

The next year, Thomas Jefferson asked Tucker to lecture at the University of Virginia in political economy, belles lettres, and rhetoric. Tucker accepted when his plantation novel, *Valley of Shenandoah* (1824), failed to capture an audience. Tucker turned his intellectual efforts to the serious study of United States society, economy, and politics; that is, political economy. It has been as a controversial political economist that Tucker has received the most attention.[3]

Although Tucker is often regarded as a liberal for his acceptance of the inevitability of industrial capitalism, he is actually socially and politically a conservative. Like many nineteenth-century men with eighteenth-century values, although Tucker would have given the average man the right to vote for his economic and social superiors, he wouldn't have allowed such "inferior men" to hold office themselves. Similarly, Tucker thought that slavery was beneficial chiefly as a social institution, and that black labor would be entirely adaptable to industrialism. He angered proslavery planters by arguing that slavery was indefensible morally, politically, and economically, and by predicting that it would soon be eclipsed by industrial capitalism. Although he recognized absentee management, slave-breeding, and slave-selling as "necessary evils" of slavery, he thought that black men and women were more content with slavery than they would be as degraded free laborers exposed to both the competition of white labor and the travails of living on their own without the protection and security that he claimed slavery provided. Since Tucker thought that slavery would die out naturally, he thought it was best for the North to let the South deal with their "peculiar institution" and "their" black people themselves.[4]

Tucker continued to be active professionally until well after his retirement from the University of Virginia in 1845. He wrote *Political Economy for the People* (1859), in which he predicted the death of slavery but the survival of America as a "white man's country," and lived long enough to oppose Southern secession from the Union. He died the day before the attack on Fort Sumter, having been struck on the head by a falling bale of cotton while he stood on a dock during a visit to Mobile, Alabama.[5]

James Ewell Heath was a Virginia state official, the author of the novel *Edge-Hill; or, the Family of the Fitz-Royals* (1828), and the first editor of the *Southern Literary Messenger* (1843–45). He was the son of a prominent planter politician, John Heath, who was a member of the Third and Fourth Congresses and the first president of the Phi Beta Kappa society. Following his father's lead, James Ewell Heath ran successfully for the state legislature in 1814 from Prince William County, and returned two more times. During his third term, he became a member of the privy council and served as the state auditor for thirty years, until 1849, when the Democrats, angry at his satire of what he called their "despicable demagoguery" in his anonymously published 1839 play, "Whigs and Democrats, or Love of No Politics,"[6] turned him out of office.

In the first issue of the *Southern Literary Messenger,* Heath goaded his fellow Southerners not to be merely the consumers of Northern literature, but to shake off their "vassalage to their Northern neighbors" and be producers of their own literature. Later on in the same essay, he supported comprehensive education for women.[7] Similarly, in December 1834, Heath published Nathaniel Beverley Tucker's "Lecture on the Study of Law" in response to a request by Tucker's students. While Tucker characteristically asserted that "the existence of domestic slavery among us has been of singular advantage in preserving the free spirit of our people," Heath as editor responded by remarking that while he agreed that slavery was an institution of private property and thus was a matter on which only Southerners could legislate, it was an institution "a great deal evil" that he was confident Southerners would gradually abolish.[8]

Heath married twice; his first wife was Fannie Weems, the daughter of Parson Weems, the prominent biographer of George Washington; in 1820, after Fannie's death, he married Elizabeth Ann Macon, the daughter of Colonel William Hartwell Macon of New Kent County. Heath is generally remembered as a public-spirited nineteenth-century gentleman who divided his time between politics and belles lettres. His novel is important as one of the last Virginia novels to celebrate the liberal values of the American Revolution.

Tucker's *Valley of Shenandoah* (1824) and Heath's *Edge-Hill* (1828) appeared at a period of transition in Southern society. These works are important because they represent planter-class attitudes critical of slavery. By the end of the 1830s, sectional divisions were much more drawn as a new industrial capitalist class forming in the North challenged those old forms of pre-industrial capitalist inequality: those based on conservative patriarchal ideals that celebrated organic, hierarchical society. While Heath seems to accept a number of the premises of the new liberalism, Tucker and the other writers in this study refuse to accept a Southern society governed by the middle classes.

Tucker's *The Valley of Shenandoah* is the first plantation novel that, as a "domestic novel," depicts the everyday lives of a plantation family as their fortunes change for the worse over time. Tucker's work is unique in this literature, not only because of the subgenre he has chosen, but also because he is critical of slavery as an institution.[9] When one first compares Tucker's work with that of the other authors considered in this study, one's initial impression is that his criticism of slavery distinguishes him as a "liberal." However, once one reads Heath's *Edge-Hill,* which is a historical romance depicting both an impoverished female orphan who marries into the planter class and an intelligent black slave turned hero who accepts his master's offer of freedom after the Revolutionary War, one realizes that "the Other South" indeed existed even if its voice was progressively ignored, then muted, and finally extinguished through coercion and violence.[10]

Tucker's work survived and he prospered because as a member of the planter class, he accepted its most conservative tenets. Unlike Heath, who seemed to champion the rights of the black and white "common man," Tucker, like the other authors considered in this study, believed that "naturally inferior" black and white men should defer economically, socially, and politically to their planter superiors. Unlike Heath, who would gradually educate and emancipate black slaves, Tucker would reform slavery into extinction as the South industrialized, keeping blacks as the South's permanent working class—a racial "solution" not unlike the one arrived at in the segregated "New South" or in contemporary South Africa.[11]

In addition to cotton, the myth of the plantation South proved to be one of the most cherished and enduring antebellum Southern products. The dashing planter heroes, captivating belles, and contented and industrious slaves are stereotypes that have been reworked in each generation since the Civil War. The genesis of these stereotypes can be found in the work of the authors considered in this study. Central to the successful depiction of these stereotypes is fidelity to particular patriarchal conventions that antebellum Southerners applied differentially to women and African Americans. "Natural inferiors" (women and blacks) were expected to defer to a "natural superior" (the planter). In turn, he was expected to provide for them and protect them. In spite of his opposition to slavery, George Tucker adhered to such paternalism, while James Ewell Heath only followed patriarchal convention in his depiction of women. In these first Southern novels written before the proslavery suppression of informed debate about slavery, one confronts a paradox: while prototypical in establishing important literary conventions, these novels are atypical in their explicit or implicit criticism of slavery. In the antebellum Southern novel, women and blacks are connected by their location on the plantation and through their relationship with the planter who contended that slavery like the family was a "patriarchal institution." Yet, in spite of this alleged connection as the planter's "natural dependents," women and blacks rarely share the same scene or figure together in a significant event in this literature. Instead, blacks are portrayed in sentimental or humorous sketches with the planter, and planter wives and daughters are depicted almost exclusively in their relations with the planter and his son, or with their friends and relatives.

Because of her race and class position, the upper-class woman—the planter's mother, sister, wife, daughter—held a pivotal position in the society. It is understandable that Southern authors and planters spent pages and pages convincing themselves and Southern women that the "Southern lady" was what Southern culture was about—if only because the Southern planter could not aspire to dominance over his society without a partner of the same race and class.

Like all women in Western patriarchal societies, the belle was expected to come to her marriage "undamaged," that is, as a virgin. Since she was sexually restricted, unlike her future husband, and since she was expected to marry within her race and class, it might be argued that she was literally responsible for reproducing existing class and race relationships in the South, and thus paradoxically, was responsible for reproducing a system that held her in a kind of bondage. Her religious training, education, and socialization all reinforced her utter dependence on the men of her race and class, and especially on the men of her family who, in turn, had been socialized to interpret criticism of her as an affront to their family honor, and to risk their lives in defense of that honor.[12]

It should come as no surprise, then, that Tucker's and Heath's plantation women play out these patriarchal scripts and are completely absorbed in their relations with the men of their race and class. That is, they fall into two large groups—unmarried women and married women—with the members of each group having various family roles. The women in these novels have no destinies of their own. They are not independent. They do not think about politics or society. They do not struggle intellectually or morally with the problem of slavery, and they do not speculate on theology. They only ask God to help them perform their duties to the best of their abilities and to accept His will. Their hopes, dreams, and fantasies center on men and the family. If unmarried, they dream about the man they will marry. If married with children, they encourage their daughters to dream those dreams of love and marriage. Well, almost. One of the things that women are allowed to speculate on and indeed are encouraged by their parents to think about in choosing a husband in this plantation literature is economics. Surprisingly, considering the amount of Southern ink expended in criticizing Northern materialism, preoccupation with the monetary aspects of class pervades this plantation literature to such an extent that one is led to conclude that class was as much of a concern as was race.

In *The Valley of Shenandoah,* Tucker creates a noble but impoverished family, the Graysons, whose children, Edward and Louisa, must cope with their father's death and the family's resulting bankruptcy. Without a patriarchal head of household to guide them economically and socially, the family is defenseless. In contrast, Heath's orphaned Ruth Elmore is courted and won over by her planter stepbrother, Charles Fitzroyal, a patriot officer in the American Revolution. In a twist unique to this literature, not only is the heroine allowed to "marry up," but the villains are from a Loyalist, planter family. Although he is writing a historical romance, Heath's solution to gender and class issues is more typical of that favored by the sentimental novelists like William Hill Brown (*The Power of Sympathy,* 1789), than that favored by his fellow Southern writers Caruthers, Kennedy, or Simms. Similarly, Tucker's writing in the sentimental tradition presents the only successful seduction of a planter's daughter (note, by a Northerner). Tucker and Heath mold patriarchal convention sacrificing the planter heroine in different ways to fit their respective critiques of Southern society.

Tucker's novel testifies to the fact that when the woman fails in her "womanly" responsibilities and duties, the very existence of the family (and the plantation) is threatened. Tucker assures his reader that Mrs. Grayson was an effective and able manager of Colonel Grayson's property, but because the Grayson family takes such an abrupt downward slide at the Colonel's death, Tucker leaves the impression that women without men to depend on are incapable of carrying on by themselves.[13]

Tucker has devised two romantic plotlines for his characters. The first romance is the ill-fated courtship of Edward Grayson and Matilda Fawkner. Although they are very much in love, Edward and Matilda provide the morally correct example by obeying their families and restraining their demonstrations of affection and their visits with each other. Furthermore, Matilda's resoluteness and steadfastness in setting the bounds of their conduct together helps Edward control his "manly" passions (1:262–65, 281–84). In contrast to Matilda, Louisa, who has been indulged from infancy and who has recently taken up the dangerous habit of reading novels, has not developed the required self-discipline or self-control that she will need to manage herself and her suitor, James Gildon, the charming son of a New York City merchant (1:91–93; 2:1–4).

They meet unexpectedly at Stanley, the estate of Colonel Barton, Louisa's maternal uncle, the most fully drawn planter in Tucker's novel. Colonel Barton presides over a four-thousand-acre estate, a fourth of which is cultivated and worked by 150 slaves. Tucker informs the reader that Barton is a gentleman-farmer of the "old school," men known for "urbanity, frankness, and ease" and possessed of a nice sense of honour; a hatred of all that was little or mean; more fond of hospitality than show; great epicures at table; great lovers of Madeira wine, of horses and dogs; free at a jest, particularly after dinner; with a goodly store of family pride, and a moderate portion of learning; never disputing a bill, and seldom paying a debt, until, like their Madeira, it had acquired age; scrupulously neat in their persons, but affecting plainness and simplicity in their dress; kind and indulgent rather than faithful husbands, deeming some variety essential in all gratifications of appetite. . . . The luxurious and social habits in which they were educated, gave them all that polished and easy grace, which is possessed by the highest classes in Europe. (2: 105–6)

Tucker's representation of the aristocratic planter signals to his readers the centrality of the patriarchal family as a source of honor and pride and as the foundation for the community. Most remarkable, is his forthright description of these planters as "kind and indulgent rather than faithful husbands." This honest admission of planter profligacy will not be repeated after the late 1820s as Southern men closed ranks in a silence meant to preserve their gender and racial privileges from abolitionist critique. In representing Barton as an admirable figure and Edward Grayson as a promising young planter, Tucker lends veracity to the patriarchal defense of slavery and thus undermines his own contention that slavery is ruinous to whites.

Although Colonel Barton would have been held responsible for Louisa's protection, Tucker holds Louisa completely responsible for all that happens in her relationship with Gildon. Tucker notes that Louisa, influenced by romantic delusions gleaned from too much novel reading, is unwilling to "refuse those little favors, which love delights in giving and receiving." Since Louisa "considered herself betrothed in the sight of Heaven," she gave Gildon "her whole heart and unlimited confidence" (2:131).

Enthroning the vaunted patriarchal double standard of sexuality, which holds women responsible for male sexual aggressiveness, Tucker implies that had Louisa not lost her self-control first, Gildon wouldn't have been tempted.[14] Fatherless and unprotected, misled by sentimental novels, Louisa's folly results in her family's ruin as Edward is killed in a duel with Gildon defending her honor and that of the family. The integrity of the family and its preservation within the planter class rests on two foundations: the careful management of the plantation and the chastity of its women. Colonel Grayson's financial bankruptcy accompanied by his daughter's moral bankruptcy spelled ruin for the family.

Unlike himself or other Victorian men and women who married often after the death of a spouse, Tucker's women display a singular romantic attachment to the one man who will make their lives meaningful. When he is lost, no other man will do. Seduced and abandoned and guilty about her part in her brother's death, Louisa declines slowly and dies. Matilda Fawkner is so shocked by Edward's death she converts to Catholicism—for Protestant Tucker a sign of emotional instability—and becomes a nun. Mrs. Grayson, buoyed by her religious faith survives to old age a widow and serves as "the lady Bountiful of the neighborhood," but with what resources Tucker never mentions.

In a society that not only makes a pretense of ignoring pecuniary considerations, and that in most of its literature idealizes romantic love, its authors produced a literature in which class dominates marriage choice and informs the other social relations. Significantly, this practice keeps wealth and power within the South's white upper class. The only escape for anyone is the frontier, but as true Virginians the Graysons would not choose to make it.

In contrast to Tucker, Heath offers the reader the classic sentimental gender conflict: the poor but virtuous woman (Ruth Elmore) assailed by a dissolute and rapacious aristocrat (Albert Monteagle). Like Kennedy and Simms after him, Heath offers a generational conflict in having Loyalist Launcelot Fitzroyal at odds with his patriot son, Charles. However, unlike either Kennedy or Simms's Loyalist characters, Heath's Launcelot Fitzroyal has few redeeming features. In Heath's hands, the conventions of the sentimental novel merge with those in the romantic novel as Ruth becomes the innocent and victimized heroine who cannot defend herself when she is lured from the plantation by Monteagle (Launcelot's nephew). Fulfilling the romantic plot, she is rescued by the courageous Charles who is aided by his faithful and resourceful slave, James. Charles, Ruth, and James (who claims his freedom at war's end) represent the liberal promise of the revolutionary new nation: social mobility for virtuous common folk and freedom for slaves. In contrast, the elder Fitzroyal and the evil Monteagle represent Old World tyranny and corruption.

Perhaps inadvertently, Heath depicts the underside of patriarchal "protection" in his portrayal of Launcelot Fitzroyal and his relationship with Ruth. Spinning the standard cavalier myth, Heath notes that Launcelot Fitzroyal is a fifth-generation Virginian descended from Sir Rupert Fitzroyal, "a loyal cavalier and gentleman of wealth and family" who migrated to Virginia after the beheading of Charles II. Fitzroyal, Senior, is described as a Loyalist by birth, temperament, and training, a "proud, aristocratical and selfish" man and a petty tyrant. In breaking with the other Southern novelists, Heath ascribes to this class of Southerner the following character: "The love of pedigree and pride of ancestry, —an inordinate desire for great wealth, and the ostentatious display of it when acquired, —a childish prepossession for everything ancient, and a lively aversion from all rash innovations and revolutionary projects, were his ruling passions and characteristics."[15]

Fitzroyal, obligated by his deceased wife's generosity years before in accepting the orphaned Ruth from penniless tenants, forbids Charles and Ruth from courting, or Ruth from leaving Edge-Hill. Declaring that as patriarchal head of the household, he is responsible for her "reputation" and well-being, he "protects" her by imprisoning her in her garret room. Paternalism, when rejected or thwarted, turns to violence as soon as the master's "dependents" demonstrate they have wills of their own. Like the worthy slave, James, on this unique Revolutionary Virginia plantation, Ruth doesn't stay bound long.

Although Heath grants Ruth admirable characteristics—honesty, innocence, courage, an independent spirit, intelligence, a capacity for friendship and love—his plot turns on her victimization. Ruth cannot leave Fitzroyal's care and establish herself as an independent person because, according to the patriarchal double standard, a young, attractive, single "independent woman"—that is, a woman without a visible male guardian—is comparable to a "fallen woman." The oppression of women within the patriarchal family is thus predicated on the assumption that women are too inept to take care of themselves economically and that they are too weak to defend themselves from the inevitable violence of lower-class males. Even though Fitzroyal loathes Ruth, his reputation rests on his "protecting" her honor at the same time as he abuses her in the privacy of the patriarchal household.

Although Ruth demonstrates considerable tenacity, independence, and daring in thwarting her imprisonment at Edge-Hill, Monteagle is one step ahead of her, arranging for her "escape" into his hideaway where he tries to force her into a false marriage—really a rape—against her will.

She resists, not by escaping from Monteagle or by physically defending herself, but by the passive "feminine" act of fainting. Only the timely intervention of the hero saves her from the traditional fate of the "unprotected" female, rape. In spite of her fine character and intelligence, then, Ruth Elmore is the classic romantic heroine. She is drawn as the suffering victim so that Charles Fitzroyal can be the moral male protector. The reader complies in her victimization by cheering on the hero. The problem with this patriarchal solution is that a higher morality is achieved at the expense of the acceptance of the inevitability of male sexual violence and of a woman who must be victimized in order for a man to become a hero. In the end, the hero's rescue of the heroine doesn't "free" her at all but only delivers her to the man of her choice—her only choice in this patriarchal fiction.[16]

Indeed, freedom is very much a theme in this literature as these Southern writers as opposed to Northern writers adhere to an eighteenth-century, preindustrial capitalist vision of freedom. While the hero of the Northern romance is an average white man "freed" from the control of a patriarchal father or artisan master to seek his fortune in the city, on the frontier, or on the high seas, the Southern hero realizes his freedom through the command and control of other people. For both Northerners and Southerners of this period, a "free" woman was a dangerous woman who threatened the very fabric (that is, patriarchal authority) of society. Her only freedom, actually part of the post-Revolutionary struggle, was to be allowed to marry the man she loved, instead of the most economically stable man. That she would get married and have children was a foregone conclusion. The "radicals" of the period argued that she should be educated and have property rights.

In contrast, Southern white men considered themselves "free" if they owned their own land, family, and labor. As long as they weren't required to work for or serve other men, they considered themselves free. What made a slave a "slave," then, was his lack of control not only over his labor, but over his family. As miserable as the lives of nineteenth-century industrial workers were, they maintained patriarchal control over their wives and children, the primary vestige of "manhood." Slave women didn't even have the fundamental protection of their womanhood or their children that the most degraded Northern working woman had. No wonder that nineteenth-century African Americans embraced the bourgeois illusion of freedom. From where they stood, anything was better than slavery. However, the African American perspective on Southern society is entirely absent from this literature, although the authors purport to represent it. While these authors created women or poor and yeomen characters who hold liberal opinions about women's rights or democratic rights, few blacks are ever depicted desiring freedom or planning revolt.

In this conservative literature, not only are women safest and most content within the well-managed patriarchal household, but slaves as well respond gratefully and affectionately to good treatment by a kind master. While Tucker shares these attitudes and depicts the plantation as a self-sustaining community of white and black families and the center of antebellum Southern society and culture, he thinks the qualities that make a kind master and a good neighbor undermine the economic efficiency of the plantation. His description of the results of absentee plantation ownership and a slave auction undermine his positive assertions about the benefits of slavery for slaves.[17] In contrast, Heath, who belonged to the Colonization Society of Virginia, creates a black hero and then frees him. Consequently, while Heath breaks with conservative thinking about class and would free blacks from both the master and the land, Tucker's blacks are inextricably connected with the land and the plantation house.

One should note that Heath's apparent liberalism in regard to slavery is tempered by his envisioning room in white man's America for exceptional blacks (whom he would emancipate gradually) and colonization for the masses, the most conservative antebellum antislavery position. Tucker, however, rejected the notion of a classless society and thought that while slavery was indefensible morally and politically, it provided the proper social barriers between blacks and whites and a stable, if inefficient economic base for the South.

More than Heath, Tucker established a series of conventions that will reappear in Kennedy's *Swallow Barn* (1832), Thomas Nelson Page's works, and books written after the Civil War when plantation mythmaking flourished. In Tucker's Southern novel, the plantation is the social and economic base of the planter class and is the symbol of Southern society. Courtship and marriage, birth and death, seduction and betrayal all take place on the plantation. The plantation represents the planter's successful domestication of nature and man's control of himself and others. The domesticated land—the fields and garden of the plantation—is contrasted to the violent and chaotic "frontier" of the poor whites and the "wilderness" of the Native American. The white and black families achieve social harmony on the plantation because their lives are predicated on the allegedly "natural" base of white supremacy. However, in his depiction of a failed planter family, Tucker implies that there is something wrong with the way in which planters are carrying out their responsibilities; thus, unlike the other authors, he fails to create the illusion of plantation stability. In fact, with planter Grayson, Tucker seems to be arguing that those qualities planters cherished in themselves—their kindness, generosity and neighborliness—translated into their spending more money than they had, and ultimately led to their undoing.

The plantation and its core, the mansion, which houses the white family, were the concrete representation of the planter class in the South. As the plantation was secluded by woods or mountain ranges and river valleys, so the mansion house on the plantation, shielded by the natural luxury of colorful and fragrant gardens and soft verdant lawns, stood aloof from the slave quarters and the fields where black slaves lived and labored.

Beechwood, the home of Mrs. Mary Harrison Grayson, is situated on a "gently sloping hill on the northeast side of the Shenandoah."[18] The house is on high ground, the fields on low ground, patched green, yellow, or black depending on their use. The plantation is surrounded on two sides by the Blue Ridge Mountains, and from the house porch one has a view of the river. Tucker describes the house as "a modest mansion of rough blue limestone, in the form of the letter L, having three rooms on a floor. Below were a passage, drawing-room, dining-room, chamber, and a large closet which had been used as a dressing room and was now the lodging room of Louisa. The three rooms above were bed-chambers (1:17).

Although the Grayson "Big House" is not the ostentatious structure of Southern myth, the proximity of the mountains and the river heighten the reader's sensation of the plantation's peacefulness and its harmonious connection with nature. Additionally, it is far removed from the bustle and toil of the fields, and its spacious comfort contrasts with the squalid poverty of the slave quarters.

In what would become a standard plantation literary convention, Tucker introduces plantation society by having his hero, Edward Grayson, escort his Northern friend, James Gildon from New York City, around the Beechwood estate. As they pass through the fields, Edward and the blacks exchange greetings, and it is clear that Edward knows them and their families well. In one incident, Edward greets Peter, a former boyhood playmate and a recent servant in the Big House. Peter has been sent to the fields for having had sexual relations with a housemaid. When Edward approaches him and asks him how he is, instead of being hostile, Peter feels "deep shame and humility" at his degradation as a field hand, gives his master a big grin, and "seize[s] his hand with the grateful bow of a courtier" (1:67). In classic paternalistic form, then, Tucker portrays a young black who has internalized the values of the master class and has accepted planter justice. What is unusual about this incident is Tucker's depiction of a sexually active young black man. In most of the novels, blacks are portrayed as asexual, being either children or old people.

Southern paternalism, then, strove to instill a sense of inferiority in slaves from birth so that blacks would internalize the racism of the Southern slave regime and the values of the planter class. Ideally, then, if slaves were "properly raised," they would need little physical coercion, would identify themselves as members of the master's extended family, and would see in their prime exploiter, the master, their unequal friend. All of this antebellum Southern literature describes the successful accomplishment of that goal in its depiction of blacks who are rarely involved with the crises of their own families, but are always involved with those of the planter family; who work cheerfully and industriously with only a word of encouragement; and who are loyal and faithful servants.[19] Tucker doesn't believe in slavery as a viable economic system; he believes in the myth of planter paternalism, and not only gives it credibility in his white-black interactions, but has his hero, Edward Grayson, defend the planter-slave relationship as the humanizing aspect of the institution.

When Edward and Gildon tour the grounds of Beechwood, they discuss the institution of slavery and the master's responsibilities to his slaves. To Gildon's remark that Edward must enjoy the "unlimited control" of being a slave master, Edward replies that good slave management doesn't involve tyranny, and "that he who has a proper sense of his own rights, has due respect for the rights of others." When Gildon notes that slavery violates that understanding of human rights, Edward responds that his generation agrees that domestic slavery is evil, but envisions "no remedy that is not worse than the disease." Although Edward thinks that colonization is the best scheme for ridding America of its black population when they are freed, he thinks that it is impractical, while merely freeing blacks to fend for themselves as "free laborers" is far worse for the blacks themselves and for public order. Edward notes that although slavery "checks the growth of our wealth—is repugnant to justice—inconsistent with its principles—injurious to its morals and dangerous to its peace," because of the basic inability of most blacks to live as free white men or with free white men, ending slavery is impossible for the planter class and for the South (1:60–70).

Next, Edward adds that blacks have a higher standard of living than any other laboring class in the West, and that blacks born in slavery and accustomed to its limitations don't miss freedom so much as white men would if they were suddenly enslaved. Edward assures Gildon that a good slave master asserts no more authority over and expresses no less concern for his slaves than a parent would over his or her children. Finally, Edward argues that slavery did even more harm to whites than to blacks in corrupting the upper classes into a life of gambling, drinking, and dissipation, and in encouraging poor whites to see necessary labor as degrading drudgery unfit for white men. Edward's defense of slavery is clearly Tucker's as well. Although Tucker frankly admits some of the chief defects of slavery and does not defend it as a "positive good" the way the other authors of this study do, he believes in planter paternalism, which he sees as the ameliorating factor in an otherwise wasteful economic system.

In contrast to Tucker, perhaps because of his choice of the historical novel as a form centered on men's lives and men's problems, Heath's plantation scenes are minimal. Two black servants, James and his mother, Alice, Edward and Ruth's former mammy, are introduced as individuals active in the patriot cause, not as members of an ubiquitous slave community. In contrast to Simms, Kennedy, and Nathaniel Beverley Tucker, Heath doesn't indulge in the usual tendency to mock black dialect; while he characterizes Alice as speaking "with the usual incoherence which distinguished persons of her color and condition," her speech is comparatively clear. In another departure, while Alice conveys her past history with and affection for the hero and heroine, her primary relationship is with her son, James. In spite of the fact that she has no husband and apparently no last name, a symbol of her slave status, few black mothers are imagined to have families who might be primary in their hearts.

The entire opening scene with Alice conveys her ongoing connection with the other house servants, her concern and affection for Charles and Ruth, and her anxiety about James, who has said that he wished Charles would give him a gun so he could kill his own British soldiers.[20] Instead of being shocked or angry at the prospect of black male violence, Charles congratulates James through his mother for his patriotic sentiments, and gives Alice the message that they will be going to war together. Although clearly describing Alice and James in the stereotypical "faithful servant" roles, Heath does not seek to justify their enslavement nor defend the institution of slavery. In fact, in James he creates a black hero.

Heath's first full depiction of James occurs as some British officers, including traitor Benedict Arnold, are having dinner with the Fitzroyals. James, who is serving the meal identifies Arnold through a dissembling act that convinces the officers and Fitzroyal Senior that he is just an ignorant slave. However, James was making sure that he had his man and his reaction demonstrates Heath's sensitivity to the game of black dissembling. Shortly afterward, however, he takes Charles's gun and surreptitiously attempts to murder Arnold, a crime that is blamed on Charles (1:112).

Later in the novel, James not only leads Charles to the captured Ruth, but distinguishes himself in the war by saving Charles's life and by serving as a spy. After the war, he accepts Charles's offer of freedom, legalized by legislative act (1:224). In contrast, John Pendleton Kennedy's Luke, in *Swallow Barn,* is freed by his master after the war, but refuses manumission; his son, Abe, who is a black hero, never achieves his freedom.[21] Heath's character James is the only free black hero in all of the Southern antebellum literature considered in this study. In fact, James, as the master's faithful servant and protector during the Revolution and then as the honest, law-abiding freeman afterward, literally takes the place of another antebellum Southern type: the sturdy yeoman farmer who is the scout in war and the plantation overseer or yeoman farmer in peace. Heath's vision of the brave and respected free black was precisely that which white males of all classes would deny.[22]

In contrast, in *The Valley of Shenandoah,* Tucker describes only five blacks in detail, all of whom are very old and share the same attributes as ancient family retainers. Primus, apparently in his sixties, is the head house servant at Beechwood who keeps the younger servants in line and who passes gossip from one family member to the next (1:159, 2:177). Similarly, Old Phil is the proud stable man, in charge of the horses, who revels in the pomp and splendor of grooming the horses and getting them ready for a visit to other plantations (1:135, 152; 2:183–84). Old Bristol (a.k.a. "Bristow") is the loyal servant at Easton who tells Edward how Cutchins, the overseer, has been neglecting the care of the blacks and has been skimming money off the top from the sale of the crops. Old Jeffery, the servant at the neighboring Fawkner estate, The Elms (2:32–33), is described as a "shrewd, artful, ready-witted knave, who, having long assumed the privilege of great familiarity with his superiors, was at length suffered quietly to enjoy it" (1:32–33). He looks on Edward as his future master and tries to placate his desires as best he can. Finally, there is Granny Moll, eighty-four-years old, who, as the mammy, has raised three generations of white and black children at Beechwood. She serves as their confidante and as family historian. After she relates the Fawkner family history, in which we learn that Mrs. Fawkner, with all of her pretensions, comes from a nouveau riche planter family, Granny Moll exclaims, "I think they are all upstarts now-a-days. There is only a few of the old families left and they can just keep their heads above water" (1:85; "Moll" is often spelled "Mott" in this edition).

The plantation novel asks the reader to believe that blacks and whites live harmoniously on the plantation under the beneficent patriarchal guidance of the white master. Male slaves as the "faithful retainer" type—the racial "Other"—allow the planter to emerge as the dominant male on the plantation and as the major character in the novel and focus the reader's attention on the white family. Ignored is the existence of the black family and the black slave community. The "faithful retainer" is a stereotype that supports the planter contention that black slaves are essentially happy and well provided for under slavery, an institution that recognizes their different and unequal capacities for achievement compared to white men.

Similarly, the nurse or "mammy" as a literary figure and cultural type provides the strongest link between generations of whites and blacks, and underscores the planter contention that harmony between the genders and races prevails on the plantation. The black woman who relates the white family's history as her own underscores the planter argument that blacks love the whites they serve, and live long lives in their allegedly mild bondage. Although Tucker is one of the few authors to portray slaves with different personalities, as servants they are minor characters who allegedly play similar "supporting roles" on real Southern plantations. These fictional black slaves do not act on their own behalf, or make or have a history of their own, but are subsumed into the allegedly ahistorical and apolitical "private sphere" of plantation society where the patriarchal planter allegedly acts in their best interests.

In this vision the family is the core of the plantation as the plantation is the core institution of the antebellum South. When the plantation breaks up, it has a reverberatory effect upon the society. At the first breath of economic crisis, the façade of planter benevolence is stripped away, since the master can no longer keep up his end of the bargain to protect "his people" from the harsh realities of the marketplace. The slaves' real value to the white family as chattels at the slave auction comes as a blow to servants protected by their master from that truth. In a realistic and touching passage Tucker comments on the psychological horror of the slave auction for the slave:

> The weight of his fetters, the negro, who has been born and bred on a well-regulated estate, hardly feels. His simple wants are abundantly supplied, and whatever coercion there is on his will, it is so moderate and reasonable in itself, and, above all, he has been so habituated to it, that it appears to be all right, or rather, he does not feel it to be wrong. He is, in fact, a member of a sort of patriarchal family. But when hoisted up to public sale, where every man has a right to purchase him, he may be the property of one whom he never saw before, or the worst man in the community, then the delusion vanishes, and he feels the bitterness of his lot, and his utter insignificance as a member of civilized society. (2:206 and 207)

That is the ultimate reality of planter paternalism and the point of contradiction for the slave: the allegedly beneficent planter father would reduce him to a commodity and sell him away from his home and family for a profit. As Tucker shows, whatever the myth of planter paternalism the master and slave have been able to cling to is shattered at the first bang of the auctioneer's gavel.

Tucker's portrayal of the sale itself is revealing of a certain consciousness that was suppressed by the mid-1830s. In spite of his affection for the planter,

Tucker understands the contradictions of slavery and freedom within the same society. Like others of his generation he sees slavery as a "necessary evil" (1:61 and 62).

The slaves on the Grayson Easton plantation have to be assured that they will not be planting indigo before they agree to be sold in a lot to Georgia. They know that in planting indigo they will be standing knee-deep in water bending over most of the day, which could result in bad backs, influenza, and pneumonia. Finally, they agree to go with a planter named Stokes from Georgia. Tucker describes a "likely mulatto girl" who would leave a husband behind if she were sold. Tucker comments quite frankly that "slaves of this description often command very high prices, when they happen to suit the tastes of some of the libertines of the French or Spanish settlements" (2:208). The mulatto girl is asked by a "very well-dressed man" if she cares to go with him, but she refuses. In the end, Truehart, the Grayson family lawyer, arranges for her to be with her husband. Absalom is the next person to be sold. He wants to be sold away from his wife because she has been unfaithful to him. The couple is reconciled and they join the group bound for Georgia.

Virginians created a myth, partly through this literature, that slavery in their state was much more humane than elsewhere in the South.[23] The references to Georgia, to the West Indies, and to New Orleans reflects the Virginian sense of superiority to other Southerners (and especially the West Indies slaveholders, who, they contended, were particularly promiscuous). Tucker's veiled references to the "fancy girl" market mostly running out of New Orleans are the only mention of it in all of this literature. Additionally, marital infidelity as the cause of separation, implies that infidelity was a problem on the plantation for blacks as well as whites.[24] Finally, Tucker takes pains in this scene to assure the reader, notwithstanding the historical record, that although friends were separated, planters made an effort to keep families, and especially mothers and young children, together.

Tucker shies away from what would be the favorite auction scene of abolitionist novelists, the forced separation of mother and child; but to his credit, he is the only antebellum Southern novelist to depict a slave auction at all. Individually, the members of the planter class knew on some level that those people they pretended were part of their "families" would ultimately be willed or sold with the rest of the planter's chattel at his death or in the event of an economic crisis. The underlying reality of plantation relationships is ignored in these other novels because their exposure would undermine the moral authority of the master and ultimately of the planter class itself.

George Tucker and James Ewell Heath provide the student of Southern culture and fiction a glimpse of that section's range of thinking before Southern antislavery positions were forcibly suppressed. Although Tucker developed many of the familiar literary conventions of the plantation novel—the primacy of the white planter family and the plantation as the setting; the swooning planter-class heroine and the valiant planter-class hero; the loyal, happy, and industrious black slaves; the unmannerly and threatening poor whites—he emerges as a critic of slavery. Tucker criticizes slavery as a "necessary evil" and as "a disease"; his depiction of the planter's family that fails because of the planter's financial irresponsibility; his allowing the seduction of the planter's daughter and the death of the planter hero; his picture of the horrors of the slave trade; and his allusions to both white and black male sexuality are unique in this literature. Similarly, Heath's egalitarianism and his creation of a black hero were themes that Southerners refused to consider by Jackson's second term.

While Heath subscribes to liberal class attitudes, Tucker shares the conservative class attitudes of the other authors. In spite of his reputation as a liberal, Tucker loathed Jacksonian democracy and thought only the propertied and wealthy elite should govern.[25] In *The Valley of Shenandoah,* his class and ethnic prejudices lead him to produce ethnic stereotypes of his social inferiors.

For instance, while Tucker claims that the adult German male is a "kind and faithful husband, and a provident master of his family," he criticizes Germans for their mediocrity, lack of ambition, lack of taste, and their contentiousness. He notes that although Germans tend to be "a useful class of citizens *in their place* (my emphasis), they are for the most part "without generosity, without public spirit" (1:53). Thus, Tucker creates a German immigrant, Jacob Scryder, who knocks Louisa Grayson's carriage off the road. Scryder comments, "lady or no lady, she has not the right to stop me from going to market" (1:129). In court, the jury found that as civilized men, they couldn't allow an "unfeeling savage" to "threaten the safety of a defenceless female" (1:233).

His assessment of the Scotch-Irish is different, but he still finds them wanting in self-control. He admires the Scotch-Irish as "ardent," "impassioned," and "imaginative" members of the yeoman and lesser slaveholding classes. Tucker notes that when Scotch-Irishmen seek to attain something "they manifest great enterprise and perseverance; but are as often idle, indolent, and improvident" (1:55). He praises them for being "hardy, restless, brave and enterprising," and notes that "they have been the most successful warriors against the aboriginal proprietors of the country, and the advance guard of civilization" (1:55). Additionally, Tucker admires the Scotch-Irish for the "lively interest" in government that makes them staunch defenders of freedom, yet he claims that the same passion which can engage one man "in a course of rapid and adventurous speculation" will lead another to pursue "thoughtless extravagance and unwarranted luxury" (1:56).

Tucker creates in a marginal planter, M'Cullough, a stereotypical Scotch-Irish type, whose improvidence and lack of foresight lead him to mismanage

his household and live beyond his means. Tucker tells us that the M'Cul-
loughs' "occasional display of luxury, together with the abundance with
which their table was supplied . . . removed the impression of poverty, which
the exterior of the house was calculated to convey; but left that of bad
management in all its original force" (1:169). M'Cullough's solution for his
periodic near bankruptcies is not to be more frugal, but to liquidate his estate
and move west, where he can start again (1:169; 2:319).

Unlike other Southern novelists, who present the planter class as stratified but ethnically homogeneous and who describe them as the section's
virtually infallible leaders, Tucker delineates stratification within the planter
class based on ethnic differences. Moreover, he shows planters who fail.
Notwithstanding Tucker's success in depicting Southern ethnic diversity, his
fictional society excluded the great majority of the antebellum population:
that is, nonslaveholding yeoman farmers from mixed ethnic backgrounds.
Tucker, like the other authors, chose to tell the story of the planter class, to
which he felt closest and which he believed was the most important segment
of the Southern population. Unlike other authors, he does not malign non-
planter classes, but conveys the impression that "Southern Civilization" was
plantation society, and that in comparison all others were insignificant.

For all their prejudices, Tucker and Heath are distinguished among these
authors for their implicit and explicit criticism of slavery and the planter
class. In spite of his generally positive depiction of the master-slave relationship, Tucker portrays a range of planters all of whom are flawed in some way.
M'Cullough is pretentious, ostentatious, and improvident, and survives by
periodically liquidating his estate and moving west; Colonel Barton, for all
his admirable qualities and judicious management of his plantation, is unfaithful to his wife and squanders his wealth; and finally, Grayson, who, with
his son, epitomizes the best in the planter class, has through his generosity
to his less fortunate neighbors, bankrupted his own family. Even Edward
Grayson, the hero of the novel and Tucker's spokesman, is uselessly killed in
a duel defending his family's honor, and with his death ruins the lives of his
mother and fiancée.

In his description of the slave auction and of the seduction of the planter's
daughter, Tucker offers an unusually critical appraisal of Southern life. Significantly, he establishes a number of conventions for the plantation novel
that will be repeated by subsequent Southern writers: the description of the
plantation grounds and of plantation society; the portrait of the faithful
black male servant and of the "mammy" who identifies the planter family
and relates its history to the younger generation; the recreational and social
life of plantation men and women; the defense of slavery as an institution
that benefits blacks more than whites.

In contrast, Heath's work is important because it renders the other side of
antebellum Southern consciousness—that which was defeated in 1831–32, in
the wake of the Nat Turner rebellion and the Virginia Slavery debates—as the

conservative strata of the planter class and their intellectual allies closed ranks in defense of slavery and of their respective gender, racial, and class privileges. The existence of Heath's novel, *Edge-Hill; or, the Family of the FitzRoyals* (1828), is an example of Southern liberal thinking that was extinguished almost before it ignited. Its significance lies neither in its form nor in its art, but in its liberal attitudes toward gender, race, and class relations.

II

REPRESENTATIONS

OF WOMEN

IN TRUTH, women, like children, have but one right, and that is the right to protection. The right to protection involves the obligation to obey. A husband, a lord and master, whom she should love, honor, and obey, nature designed for every woman—for the number of males and females is the same. If she is obedient, she is in little danger of mal-treatment; if she stands upon her rights, is coarse and masculine, man loathes and despises her, and ends by abusing her.
—George Fitzhugh, *Sociology for the South*

There is no great danger—none to you, my dear, so long as Willie Sinclair can strike a stroke, or lift an arm at all for your protection. (Willie Sinclair to Carrie Sinclair)
—W. G. Simms, *The Forayers*

We learn ourselves through women made by men.
—Sheila Rowbotham, *Woman's Consciousness, Man's World*

5. Representing Southern Women's Lives

THE LIVES of antebellum Southern women were determined by their gender, race, and class, as well as by choice and by chance. While they shared similar life problems—establishing a feminine identity, deciding when and whom to marry, asserting their authority within the family and their community, surviving materially and supporting their dependents, dealing with old age and the deaths of loved ones—women of different races and classes obviously had different and unequal options. White and black women of the "Big House" formed alliances designed to nurture black and white children and to operate the plantation household. However, because of the differences in the conditions of their lives and those of their families, they never quite achieved the "sisterhood" of planter myth.

Depending on their talents and temperaments, on the ability of the planter to manage his estate profitably and his willingness to remain faithful in marriage, a plantation household could be efficient and harmonious or it could be wasteful and disorganized, riven by numerous intrigues, daily squabbles, petty jealousies, and violence.

One suspects that over a twenty-year period any given plantation may have had cycles of efficiency and inefficiency, harmony and disharmony, depending on market factors and the disruption of its human society due to marriages, births, sales, and deaths. More important, it is clear from the testimony of women and blacks that the times of greatest "harmony" were the times of greatest violence and oppression toward them. A white or black woman might grow up on a plantation that was managed quite differently from the one on which she would spend her adult life. If it were traumatic for a young planter's daughter to leave her own family and join her husband's household, it was even more traumatic for the black slaves accompanying her who were forced to leave their families, sometimes forever. The initial years of marriage not only meant mutual adjustments between spouses, but reconciling differences between two groups of household servants. That work, like other domestic work, fell largely on the plantation mistress.

One of the myths dispelled recently is that of the idle leisure plantation mistress, who lived a life of luxury, and was more a human ornament than a household worker.[1] In reality, she was a wealthy farmwife. If somewhat free of anxiety about her social standing and material well-being, she was nonetheless responsible for the day-to-day management of the household: for overseeing the dairy and the care of poultry; for supervising the gardening, the laundering, the cleaning, the food preparation, and clothesmaking; for nursing the sick and caring for children. Her own labor varied with need and her own inclinations and talents. Additionally, she had sole responsibility for the religious education of her children and for maintaining correspondence with her family and friends. If any women on the plantation came close to living the life of the mythical "Southern Lady," it was perhaps her teenage daughter who was in apprenticeship in learning these domestic skills, or perhaps an aged female relative who could assume some but not all of the daily domestic tasks.[2] The recent social history of the antebellum plantation reveals a plantation mistress who worried about her health and that of her family; about her soul and those of her children, relatives, and slaves; about her husband's fidelity; and about her ability to carry the domestic burden placed on her. Although she was of the upper class, her life choices were severely circumscribed by her sex. Her education and her socialization were designed to make her a pious planter's wife, and the only "choice" she ever made was when and whom, not whether, to marry.[3] Since family concerns often outweighed her individual choice, even that choice was often made for her.

The lives of black plantation women were even more circumscribed than those of white women. Ironically, if the planter's daughter was oppressed because her life was predetermined, then the slave's daughter was oppressed because very little about her life was certain or predictable. Like all those living in the antebellum era, she knew the fear of disease and epidemics; but owing to an increased vulnerability to disease due to her inadequate diet, her working conditions, and lack of proper medical care, she ran greater risks of dying early than did the white plantation woman.[4] Black women had to worry about being maimed by faulty household and farm equipment or about being physically abused by members of the planter family.[5] Additionally, black women had to thwart the sexual advances of white planter-class males, overseers, and their friends and relatives, while restraining themselves and the men of their families from seeking just revenge for such abuse. In addition to constant hard work under the most oppressive situations with minimal opportunity for learning any but the most basic domestic and agricultural skills, black men and women faced the additional burden of trying to keep their families alive and together.[6]

The images of women that emerge in the fiction under review bear almost no resemblance to the realities of the lives of white and black women on the antebellum plantation. As historical romances, in addition to recording male political struggles, they sought to re-create the "very best" possible male and female characteristics in their white heroes and heroines and to establish a conservative "ideal type" for male and female readers. The creation of the historical romance allows these Southern authors to evade the daily plantation reality. Instead, an ideal white planter-class hero and heroine are portrayed, while it is claimed "realistic" "lowlife" characters—that is, black slaves and poor whites—are also depicted. Thus does the white plantation family emerge as the best representative of its race and class; everyone else falls into "good" and "bad" categories. Like his European and Northern counterparts, the Southern romancer took the sentimental heroine—the assertive woman who like Richardson's Clarissa coped alone with the advances of her suitor/seducer without male intervention—and transformed her into the "romantic" heroine as the embodiment of passive femininity. The hero emerges as the embodiment of transcendent masculinity, and the villain represents human evil as well as the baseness and inferiority of his particular race, class, or nationality. In that transition from the sentimental heroine to the romantic heroine, the woman loses her capacity to act on her own behalf. The heroic male becomes her savior and thus establishes himself as a "moral man," his heroism, in effect, rests upon her victimization. Additionally, in the Southern romance, the male hero represents the men of his race and class, and thus emerges as the "natural leader" of Southern society.

If Richardson's Clarissa and Pamela are bourgeois and working-class virgins fighting off the lechery of aristocratic men, then the Southern heroine is an aristocratic virgin whose male protector guarded her from the lechery of planter enemies. Many of the Southern novels combine both modes so that the planter-class heroine holds out until she can be rescued, very similar to the way Ruth Elmore in Heath's *Edge-Hill* held out against the villain Monteagle. Significantly, in contrast to Tucker's *Valley of Shenandoah,* none of the historical romances depicts a planter's daughter who is either raped or successfully seduced. The romantic heroine, then, emerges from the Southern antebellum novel as a "man's woman" who exists to solve male problems.[7]

Northern and Southern antebellum fiction have different emphases and perspectives and create different myths. If bourgeois romanticism celebrates individual uniqueness, emotional spontaneity, and the possibility of human progress, then the Southern novel with its emphasis on the values of the organic society—individual self-sacrifice, family honor, patriotic loyalty, emotional conservatism, and the mutual obligations of natural superiors and inferiors—is anti-bourgeois to its core. Whereas the Northern bourgeois romantic hero tests himself against his own moral frailty, nature, and the competitive marketplace, and is often engaged in a lonely rejection of "civilization" (which he associates with femininity), the planter hero strives to conserve the traditions and institutions of his gender, class, and race against what he perceives as an assault from the outside.[8] Even when the planter ventures into the wilderness, he takes the plantation with him and has no desire to be a "freeman" in the bourgeois sense; he is a freeman in the eighteenth-century, conservative meaning of the term: a patriarchal owner of property, the head of his household, and a "natural aristocrat" who controls a single workforce.

For her part, the Southern heroine is what we would call a Victorian woman. Her most laudable qualities are purity and piousness, which allegedly inspire men to noble deeds; self-sacrifice, altruism, and submissiveness, which make her a loving wife and mother and a charitable mistress; and her domestic talents, as opposed to her intellectual ones, which bind her to the plantation household instead of giving her "exaggerated notions" of her ability.[9] Katherine Rogers notes that Victorian men "told women that they would cease to be women, and thus forfeit all masculine love and respect, if they aspired to strength of body or mind, and that such aspirations would be further disastrous because women are weak—physically, mentally, morally."[10]

No longer perceived as the source of temptation for male corruption, the Victorian "lady" became trapped in its opposite: the bind of pious purity that totally denied their sexuality. If Northern Victorian women admitted to or acted on their sexual passions, they were denigrated as being no better than the working-class prostitutes that bourgeois men increasingly sought for sexual gratification. In comparison, the sexual Other for Southern mistresses were black slave women, "Jezebels," who allegedly seduced their husbands and turned their plantation households into "harems."[11] The earliest colonial literature reveals Southern planter projections of their sexual fears and sexual fantasies onto black men and women, reflecting planter perception of black women as their lewd seducers while attributing chasteness and sexual purity to their own white mothers, daughters, and wives. Nineteenth-century Victorian morality did not change that tendency in the South; indeed it enhanced it.[12] What is significant about Southern literature after 1831 is the authors' failure to mention sexuality, especially miscegenation between black people and white people. Although planters freely boasted about their sexual conquests in the camaraderie of intimate all-male gatherings, they were publically silent about this aspect of their lives, especially after abolitionists started attacking them for licentiousness. What others saw as hypocrisy, they considered as upholding their family's honor.[13]

Even the most privileged woman was denied fundamental civil and political rights and educational and economic opportunity that the men in her family enjoyed. Her oppression was forever before her: she left her own family and took her husband's name; her husband was the legal guardian of their children who bore his name; her property became his and her wages were his; she had no citizenship rights and could not serve on juries or be tried by her peers; rape was a crime against her father or husband; she could be beaten by her father or husband at their will; she could not easily obtain a divorce for abandonment or cruelty; it was considered "unfeminine" for her to speak or write in the public sphere.[14] However, she was trained to see these disadvantages as "privileges" and to think of those women who protested against their lot or who acted against male-prescribed law as "unfeminine" or "unruly."

In the antebellum South, as in most Western Christian societies, men perpetuated the myth of female inferiority and represented them as the sexual Other: the adored "Virgin," revered "Mother," dissolute "Whore." Woman stands for the immanence of nature, which man must conquer if he is to realize himself as the transcendent hero, the fallen God. "She is the privileged object through which he subdues Nature," Simone de Beauvoir argues.[15] Thus men form their philosophical construct of the world based on the inherent violence of the social relations between the sexes. Their dualistic worldview is expressed in binary oppositions: me/not me, good/evil, male/female, rationality/irrationality, white/black, civilization/Nature. Constructing the woman as the sexual Other, the patriarchal male distances himself from her and from what he calls her "femininity," which he loathes. She selflessly serves, he commands; she is fragile and timid, he is resolute and courageous; she gives and preserves life, he takes it in war; she is naive and gullible, he is worldly and resourceful. Although the styles of femininity and masculinity change with each historical period, each generation has its own feminine and masculine gender conventions, the primary principle being male dominance of women. From the time they are little boys, especially in emotionally conservative families, males are taught to loathe "feminine" qualities in themselves as they insist on them in women. Although they require feminine deference, the patriarchal male loathes women for their weakness and inferiority and hates them for making him their oppressor. At the same time, he is trapped because his social, economic, and political privileges are gained at woman's expense; he is the "man" only as long as she is willing to be the "woman." If the race and class stakes are high enough, as they were with Southern mistresses, she might be willing to play for perpetuity.[16]

To escape from the implications of his violence against women, the patriarchal male convinces himself and them that they are essentially inferior to him, thus absolving himself in their victimization and projecting himself as their virtuous and superior protector. Unfortunately, seeing no positive examples of free and independent women before her and taught to fear and loathe "unfeminine" women and those independent impulses in herself, the average woman believes in the legitimacy of male dominance and patriarchal law and allows herself to be silenced. Thus dominant males assume the mythmaking authority for their respective societies, writing women into submissive roles and out of history.[17]

It should not be too surprising then, that this Southern literature written by men ignores women's hopes, dreams, fears; their relationships with other women; their speculations on politics and philosophy; their complaints and protests about their lives, and refuses to grant them any sense of worth and value except as they nurture men and children. Instead, the authors follow traditional Western European patriarchal convention by creating female characters who live through men and who are variations on the "Virgin," "Mother," and "Whore." With the exception of the heroine whose destiny is marriage, the unmarried woman is the object of pity, scorn, and hatred;

she is characterized as the "coquette," the "spinster," and the "intellectual woman." For such authors, the "masterless woman," like the masterless
slave, is a victim helplessly adrift and subject to social predators, usually the
enemies of the planter class. Planter-class ideology instructs that both the
woman and the slave need the material and emotional security of the patriarchal family under the benevolent guidance and protection of the planter.
Of course, without a woman of his race and class to reproduce the next
generation, or black laborers to produce the crops he needs to generate
wealth, the planter has no social or economic standing and therefore no
political power.

What paternalism does, then, is mask planter dependence and institutionalized violence and reverse the nature of the social relationships, by
claiming that women and blacks are his dependents. It is only in the planter's imagination and in his worldview—in his understanding of himself as a
"man"—that women and black slaves are connected as his inferior dependents. In reality, white plantation women and black slaves stood in fundamentally incomparable positions to each other and to the planter. They were
"connected" only through their relationship to the planter. Planters' wives
and daughters comprehended their oppression to a relatively greater extent
than did their fathers, husbands, and brothers, but since such oppression
was so psychologically bound with their understanding of themselves as
women, they internalized the anger born of passivity. On those occasions
when they did express it, this anger was more often than not directed against
their slaves than against their male relatives.[18] In contrast, slave testimony
indicates that black slaves were much freer psychologically from their masters and mistresses than they revealed in everyday behavior. They were able
to forge a culture of resistance that sustained them in their continuing struggle against new forms of white racism.[19]

Motherhood is the only female role depicted in this literature that transcends race and class barriers to unite all women. "Good" married women
include self-sacrificing and pious mothers and widows; "bad" ones are undisciplined, unskilled, or neglectful mothers, or the mothers of poor-white
men who encourage and aid their sons' lawlessness against the planter class.

For the most part, women and blacks submitted to planter government;
the price for not doing so was too great. The planter read their submissive
behavior as acquiescence to his assertions of superiority. Those relations
were defended in proslavery essays and speeches and in this proslavery
literature reaffirming paternalistic ideology. This antebellum Southern literature, written by white males allied with the planter class or by planters
themselves, justifies the planter's economic, social, and political oppression
of women, blacks, and poor whites in the South. Its proslavery ideology
supports both male supremacy and elitism. It not only offers a vision of male
power that reflects eighteenth-century conservativism, but in its class analysis is antagonistic to the tenets of bourgeois democratic thought.

6. Unmarried Women: The "Belle," Passive Sufferer versus Spirited Woman

THE UPPER CLASS of Southern society was reproduced when members of the planter class intermarried, had children, and passed down property in land and slaves from generation to generation. Patriarchal inheritance customs legitimated the dominance of ruling-class males in antebellum Southern society as they did elsewhere. The romantic plot, then, becomes more than a frivolous diversion for female readers. Its subtext is justification for planter rule. The most significant woman in this literature is the planter's unmarried daughter, the "belle," because her consent to marriage enables the planter to establish or reestablish a family claim and in attendance, a racial and a class claim to the land. Although a planter might operate a plantation without a wife, her companionship, work, and reproductive capacities tie him to his past, present, and future in a way which is impossible with any other social relationship.

The fictional images of women, then, are always two-sided: they reflect the gender conventions of antebellum Southern society and offer a fusion of planter fantasy, longing, and desire. As already seen, in reality planters' wives were most unromantic. Wealthy farmwomen, they absorbed the cares of household management, childrearing, and family religion. For the planter, the adventure and uncertainty of life were not found in private, daily household events—the subject of the novel—but in the public sphere of war, politics, and courtship dominated by men and male problems, the subject of the historical romance. Women, it follows, may be central to the plot, but they are not actors in their own behalf. Rather, they are the vehicles through which ruling-class men maintain their gender superiority and their race and class dominance. The belle's victimization by a planter enemy allows the planter hero to establish himself as the prime enforcer of public morality, law, and justice. The form of the romance establishes a conservative social philosophy that confirms male violence and female passivity as "natural" and immutable.

The dominant belle remains the virtuous, domestic, and essentially passive and suffering Victorian woman. The "Scarlett O'Hara" type—the willful, indulged and flirtatious coquette (created by a woman, after all)—is almost entirely absent from this literature. When she does appear, she is severely

censured. The more assertive spirited and/or intellectual woman is a variation on this type and given the absence of the plantation mistress in this
literature may stand in for her. Only Nathaniel Beverley Tucker succeeds in
making all of his heroines saccharine and passive to the point of total depen-
dency. In contrast, the other authors offer a somewhat more diverse range of
female characters, although one should emphasize that all of these fictional
women seek in men and marriage the essential meaning for their lives.[1]

Two types of heroines will be discussed below. The passive heroines of
Nathaniel Beverley Tucker (Gertrude Courtney, *Gertrude,* and Bet Balcombe,
George Balcombe) and William Gilmore Simms (Bertha Travis, *The Forayers*
and *Eutaw,* and Virginia Maitland, *Border Beagles*) emerge as stereotypes:
innocent, fragile and passive creatures who need protection from the sordid
and violent "real world." These heroines' passivity and victimization not
only set the stage for male heroism; they are necessary for it. Indeed, their
victimization is a prerequisite for proving the conservative contention that
the average man is inherently violent and needs the discipline and leadership of the planter class. Even the more assertive heroines discussed below
are eventually subordinated by the "superior" men of their race and class. Of
these self-assured and intelligent young women, only Bel Tracy is mocked
by Kennedy for her attachment to the medieval (and Southern) chivalric
tradition. Interestingly, Simms's depiction of Janet Berkeley undermines his
hero, Mellichampe, but tips off the careful reader to the underlying structure
of the historical romance.

The primary question posed in *Gertrude* is whether one marries for love
or for money. Tucker's solution is expressed by Gertrude Courtney's stepfather, Doctor Austin, who tells Gertrude that a woman "should neither marry
a man she does not love, nor one who cannot support her."[2] Gertrude lives
with her mother, her stepfather, and his son, Henry Austin, with whom she is
in love. Mrs. Catherine Austin, with a more pragmatic vision of her daughter's prospects, first discourages Gertrude and Henry, and then thwarts their
romance by arranging for Gertrude to think that Henry no longer cares for
her. She manipulates Gertrude into marrying a wealthy South Carolinian
planter, Harlston.

Tucker thus presents Mrs. Austin as the villainess and treats all three characters—Gertrude, Henry, and Harlston—as wronged victims of her avarice.
What dominates this novella, however, is Tucker's feeling that given woman's "natural" emotional passivity and economic dependence on men, her
only life choice is marriage. However, the worst sin is to marry for money not
love (11:706 and 707). His fictional women are caught in the classic patriarchal double bind. Economically helpless, they must marry someone who
can support them, but they can only marry for "true love." Further, they must
be passive recipients of male attention, not active seekers of men who attract
them. Psychological and economic power, then, remains vested exclusively
in one gender.

Women, Tucker believes, are always passive sufferers. They must bear whatever nature and society have in store for them. Tucker clearly delineates the advantages men have in a patriarchal society: "In his intercourse with the other sex, man is always the regulator of circumstances, and thus master of himself. He is free to choose his company, his occupations and amusements, all of which, in the case of a young woman, depend on the choice of others. Passive, yielding and accommodating from the necessity of her position, the very excellence of her nature makes her the victim of the artful or inconsiderate measures of those who regulate her destiny" (10:644 and 645; see also 11:708). Woman's oppression, then, is attributed to her nature and not to the violence of men. She is "born to suffer" in a socio-economic system that reserves its harshest penalties for those who fail to conform to planter domination.

Patriarchal power, thus reproduced in generation after generation, re-creates the allegedly naturally inferior and suffering woman as victim. The independent woman, for Tucker, is as much of an anathema as the "free" or masterless African American. The former flouts patriarchal gender authority, the latter flouts patriarchal racial and class authority. For Tucker and others, the oppression of women, much like that of blacks, results from their alleged incapacity for independence. The planter learns to be their "master" within the patriarchal family where he first gains confidence in his ability and right to dominate those different and therefore presumably inferior to him. If he has the right to dominate that other human being—the ruling-class white woman—who shares his race and class, then surely, he might reason, he is justified in dominating all other groups. Tucker's work contributes to and justifies this Southern mythology of planter domination. In a most revealing passage, Tucker laments: "Oh Woman, Poor Woman. She is the slave of circumstances, and bound by an invisible chain she is dragged along to whatever destiny the interested views of others may prepare for her" (11:180).

The nineteenth-century Southern woman was not dragged along by "invisible chains." Her oppression was everywhere apparent: in her family, her education or lack of it, her lack of economic options and property rights. In making the case for patriarchy, Tucker exposes the violence inherent in paternalism. He demonstrates forthrightly that, like slaves, women must be taught submission and obedience to their "natural" masters. If they obey, they will not be beaten, raped, starved, or turned out into the society or the wilderness to be abused by others. Furthermore, they have the ever-present example of slave resistance met by the master with unconscionable brutality to discourage them from standing upon their rights in a "coarse and masculine way."[3]

From his own experience in Missouri and as in Simms's border novels, Tucker's *George Balcombe* reproduces Eastern plantation culture in frontier Missouri.[4] The main action of the novel centers on Balcombe's pursuit in Virginia of a dishonest lawyer, Montague, who has cheated him and a young friend, William Napier. As Balcombe and Napier ride from Missouri to Virginia to hunt down and punish Montague, Balcombe, the conservative paternalist, tries to dissuade Napier from his liberal notions on the education of women and slavery. Balcombe explains that the woman who has made men the most happy is the "housewifely girl, who reads her Bible, works her sampler, darns her stockings, and boils her bacon and greens together."[5] In Tucker's view, educating women "unsexes" them and makes them unfit for marriage. He concludes that the worst thing for a marriage is competition between the sexes, and that nothing fires that competition more than when a woman thinks that she knows more than her husband or feels she can manage just as easily without him.

Balcombe describes how a woman should be properly socialized from infancy to subordinate herself to men. He intends to educate his own daughter "to be the wife of a great and good man" (2:51). That process starts at home in training her in "the habitual subordination of the heart and the mind . . . to the wisdom, real or fancied, of her parents." Learning her lessons of humility and subordination well, the little girl, now a young woman, is ready for marriage. If her parents (especially her father) have done their job properly, her so-called education "will prepare and dispose her to enthrone, as the master feeling of her heart, a cherished sense of her husband's superiority, from which will spring an assurance of his virtue, a reliance of his wisdom, a zeal for his honour, a pride in his distinction, and an undoubting confidence in his fortunes and his prowess" (2:52).

In Elizabeth (Bet) Balcombe, Tucker has created as his feminine ideal a most insipid and self-abasing woman. We are told that Balcombe admires his wife's "primitive qualities": her childlike faith and fawning devotion to him. Described as "the proudest and happiest woman on earth," Bet Balcombe's moods are determined by those of her husband (2:51). If he is happy, she is joyful; if he is wary, she is afraid; if he is despondent, she is depressed. We are told that "when he was silent, her eye dwelt on him. When he spoke, her ear seemed to drink in greedily all his words. She seemed impatient that anyone should differ from him in opinion, and indignant that all did not reverence him as she did" (1:257). Her only wish was that she be worthy of his love and respect. Indeed, in the event there is any doubt about her lack of self, the reader is told that Bet "seemed to feel her individuality merged in her husband, and to rest undoubting confidence on his wisdom, his courage, his prowess and resources" (1:210).

Significantly, her type of womanhood is paralleled by the "Sambo" caricature these writers created of blacks. Passive, fawning, grateful, loyal, happy, and lazy, "Sambo" lived for the approval of his master. But that is the point of paternalism after all: to take adults and infantilize them into willing servants. The paternalistic ideology reinvented by Southern planters as part of the "positive good" defense for slavery emerged from the social relations within the patriarchal family. Paternalism justified both the male coercion of women and children within the patriarchal family, and slavery itself. If there is any doubt that Southerners like Tucker are making this connection, he eliminates it by having Balcombe explain to Napier, "No, William. Let women and Negroes alone. Instead of quacking with them, physic your own diseases. Leave them in their humility, their grateful affection, their self-renouncing loyalty, their subordination of the heart, and let it be your study to become worthy to be the object of these sentiments" (2:166).[6]

Surely this kind of excessively dependent woman and the "Sambo" kind of slave existed in reality as well as in the planter imagination. But the numbers are impossible to quantify and we may believe they were fewer in number than the planter myth would have it; their respective labors and family responsibilities alone would mitigate the full realization of this totally passive personality as a dominant type. The creation of the woman-as-passive-sufferer in antebellum Southern literature constituted a psychological attack on women that justified at once their alleged inferiority and male power over them. Blacks, however, at least in this period, were spared this level of psychological manipulation; unlike plantation white women, they were not the consumers of such literature. Possibly some or most white plantation women dismissed these images of themselves as male fantasies; but, whatever the actual effect, one cannot mistake its intent. It was to justify white male planter domination of women in marriage and blacks in slavery.

In *The Forayers* and *Eutaw,* Simms gives us a comprehensive if skewed depiction of eighteenth-century South Carolinian society.[7] Every relationship in these works reflects gender relationships and class politics. For instance, the most important issue between William Sinclair and Bertha Travis is the question of class. William Sinclair is a handsome young man, a gentleman from one of South Carolina's "best families." Although Bertha's father is a planter, he has come from a Southern family of only moderate means and has made his money by cheating the Indians during South Carolina's Cherokee War; as the novel opens, he is trading with both sides in the Revolution. He is regarded by established planters as a corrupt "new man." In fact, Colonel Sinclair, William's father, threw Travis out of his house when he came to discuss his daughter's engagement.[8] The romantic and revolutionary plots mesh when Tory Captain Richard Inglehardt, who is the son of Travis's former overseer, has Bertha, her father, and her brother abducted by his poor white confederates, so he can bribe Bertha into marrying him. Fulfilling romantic convention, William Sinclair, the patriot hero, is victorious in the battle against the British and returns to rescue Bertha from the villainous Inglehardt.

Simms's portraits of William's sister, Carrie Sinclair, and of Bertha Travis are paradigms of idealized Southern womanhood. Describing Carrie and her sister Charlotte ("Lottie"), he writes: "Both had very fair complexions, and very long, silken brown hair, and Carrie had large swimming blue eyes, and a soft, small delicious mouth" (82). This description is interesting given

the dominant tendency for white male American authors to portray heroines as blonde, and their female foils as darker-haired. Perhaps because they
had black women to symbolize uncontrolled emotions, especially sexuality,
Southern authors felt free to depict both fair- and dark-haired heroines,
while their Northern counterparts usually chose blonde, blue-eyed heroines.[9] An attractive and loving friend and sister, Carrie is also a dutiful and
patient daughter, who spends most of her day looking after her demanding
and irritable father. In contrast, Bertha Travis is described as having a pale
complexion and "dark and brilliant eyes" (*The Forayers,* 279). She is "of fine
shape, medium size, graceful movement, and dignified yet eager carriage."
Bertha's love for William "was a very artless, ingenuous passion, and betrayed itself without reserve" (279, 281). However, she refuses to enter a
family that scorns her and her family; and William's assurance that in due
time she will be loved and accepted by his family does not entirely convince
her.

The denouement of the novel occurs when Carrie and Bertha are taking a
walk and are accosted by "Hell-Fire Dick" (Joel Andrews), predictably a poor-
white outlaw, Inglehardt's outlaw comrade. Carrie is hit with a "terrible blow
planted between her eyes," and Bertha is abducted by the gang to Inglehardt's hiding place. Bertha refuses to believe Inglehardt's claim that her
father had given permission for their marriage. Like the typical sentimental
heroine, Bertha is deliberate, patient, and resolute in her rejection of Inglehardt; she lets him know that she will be neither bribed nor bullied into
submission. In the final scene with the three Travises standing before him,
Inglehardt announces his plan to kill the father and son and take Bertha as
his wife against her will. As Bertha begins to waver, fearing her purity is
being bought at an unacceptable price, her father breaks loose and bashes in
Inglehardt's skull with his handcuffs as Inglehardt's sword passes through
his body killing him. William Sinclair appears at that moment to rescue the
fainting Bertha and her brother from the remaining outlaws. Bertha has
been passed literally from her father to her future husband. Thus, all of the
patriarchal and class conventions are established and observed by Simms.[10]

Simms establishes William Sinclair and Bertha Travis as hero and heroine
in a way that serves both gender and class politics. Although Bertha displays
some of the sentimental heroine's fortitude, ultimately she must be rescued
by a man: her father redeems himself by ensuring his children's survival;
William Sinclair ensures their deliverance. In fighting his way successfully
through the gang of outlaws, William Sinclair earns his heroism. Additionally, Bertha's passive resistance to Inglehardt, a man of the middle classes,
stands the sentimental tradition on its head, since it was originally established by new middle-class men to protect the virtue of their women from
aristocratic lechery. In making the case for the planter aristocracy, Simms
contends that "class" is defined by more than wealth. It also encompasses
intelligence, manners, and morality that are inherited and "bred" in each

generation. Like many poor men, Travis and Inglehardt have confused the symbols of wealth—land, women, slaves, and money—with "class" itself.

Similarly, in Simms's border romances, the heroes compete against other men in a rough and democratic male world in which the women they court play passive and submissive roles. Significantly, because these novels are set in what were then border states (Georgia, Alabama, Missouri, Mississippi), the frontier overshadows the "big house" of the old plantation. The heroes and heroines of these novels have families that have moved from the old planter states to the territories. Although patriarchal planter values and the plantation with slave labor is replicated in the new location, it is done on a smaller scale than in the East. Further, there is a primitive masculine lawlessness implicit in Simms's settings. Outlaw gangs control sections of some territories and Native Americans are never far off. Simms argues on several occasions that only the strong survive on the frontier; hence he creates heroes and heroines, allied with the planter class, who will meet the challenge of Indians and outlaw gangs.[11]

Simms's *Border Beagles* (1840) is a sequel to *Richard Hurdis* (1838), which introduced frontier lawlessness in the person of Clement Foster. Foster reappears in the latter romance as "Edward Saxon." Saxon, an ingenious outlaw, leads a band of fifteen hundred poor white outlaws who rob their way through the Southwest. In a classic scene that anticipates the Western novel, Virginia Maitland and her family, riding west in a coach, are attacked by members of Saxon's gang. Predictably, handsome "lively, bold, frank and generous" Harry Vernon is nearby with his traveling companion, woodsman Walter Rawlins.[12] They fight the robbers and rescue Virginia and her family. In the course of the skirmish Vernon is wounded, yet before he faints he catches a glimpse of Virginia: "a lovely virgin . . . a form of chiselled symmetry, and a face, of the exquisite beauty of which the soul, alone, could feel the perfection and the charm, in those vague and spiritual imaginings which come to the youthful heart when it first dreams of love" (182; see also 170–182). Virginia has a similar reaction to Harry. She thinks that "the face of the stranger youth was one of the most noble she had ever seen, and distinguished by that delicacy of feature and expression which are conjectured to denote equally aristocratic birth and natural genius" (190).

Simms's initial description of Virginia is as a helpless, innocent child-woman, who matures into a woman by suppressing her girlish squeamishness about dealing with a stranger's wounds and her romantic fantasies about Harry as she assumes the role of the nurse. Simms notes: "It was then that she became the woman . . . following her father to the chamber of the patient prepared to assist in the labor of the nurse" (282). What is the nature of the "womanly character" that has now emerged in Virginia, one might ask? What is the difference between a girl and a woman? What gives nursing its special quality that, as author after author believed, evokes special womanly traits? Simms's answer is revealing:

> The affections of women are usually unselfish. They love the more
> profoundly, the more they serve. Their love grows with their labors—
> with their toil for the beloved—and, the idea of all injustice or op-
> pression excluded, their passion is proportionately increased by their
> cares. To be allowed to serve is, with them, to love the object of their
> devotion. It is for the man to show himself grateful for the service. . . .
> Yet even when this acknowledgement is withheld, the service itself, to
> the dependent spirit, is a joy; and they will ask little more than the vine
> that only prays the privilege to be suffered to cling around the tree.
> (282–83; the "clinging vine" metaphor recurs in this literature)

Stripped bare of its romanticism, an act of kindness if not of love is turned on
the woman and becomes an instrument of her oppression. In this case, nursing a sick person, an admirable act, becomes the justification for Virginia's
exploitation. If women "love the more profoundly the more they serve," asks
Simms, then who are we as men to question this obvious God-given natural
trait? Simms had earlier written that, were men to exhibit similar nurturance
and care toward one another instead of being "proud" and "independent,"
their "effeminate" trust of other men would leave them vulnerable to attack
(25–26). Women are unfit for the world because they not only fail to comprehend this basic reality of aggressive male nature, but, once confronted with
it, they are helpless to defend themselves. In this instance, Vernon returns
Virginia's compassion and concern not by nurturing her—a female form—
but by rescuing her from criminal violence, thus proving his masculinity
and confirming conservative views about human nature.

The construction of passive femininity, then, depends on a similar construction of a contrasting masculine type. In this literature, the "true man"
was honorable, intelligent, courageous, and protective. While true men are
present in all white classes in this literature, each class is distinguished by its
own characteristics. All the authors considered in this study assume that
masculine nature is inherently violent, yet the more "civilized" men shed
blood only to advance or protect "civilization," while poor white and inferior
men turn their naturally violent and undisciplined natures against society,
law, and order as denizens of the criminal world. These authors depict a kind
of "cult of masculinity" in which the men of the planter class are not only the
"toughest" men, but the most intelligent and moral. Thus, they are the most
fit to govern. Although they are paired with both passive and spirited heroines, the most attractive couples are those in which both hero and heroine
are assertive, intelligent, and ethical.

While Tucker didactically contends that women are naturally weaker and
more passive, Simms, Kennedy, and Caruthers consistently portray women
who are spirited and intelligent and who cope with crises courageously.
While they defer to masculine authority, they assert themselves at critical
junctures in the narrative. Unlike the passive heroines, they are opinionated
and often take action that resolves family difficulties or furthers their par-

tisan interest. These self-assured and competent Southern women may fill the void created by these authors' failure to depict the plantation mistress in any other than a cursory way.

Katherine Walton (*The Partisan* and *Katherine Walton*) was drawn "after our best models of good manners, good taste, good intellect, and noble, generous sensibilities; frank, buoyant, and refined; yet superior to mere convention," Simms notes.[13]

He describes her as having brown hair, dark eyes, an "elevated and intellectual forehead," and a face that is "finely formed, delicately clear and white, slightly pale, but marked still with an appearance of perfect health."[14] She is beautiful, virtuous, and dignified, "one of those high-souled creatures that awe while they attract; and, even while they invite and captivate, control, and discourage" (104). In short, Katherine was a "lady": "sensitive, yet firm; pure and chaste, yet without any affectations of delicacy" (271). She is Simms's perfect heroine. No other woman in his work so captivates him except perhaps for the "fallen" intellectual, Margaret Cooper.[15] Unlike Cooper, however, Katherine, or Kate, acts always with propriety suitable to her class and sex, and faces her life with admirable unflinching courage.

Typically, Katherine's mother has died and she has the responsibilities of the plantation mistress on her shoulders. She supervises the household servants and oversees the daily household tasks. She nurses her invalid cousin, Emily, and cares for her father, Colonel Richard Walton, and cousin and suitor, Robert Singleton, who is a member of Francis Marion's troops. Robert wants her to be his wife, but she tells him that she cannot think about becoming anyone's wife until the war is over (165–67, 275–80).[16]

In contrast to Katherine, her cousin, Emily Singleton, is a pure Christian; a young female who is naturally a pacifist and who therefore cannot exist in a war-torn society. She dies with Katherine at her side.[17]

Katherine is everything to everyone. She nurses Emily; protects the family estate in the absence of her father and Robert Singleton; and, when Emily dies, provides emotional support for Robert. Throughout it all, she is compassionate, calm, and clearheaded. In effect, the woman they are all supposed to protect is actually taking care of them—but perhaps that is one underlying lesson of patriarchy.

Katherine faces another crisis when her father is taken prisoner by the British. Considered a traitor, he will be hanged in Dorchester unless he can be rescued. Katherine turns to Robert Singleton, "a man of sterling character, and deep, true feeling," for help. An idealist with a deep passion for Katherine and for his country, Singleton is also a leader of men. In a society that equates manliness with qualities of honesty, courage, familial loyalty, and a sense of obligation, Robert is clearly unique (389–99). These are the heroic qualities admired by antebellum Southerners, and Singleton is one of Simms's most convincing heroes. The patriarchal social compact is based on the proposition that women create and nurture life while men hold the "sacred duty" and power in being able to take life. In this context, male violence and aggression are perceived as being "natural." Honorable men serve to protect women and children in war, which justifies their patriarchal rights over women and children in peace. Simms's work clearly delineates and defends this critical division between the sexes.

In Katherine and Robert, Simms embodies both gender and class values. Although Katherine is one of Simms's strongest plantation heroines, she must finally turn to a man to deal with other men in a man's world. Specifically, in war—the time-honored domain of men—she has no influence or power. But in peace as well as war, she can only effect her will on her own black slaves. Other people's slaves and poor white men stand outside her influence. Second, Simms underscores the family/class relationship by making Katherine and Robert cousins. Singleton is the most worthy man of her class for her to marry. As her husband and her protector—played out in the hero-heroine romance—Singleton will protect her from want and danger.

In a discussion with Singleton about why he has hesitated to join the patriot cause when his heart is so much with them, Walton explains: "The wealth is nothing, Robert; but I have a strange love for these old groves—this family mansion, descended to me like a sacred trust through so many hands and ancestors. I would not that they should be lost" (163).

As expressed by Simms through Walton, planters rule because they are "naturally" superior, as witnessed by four generations of successful economic and political leadership. The "sacred trust" that Walton must uphold is his responsibility to reproduce the plantation society in his family and to protect his family's ownership of the land. That means that the family is the prime social and economic unit in the society. Its reproduction re-creates both the planter class and the black laboring class, and women, of course, play a primary role in that endeavor.

Janet Berkeley (*Mellichampe*) is another of Simms's strong heroines, but unlike Katherine Walton and more like Kennedy's Mildred Lindsey, she completely overshadows the hero. Described by Simms as being "small and slender," "soft and delicate," she has black eyes and dark hair, which is gathered simply on the top of her head. She is composed and graceful, and her outward calm reflects an inner "strength of soul."[18] She, too, serves as both belle and plantation mistress, residing on her "Piney Grove" estate in Dorchester County, with her father, Philip, a Loyalist planter, and her cousin, Rose Duncan.

Like Katherine Walton, Janet displays fortitude and courage when she and those she loves are threatened. In one series of events, her fiancé Ernest Mellichampe's unit, commanded by Robert Singleton, skirmishes with yeoman Tory Owen Barsfield's troops and sends them fleeing back to the Berkeley plantation where they have been given refuge by Philip Berkeley. Janet, escaping to the overseer's cottage at the first sign of trouble, suggests to Singleton that they shoot burning arrows at the mansion roof and burn the Tories out (196–97). The tactic works and Barsfield's men are close to defeat when British Colonel Tarleton comes up with his detachment and runs Singleton's men off the plantation. In the second phase of the skirmish, in revenge for his earlier humiliation at the hands of Mellichampe's father, Barsfield was about to kill the wounded Mellichampe, but Janet "threw herself under the weapon," and "lay prostrate upon the extended and fainting form of her lover" (238). She persuades Tarleton to send Mellichampe to Charleston for trial as soon as he has recovered.

Simms demonstrates Janet Berkeley's superior character and courage in several different ways. Although she is frightened when the fighting starts, she does not hide from sight of the battle. Rather, she pulls up a chair to the window and watches in case she might be of help to Mellichampe or some other patriot. Then, when it seems as though the armies would fight to a standstill or that many patriot soldiers would be lost storming her mansion, she suggests they burn it down in a "noble" and "patriotic" gesture. Finally, she confronts death itself in throwing herself between Barsfield and Mellichampe (although, as with Virginia Maitland, Simms claims she reacts instinctively, not rationally). "The instinct of love," Simms notes, "is woman's best reason" (238).[19]

Janet is considerate with even the meanest of men. When Ned Blonay, the grotesque half-breed who works for Barsfield, introduces himself to the Berkeley family, Janet asks Blonay to dine with them as an insult to Barsfield. When Barsfield objects, she stops him short by declaring pointedly: "we can take no exception to his poverty, or his occupation, or the place from which he comes. We have not heretofore been accustomed to do so, and it would be far less good policy now, when the vicissitudes of the times are such, that even a person such as you describe him to be may become not only our neighbor but our superior, tomorrow" (74). Janet, moreover, is polite and gracious to Blonay, a favor he will remember later when Barsfield tries to enlist him in killing Mellichampe.

Similarly, in a rare fictional mistress-slave depiction she treats the "faithful slave," Scipio, with respect and kindness, if with paternalism. When they are in battle and he is frightened, she touches Scipio gently and bids him to "fear nothing, but come quickly" to lift Mellichampe to safety. In both cases Janet is clearly their superior, and her "charity" reinforces racial and class distinctions: Janet is braver than Scipio, and more gracious, mannered, and intelligent than the rude Blonay. These positive qualities, then, must be seen in their complete social context. E. P. Thompson has pointed out that charity and "goodness" have class dimensions that, unless reciprocated, become instruments of class power. Embodied in an upper-class woman, in this case Janet Berkeley, these qualities serve to reinforce the paternalism that the planter class uses as ideological justification for its power (236).[20]

The antebellum Southern historical romance as a form is essentially conservative in its insistence that hierarchies of gender and class be maintained.

By this standard, *Mellichampe* fails because Simms allows the hero to be overshadowed by his "natural inferiors." Ernest Mellichampe has all of the superficial qualities of a hero. Attractive, brave, honest, he also possesses that most essential ingredient: he is a gentleman planter. But he lets passion control his reason, and thus makes a series of foolish mistakes.[21] His recklessness runs against him in both love and war, and almost ends his life. Rather than being in control—the guardian of women, children, and servants and a leader of men as Singleton is—Mellichampe is saved by the very people he is supposed to protect. Janet and Blonay plot together to free Mellichampe, and Scipio actually kills Barsfield. Thus this "hero" is eventually saved himself by a woman, a yeoman white, and a slave. Ironically, in terms of the structure of the novel, Mellichampe is so inferior and ineffectual as a hero that he is clearly mismatched and unworthy of Janet Berkeley. *Mellichampe* was Simms's second Revolutionary romance and its plot resolution and character development is a complete aberration from his other work; perhaps it is thus a more honest novel. Yet, Simms never again makes the same "mistake" in portraying a hero and a heroine. If Simms had created this story later in his career, one might argue that he had transcended the stereotypes and plantation convention that he established by portraying a set of characters who exist against type. Given Simms's criticism of certain plantation practices, this kind of portrait would not be that unusual. However, not only did Simms write this novel early in his career, but the character of Mellichampe and the novel's plot structure are unique in Simms's work and in this literature.

Additionally, there seems to be space in these historical romances for only one well-drawn plantation woman. The heroine is thus asked to do "double duty." Not only must she be innocent and submissive to the men of her race and class, but she must also be as mature, self-confident, and competent as a plantation mistress. Even if she lives with other women like Rose Duncan or Emily Singleton, female friendship is never explored. Instead, their lives are dedicated to their doting fathers. They are girls who substitute for their mothers—a pervasive patriarchal fantasy—and thus emerge as their father's daughters. Kennedy's Mildred Lindsey is a case in point.

In *Horse-Shoe Robinson,* a historical novel set during the Revolution, Kennedy makes the same mistake as Simms in *Mellichampe.* His "supporting" characters are more interesting and effective than the hero, planter Arthur Butler. While Butler is clearly the "superior" Southern gentleman and a military and political leader, Robinson, a blacksmith, dominates the action, including several rescues of Butler and Mildred.[22]

Although Mildred is stereotypically described as blue-eyed and blonde-haired with pale cheeks, clear skin, and a soft and gentle voice, she is also an expert horsewoman with "a degree of steadiness and strength that might be denominated masculine."[23] Mildred is described as a "boyish girl" who possessed "a feminine courage that was sufficient for any emergency." A confirmed patriot with "her ready genius, her knowledge and her habits of reflection, much in advance of her years,"[24] Mildred Lindsey will not be just another retiring Southern belle who passively waits for the hero to rescue her. Indeed, Kennedy creates an admirable woman character who is intelligent, capable, and assertive.

However, in an unconventional twist at the end, Kennedy discloses that Mildred and Butler had been secretly married and they get Philip Lindsey's deathbed blessing. So Mildred Lindsey is revealed as a married woman and not a belle, which explains her unguarded concern for Butler and her daring actions on his behalf. The lingering promise of the assertive and spirited belle is thus realized in the depiction of Mildred Lindsey. She will inherit her father's estate as a fully realized plantation mistress and not a passive and untried girl. One suspects that these latter portraits of Southern women are closer to the reality than the passive and suffering heroines of romantic literary convention. But what that means is that she requires a superior hero to "handle" her; a Robert Singleton, not an Ernest Mellichampe.

In contrast to Mildred Lindsey, Bel Tracy appears to be a girl-child playing at being a woman. *Swallow Barn* is a domestic plantation novel and a successor to Tucker's *The Valley of Shenandoah*. While it develops one of the most critical antebellum proslavery defenses, its romantic plot parodies the Southern fascination with medieval courtly life.[25]

At Bel's insistence, Ned Hazard, the hero, conforms to her standard of chivalric behavior, but Kennedy makes him look foolish. Throughout the novel, Kennedy pokes fun at Southern pretense to the chivalric tradition and playfully exaggerates the Southern male and female "types," as his construction of Ned's history demonstrates. Witness also Bel's "court," with a semiliterate poor white, who as the "minstrel" plays the guitar, not the mandolin. Kennedy explains that "Bel Tracy is a little given to certain romantic fantasies, such as country ladies who want excitement and real novels are apt to engender. Her vivacity and spirit show themselves in the zeal with which she ever cultivates the freaks that take possession of her mind" (228).

When Ned rescues Bel's pet hawk, he scuffles with Miles Rutherford, a local bully who had insulted Isaac Tracy, Bel's father. Since Ned, like everyone else, concluded that "an attack upon her father was an attack upon her" (391), he felt justified in fighting even though Rutherford was of a lower class. When the story of the fight (not its cause) was related to Bell, she was appalled that Ned would grovel to fight with anyone so beneath him. Because of his unbecoming conduct and notwithstanding his heroic service in rescuing the hawk, Bel decides that she should not see him again (384, 388–91). Ned at this point confesses his desire to marry her. After some uncertainty, Bel decides that she will accept his proposal. In the end, traditional gender conventions prevail: although she is a spirited young woman, Bel is put in her place. She learns to want a man who will dominate her (431–34; 504 and 505).

Similarly, in *The Cavaliers of Virginia,* Caruthers describes Virginia Fairfax as having blonde hair, brown eyes, "white and regular" teeth, and a lovely face "not disfigured by a single freckle, scar, or blemish." She dresses simply and tastefully "exquisitely appropriate to her style of beauty." Everything about her suggests "virginal" innocence.[26] The most prominent character-istic of Caruthers's heroine is her intelligence and integrity. Like Kather-ine Walton, she is resilient and able to cope with material and emotional hardship.

From the outset, Virginia demonstrates an independent streak. Abetted by her suitor, Nathaniel Bacon, she sneaks out of her parents' home on a night visit and from there they go to visit the mysterious "Recluse," Charles Whalley.[27] Having researched her life and that of Bacon and her parents, Whalley warns Virginia to stop seeing Bacon. She refuses to listen to him and remains steadfast in her loyalty to Bacon.

Because of Bacon's unknown class origins, her family wants her to stop seeing him and court her kinsman, Frank Beverly. Only her mother allies with her. However, Virginia loathes Beverly, not only for his hostility to Bacon, but because "he treated her as a child" and taunted her with his "proud self-sufficiency" (2:114). Here, then, Caruthers seems aware of wom-en's anger at being patronized by men, and seems to reject the patriarchal posturing of someone like Nathaniel Beverley Tucker.

Similarly, in Ellen Evylin and Ann Catherine (Kate) Spotswood (*The Knights of the Golden Horse-shoe*), Caruthers offers unconventional female characters. One would expect blue-eyed, blonde-haired Kate, as the gov-ernor's daughter, to be the heroine. Yet, Caruthers has developed brown-haired, moody, and orphaned Ellen Evylin as his heroine. Even more un-usual, Kate and Ellen are one of the few examples of female friends repre-sented in this literature.[28]

While growing up with intellectual Frank Lee, Ellen read and discussed politics, history, and moral philosophy. Although she thinks the experience gave "a masculine cast" to her thoughts, Lee disagrees: "No, no, I cannot say they are masculine; at all events they are not unfeminine. Whatever relates to our higher sentiments and our spiritual natures, certainly belongs in com-mon to the sexes, and if man has usurped the whole claim to discuss them, he assuredly has no right to do so."[29] Later, Dr. Evylin asserts that women are "purer in heart . . . much more elevated in sentiment, more patient and hopeful in suffering" and more faithful in the powers of God than men, and that it seems wrong to him that they are "excluded from *active participation* in more than half of all the concerns of life" (1:116 and 116; my emphasis).

In both *The Cavaliers of Virginia* and *The Knights of the Golden Horse-Shoe,* Caruthers emerges as the most liberal of the authors on the issue of gen-der in asserting that the moral and intellectual capabilities of women are equivalent to those of men, and that women should not be excluded from their rights to be educated and to assume the responsibilities of citizenship.

Though this position is linked to the questionable "superiority of women" axiom (a positive stereotype), Caruthers is the only Southern author to take such a stand. However, he is still captivated by romanticism. Ellen internalizes her sadness and anger by becoming physically sick when it appears that Frank Lee is dead. She is neither intellectually nor emotionally independent of Lee, a most romantic vision.

If melancholia and a brooding intellectuality mark the character of Ellen Evylin, then her opposite is surely Kate Spotswood. When Kate is first introduced she is cheerfully strolling down the lane from the Big House to the slave quarters to attend those who were sick and is greeted warmly and responsively by her African American patients. After an alcoholic madness seizes him, she nurses her brother John day and night. One of her suitors and her favorite, Bernard Moore, stands by and, watching her, falls in love.

Although Caruthers might give women more say in the day-to-day politics of a town or a city, he would not have them become active at the expense of abandoning their "proper sphere" in the home and especially in the sickroom. Caruthers notes accordingly: " 'tis purely because it presents woman in her true sphere; it is because it presents her in the attitude of a ministering angel. . . . There is no impatience—no drowsiness—no yawning—not even talking when out of place—they endure all things and suffer all things" (1:80). Like Simms's Virginia Maitland, Caruthers's Kate Spotswood is most feminine when she is nursing others. Additionally, Caruthers's portrait of Spotswood clearly demonstrates the emotional burden that women are required to bear under patriarchy. They must "endure all things and suffer all things" for the people they love. Even Caruthers, who for the most part created unusual heroines, capitulates to the dominating Victorian stereotypes.

Thus Caruthers's heroines, like Kennedy's, challenge certain stereotypes as they confirm other ones. Virginia Fairfax, Ellen Evylin, and Kate Spotswood are all young women who are protected by their families and who are soon to be wed. In comparison with the passive and suffering heroines, they are allowed some independence of spirit and some intellectual interests. In the end, even Caruthers's "intellectual" woman, Ellen Evylin, has had her intellect molded by the man she will marry, and optimistic Kate Spotswood looks forward to a life of service and suffering for others.

In this fiction the unmarried planter's daughter emerges as the heroine through her beauty and her breeding. Deferential to the men of her class, she is allowed some measure of ability and assertiveness, but never any real independence. Her gifts are most often employed to aid the hero and his cause. She rarely argues with him and never gives precedence to her own needs. Indeed, as readers we never know what those needs are. Like the plantation mistress whose surrogate she is, she is singlemindedly devoted to others, and especially to men of her family. Finally, even the strongest and most capable heroines turn to the planter hero as protector. Through his defeat of planter enemies and/or his rescue of the heroine from them, the planter hero is established by these authors as woman's natural superior and as the natural leader of Southern society.

Such heroinism is denied the African American woman slave. She is not a "belle" (though she might well be a planter's daughter, a relationship suppressed in this literature as it was in Southern society). Dark-eyed and dark-skinned, her beauty serves as a counterpoint to the paleness of the white heroine. While these authors displace their miscegenation fears to Native Americans, fairness becomes associated with modesty, virtuousness, and chastity, while darkness is associated with sensuality, uncontrolled passion, and promiscuity. In deflecting the reader's attention to the fate of the belle and the planter's son, these authors never depict a parallel African American couple. Similarly, as will be discussed later, the "fallen women" is an ambitious woman," white or black. The patriarchal virgin/whore dichotomy plays itself out in a peculiar way in this literature. While there are white, planter-class virgin heroines, there are no black slave "Jezebels." Instead, these authors omit any reference to sexual relations between planters and their female slaves; the threat to planter-class women is from lower-class white males, not black men. One is left to conclude, then, that African American slaves remain depicted as either asexual old people or as childlike adults. They are seen, but not heard.[30]

To the conservative patriarchal thinker, liberating a woman from the joys and burdens of motherhood (like manumitting blacks from the "civilizing influences" of slavery) constitutes a crime against her, against society, and against God. On another level, such freedom represents a personal threat: free blacks and free women have no need for a "master." The power relationships on the plantation form in the family, in the patterns of dominance and submission learned by children watching their parents, and by being loved and nurtured in sex-specific ways. The white male planter was trained from boyhood to dominate women, blacks, and men from the lower classes. To the conservative planter, white womanhood, racial purity, the family, the plantation, and the South were inextricable from each other, and represented the interlocking and mutually supportive psychological and material basis for his existence and his power. A threat to any one of these relationships was a threat to the planter, and he fought to the death in the Civil War to protect his way of life.

7. Unmarried Women: The "Spinster" and the "Fallen Woman"

PATRIARCHAL proscriptions North and South indoctrinated young women to the necessity of becoming wives and mothers. Although some women successfully resisted marriage or were unlucky in courtship, they had far less social status and little psychological and economic security. One historian has estimated that between 1795 and 1835, Southern women who failed to marry dropped from 3 percent to 1 percent.[1] Clearly, there was extreme pressure exerted on both men and women in planter families to marry, raise children, and otherwise preserve the family estate. But upper-class male experience was distinguished from female experience, since men enjoyed both political standing as voters and potential officeholders, and economic security as property owners. Women, however, were not only excluded from the political sphere but could not legally own their own property, especially if they married. Instead, they were expected to be under direct male supervision and control—"protection" in patriarchal rhetoric—and paid an additional psychological price in being deemed "unfeminine," or immoral, if they sought political and economic rights or otherwise eschewed male "protection."

These authors divided all women into two groups: unmarried women and married women. Unmarried women were further divided according to their sexual behavior and their adherence to patriarchal norms. In addition to the belle, the "spinster" and the "fallen woman," were the most common types. While the spinster is often tangential to the plot or is an object of pity, scorn, and condescension, the fallen woman often presents a direct contrast to and moral foil for the heroine. In spite of their condemnation of the fallen woman's errant sexuality, these authors display far more compassion for her than for the spinster, whom they ridicule. However, while the spinster can be a member of any class, the fallen woman, who is dark-haired and dark-complexioned, is from either the yeoman or the poor-white classes.

That it was possible for women to function without men apparently didn't occur to such authors or, for that matter, to many women of the South who paid a very high emotional price for remaining unmarried.[2] That both men and women might choose not to marry threatened a patriarchal class system based on the orderly transmission of property from generation to gener-

ation. Moreover, there was an additional affront in a woman's refusal to
marry: her real or imagined rejection of male control, especially of her body
in reproduction.

While the spinster sins on such counts, by conventional standards the
"fallen woman" has failed to observe patriarchal custom in courting. She can
be partially forgiven because she hasn't rejected men; indeed, she has allowed her passion for a man to overwhelm her reason. None of the authors
of course claims that the unmarried man is "unmasculine," but they all
view the unmarried woman as being not only "unfeminine" but "unnatural."
Since marriage was designed for women's protection, they contend, the
fallen woman has foolishly victimized herself. Finally, only Simms portrays a
"mistress" and none of these authors, probably in deference to their readers'
sensibility, depicts a fictional prostitute. The prostitute's chief "crime" in
traditional society is economic independence and her nonmonogamy. Like
the lesbian, she is an outlaw; unmentionable in this literature.

THE SPINSTER

Of the spinsters in this literature, several are noteworthy either for their
unusual characterization or for the conservative patriarchal values they establish. The discussion about Ellen Evylin (in Caruthers's *Knights of the
Golden Horse-Shoe*) is an example of the former, while John Pendleton Kennedy's Prudence Meriwether and Catherine Tracy (*Swallow Barn*) are examples of the latter. In contrast, William Gilmore Simms's Ellen Floyd (or, "Hurricane Nell," *Eutaw*), a kind of antebellum Southern tomboy, is unique in this
literature.

Antebellum Southern fiction portrayed the unmarried woman as undermining the patriarchal family, and deemed her pitiable or contemptible. Her
status was attributed to her own inadequacies as a woman or occasionally to
unpleasant experiences with men, but never to hardships involved in being
a planter's wife. That a woman may have made a conscious choice not to
marry, or not to settle for any "eligible" male, usually escapes these authors;
or, having thought of these possibilities, they accuse her, "a mere woman," of
false pride and "unfeminine" self-love. Caruthers's male characters, for instance, engaged in two revealing conversations about unmarried women. In
one, Kit Carter and Bernard Moore (*Knights of the Golden Horse-Shoe*) are
discussing Ellen Evylin and her marital prospects. Carter notes, "She is no
man-hater, take my word for it. It is only your broken-backed girls and old
maids scarred with the smallpox, that truly hate the men, and then it is only
because they discover the aversion in us first. I never saw one of your man-
haters who was a pretty girl, in my life."[3] In a separate incident Frank Lee,
posing as "Henry Hall," warns Ellen: "you are a candidate for admission into
that abused sisterhood ycleped [*sic*] old maids—that slandered traduced
class—nearly every one of which are living monuments of the infidelity of

men—that noble sisterhood, which lives forever upon the memory of the past" (1:97). For Caruthers, it follows, women remain unmarried, either because they are unattractive or because they have been betrayed in love. In effect, even unmarried women, make no real decisions about their lives, but simply respond to the actions and reactions of men.

John Pendleton Kennedy in *Swallow Barn* depicts two classic "old maids," Prudence Meriwether and Catherine Tracy. Prudence Meriwether, Frank Meriwether's sister, is "rather comely to look upon—very neat in person." She suffers from an "exaggerated thoughtlessness" and "a little too much girlishness," though intelligent and active.[4] Indeed, she has helped establish three Sunday Schools, belongs to an African colonization society, manages a tract society, and is involved in the temperance movement (47).[5] Her friend and next-door neighbor, Catherine Tracy, is "well-educated" with a "thoughtful and rather formal cast of character—a certain soberness in the discharge of the ordinary duties of life—and a grave train of conversation, such as belongs to women, who, from temperament, are not want to enjoy with any great relish, nor perceive with observant eyes, the pleasant things of existence" (78). They are both attracted to Singleton Oglethorpe Swansdown, a bachelor their age, who has been engaged as Mr. Tracy's lawyer in a land dispute with the Meriwethers. Swansdown is described as having "a tall figure, and an effeminate and sallow complexion somewhat impaired perhaps by ill health, a head of dark hair, partially bald, soft black eye, a gentle movement, a musical low-toned voice, and a highly fashioned style of dress" (122). A wealthy Tidewater planter who has traveled in Europe and run for public office, he is also a successful lawyer. He has courted many women and seems "to do remarkably well for the first two weeks" and then "falls off unaccountably." Just as Prudence's social-reform activities suggest a misdirected ambition and aggressive disposition disguised by a false girlishness, so Swansdown's appearance and character suggests a kind of effeminacy and effeteness (123; see 123–29 for Kennedy's description of Swansdown).

Swansdown courts both women. Each praises him and makes kind observations about why he hasn't married. Prudence thinks he is "too sensitive for such foolish things" and Catherine believes him a little shy. Exchanging information, they realize that Swansdown has been courting both of them insincerely. After ignoring him, they display hostility; Swansdown, realizing the game is up, leaves the plantation.

Kennedy intends this section to be humorous, and indeed it is, but at the expense of exposing his contempt for unmarried men and women. In one passage, he describes Prudence and Catherine in conversation. They "talked—heaven knows what!—or, at least, they only know, who know what ruminative virgins, on river banks at dewy cue, are wont to say" (296). Hostility to the unmarried woman is rooted in ideas about woman's "true" nature, about the power relations between men and women, and about the "community." Under patriarchy, women are perceived as the bearers and socializers of children, and as domestic workers. The older, unmarried woman, especially one beyond childbearing age, is useless to men. In her "master- less" state she is despised and feared. If a woman chooses not to marry, she might become a financial strain on her family. Thus, the "spinster" was con- sidered a pathetic creature deserving of pity, scorn, and contempt. These novelists were simply unable to accept that a woman might be happy living without a man and children.[6]

Like Kennedy, Simms is interested in the unmarried woman, and draws a unique one in Ellen Floyd, or "Hurricane Nell" of *Eutaw*.[7] She is introduced when rescuing her brother, Mat, from hanging by Lem Watkins's gang. She climbs to the roof of the barn where the hanging is to take place, drops down noiselessly among the outlaws, cuts the rope that Mat is dangling from, points a gun at the outlaws, and makes off with her outlaw brother. "No ordinary woman" she possesses

> the most singular fearlessness of character, a masculine decision, an
> intense will, and an impulse that always declared itself without re-
> straint. . . . Nell was not a mere woman—not, certainly, an ordinary
> one; she did not act as is common mode with her sex. She did a thou-
> sand things which have never entered the brain of an ordinary woman
> to conceive, and never gave herself much concern about that influ-
> ence which women usually feel so coercive a power—"what my neigh-
> bor thinks." (63 and 64)

Simms writes of her "untameable" masculine nature, her unselfishness, and her generosity, her "highspirited, logical, fearless, ingenuous speech" and her intelligence as she humiliates William Sinclair's (admittedly alcoholic) scout, Jim Ballou (458–60).

The other characters in the novel treat Nell as if she were mad. But Simms explains she is a woman who acts in conflict with the assumptions and expectations of the society, and consequently is misunderstood (63–75). Though he is sympathetic toward this heroic woman, Simms doesn't know quite what to do with her. There was, after all, scarcely any way for a woman to survive off the plantation or outside of marriage, as she was barred from both business and the professions; thus no realistic solution that would conform to literary conventions or reader expectations offers itself to Simms. Simms cannot match her with Sherrod Nelson, the man she loves, because of class considerations, and she is too exceptional for Ballou, the scout.

Disturbed by contemporary women's-rights activists, Simms is fascinated as well by the "aberrant human nature" of the intellectual woman, the am- bitious woman intelligent enough to succeed in male society and to escape her fate as the subordinate of men. He repeatedly returns to this type and, although ultimately deciding upon patriarchal condemnation of her, he also conveys his respect for her intelligence: many of his most attractive heroines may be characterized by their intelligence, independence, and strong character.[8] Admittedly, the traits he admired in Nell—her fearlessness, her intelligence, her knowledge and ideas, her logical mind—are attributed to "masculinity." In effect according to patriarchal prejudice, these are not female characteristics, and she is unnatural in having them. Hence the game is rigged against the "intellectual woman." Nell is treated as an exception, a freak, an aberration. It is to be expected that Simms admired the dainty, simple, frail women who fill his pages, but he doesn't. He may praise "feminine sensibilities," but clearly he admires the independent and intellectual types, and shows a thinly veiled contempt for the ineptness of his weaker heroines. Because Simms, like Nathaniel Beverley Tucker, thinks that marriage is the only proper institution for women (as slavery is for blacks), and that the only way men and women can coexist peacefully in marriage is for the male to be superior, he concludes that Nell, as a superior woman is unfit for marriage. However, she is too passionate and attractive to fit the "old maid" stereotype and she is too religious to be a "fallen woman." His solution is to consign Nell to a heroic death. Like the masterless slave, the masterless woman, is an anomaly and a threat to the rationalizations that sustain patriarchy.

THE FALLEN WOMAN

In contrast to the spinster, the "fallen woman" is a victim of her own passion. Since she covets male society and is often its victim, she is treated sympathetically. She is to be pitied but not censured. Florence Marbois of Simms's *Border Beagles,* Wingina the Indian Princess of Caruthers's *The Knights of the Golden Horse-Shoe,* Mary Scott of N. B. Tucker's *George Balcombe,* and Mary Clarkson of Simms's *The Scout* are examples of four kinds of women seduced and abandoned by dishonorable men. Rejected by society, they are treated compassionately by their creators because they are weak women who are ultimately supportive of male power.

Virginia Maitland as an honorable woman is contrasted in *Border Beagles* to the "dishonorable woman" Florence Marbois, one of Simms's most intriguing female victims. A creole from New Orleans with dark hair and black eyes, "her person was rather masculine—her carriage majestic."[9] Her parents died when she was young, leaving her with "indifferent relatives" (356). While still an adolescent, she met Edward Saxon whom she perceived as "noble in form, handsome in features, proud in spirit and intelligent in mind far beyond the average intellects to which she had been accustomed" (356).[10] And she ran off with him, accepting his love and protection. Simms, ever the moralist, notes that although the illicit relationship originated in love, it had "its termination in disgrace" (356). However, he gives Florence a "disadvantaged" background that in part accounts for her behavior. She is "tainted" with inferior "blood" as a creole, and she had not enjoyed the "protection" of her natural father. Drawing her in patriarchal terms, Simms makes her a parentless "wretch," vulnerable to the worst influences and because of them and of the absence of paternal control, a threat to herself and to the social order.

Florence's chief characteristic is her passion, caused by "the tempestuous blood that coursed through her veins" (347). She is a "creature of impulses, not of thought," who flies into jealous rages when she thinks her beloved Saxon is being unfaithful (360). Saxon does indeed fall in love—with pure and innocent Virginia. The only way he can have her, he realizes, is by abduction. He tricks her into a forest meeting and forcibly takes her to his hideout in the swamp. Florence has learned of Virginia's capture and concludes correctly that her own affair with Saxon is over. "I am but a woman," she declares, "a frail, feeble, desolated, abandoned woman." She is, however, anything but frail and feeble (369). She plots to avenge the wrong done to her.

Florence plots to kill Saxon, then herself, and free Virginia, whom she pities (394, 400). For his part, Saxon plans to force himself on Virginia. First, she will fear him, he thinks; but then realizing that he is her only protector, she will surrender, much as Florence did, and will grow to love him. That Saxon plans to rape Virginia—to take her against her will—defines him as a lower-class rogue. Like most women, he concludes, she will submit when she realizes her fate. He confides these plans to Florence, who maintains an outward calm, but is inwardly seething. At the first opportunity, Florence strikes at Saxon with a small dagger, but he escapes, and she then sends for Harry Vernon.

In the melodramatic and primal climactic scene, as Vernon is about to engage Saxon in combat, Virginia Maitland offers a self-sacrificing diversion by rushing Saxon; then Florence Marbois grabs him from behind, allowing Vernon to capture him (482 and 483).[11] When Saxon accuses her of betrayal, she replies: "Your death, Edward Saxon, were you thrice to die, could never atone for the wrongs you have inflicted on the frail, foolish heart of Florence Marbois! You have taken from her all that made life precious—and the life which seems so desirable to you is her scorn! . . . She to whom you ascribe your fate will show you how completely indifferent you have made her to her own" (483). Whereupon Florence drives a concealed bowie knife "deep down into her breast," and dies (404).

Although it was an act of independence, Florence's suicide attests to Saxon's mastery over her. Florence's behavior responds to Saxon's actions just as Virginia's seemingly independent acts are reflective of her socialized need for male approval and love. The patriarchal ideology of paternalism applies to women as well as to slaves. Just as planters fantasized that blacks would protect them if they were in danger, so they thought that women overcoming their natural timidity would respond with their fierce maternal protective instincts to defend the ones they loved. Like Janet Berkeley in *Mellichampe,* Virginia, as such a true woman, does exactly that for Vernon.[12] "Mastery," Simms believes, was the essential quality of all white Southern men. If poor, like Edward Saxon, they master "their woman" and a band of criminal outlaws. If "noble and aristocratic," like Harry Vernon, they are destined to master women, blacks, and poor whites.

As "master," the white male planter considers himself superior to all his dependents, including his wife, who in part shares his race and class authority. Love is enslaving only for the woman who gives herself up physically, psychologically, and socially to the dominant male. The context of the male-female relationship, like that of the white-black and upper class–lower class relationship, is an unequal one, permeated by paternalistic values and psychological sets that at best assign the white male the role of beneficent protector, but at worst denigrate otherwise positive qualities like love and nurture, transforming them into qualities characteristic of the weak and dependent. Hence writers like Simms not only debase women in thinly disguised masochistic roles, but deny men the possibility of nurturant behavior that equal social relationships foster. What Virginia Maitland and Florence Marbois have in common, then, is their self-effacing submission to the authority of the men they love. Virginia, however, has played by patriarchal rules and so will be allowed to live and to be protected from economic insecurity and the sexual aggression of men of other classes. In contrast, Florence, an allegedly innately inferior creole who has defied patriarchal law, has given in to her passions, thus contributing to her own debasement and death.

Unable and unwilling to depict planter sexuality with their female slaves, these authors turn to Native Americans to deal with the miscegenation issue. Wingina, of Caruthers's *The Knights of the Golden Horse-Shoe,* is a sixteen-year-old Native American "fallen woman" and the sister of Chunoluskee, a Native American prince. Seduced by Governor Spotswood's dissolute son, John, she becomes pregnant. Their sexual relations raise the whole question of amalgamation or miscegenation.[13] Wingina is described as follows:

> She had the general appearance of her race, so far as color and general outline of features went . . . she had been delicately nurtured, and had learned many of the customs, as well as the language and costume of the whites . . . she wore moccasins, on a pair of the most diminutive feet imaginable; and over her ankles and wrists, broad silver clasps, and large gold rings in her ears. Her hair was plaited, and usually hung down her back; and round her neck were many strands of gaudy colored beads. She was as perfect as any of that race ever is; preserving nevertheless, all their distinctive characteristics, such as the high cheek bones and wide-set eyes. These were softened by a childlike simplicity of expression in her countenance, and a general air of dependence and deference in her manners. (1:62)

Hence, although a woman, she is primarily defined by her racial characteristics. Not as perfect as an Anglo-Saxon Virginian maiden, she is "as perfect as any of that race ever is." Her father had been killed in an Indian war and she

supports her blind mother as a household servant. Wingina was "too elevated to associate with the negroes and scarcely considered equal to the
whites" (1:63). Her lonely life is changed by the attentions of John Spotswood.

Although confessing to Wingina that he loves her well enough to marry
her, he doesn't love her well enough to "brave the scoffs and jeers" of his
"race" (1:60). The two of them, he asserts, should commit suicide together
because the two "races were never formed to amalgamate" in this world, and
they might have some justice in the next. Wingina is not completely alone.
Her brother Chunoluskee, who has been educated by the Virginians, is "the
interpreter to the Queen," and chief guide for Governor Spotswood's pro-
posed Tramontaine expedition. He believes that John has insulted the honor
of his tribe and his family. As a woman, Wingina is seen not as an independent agent, but as her father's daughter and her brother's sister. Her relationship with Spotswood is not perceived as a decision made by her as an
individual, but one that has brought crime and shame to her family. Her
seduction, then, is perceived by her male relatives as an insult against *their*
masculinity and against the integrity of their family; her feelings are largely
irrelevant. John and Wingina decide to flee to the frontier to start a new life,
but Chunoluskee apprehends them, tomahawks Spotswood, and kidnaps
Wingina.

When the hero, Frank Lee, is charged with the crime, Wingina comes forward at his trial and testifies to his innocence. Caruthers notes that "woman
like . . . she took the whole blame upon herself, and almost wholly exoner-
ated her deceased lover" (2:152). Chunoluskee is caught, tried, and banished.
Then there is the question of what is going to become of Wingina. The scout,
Joe Jarvis, wants to marry her, but to everyone's surprise she will not marry
him because as an Indian princess, she considers Jarvis too lowborn (2:236,
240, 242). Nonetheless, Caruthers finds her essential nature "uncivilized."
She "could not comprehend the full measure of her disgrace . . . she could
not comprehend her fallen position in the eyes of those around her; she felt
bereaved, but much in the way she would have done if she lost a husband,
after the aboriginal manners and customs" (2:158). Wingina and her child
finally leave "civilization," and nothing more is said of them. Her fate is contrasted to that of the heroines, Ellen Evylin and Kate Spotswood, both of
whom have paternally arranged marriages. Wingina is an outlaw on two accounts. First, as a woman, she thwarted male-dominated society (her brother
in this case) by having an independent sexual life; worse, she has chosen a
person of another race.

Like Florence Marbois who has "creole blood," Wingina falls in part because of her race—her "uncivilized" nature and her "aboriginal habits" pre-
cipitate her disgrace, but these qualities also temper her banishment. Allegedly, living in the wilderness was no hardship on her or her child. In
contrast, Tucker's Mary Scott (*George Balcombe*) and Simms's Mary Clarkson
(*The Scout*) are seduced by men of a higher class and then rejected by those

of their own. Mary Scott, the overseer's daughter on the Raby estate in Virginia, had been courted by George Balcombe when he lived there as Raby's ward. She was seduced by Edward Montague, Raby's lawyer. Balcombe tells William Napier that Mary had been an articulate and eager scholar who was "cheerful, imaginative, witty, ardent, and confiding."[14] She was a beautiful woman who "often gushed forth in stream of fervid eloquence, or sparkling wit, or bubbling gayety [*sic*], or deep, low murmured tenderness" (1:47). Edward Montague wanted her simply for the joy of masculine conquest. Pursuing her for more than two years, he finally "found the unguarded moment when a woman can deny nothing to the man she loves" (1:63). Had Mary been coquettish, Balcombe observed, and played him off against Montague, Montague would have married her. Balcombe knew only that she had been abandoned; he did not know why. When Mary told him of the "crime," Balcombe was horrified. She was "polluted" in his eyes. Her beauty became "loathsome." "The plague was on her breath," Balcombe told Napier, and "I shrank from her as from a hateful reptile" (1:63).

Because she is basically a good woman and not a rebel, Mary accepts Balcombe's assessment of her. Berating herself, she confesses: "Pride led me to the precipice. Pride deepened the abyss below. Pride urged my fall; and pride prepared the flinty bed of shame, remorse, and horror where all hope of recovered happiness was crushed" (1:133). Tucker argues again that as a poor woman she had no right to expect a man richer than the yeoman George Balcombe. False pride and ambition blinded her to George's qualities as a man. When her parents die, Mary is even more bereft of friends and family. In the end, she redeems herself by helping William Napier recover his estate and is taken into Major Swann's household as his wife's companion, but she will never be accepted as anyone's wife.

Again, patriarchal law in its gender and class forms prevailed. Mary Scott has no right to her own sexuality. Her body is not hers, but is owned by her father, who would deliver it "undamaged" to an appropriate male. In choosing to follow her feelings and give herself to the man she loves, she is guilty of thwarting one of the fundamental tenets of patriarchal law. Additionally, her pride and ambitiousness led her to betray an appropriate man of her class for a professional. Such upward mobility is severely censured in this literature. She partially redeems herself by accepting society's condemnation of her. In this way, then, especially in traditional societies like the antebellum South, patriarchal law and convention reinforce both gender- and class-specific conduct.

Similarly, William Gilmore Simms creates in Mary Clarkson an attractive and simple young girl, whose pride leads to her seduction and betrayal. In an unusual twist, Simms makes the villain, Edward Conway, a planter's son and also a Tory.[15] Rejected by her family, her neighbors, and her former lover, woodsman John Bannister, she abjectly wanders in the woods, living off the land, looking for Conway, while her family presumes she has drowned herself. Upon finding him, she begs him to take her with him, but he rejects her outright, exclaiming: "You were a fool for believing. How could you suppose that I would marry you? Ha! Is it so customary for pride and poverty to unite on the Congaree that you should believe? Is it customary for the eldest son of one of the wealthiest families to wed with the child of one of the poorest?" (*The Scout,* 168). Class again is the issue here, as race was with Wingina. In both instances the men of the most powerful class exploit women of the least powerful classes.[16] Like Tucker, Simms attributes such exploitation not to the baseness of the males, though they are hardly admirable characters, but to the women's lack of self-control, their pride in thinking themselves better than the other men and women of their class, and their dependence—their need to cling to a man even though his "heart is rotten" (177–79).[17] Like Florence Marbois, the wages of Mary Clarkson's sin are death.

In all four cases, then, a poverty-stricken young woman is seduced by an upper-class man not merely because *he* is corrupt—the message of the sentimental novel—but because of *her* false pride. The fallen woman believes that a man of a higher caste and class will provide her with a better livelihood and will treat her more respectfully than those of her own class. Such women are depicted as creatures of impulse and passion. However, they are more "natural women" than the cold and passionless spinsters. Caruthers, Tucker, and Simms regard the fallen woman as someone to be pitied, but not condemned. Additionally, by having poor women love upper-class men, they reinforce conservative values, stress the superiority of upper-class men and argue that societal order is maintained when hereditary class lines are respected. (This problem of marriage and class will be discussed in Chapter 13.)

Possibly Simms's most fascinating female portrait is that of Margaret Cooper. In Margaret Cooper (*Charlemont,* 1856; *Beauchampe,* 1842), he tried to confront the problem of the "intellectual woman." His heroines Katherine Walton and Janet Berkeley are intelligent women, but in Margaret Cooper, he confronts directly the claims of the antebellum women's-rights movement that men and women should be equally educated. In comparison with Nathaniel Beverley Tucker, who rejects any form of female education except the most elementary kind of literacy, Simms is both intrigued by and threatened by the idea of the intellectual woman. In the end, although he flirts with the intellectual woman, he rejects her as a heroine.

Margaret Cooper is a most sympathetic, even heroic, character. She is "tall, erect, majestic . . . a brunette with large dark eyes," a natural beauty of an impoverished but middle class family living on the frontier.[18] Her character embodied all that was "vital, spiritual, expressive, animated," and her "intelligence was keen, quick, and penetrating." Her "mind was at the control of her blood," and yet, rather than possessing a cold, calm intellect, she was a wild, impassioned dreamer "filled with ambitious thoughts—proud, vain after the vague, the unfathomable!" (171, 165, 125).

This, then, is the Margaret Cooper to whom "Alfred Stevens," better known as Colonel Sharpe of Kentucky, was attracted as he passed through the hamlet of Charlemont. Stevens, unprincipled and predatory, wants to conquer her. He senses her restlessness and boredom: "her mind was of a masculine and commanding character and was ill-satisfied with her position and prospect in Charlemont" (37). Her father, who had encouraged her, had died and left her with her doting but ineffectual mother. Poor and isolated from the other village girls, Margaret read not only the romances in his library, but the history and philosophy volumes as well. As she matured and mastered these disciplines, she grew in self-confidence and considered herself superior to the young men and women of her village, demonstrated in her rejection of William Hinkley, a poor but promising youth who had been her suitor for years. Like Simms's other ambitious characters who forget their place in Southern society, Margaret thinks that the courting conventions of her day are meant only "for the protection of the ignorant and feeble of her sex." She ignores them and therefore sets herself up to be seduced and abandoned by Stevens, who feeds her vanity (296).

For Simms, then, Margaret Cooper represents what conservative Southerners most feared: the unmastered, natural inferior who aspires to an individuality apart from her preordained place in society. Her father had originally led her to the library, but his untimely death meant that she was never firmly shown her way back to the kitchen. As a result, "unguided" and "unprotected," Margaret Cooper creates herself as an "unnatural" intellectual woman. However, because she is a woman, her intelligence (unlike male intelligence, which is cool and disciplined) is governed by her passions. Thus she aspired to status, wealth, and fame beyond her rightful place in society.

In his preface to *Charlemont,* Simms criticizes his contemporary "strong-minded women" who sought "to pass from that province of humiliation to which the sex has been circumscribed from the first moment of recorded time" as the "mother of men."[19] Like fellow conservative Nathaniel Beverley Tucker, Simms thinks that civilization requires that a woman be educated and socialized enough to guide her children intelligently, but that she must remain subordinate to her father's and husband's authority. She has only the right to protection under patriarchal law; if she rejects this "right" and insists on her own rights, she will be, as Fitzhugh notes, justly abused by men, in the interest of maintaining social order. For Cooper's temerity in challenging her oppression, Simms relegates her to the fate of the fallen woman. Trying to thwart male domination and control, she is snared by the oldest male trap (402 and 403; see the opening epigraph to this part).

What is more, as Simms creates her, Margaret Cooper is in rebellion not against the masculine world, but against the female one. Simms creates her as a "feminist" who hates women and hates herself as a woman. She doesn't move into the male world from a feminine base or with other women—as Simms's contemporaries actually did—but by denigrating women and their lives and by asserting herself as an exceptional woman. She rails against women's domestic duties as being devoid of thought and as only fitting only for the "meanest slave" (177). She despairs at one point—"I am a woman!—and her name is weakness. . . . But what am I? . . . I feel I can be nothing!" (176).[20] Instead of being an independent woman, a true feminist, however, Margaret Cooper has been colonized. She has internalized her oppression by identifying with her oppressor, which leads her to discredit her own kind. Even her weak and ineffectual mother enhances her contempt for women.

The antebellum feminists who inspired Simms's attack did not envision themselves as exceptional women seeking admission to the male citadels of power, but as women organizing themselves and other women to take what was rightfully theirs. It was not individual genius that troubled Northern and Southern conservatives. It was the collective movements of oppressed people seeking to take power over their lives as a group. In isolating his heroine and having her contemptuous of other women, Simms simply underscores his contention that the majority of women are incapable of even Margaret Cooper's achievement, and that those who strive beyond their true station in life will justifiably suffer abuse and scorn, or, worse, seduction and abandonment. Additonally, in having Cooper condemn women's work as that of "the meanest slave," Simms articulates a certain form of racism that many white plantation mistresses expressed; they felt that they, like their brothers and husbands, should be free to pursue the higher aims of "civilization" and leave the hard labor of the plantation household to the allegedly inferior slaves.[21]

However, Simms is not content to let Margaret Cooper be seduced and abandoned. He gives her a rebirth, but again on patriarchal terms. She goes through several cycles of guilt and shame—"the gnawing misery of hopelessness; the consciousness of sin and weakness; the bitterness of defrauded hopes and aims and powers; the loss of name, position, love"—counterbalanced by a "prodigious strength of soul, indomitable resolution, and the courage of a *gigantic man*" (my emphasis) in seeking to avenge her dishonor by learning to shoot so she can kill Sharpe.[22] But she is saved for the role of dutiful wife and loving mother, not by her own action and strength, but by the love of a good man, Orville Beauchampe, who swears to avenge her dishonor. In this act of protecting Margaret Cooper, Beauchampe in fact "domesticates" her. Her anger, seemingly so justified, is an affront to "nature," as well as a threat to male power. After all, only men are allowed to be angry and violent. Instead of allowing Cooper to have her own revenge, Simms converts her to a "true woman" who turns to a man to protect her. Simms doesn't argue that Cooper has no issue with Sharpe or that revenge of this nature—shooting someone—isn't an appropriate "civilized" response; but a *woman's* killing her seducer threatens the social order and undermines the central convention of the romance: the heroic male rescue of the helpless heroine.[23]

In these sagas of female victimization and male deliverance, Southern writers spin out the patriarchal fantasies of ruling-class planters. While man as "human being" assumes his "right" to know, share, and dominate the worlds of the plantation, the marketplace, politics, and war, plantation women are like some exotic and precious species, caged in the rarefied atmosphere of the Big House where they are condemned to serve in a subordinate role. The conventional wisdom found such imprisonment coterminous with protection from a hostile and sordid world.[24]

In spite of the individuality allowed assertive heroines such as Virginia Fairfax, Mildred Lindsey, and Katherine Walton, they are defined by their relationships with men and their ultimate fate in each novel serves male needs. They dream no dreams of their own; they think no thoughts unconnected with their ideal of marriage; they fail to reflect on social or political relationships or on their lives as plantation mistresses. They rarely have political or religious experiences or ideas except as these reinforced their subservience to men, and they never discuss the literature to which they were allegedly so attached. As Sander Gilman would point out, they are positive stereotypes which embody the ideals of their society.

Only Caruthers creates women who are friends with other women and only Simms's Janet Berkeley has a lifelong relationship with a slave. Indeed, there is scarcely a scene in all of this literature that depicts the heroine and slaves alone. Consistent with the masculinist bias of the culture, the spinster who appeared to have rejected men and male society was herself depicted with contempt and derision, while the woman who has flouted patriarchal law in premarital sexual relations was considered pitiful or at worst "polluted." Those who, like Hurricane Nell, don't fit easy classifications, must perish.

The woman that intrigues these Southern male writers is the unmarried white plantation woman, the belle, who symbolizes ideal Southern womanhood. She is contrasted with the comic "spinster" and the degraded "fallen woman," both of whom thwart patriarchal gender conventions. These authors rework the Western virgin/whore dichotomy to their own ends, stripping these women of their individuality and volition, requiring that they be responsive either to honorable men or to criminals. In both cases, men control their destiny. Only William Alexander Caruthers recognizes the positive aspects that cultivation of the female intellect could bring, but even he capitulates to the racism endemic in American culture in his portrait of Wingina.

Significantly, in spite of these themes, there is no portrait of the planter–black female slave relationship. The code of silence strictly forbids its mention especially after abolitionists used it as an example of the inherent corruption of the planter class and of slavery. What that means is that the "Jezebel" stereotype does not appear in this literature. Additionally, in their refusal to depict a young black woman of the same age as the belle who might also have family and romantic attachments, they have constructed the white plantation family as the center of plantation life and have re-directed the reader's attention from thinking about slaves as human beings with their own needs and desires. Their exclusive focus on the planter's family also abets the planter class's persistent undermining of the viability of the slave family and slave community.

But that is not all. It is curious that these authors persistently fail to offer compelling portraits of the plantation mistress. As will be apparent from Chapter 8, these authors are content to kill off the plantation mistress and allow her daughter to stand in for her. Perhaps the mundane realities of the mistress's life, combined with the demands of the historical romance, limited their choices. Given the portraits of mistresses like Kennedy's Lucretia Meri-wether (*Swallow Barn*) or Simms's Travises (*The Forayers* and *Eutaw*), one would expect a greater representation of plantation mistresses.

At any rate, the depictions of unmarried women that these authors offer are largely idealized distortions created to attest to the superiority of the members of the planter class and especially of the planter hero. The fictional planter hero does more than bring order to wartorn Southern society and to the Southwestern frontier; within plantation society, his preference for the "pure and chaste" white plantation maiden reconstructs fictional order where true chaos reigned.

8. Married Women: Mothers

GIVEN the patriarchal ideology that dominated Southern life and informed its literature, one might assume its authors would have created married women happily ensconced in large families with proud and doting husbands. In fact, only John Pendleton Kennedy's Lucretia Meriwether (in *Swallow Barn*) provides a portrait of the daily routine of the plantation mistress. For the most part the plantation mistress is invisible. In this era, the historical romance concentrated on the public life of men in politics and war rather than the "private life" of domesticity and plantation life. Consequently, fictional plantation mistresses, like their real-life counterparts, are the hidden and submerged workers and nurturers.[1] Furthermore, the difficulty these authors had in portraying plantation mistresses is evident by the number of their heroes and heroines whose mothers were deceased. Perhaps they realized the "romance" of the historical romance would be compromised if the promised end for the heroine, as evidenced in the life of her mother, was years of pregnancy and fear of death in childbirth, unceasing toil, isolation, and loneliness, and possibly ruined marriages due to planter bankruptcy or vice.[2]

Plantation mistresses are primarily depicted as mothers. Small wonder, since the positive images of mothering remind young female readers of their proper place and roles, and perhaps, too, allowed the authors to relive these now-idealized relationships with their own mothers. Southern women, like their Northern sisters, were expected to confine their activities to the house, the nursery, the sickroom, and the garden, and to leave planting and slave management, the marketing of the crop, and politics to their husbands. As this literature attests, women who obeyed these patriarchal constraints on their intellectual, economic, and political rights were respected if not revered.

Just as these authors can only imagine women dualistically as either married or unmarried, so their portraits of women are divided in similar bipolar oppositions of "good" and "bad" mothers. All plantation sons and daughters have "good" mothers, while "bad" mothers are found exclusively in the yeoman and poor-white classes and among slaves. However, those latter groups can also produce "good" mothers, who like their plantation counterparts train their children to obey planter rule, to defer to their betters, to accept their responsibilities to their families, and to avoid aspirations to social mobility. Being a "good mother" enables the slave or poor white woman to transcend the "natural inferiority" of her race or class and represents one of the few attempts by the authors to offer positive portraits of slaves and poor whites in the literature.

In shifting the focus of the novel from the private sphere of the family to the public sphere of politics and commerce, the role of the mother is diminished, except in one instance. A recurring theme in this literature and especially in Simms's border romances is the importance of a young man's leaving his mother's home to establish himself "as a man" on his own frontier plantation. Like their Northern counterparts, then, there is a tendency among these Southern writers to equate "home" and "civilization" with a smothering female nurture that the "real man" must escape to remain masculine. These fictional planters reestablish a patriarchal slave society on the frontier and often travel there in the company of their families and slaves; the harshness and violence of frontier life reinforces the most conservative patriarchal gender conventions. Motherly protection of her son, unlike the planter's protection of his dependents who "naturally" require his dominating paternalism, is depicted as emasculating and infantilizing. Indeed, these authors require their young male heroes to achieve a state of independence they deny women and slaves. And thus, "mother love" emerges as a disabling love for sons and can even corrupt them, while "father love," which toughens sons and emotionally releases them, is depicted as necessary for masculine independence and for social harmony.

"GOOD" MOTHERS

Adrienne Rich has argued that although women give birth to children, "mothering" is a product of culture.[3] That is, the material circumstances a woman finds herself in—the resources at her disposal, how much parenting men do, whether childrearing and child-socializing are individual or collective responsibilities—depend more on the society and era in which she lives than on her own allegedly "natural" attributes as a woman. In this antebellum Southern fiction, the image of the mother is shaped by the consciousness and prejudices of male writers. If it is impossible to find unmarried women who stand on their own as independent individuals, then it is virtually impossible to find any women—plantation mistresses, slave women, middle-class women, or poor women—who are distinctive as people apart from the biological fact of their motherhood. The fact of being "mother" outweighs all other traits and defines a woman's relationship to society.[4]

Although she is a widow, Mrs. Mary Harrison Grayson in Tucker's *Valley of Shenandoah* serves as an appropriate prototype for the later development of the plantation mistress. We have seen her portrayed as attractive and poised, gracious and considerate. When her husband was alive, she supported him through her hard work, devotion, and respect. When her opinion was solicited she gave it; otherwise she did not interfere in the decisions her husband made. Devoted to her children, she nursed them when they were sick and trained them to be proper upper-class Virginians. However, when her husband died and left her penniless, instead of being a frail and helpless creature, she emerged as a very capable administrator of her husband's estate. The untimely death of her son, Edward, not her own inadequacies, brought about her final bankruptcy. Mary Grayson as both a wife and a mother exemplifies the qualities that antebellum Southern writers most admire in women: deference and loyalty, strength and competence.

Lucretia Meriwether (*Swallow Barn*), Emily Fairfax (Caruthers' *Cavaliers of Virginia*), and Lucy Travis (Simms's *The Forayers* and *Eutaw*) are among the few plantation mistresses who are portrayed vividly as both wives and mothers. Lucretia is noted especially for her household management, which she has made "a perfect science," and for her reproductive capabilities, in which she "seldom fails in her annual tribute."[5]

Notwithstanding comfortable surroundings, she is essentially a farmer's wife who rises "with the lark and infuses an early vigor into the whole household" while making one of her famous breakfasts (38). She supervises the cleaning, laundering, leads the black and white children in their daily prayers, and in her one peculiarity, forces a "death-routing decoction," a health medicine, down their throats (39). In spite of her concern for the health and happiness of the people around her, she is not very well herself. She is thin and feeble "with a sallow complexion, and a pair of animated black eyes" in a "countenance otherwise demure from the paths worn across it in frequent travel to low country ague" (39). Indeed, if true status of the Southern plantation mistress can be inferred from this portrait, she is expected to suffer and be silent, growing old before her time from overwork and multiple childbirths.

Lucretia presents a striking contrast to her husband, Frank Meriwether, the jovial, proud host of Swallow Barn, but their work is very different. He directs the planting and harvesting, oversees the purchase of labor, supplies, and equipment, plans the family and plantation budget, and confers with Carey, his chief stable hand, about the breeding of his horses. He is also the plantation emissary to the outside world, and once a month rides to the county courthouse to catch up on the news and transact his business. In all of those activities, especially those on the plantation, his authority is established, and people approach him with restraint and respect. He doesn't involve himself with the emotional outbursts of small children or the anger of recalcitrant servants. These are left to Lucretia. Most of all he doesn't labor in any real sense. Lucretia's labor and that of his slaves allows Meriwether the freedom to dabble in law and literature and to play the gracious host. Southern writers were very aware of these gender, race, and class privileges, but argued that such patriarchal arrangements were what distinguished the South as a superior civilization.[6]

Similarly, although one does not get the sense that she is living in a busy household, Mrs. Emily Fairfax, like Lucretia Meriwether, defers to her husband in all matters except those that concern the household and the children. Unlike Lucretia, however, there is a mystery in her past. In spite of her "mild, lady-like and placid serenity," she lapses into occasional melancholic depressions that alarm her family and friends.[7] Although she is loyal to and supportive of her husband, Gideon, her strongest attachment is to Virginia, her daughter. Her own unhappy first marriage to Charles Whalley, against the wishes of her family, shapes her response. The qualities that one comes to admire in Emily Fairfax are her courage, passion, and egalitarianism rooted in her own history. One wishes that Caruthers had the interest and stamina to do more with her character than to leave her to madness and death on the frontier.

Both Lucretia Meriwether and Emily Fairfax are described as they fit into the household economy or into the romantic plot, and then they are forgotten. In contrast, Mrs. Lucy Travis (Simms's *The Forayers* and *Eutaw*) is an important minor character as her husband's friend and her daughter's companion. Her own family, a "good family in the Low Country," was horrified when she married Travis, "an obscure Indian trader," and disowned her.[8] That brought her closer to her husband, and meant that both of them had to rely more on each other and less on their families for support. When Travis left the plantation for the last time, he suspected that he would not return. In a touching scene, he parted from his wife of thirty years, after explaining the details of how Lucy was to manage without him. Moved by his uncharacteristic generosity toward their children and his love for her, she felt justified in her faith toward him.

The first images of Lucy Travis, then, are of a compassionate woman who exercises some authority over her household and her children. She counsels her daughter, Bertha, on the proper courting behavior, she serves as a confidante and companion to her husband, and she manages the plantation in his absence (273). In *Eutaw,* the sequel to *The Forayers,* Lucy Travis continues to be self-composed and self-assured even when she and Bertha are captured by poor-white bandits who hold them for ransom. She assures Bertha that their abductors only want plunder and money, and convinces the bandits that they will get the money if she and her daughter are well treated. Finally, she bargains for their release by promising to pay for their safe conduct. In short, she uses the resources she has and turns her potential enemies into protectors.[9]

Later, when she and Bertha and Colonel Sinclair and his daughter Carrie arrive at the Widow Avinger's plantation as refugees from the war, she organizes the young women to help with nursing Colonel Sinclair (410). The only time she loses her composure is when she hears that their home has been burned by the British and that her son and husband have been captured (106 and 145). As a character, however, she is forgotten after Bertha is reunited with her father. In the epilogue, Simms announces that after William and Bertha are married, Lucy lives with them at the Sinclair home and that she and Colonel Sinclair are doting grandparents.

Although Kennedy, Caruthers, and Simms create believable even admirable female characters as wives and mothers, they don't sustain the reader's interest in them. Kennedy's Lucretia Meriwether is initially well depicted, and then she disappears, and Caruthers's Emily Fairfax suffers madness and death. Simms's Lucy Travis exerts some influence, but Simms fails to imagine her thoughts, dreams, and politics. Since romantic literature is given over to exploits of the unmarried hero and the heroine, it is relatively simple to accept mothers as stereotypes and to expect them to defer to their husbands and nurture their children. Significantly, the strongest heroines are without mothers.[10] It is almost as if the authors couldn't manage two distinct and compelling female personalities in the same novel.

Additionally, these writers were transforming the sentimental domestic novel, which had as its focus women's feelings and women's lives—the "private life" of the home—to the historical romance, which put men at the center of the action. In this shift of context from the private sphere of the home to the public sphere of politics and war, men's life problems supplanted those of women as the subject for fiction. The masculine protest against the sentimental novelists of the 1850s not only lay in their jealousy over the women's financial success, but stemmed also from their anger at women's choosing "inappropriate" subjects and trivializing their "art." Significantly, the dominant theme of these women's novels was the heroine's ability to cope with terrible personal and economic hardships when patriarchal promises of "protection" often in marriage failed to materialize.[11]

Wives who are friends and companions of men hardly figure in the novels. Some women are closer to their husbands than to their children, but virtually all of the wives are also mothers.[12] In contrast to the first group of women who have relationships with both husbands and children, the second larger group of women as mothers are depicted as relating primarily to their children. They are portrayed as either "good" or as "bad" mothers. Married women are defined, then, solely by their biological capacity to give birth. Clearly these authors believe that if a woman is a mother, she should want nothing more in life.

Kennedy and Simms are the most reverential in their attitudes toward mothers. That role transcends all other aspects of a woman's character. Both depict blacks and poor whites disparagingly, but their most sympathetic portraits of each group are reserved for women who are mothers. Similarly, although Simms and Tucker are ready to excuse the behavior of a fallen woman, they do not forgive the errors of a bad or inept mother. All the novelists, moreover, wax rhapsodic about the mother-child relationship especially when describing a young man's feelings about leaving his mother. John Ramsay (Kennedy's *Horse-Shoe Robinson*) leaves to join the patriot

cause; William Hinkley (Simms's *Charlemont*) is cast out by his father; and
Richard Hurdis (Simms's *Richard Hurdis*) in a feud with his older brother
departs for the frontier. In all of these instances the mother is depicted as
nurturing and protective of her son, while the father is depicted as a distant
and judgmental taskmaster who bids the son to do his duty or is his adversary. Most significant, none of the mothers of the major romantic heroes is
alive.[13] The most fully developed maternal figures are in Simms's border
novels where the hero's quest involves his leaving the comforts of his home
and accepting the "masculine" challenges of frontier life. That Simms would
articulate this kind of gender politics is especially significant, given his own
choice to remain in his maternal home of Charleston rather than join his
father in frontier Mississippi.[14]

In *Horse-Shoe Robinson,* Mrs. Ramsay is the wife of a patriot yeoman,
David Ramsay, and the mother of two sons, John and Andrew. When first
introduced, "Mistress Ramsay" is shelling beans for dinner. When she sees
Horse-Shoe Robinson, she immediately inquires about her son John, a soldier with the patriot forces. She worries that John "is often without his natural rest, or a meal's victuals," and then she adds proudly that "the general
thinks so much of him, that he can't spare him to come home."[15] At once the
classic role is recognizable. The mother worries about her son's health, but is
proud that he is doing his duty. If it is "womanly" not to know about "man's
business," especially war—the most masculine of occupations—it is equally
"motherly" to assume that the American cause especially needs the services
of her son. In creating the type, Kennedy underscores the mother's helplessness and vulnerability in coping in a "man's world."

In one incident, Horse-Shoe wants to borrow her younger son, Andrew,
for a bit of a ruse on the British, but Mrs. Ramsay is hesitant to let him go. She
implores Horse-Shoe: "Ah, Mr. Robinson, I have one son already in these
wars—God protect him!—and you men don't know how a mother's heart
yearns for her children in these times. I cannot give another" (266). In Kennedy's view, if mother love involved sacrifice and the pain of parting from
one's children, it also involved being overprotective and unwilling to let go.
One is always a child to one's mother. In this way, then, the protectiveness of
the mother emasculates the son and is subversive of the higher claims of
patriotism and civilization that call him out of the home to work and to war.
John Ramsay dies a hero's death in a special mission for Butler, the novel's
hero. Expiring in Butler's arms he whispered that he "did not fear to die"
except for the reaction of his fiancée and "for the sake of my poor mother"
(468).

The family responses were predictable. His fiancée Mary Musgrove
fainted, his mother wept silently, his father recovered first and affirmed:
"Dead! He fell doing his duty to his country, that's a consolation. A man
cannot die better. If it please God, I hope my end may be like his. Andrew my
boy, come here. You are now my oldest living son. . . . I am willing, as much

as I love you, that the country should have you" (476). Mrs. Ramsay, horrified by such insensitivity, is sharply told: "Silence, wife, this is no time to hold back from our duty" (476). In spite of maternal love, then, a man must go into the world and do his duty. That is what it means to be a man. In depriving him of his opportunity, the mother would deprive him of his manhood. Like all feeling, then, mother love is irrational, and must be overcome. But it is never forgotten, and remains the ideal love.

Because all nurturing is undertaken by women, the world of men, especially in the army, is emotionally brutalizing. The hierarchies that form among men based on force are justified in part by a ruling class that perpetuates the myth of masculine "toughness," or, in a later era, "fitness." Those men who hold power in the society, it is implied, are not only the most intelligent and talented, but the "toughest" and most masculine. Thus do class and racial hierarchies among men enhance this "cult of masculinity," which is celebrated by the most conservative patriarchal societies from ancient Greece to the Third Reich.[16]

Although the antebellum South had not achieved the total separation between home and work that would come with the triumph of industrial capitalism, the social base for that transformation was laid by the patriarchal insistence on separate and unequal spheres for men and women where men hold the balance of power. Once these gender dichotomies were established it was not difficult to make a case for "natural" feminine passivity and masculine violence which, along with the assumption of inevitable human evil, form the core of conservative patriarchal thought.[17]

For instance, Simms is much more straightforward in describing and sentimentalizing the mother-child bond than any of the other writers. The standard motif of his border novels has a young man leaving his yeoman family farm to seek his fortune on the frontier.[18] William Hinkley (*Charlemont*) is driven away and disowned by his fundamentalist father, who believes he committed a terrible transgression in dueling with "Brother" Alfred Stevens, a charlatan preacher who eventually seduces Margaret Cooper, Hinkley's love. The father, portrayed as a pious man and a rigid disciplinarian, is prone to violence when his authority is questioned or his will thwarted. When father and son argue about Brother Stevens, Mrs. Hinkley, sensing her husband's intemperate response to his son's disrespect, urges William to "be submissive or fly." William Hinkley replies: "Here I will remain. I will not fly. It will be for my father and mother to say whether they will expel their only son from their home to make room for a stranger."[19] His father meets his words with a whip to his shoulders. Stunned, William wrests the whip from his father's grasp and turns to use it on Stevens, but his mother's cries and fearful admonitions arrest this act, and he flees from the house. Unlike his mother, William cannot submit: he must stand his ground as a man.

Hinkley next challenges Stevens to a duel, which Stevens accepts. Hinkley's father intercedes and strikes William on the head with a wooden rod.

Before he can deliver a second blow, in a now familiar scene, Mrs. Hinkley throws herself between her husband and son, admonishing her husband:

> Shame! Shame! you bloody-minded man . . . to slaughter your only son—to come behind him and knock him down with a club as if he had been an inhuman ox! You are no husband of mine. He shan't own you for a father. If I had the pick, I'd choose a thousand fathers for him, from here to Massassippi [*sic*], sooner than you. He's only too good and too handsome to be son of yours. And for what should you strike him? For a stranger—a man we never saw before. Shame on you! You are a brute, a monster, William Hinkley, and I'm done with you forever. (270)

As it turns out, William recovers and is adopted by his tutor, Calvert, and his mother stays with her husband. Hinkley Senior was clearly cast in the patriarchal mold, requiring the absolute obedience of his son. While William submitted, he was treated affectionately and paternalistically; when he did not, he was cast off.

One sees in Simms's depiction of this family his assumption that the mother-child bond is greater than that of husband and wife. In Simms's scheme, the mother's affections go with her child, though her duty is with her husband. When it becomes clear father and son are finished, his mother assures her son, "I have none, none but you. You know how I have loved—you know I will always love you" (274). William returns her love, swears to continue as a dutiful son to her, but declares that he now must leave home. Even when parted, therefore, they are emotionally connected in a way that excludes his father.

Similarly, Richard Hurdis (*Richard Hurdis*) must leave the household. Although he worked industriously on the family estate, his indolent oldest brother John will inherit it.[20] More infuriating to him, his love, Mary Easterby, is rumored to be involved with John. Instead of asking her about it, Richard decides to leave before being forced "as a man" to make trouble. About his leave-taking he comments:

> I effected no small achievement when I first resolved to leave my mother. It was no pain to leave my father.
>
> My father, though a phlegmatic and proud man, showed much more emotion at the declaration of my resolve to leave him, than I had ever expected. His emotion arose, not so much from the love he bore me, as from the loss he was about to sustain by my departure. I had been his best negro, and he confessed it. (16)

On the day of his departure, his mother is distressed. He commented that he "had never seen her exhibit so much mental suffering before." She staggered to a chair and "wept without restraint," until they both heard his father approach. The older Hurdis is described as a "stern man" who "gave little heed and no sympathy to such emotions for any cause" (54). At his son's departure, he hugs him and confesses: "I won't palaver with you about my love and all that soft stuff, but I do love you, Richard, as a man and no sneak. Good-bye, boy, good-bye, and take care of yourself" (56).

In spite of his love for his son, the patriarch Hurdis cannot openly express his feelings as his wife had done; to do so would be considered "unmasculine." As a result, Richard is unsure of his father's love and leaves feeling rejected and unappreciated. The father, in turn, loses both his son and his best worker. Richard's mother makes him promise to forgive his brother because it is the Christian thing to do, and because it grieves her to have two sons fighting. Richard comments that their parting "was one of mixed pain and pleasure" (57). Troubled over her suffering, he was comforted by the knowledge that she loved him.

As Richard rides away from his home, he reflects on his mother's love for him:

> They [his memories] cling to me with a mother's love; the purest, the least selfish of all human affections. The love of woman is a wondrous thing, but the love of a mother is yet more wonderful. What is there like it in nature? What tie is there so close, so warm, so uncalculating in its compliances, so unmeasured in its sacrifices, so enduring in its tenacious tenderness? . . . It refines vulgarity, it softens violence, it qualifies and chastens, even when it may not redeem, all other vices. I am convinced that, of all human affections, it is endowed with the greatest longevity; it is the most hardy, if not the most acute in its vitality. (58)

Thus does Simms join other Victorian writers in sentimentalizing a mother's love as the purest and most spiritual of human emotions, surpassing even that of a wife or a husband. And yet a young man, if he is to be a man in this frontier democracy, must leave his mother and his past behind. This coming-of-age theme in the border romances is fundamental to American fiction. Rejection of the father's power is complemented by the assertion of one's own identity. It is the American male's rite of passage. A boy becomes a man when he takes his place among men as their equal: on the battlefield, on the frontier, in the marketplace. It is the message of a mobile society that provides sons with a place to move and a way of resolving conflict in the family in a manner supporting both masculinity and family-building.

What is unusual about this theme in this antebellum Southern literature, especially in Simms's work, is that the planter hero usually inherits his father's or his father-in-law's estate. Family wealth in land and slaves is transmitted to the male. The crimes of Richard's brother John lead to his death and Richard returns to claim the woman he loves and his patrimony. Most of the novel, however, unwinds like a typical "Western"—the ultimate American romance.[21] Finally, one should note that the same author who could draw such oversentimentalized scenes of a grown man leaving his mother was incapable of being moved to similar compassion for black slaves who were often parted from beloved family members. Simms argued that black slaves bore their family separations more lightly than whites because they were less civilized. And he even went so far as to claim that many, especially lustful black men eager to find a new woman, looked forward to this change.[22]

In these border novels Simms repeatedly develops three major American themes: the democratizing effect of the frontier, the roving and adventurous pioneer spirit of the "Anglo-American," and the kind of *man* it takes to settle a continent.[23] *Charlemont* emphasizes the absence of inherited wealth and accompanying class structure on the frontier, which Simms argues "leads to a singular and unreserved freedom among the people" while the region's loneliness tends to break down most of the barriers of sex and class that are fundamental to "civilization." The frontier also breeds a special kind of man, a "singular combination of simplicity and sagacity." Coarse and unrefined, in manner, he nevertheless appreciates the "fine delicacy" of a woman, which is reason enough to defend her heroically (7–11, 13–21).

The pioneer represented that new breed of Anglo-Saxon, the American or "Anglo-American" as Simms named him. His conquest of the frontier and Native Americans is celebrated as a triumph of civilization over barbarity. This view, an unabashed racism, appears in Southern as well as Northern fiction and gives it a distinctly American character.[24] Further, the "silk-shodden and sleek citizen of the European world," or the clerk of the American (read Northern) city "who lives by measuring tape and pins by the sixpence worth" is "scarce a man" compared with the pioneer with his physical strength, "noble restlessness," sense of fair play, and egalitarianism.[25] Hurdis, angry at his father for working him hard and at his brother for trying to steal "his woman," must also, like many of his countrymen, "burst his shackles" and prove himself a man among men. This involved leaving his mother, which, he understood, was integral to his coming of age. He explains: "The love of the young for each other is a property of the coming time, and it is for the coming time for which the young must live. That of a mother is a love of the past, or, at best, of the present only" (59). To become a man one must give up "effeminate" dependencies and find a new life in a masculine world. It is this knowledge that leads Hurdis to conclude that mother love exists largely on memory and is of the past; in that spirit he "would have given up the love of a thousand mothers, to be secure of that of Mary Easterby" (60).

What distinguishes the Southern novel from the Northern one of the same period is its insistence upon transplanting the plantation to the frontier. The "democracy" of the Southwest was not destined to be the rough egalitarianism of the Northwest, though it was more egalitarian than the Southeast. Rather, these Southern writers would replicate their own society of "natural inferiors" deferring to "natural superiors." It is this departure from masculine egalitarianism that distinguished the antebellum Southern novel from that of the North and which makes the former seem anachronistic, if not "un-American," to modern readers (see Chapter 14 for development of this idea).

Significantly, the black mother, as nurturer of both black and white children, is the most respected black person in this literature. Lucy, in Kennedy's *Swallow Barn,* is the paradigmatic black mother, "the mammy," and she embodies the idea that blacks have the most familiar and fundamental human attachments. She lives alone in a small, sparsely furnished cottage set apart from the rest of the cabins as she had been separated from fellow slaves all her life. She is cared for by her daughter, underscoring Kennedy's rebuttal to the abolitionist contention that slavery broke up slave families and led to the premature death of slaves. As chapter 47 opens, Frank Meriwether, the proprietor of Swallow Barn, escorts his wife's cousin, Mark Littleton, also the narrator, around the plantation. Meriwether introduces Mark and Lucy and later Littleton recounts the scene for his readers.

Littleton notes that Lucy "showed the double havoc of age and disease," rocking back and forth in front of the hearth, lost in "the weak and childish musing of age." She was tapping one foot on the floor with a regular beat "such as is common to nurses when lulling a child asleep" (461 and 462). At first she is insensible to their presence, but then she recognizes Frank and exclaims in her high, creaking voice: "God bless the young master! I didn't know him. He has come to see poor old mammy Lucy!" (462). She begins to talk with them in an incoherent jumble about people coming to see her and get her, and about a ship that had been gone for five years. Impatient with "this exhibition of driveling dotage," the two men leave, and Frank tells Littleton Lucy's life story (463).

During the Revolution, Meriwether's father-in-law, Walter Hazard, had commanded a troop of cavalry from the county and had been accompanied by "a faithful negro" named Luke. At the war's end Hazard offered Luke his freedom but unlike James Ewell Heath's James, "the domestic desired no greater liberty than he enjoyed, and would not entertain the idea of any possible separation from the family" (465). Instead, Luke settled for a few acres of land and married Lucy, the family's lady's maid at Swallow Barn. Lucy and Luke went on to raise a family, one "remarkable for its intelligence," and their children had served on the plantation as shoemakers, weavers, or carpenters (466).

Their youngest son, Abe, was more spirited than the rest and chafed under his bondage. He started to get into trouble—playing pranks, staying out late, leaving the plantation without permission. But Lucy only defended Abe, thereby spoiling him, according to Meriwether. Rather than curb his antisocial behavior, she merely protected him: "a common effect of strong animal impulses, not merely in ignorant minds" (467). Finally, Meriwether, who had married Lucretia, Hazard's daughter, and was now running the plantation, could not tolerate Abe's disruptive behavior, and concluded that he would have to hire out Abe, notwithstanding his hesitancy about separating slave families (467 and 468). It was going to be difficult, he realized, to convince "the mind of a mother of the justice of the sentence that deprives her of her child—especially a poor, unlearned negro mother" (468). Lucy heard Meriwether's arguments and seemed to agree to an act that would save her son from the horrors of a Southern prison, but his parting "was a source of unutterable anguish to her, which no kindness on the part of the family could mitigate" (468).

Kennedy uses this portrait of Lucy and her family to make several classical planter defenses of slavery. First, he argues that if blacks like Luke were well cared for, freedom was unnecessary; given the choice, slaves would prefer to stay in the comforting plantation situation. Second, he notes blacks were naturally deferential and loyal to the master. Third, he establishes Lucy as a loving but inept mother who spoiled her son and was probably responsible for Abe's behavior. Thus Kennedy establishes the attachment of a black mother to her children.

Abe, upon hearing of the decision, seemed to react with "callous unconcern." But as his departure neared, Meriwether reports, he went through stages, from buoyant confidence to deep sadness in parting from the security of plantation society and from his mother. Lucy saw him off at the ship on which he would be a deckhand; for the most part she was stoical throughout, until the final moment of parting, when she "flung herself upon his neck" and "wept aloud" (473). Abe rejected the silver Lucy wished to give him, preferring instead the handkerchief she wore around her neck. He became a responsible and able seaman and died a hero in a shipwreck. When told the story of his heroic death, Lucy's shock is so great that she refuses to believe it and continues to make preparations for his arrival home. Within the year, her grief turned into insanity (484–90).

To a group in which he credits very few of the "civilized attributes," then, Kennedy ascribes, at least to this black woman, and by implication to others as well, the bonds and affections of motherhood. Apparently some planters realized the human toll being exacted when they sold off members of the same family.[26] It must also be remembered, however, that Kennedy uses this instance as an exception to answer the most effective criticism of antislavery propagandists; namely, that the forced parting of mother and child was barbaric and inhuman. First, Abe is not a child, he is a young man, perhaps even in his early twenties and like other young men ready to leave. His leave-taking like Richard Hurdis's is depicted as an opportunity. Second, arguing for the planter defense, Kennedy takes great pains to depict the continuity of the black and white families with their shared past, and to argue that the selling of slave family members was an economic or a social necessity, not lightly or often undertaken. Through his positive portrait of the black mother and her family and their intergenerational ties to the white family, Kennedy justifies slavery as a social institution, even though he was opposed to it economically and thought it would die out.

In *Woodcraft,* one of his most difficult and fascinating novels, William Gilmore Simms depicts the same connection—the love and loyalty of white and black families for each other—through the person of a black woman, Porgy's "Mauma." Captain Porgy and his small troop of soldiers return to Porgy's devastated plantation on the Edisto River. It had been ransacked and robbed by both the British and their poor-white allies, and the blacks had been run off to the swamps. Porgy despairs because even though he can borrow money and equipment, he cannot make a crop without his black labor force. One evening an old black woman returns to the plantation. She is Sappho, Porgy's mammy. She mistakes the overseer, Millhouse, for Porgy because Millhouse is sleeping in Porgy's old bedroom. She says to him, thinking he is Porgy: "It's me, my chile! It's you own ole woman—Sappho! Enty you member de ole woman—you own nuss,—de same Sappho wha' bin mind you a t'ousand times. De Lawd be praise for bring you back—dat de ole woman kin hug he child once more, fore he dead for ebber."[27] Comforted when the error is discovered and he finally finds her, Porgy embraces her as his "poor old mauma" and gives her a kiss (310). As it turns out, she has kept her family together by running them off to the swamps to hide from the British and the outlaws. When she tells Porgy the "news," it is of her children's marriages (313 and 314). Here again in the planter version white and black families have a shared past, one represented by the old black woman. Porgy feels he has come home only when he sees Sappho; she is the link with his past. Simms, like Kennedy, endows a black mother with the most humane and admirable qualities of blacks.

For both authors, the characterization of the black mother becomes another way for planters to deny the existence of conflict on the plantation, especially the rape of the black woman, who appears in these novels as the unsexed, mammy.[28] Planter enemies are the enemies of the black family. The mother-child tie binds the two families together as the black woman becomes the bridge between them.[29]

Kennedy and Simms seem freer to acknowledge their loathing of poor whites, so their portraits of poor white women are even more revealing of their veneration of motherhood. In Peggy Adair (*Horse-Shoe Robinson*), Rachel Bostwick (*Woodcraft*), and Betsy Pickett (*Richard Hurdis*), Kennedy and Simms create three women who live similarly squalid material lives, yet react differently to their situations. While Adair is completely defeated by her life, Bostwick and Pickett find meaning in caring for their children. Additionally, Pickett betrays an unusual class consciousness in her hostility to the planter class, and her mistrust allows her to protect her child from a corrupt planter. While Kennedy affirms his prejudice that only the most morally debased whites become poor, Simms finds good qualities in the poor but virtuous woman who learns to accept her impoverished place in Southern society, deferring to superiors in the planter class, and training her children to do the same. Peggy Adair (*Horse-Shoe Robinson*) is the wife of poor-white woodsman Wat Adair, whom Kennedy describes as "cunning," "savage," "slovenly," and ungraceful (156). Peggy, Kennedy notes, "was a woman who could scarcely be said to have reached the middle period of life, although her wan and somewhat ragged features, and a surly discontented expression of face, might well induce an observer to attribute more years to her worldly account than she had actually seen" (149). She spends her life cooking, cleaning, and caring for children under the utmost deprivation. Her husband is a hunter and a lumberjack so they eat slightly better than their neighbors, but she is burdened by too many children, whom she characterizes as "troublesome brats," adding that "poor people generally have the luck that way" (151). She leads a joyless life catering to the needs of both her husband and her children, and for her efforts, she gets little affection or respect. She does no more than survive in a desperately alienating existence with an uncouth, disrespectful brute for a husband. Kennedy pities Peggy Adair demoralized and degraded in her barbaric existence, but otherwise leaves her with no dignity.[30]

In contrast, Rachel Bostwick, the poor-white wife and mother in Simms's *Woodcraft,* is one of the few salvageable people he finds in the lower orders of Southern society. She is married to Samuel Bostwick, one of Simms's most despicable poor-white criminals. She is scrupulously neat and clean and makes every effort to care for her children, though they are given nothing to live on. She is described as being a "poor, subdued, faint-spirited woman," with a "thin, frail, pale-faced body [*sic*], with fair complexion still, or soft sad eyes, the only remains of a once girlish beauty" (215). Like Peggy Adair, she cooked, cleaned, and nurtured her children, and in addition spun for the rich Widow Eveleigh on whose land they live. Although Bostwick is kind to his children, especially to Dory, his attractive teenage daughter, he treats his wife with disdain and contempt. He returns home only when sick and hurt and when he wants something. Then he demands nursing, food, and shelter from the woman he is supporting. Simms comments: "Rachel—poor Rachel— his wife! He thought of her at that moment, not as one whom he loved or cared for, but as the creature from whom he might find shelter" (214). Broken-spirited and poverty-stricken though she is, Rachel devotedly cares for her three children, teaches Dory how to read the Bible and how to spin. Most important, she makes sure her daughter knows her place and is properly deferential in her contacts with the members of planter class (219–25, 475 and 476).[31] When Bostwick finally dies, as their reward for their humility and piety, Widow Eveleigh provides Rachel and her children with a farm of their own with their own black servant (507).

For Simms, then, the poor-white woman is saved from the degradation of her class by her maternal instincts and by planter charity. For Kennedy, even those basic instincts are snuffed out by a brutish existence. Like the African American mother, Rachel Bostwick is "good" because she fulfills her domestic responsibilities without questioning the authority of either her degraded husband or the planter class. The offspring of both are similarly socialized into an acceptance of their places in Southern society. This is the true value of the good mother: to inculcate deference to patriarchal authority.[32]

Similarly, in Betsy Pickett (*Richard Hurdis*), Simms creates a self-conscious poor-white woman who attempts to keep her weak husband from being corrupted by Richard Hurdis's wayward brother John. To most Betsy Pickett seems "sour and vacant," "dark and threatening" (83). Simms notes, however, that "her mind was something stronger, as it was more direct and less flexible than his [her husband's]. She was a woman of deliberate and composed manner, rarely passionate, and careful to accommodate her conduct and appearance to the well-known humility of condition in which she lived" (83). As a wife she tries to discourage her husband from following John Hurdis. But her objections, he tells her, are just "woman's talk." She argues:

> What would the rich Squire Hurdis want of Ben Pickett the squatter? Why should he come palavering you, and me, and that poor child with fine words; and what can we, poor and mean and hated as we are by everybody, what can we do for so great a man as him? I tell you Ben Pickett, he wants you to do dirty work, that he's ashamed and afraid to do himself . . . these rich men ask what right a poor man has to be good and honest; they expect him to be a rascal. (92)

She loses the argument, but wins her point with the nineteenth-century reader who understood the irreconcilable class differences in the South. Despite her poverty and her lack of education or social refinement, she has the one great virtue Simms finds in all women: she is a mother first and displays the kind of passionate "mother love" that makes women the fiercest of fighters in defense of their children. Additionally, at least in this portrait, Simms has acknowledged the advantages that upper-class men take of lower-class women. This acknowledgment is important because in Simms's heroic tales, poor whites and yeoman-class men are a threat to upper-class women. What these incidents make very clear is that men of both classes use women to make war on each other.

If Betsy is adamant and demanding with her husband, she is even more forceful in her defense of Jane, her impaired daughter. John Hurdis has been taking Jane for long walks in the woods to pry information from her and to steal a kiss or two. One day Betsy Pickett follows them. Simms feelingly evokes the enraged mother protecting her child:

> Her meager, and usually pale and severe features, were now crimsoned with indignation; her eyes flashed a fire of feeling and of character which lifted her, however poor and lowly had been her birth and was her station, immeasurably above the base creature whose superior wealth had furnished the facilities, and too, frequently in the minds of

men, provided a sanction for the vilest abuses of the dependence and inferiority of the poor. (110)[33]

When Hurdis tries to defend himself, she assails him with her evidence:

> It was a mother's eye that watched—not you, sir, but her child; it was a mother's ear that sought to know—not the words spoken by John Hurdis, but all words, no matter of whom, which were poured into the ears of her child. . . . You have appealed to the blood and passions of the child, and, but for the mother that watched over her, you might have succeeded at least in your bad purposes. (114)

Though they might be "low and poor," she assures Hurdis, Ben Pickett would come looking for him "to avenge our dishonor" (114), and she chases him off their land.

"Good" fictional mothers, regardless of race or class, are women who as wives and mothers have subordinated their own needs, dreams, desires, and ambitions to those of their husbands and their children, and, in the case of black women, to those of their masters. Most important, good mothers labor, without complaint, and love selflessly, expecting respect and gratitude in return, but not real power. Because of their domestic responsibilities and their devotion to children, they exist in a world that is tangential to if not totally removed from the competitive and hostile one of men. They possess a blind faith in their husbands and children, naively assuming that the world will share their opinion.

Mother love, then, is innocent and boundless. It is sentimentalized in Northern as well as Southern literature in this first great period of the women's-rights movement to convince women that, whether they are safely tucked away in their urban Northern homes or hidden on their plantations, their greatest contribution to society is as hard-working wives and nurturant mothers rather than as passionate, self-centered, and "unsexed" social reformers and intellectual women. As William R. Taylor observed more than twenty-five years ago, "it is impossible to read widely in the literature of the South without gaining the impression that Southern women in a certain sense were being bought off, offered half the loaf in the hope they would not demand more."[34] Judy Grahn would remind these authors that it is the woman who bakes the bread and like it, she too will rise.[35]

"BAD" MOTHERS

The overwhelming number of the women portrayed as mothers in this literature are nurturant, affectionate, and understanding. They are the sources of love and guidance. They prepare their teenage daughters for courtship and marriage, and their teenage sons for war and/or for life as a planter. However, Southern authors have also created a series of "bad" mothers that tells us more about what they believed were the requisites for motherhood than about mothering per se. Women are "bad" mothers either because they have an overwhelming character flaw or are degraded members of the poor-white class. As with all mothers, their worth and effectiveness are judged by the behavior of their children. The principle is clear: good women are good mothers and good mothering produces good children. Most important, the best and worst people reproduce themselves.

One exception to this general practice, however, was Catherine Austin in N. B. Tucker's *Gertrude*. Although her daughter Gertrude Courtney is a para-gon of virtue, Catherine Austin suffers from being overly ambitious, "bor-dering on avarice." More typical are Simms's Widow Cooper (*Beauchampe* and *Charlemont*) and Guy Rivers's mother (*Guy Rivers*) who are tyrannized by their children. Simms argues that as a result of their mothers' inability to curb the passions of their offspring, Margaret Cooper and Guy Rivers fail to develop enough self-discipline and self-restraint to face the critical moral choices of their adult life. Mrs. Cooper is characterized as a dimwitted gossip who has no control over her teenage daughter, Margaret. She is obviously proud but puzzled over Margaret's intellectual curiosity. She notes Marga-ret "cares for nothing half so well. Morning, noon, and night, all the same, you find her poring over them; and even when she goes out to ramble, she must have a book, and she wants no other company. For my part I can't see what she finds in them to love so" (103). Simms creates Margaret Cooper as a woman who has been "corrupted" by books and encouraged to depart from her "proper sphere" of wife and mother. Thus she feels superior to other young women. Her own mother is culpable, because she has indulged Margaret's fiction and poetry reading, her egotism and ambition, and has scorned the counsel of Mr. Calvert, the schoolmaster, who tried to warn them both about Albert Stevens, Margaret's eventual seducer.[36]

When Calvert comes with his well-intentioned warning, Widow Cooper flies into a rage. His advice, she declares, reflects the disappointment and jealousy of his adopted son, William Hinkley. Calvert rejects these sugges-tions, and leaves with the satisfaction that at least he has done his duty, but he is aware that Widow Cooper is ineffective in controlling her daughter. The conversation between them takes place on the same night that Margaret is being seduced by Stevens. When Margaret arrives home, she is upset to the point of frenzy. Her mother, lacking the instincts of the "true mother," doesn't even notice. Rather, she babbles on about how she sent Calvert off "with a flea in his ear" (323). Margaret excuses herself and escapes to the privacy of her room, where she sobs herself to sleep in "hopeless despera-tion" (326). Thus, Mrs. Cooper fails in her primary task to protect her daugh-ter from the wiles of dishonorable men. By assuming that Margaret is capa-ble of taking care of herself, Simms argues, she had made Margaret's mistake of not recognizing her own frailty as a woman.

If poor mothering leads a young woman to dishonor and social death, then poor mothering leads a young man to what Simms contended was the male equivalent: crime. He is most explicit in attributing Guy Rivers's moral failings to his mother's indulgence of him as a child. Rivers laments: "her schoolings have made me the morbid, fierce criminal, the wilful, vexing spirit, from whose association all the gentler virtues must desire to fly. If, in the doom which may finish my life of doom, I have any one person to accuse of all, that person is—my mother!"[37] And what terrible thing did she do that set him on the high criminal road? Did she teach him to lie, to swindle, or to murder? Not at all. She indulged his "passions." When Rivers's father sought to discipline Guy, his mother defended him and lied for him. In undercutting respect for his father, she subverted his respect for all authority as well as his capacity for self-government. She told him not to lie, yet she lied daily to his father to protect him. She bribed him to do what was right, so he never learned that "virtue is its own reward." Aware that she loved him, he also recognized that she "ruined him" by yielding to his boyish passions. Thus does Simms describe the making of a criminal. Criminality is not caused by economic deprivation or by social conditions, but by unruly passions that have never been curbed. In most cases, Simms attributes criminality to the "inherent viciousness" of the lower orders, but among the yeoman class it derives from well-intentioned but blundering mother love (452–55).

For Simms the truly evil mothers were aged poor whites. Even though she suffers from rheumatism, Jenny Blodgit (*The Forayers*) masters enough spirit to urge Pete, her lame and cowardly son, to greater and greater crimes, from fraud to theft and murder. Pete is the overseer of William Sinclair's estate. As Sinclair's agent, Blodgit is supposed to sell the plantation's produce and return half the sales money to Sinclair's family and use the other half to buy guns for the patriots. But at his mother's urging, he has been defrauding the estate, and Sinclair discovers it. Blodgit is too stupid to know that he will never again be trusted by Sinclair, something his mother immediately realizes and urges him to murder Sinclair:

> Lord! ef it had been me, I reckon I could ha' found a hundred chainces for laying him over the head with a hickory, or driving a sharp knife cl'ar down into his ribs. Thar's always chainces enough for any man that's got a man's heart in his buzzom, Pete Blodgit! But you ain's no man at all, as I've told you a thousand times. . . .
> Oh! ef I was a man, I wouldn't waste words on you nor him! I'd do it myself, and nobody'd be wiser of what was done till it was too late to put in with a 'stop you thar!' (44 and 45)

Deceptive, avaricious, and emasculating, Jenny Blodgit, then, is a representative of the most degraded class in the South. Simms, like his protagonist, William Sinclair, expects little from these people but ingratitude.

Similarly, Polly Blonay (*The Partisan*) is the mother of the misshapen and wayward son, Ned Blonay, also known as "Goggle." Bloney got his nickname

from his blear eye, and is one of Simms's most desperate poor-white characters. Polly is a poor-white woman who lives in absolute squalor, depending
on Ned for support. Her hut, scarcely a home, is "dreary," "cheerless," and
"barren," filled with the foul fumes from the pipe she smokes.

> Her thin, shrivelled, and darkly yellow features were hag-like and
> jaundiced. The skin was tightly drawn across the face, and the high
> cheek-bones and the nose seemed disposed to break through the slen-
> der restraints of their covering. Her eyes were small and sunken, of a
> light grey, and had a vicious twinkle, that did not accord with the
> wretched and decayed aspect of her other features. Her forehead was
> small, and clustered with grisly hair of mixed white and black, disor-
> dered and unbound, but still short, and with the appearance of having
> but lately undergone clipping at the extremities. These features, repul-
> sive in themselves, were greatly heightened in their offensive expres-
> sion by the severe mouth and sharp chin below them. The upper lip
> was flat underdeveloped entirely, while the lower was thrust forth in a
> thick curl, and, closely rising and clinging to the other, somewhat
> lifted her glance into a sort of insolent authority, which, sometimes
> accompanying aroused feeling, or an elevated mood of mind, might
> look like dignified superiority. The dress she wore was of the poorest
> sort, the commonest white homespun of the country, probably her
> own manufacture, and so indifferently made, that it hung about her
> like a sack, and gave a full view of the bronzed and skinny neck and
> bosom, which a regard to her appearance might have prompted her to
> conceal.[38]

"Mother" Blonay, then, embodies the characteristics despised by Simms
and his class. She is superstitious, immoral, careless, lazy, repulsive. Even
worse, she is jealous of and hostile to the planter class. When questioned
about her son's whereabouts, she threatens to put a curse on her interroga-
tors. Furious with Sergeant Humphries because he calls her son Ned, "Goggle," she gets her revenge by setting a trap for his gullible sister, Bella, where
a British sergeant tries to rape her. Once again, in conflicts in patriarchal
societies, men of the different classes fight each other through the seduction
and rape of one another's women.

Ned is largely indifferent to his mother, though she obviously dotes on
him: "She fondled upon her son with all the feeble drivelling of age; called
him by various affectionate diminutives, and busied herself, in spite of her
infirmities, waddling about from corner to corner of the hut to administer to
his desires, which were by no means few" (191). His reaction to such attention
is one of "the most brutal indifference" (191). Teased most of his life about
being illegitimate, though he always lived with both parents, he had mostly
ignored such talk, but in having heard himself being described as the illegitimate son of an Indian, he demanded to know the truth. His mother "poured

into his ear a dark, foul narrative of criminal intercourse, provoked on her part by a diseased appetite, resulting, as it would seem in punishment, in the birth of a monster like himself" (198).

Simm's writing here is passionate and vivid, dripping with contempt for this hated lower class. First, Polly has committed adultery. But what makes her adultery criminal, Simms concludes, is that her sexual partner was an Indian. Ned Blonay's deformity, Simms thinks, is thus a result of God's fury at such an immoral and "unnatural" union (197 and 198). Second, as a poor white woman, she is portrayed as having instigated the illicit act. Like the Widow Blodgit, she is the partner of a criminal son. Their bond remains unbroken. When she dies a hideous death mashed to a pulp beneath the hoofs of galloping horses, Blonay carries her to the gravesite she had marked by their home. Thus, notwithstanding his hostility and contempt for poor whites, Simms still grants them basic human compassion. In the end, for all their brutality, the mother-child bond is the most enduring.

For antebellum Southern writers, it has been suggested, the "bad" mother is not found in the planter class; rather, she may be found among the yeoman and poor-white classes. In this literature, bad yeoman mothers are portrayed as inept and indulgent, while poor whites are characterized as immoral and criminal. Interestingly, black mothers tend to be depicted more like yeoman mothers; they are overindulgent and inept, not immoral. A writer like Simms would attribute such a condition to the ameliorating aspects of slavery as an institution and to planter discipline, rather than seeing any particular strength in African American culture.

In addition to physical repulsiveness, which older planter-class women never display, the poor-white mother's outstanding characteristics are her indifference to the feelings of her children, her lack of self-discipline, her greed, and her hatred for the ruling planter elite. At her worst, she encourages her children's crime much as the fictive good mother would be horrified by an imputation of criminality in her offspring. When a woman is ambitious and ignores her true gender, race, and class position, only social disorder can occur. In contrast, the "good" poor-white woman, such as Rachel Bostwick, knows her place at home and in the society—endures her husband's abuse and scorn, suffers the hardship of poverty without complaint, and manages to raise her children to be submissive to their superiors, pious, and grateful for the crumbs that they have. She is the model for all, especially for the poor women in the society.

The representations of mothers in this literature conform to patriarchal expectation. While the plantation mistress as mother is notably absent from this literature, she more often than any other women embodies the Victorian ideal of the "true woman." She is deferential to her husband and is entirely focused on the well-being of her family. All "good" mothers have deep emotional attachments to their children and protect them without regard to their own safety. They also school their children in their initial lessons in self-discipline, the basis for morality. It is clear that these authors think that mothers shape the moral destiny of their children and thus of the nation. Planter sons are the most fit to lead Southern society because they have benefited from superior mothering. When the son marries, he looks for a woman like his mother to nurture his own children as they reproduce their racial and class relations. But he must leave his mother, a wrenching yet necessary step in his achieving manhood. In failing to depict plantation mistresses in any great detail, perhaps these authors were not only following the conventions of the new historical romance, but unconsciously writing their own declaration of independence.

9. Widows

AS THE CHARACTERIZATIONS of Widow Blodgit and Widow Blonay suggest, widows, like unmarried women, pose grave problems for a conservative patriarchal society. They are not only women without masters, but are often older women whose childbearing days, and thus usefulness to patriarchal society, are over. This prejudice is underscored by these Southern writers who limit the witchlike stereotype to poor-white women.

Those of the planter class, like Mary Grayson (*The Valley of Shenandoah*), Mrs. Markham (*Horse-Shoe Robinson*) the war widow, and Emily Fairfax (*Cavaliers of Virginia*) are "brave widows." They mourn their dead husbands, but manage to carry on their obligations to their children and communities. Southern authors portrayed their fictional upper-class widows with respect, but usually did not allow them to prevail, and rarely gave them major roles, unlike those assigned to widower Richard Walton (*The Partisan* and *Katherine Walton*), or Baron Sinclair (*The Forayers* and *Eutaw*). For example, although she is quite capable, George Tucker's Mary Grayson lived out her life as an impoverished widow when her son, Edward, was killed in a duel defending his sister's honor. Similarly, Kennedy introduces Mrs. Markham as "the personification of a class of matrons that—for the honor of our country and the human race—was not small in numbers," but then drops her as a character.[1] Caruthers's Emily Fairfax (*Cavaliers of Virginia*), without the protection of her deceased husband, left her home, was captured by Native Americans, and went mad. Finally, Simms's Mother Ford (*The Forayers*), though very poor, raised three orphaned children, two of whom turned to crime and one became "Hurricane Nell," the heroic mystic, who was killed in a gunfight. The message of these novels is clear. While widowers survive and even prosper, widows, helpless and impoverished, perish. But what about those legendary widows who do carry on and succeed? What kind of women are they? What are their relationships with men and how do they survive? Simms answers such questions in *Woodcraft*, in his portrait of the widow Mrs. Eveleigh.[2]

Originally, *Woodcraft; or, Hawks About the Dovecote* had been entitled *The Sword and the Distaff; or, "Fair, Fat, and Forty"* (completed in 1852). As the original title suggests, Simms focused on the relations between the sexes that combined the "needed union of the man's military skills with the woman's domestic arts in practice."[3] The subtitle, "Fair, Fat, and Forty," referred directly to the leading lady, Widow Eveleigh, though it could easily refer to the hero, Porgy, or to Simms himself.[4] The novel's major action centers on the reconstruction of the plantation, Glen-Eberley, after the Revolutionary War; that is, on the accumulation of credit, land, tools, slaves, an overseer, and a wife as necessary for a properly functioning plantation. The plantation cannot be operated by the planter alone; rather, an efficient plantation requires a mesh of social relationships in which he plays a dominating role (though the ironic comedic line in *Woodcraft* is that the planter's subordinates rule him).

When Porgy begins he is a planter without land or credit, a master without slaves, and a lover without a woman. The social reproduction of the plantation involves reestablishing a family. Porgy apparently has the choice of marrying one of two widows: middle-class Widow Griffin or upper-class Widow Eveleigh. Simms had already introduced Widow Griffin in *Katherine Walton* (1851). He describes her as "a comely woman, not much beyond the middle period of life . . . plainly, but neatly dressed, with a face smooth yet, and fair with the bloom of health upon her cheeks."[5] Heartbroken, and anxious about supporting herself and her daughter, like many "humble" people of the South and the Southwest, Simms explains, she assumed "an appearance of stoicism under grief" (374) as she prepared Porgy and Lance Frampton a good meal and looked after them properly as guests. Mrs. Griffin, is thus defined as a true woman: she puts her own needs and feelings aside for others.

On their way to the Griffin cabin, Porgy and Lance had discussed women and marriage. Porgy states that he is getting old and that he must marry soon, and startles Lance, who assumes he will seek to marry a young woman. Porgy assures him that he will choose "the ripe . . . not the green fruit":

> I require a woman who has some knowledge of life; who is skilled in housekeeping; who can achieve success in the culinary department; . . . there is another quality which a woman of this description is likely to possess, and that is a due and reverent sense of her husband's authority. It is because of her deference for his authority that she acquires her art. She has learned duly to study his desires and his tastes, and she submits her judgment to his own. She waits to hear his opinion of the soup, and is always ready to do better next time. I feel I could be happy with such a woman. (368)

And how are such woman found? Lance asks. Porgy then makes the feminist argument for women's oppression as he explains, echoing Nathaniel Beverley Tucker that wives are made, not found: "They come from training. A wise father, or a wise husband will make such a woman; she cannot make herself" (368). However, shaping a woman into the wife he wants—a woman who serves her husband faithfully, obediently, diligently—takes time and patience, and Porgy has neither. What he requires, he tells Frampton, is a someone already broken in, a widow, in other words: "widows are, after all, the best materials out of which to make good wives; always assuming that they have been fortunate in the possession of husbands like myself, who have been able to show them the proper paths to follow, and who have had the will to keep well them [*sic*] always in the traces. I am clearly of the opinion that widows afford the very best material out of which to manufacture wives" (369). With this attitude, Porgy meets Widow Griffin for the first time and is impressed by her domestic abilities and strength of character, especially by her deference to him. In *Woodcraft*, she is reintroduced as a possible partner for Porgy.

However, the most compelling person in the novel is Widow Eveleigh. When *Woodcraft* opens she has made her way to the headquarters of Colonel Moncrieff (British commissioner for Charleston, South Carolina. Her husband had been a Loyalist officer; since his death, she has been in charge of running the plantation. She has come to Moncrieff's headquarters to claim her family's slaves stolen by the British. While Moncrieff and M'Kewn, a Loyalist spy, are conferring about how to respond to her claim, she spies a paper on Moncrieff's desk. It reveals that M'Kewn has supplied Moncrieff with slaves from both her estate and Porgy's to be shipped to the West Indies. A woman of strength and resolution, now realizing that she is "dealing with enemies" and that the paper might prove necessary to legitimate her claim, she seizes the document muttering: "The villains! Shall I scruple when I am in such hands? Shall I suffer them to defraud my son of his rights, when it is in my power to prevent them? Away with such childish scruples. It is war between us, perhaps, and I owe them no courtesies, no forbearance."[6] She sees Bostwick, who was a squatter on her property and whose family she has fed and cared for during the war; and immediately she makes the connection. Bostwick and his poor-white cronies procured slaves for M'Kewn, and M'Kewn transferred them to Moncrieff, who then sells them to West Indian planters. From the beginning, then, Widow Eveleigh appears as "no ordinary woman." She is decisive and intelligent, principled, and willing to act when higher things are at stake.[7]

Moncrieff rejoins the widow and denies knowing the Captain Dort whose ship would transport her slaves, but he gives her a release for them. Although it is clear to her that he is deeply involved in the matter, both of them are being "correct" in their exchange with each other. Then Eveleigh announces that since her own affairs are now settled, she feels compelled to free Porgy's slaves as well. Since Christians are taught to love their neighbors, she notes, she is simply doing her Christian duty to look after Porgy's property, as he would for her. Moncrieff reacts by observing that Porgy is a "fierce and pestilent fellow—one of the gang of Marion" and undeserving of a favor from the British. Their exchange reveals her tenacity:

"Oh! surely not a favor! The question is one of right, simply. Either these negroes are Captain Porgy's or not. I can prove them to be so."

"But not that he has not sold them?!"

"His bill of sale would show that."

"Madam, you should have been a lawyer."

"But a little while ago, your opinion was that I should have been a soldier."

"Egad! madam. It is difficult to say what profession you might have chosen successfully."

"Thank you, sir, for the compliment, however equivocal. But you will give me the order, will you not."

"Oh! to be sure, if there really be such negroes in our possession." (12)

After Eveleigh leaves, Moncrieff and M'Kewn discover the paper with the list of slaves is missing. M'Kewn suggests that Mrs. Eveleigh has purloined it, but is sharply rebuked by Moncrieff:

> "But, permit me to say, M'Kewn, that your habits in life, and business, are not, perhaps, the best calculated to make you a judge in such matters. The rules which govern the conduct of ladies and gentlemen do not necessarily occur to persons in trade. They are, perhaps, almost exclusively understood by those whose life from the beginning has been in society, and among that class which finds its chief occupation in this very study. Now, you are a shrewd man of business, M'Kewn . . . but you will admit that you have paid but small attention to the affairs of polite society. You can not well understand them, my good fellow—Permit me to repeat that Mrs. Eveleigh, who was born in the purple chamber of aristocracy, never could have taken this paper—never! never!" (32 and 33)

This passage conveys something of the gender, racial, and class relationships that dominate the novel and inform most of Simms's work.

First, as the character of Mrs. Eveleigh is drawn, she is intelligent and cunning, assertive and resourceful. Her passionate assertion of what is right and her shrewd assessment of Moncrieff's character and of his connection to M'Kewn and Bostwick guide her in a very complex and dangerous business. Clearly, Simms has given us no ordinary heroine, but one of his attractive intellectual women. Second, black people are slaves, and as slaves they have dual features: on the one hand, they are commodities desired by and fought over by whites; on the other, they are human beings who serve as loyal retainers and are regarded as extended family members by their masters and mistresses. Third, class relationships dominate social relations among whites. Mrs. Eveleigh's husband had been a Loyalist planter who knew Moncrieff, which should have prompted distrust, if not animosity between Widow Eveleigh and Porgy. However, not only did she acquiesce to her husband's wishes and not disclose her patriot sympathies but, being of the same class, she defends Porgy's interest in his slaves. Even after she has persuaded Moncrieff to return her own slaves and has stolen a crucial document, his own class prejudice led him to reject M'Kewn's correct assumption that Mrs. Eveleigh is the thief. In Simms's world, the bonds of class bind Eveleigh, Porgy, and Moncrieff, a war notwithstanding, while the middle-class M'Kewn and the poor-white Bostwick are excluded. Established in these first chapters, the class connection dominated Simms's depiction of community in the South as did gender and racial relationships.

The next series of adventures for the intrepid Widow Eveleigh happens when she, her overseer, Fordham, and her son, Arthur, are escorting their relieved and happy black slaves home. They are attacked by Bostwick and his poor-white confederates who try to take their slaves and valuables, but are rescued by the fortunate intervention of Captain Porgy and his men. Throughout it all, Mrs. Eveleigh, while unconcerned for her own safety, is anxious about her son, Arthur. In contrast, her black maid, Jenny, becomes hysterical as soon as the bandits appear (59–68). Consistently, in all her dealings, Widow Eveleigh's deepest passions and strongest fears are reserved for her son. Porgy watches their reunion: "his eye took in all the sweet picture of maternal love; of all the forms of love, perhaps the most pure, the least selfish, the longest lived!" (138). Though a widow and forced into the harsh and violent world of men in war, she remained a mother, which endowed her with a great capacity for love. The slaves secured, mother and son reunited, and the outlaws killed or run off, the parties make their way to the respective Porgy and Eveleigh plantations where, Simms implies, they will be safe.

Returning to Glen-Eberley, Porgy finds it in ruins. The slaves have been run off to the swamps or stolen or sold, leaving him with only the handful of men Widow Eveleigh had rescued. That means that the fields have lain fallow for months, perhaps years. His own parents have died and their house has been sacked and partially burned. Moreover, his lands have been mortgaged at five times their present value, and a foreclosure of his mortgage would take away everything: house, land, slaves. What was even worse, in his profligate and dissipated youth he had neglected to learn the requisites of being a good planter. Understandably, the burden of reconstruction weighed heavily upon him.

Porgy does not know where to begin, but Millhouse, his former sergeant, now his overseer, does. In discussing the plantation with Porgy, Millhouse set forth their mutual responsibilities. First, he will be the overseer (his "sense-keeper") and will supervise turning out the crop. That is, he will make the decisions about planting crops and rotating them, procuring domestic tools and supplies, and organizing and disciplining the slave labor force. Millhouse is most precise in all this: "I'm overseer, and you mustn't come between me and the niggers. I'll do my work and will make 'em do theirs. Ef there's any licking to be done, I'll lay it on. You may look on, but you mus'n't meddle. You may think what you please, but you mus'n't say nothing. We kin talk over the matter every night, and I'll show you the sense of what I've been doing in the day" (190). Porgy must establish himself as a respectable citizen, so that he can obtain credit enough to purchase the necessary tools, grain, and labor. Porgy is at a loss about how to do that, since his lands are mortgaged. Millhouse has a solution: Porgy should marry a rich war widow. Widow Eveleigh is the obvious choice.

The Millhouse–Porgy exchange on women is more than a satirical view of the relations between the sexes. It also parodies Millhouse's middle-class utilitarian philosophy, in which everything, even human relationships, are measured in terms of their cash value. In that way, Simms is also presenting Northern capitalist values as a contrast to the "Southern way of life," which he alleges values the unmeasurable worth of human relationships. However, what this debate reveals is the centrality of marriage and the patriarchal family in the establishment of the plantation community.

Millhouse's view of courting, is analogous to war: "a woman of ixperance likes a man the better if he gives her no time for long thinking. Courtin' is like storming an inimy's batteries. Women expects naturally to be taken by storm. They likes a good ixcuse for surrenderin'. You must go it with a rush, sword in hand, looking mighty fierce, and ready to smite and tear everything to splinters; and just then she drops into your arms and stops the massacre by an honest givin' in" (298). When Porgy protests that a woman might find that approach aggressive, Millhouse assures him, "woman is born with a knowing that some day she's got to find a master," and the man has only to assure her that he is that master. A younger woman expects a man to capture her "by insinivations," but older women like Widow Eveleigh will appreciate the straightforward approach. When Porgy observes that his idea is very practical, but Millhouse hasn't considered romance or love between the sexes, Millhouse grows impatient with Porgy's naiveté about women and marriage: "Marriage is business; 'taint love. It's airnest work; 'taint sport. Nobody, I reckon, marries for the sport of the thing ef he's once cut his eye-teeth. Your boy and girl marriages is sort of baby house-business. When we talks to grown men and women about the thing, we means an argyment, and a reason, and a sense, and needcessity" (300). Finally Millhouse tells him that "'fections mustn't stand in the way of business," that he has two attractive widows in the neighborhood, and that although he finds Widow Griffin "more comely," she is decidedly poorer than Widow Eveleigh, and so of little value to him.

Porgy is both amused and aghast by Millhouse's discourse on women. It represents a viewpoint that he as a principled planter rejects. Millhouse's utilitarian philosophy "succeeds pretty generally, in the world," Porgy admits, but he would never succeed as planter: "the chief secret of the success of such a philosophy as yours is that it never vaunteth itself. It's professors never publish their virtues as you do. They are content to practice in secret what you mistakenly praise. They *do* what you *preach,* and *preach* against what they themselves *do.* Pride thus discourseth of humility with moist lips, selfishness thus becomes eloquent in its exhortations to self-sacrifice; and the good preacher will possess himself of the fattest lamb of the flock while insisting on the beauties of a perpetual lent" (303; Simms's emphasis). Or, Simms might have added, Northern abolitionists living off the profits earned by the Southern economy attack its allegedly dissipated planter class and the poverty of their slaves without considering their role in perpetuating both, or the treatment of Irish "wage slaves" in their own Northern cities.[8] This "masculine" argument about women allows Simms an opportunity to air some of his grievances against capitalism and its utilitarian philosophy, and highlights some of the differences between the political economy and social relations of each section.

In reality Porgy's attitude toward women is the same as Millhouse's, although not so crudely expressed. Nor does he attach a cash value to a wife although it is clear that her family wealth and labor have value. This is a remarkable passage. It was meant to be humorous, but it reveals patriarchal vision of women. Feminists have argued that wives and mothers are not found, but are made through years of social conditioning and outright oppression. Here is conservative Simms, like Nathaniel B. Tucker before him, affirming that very point. Porgy requires that a woman, as wife and mother, be skilled at housekeeping—cooking, cleaning, laundering, and child care. Additionally, he requires that she subordinate her needs and desires to those of her family. In effect, a wife must be tractable and loyal, and must willingly do household labor in exchange for the security and society of a man. Porgy is the voice of the Southern white male planter class. Such a class must assert its authority over poor whites as well as women, children, and slaves. It avoids the implicit racial and sexual exploitation involved in the social arrangements with one's inferiors. The idea of molding one's inferiors "to their better selves" is the coercive voice of paternalism and informs the social relations of a patriarchal society.[9]

In *Woodcraft,* when Simms returns to Porgy's marital problems and his choice of two widows, the focus is exclusively on Porgy and Porgy's attitudes. That the women themselves might have private thoughts about Porgy go unexplored, but the reader's ignorance of their preferences becomes the basis for Simms's humorous resolution of Porgy's problem. Instead, the reader's attention is focused on Porgy's weighing the qualities of Widow Griffin against those of Widow Eveleigh so that *he* might make a choice. Widow Eveleigh and Porgy are social equals and friends. Porgy has borrowed a considerable amount of money from her to run his plantation, and appears capable of getting out of debt within a few years. He finds Eveleigh "almost free from affectations; . . . frank and ever gay of mood; always cheerful; always ingenuous, and never labored at the concealment of her sympathies" (369). Capable of being both humorous and serious, she has an expansive knowledge of the best European poets, dramatists, and philosophers. She is a "fine looking woman" who is charming, graceful, kind, and generous. Porgy says she is "vastly superior, as a lady—as a woman of sense and sweetness—grace and intelligence—to any I know" (371). But then there is Widow Griffin. Once "very beautiful," she is "good, gentle, humble, and affectionate." But in contrast to Widow Eveleigh "she is not wise, nor learned; is really very ignorant; has no manners, no eloquence; is simple, humble and adhesive . . . she has no resources, no thoughts, no information; has seen nothing, knows nothing" (372). Widow Eveleigh's class advantages have made her superior to Griffin in most objective respects. However, Porgy is troubled because he has never seen Widow Eveleigh cooking or cleaning or "attending to household affairs at all." He has only seen her command and as a prospective husband that bothers him (373 and 374).

Widow Eveleigh is a dominant figure physically as well as intellectually, and that also is troubling:

> Still, there was something wanting to the perfect sway of the widow over her admirer; something which he felt, but could not explain, or account for to himself. She was a fine-looking woman, "fair, fat, and forty"—but he found himself occasionally objecting to "the fat." The very fact he was, himself, too much so, was enough to make him quarrel with her possessions of the same sort. (370)

Perplexed, Porgy asks himself,

> Do I—can I love this woman?—as a woman *ought* to be loved, as a man ought to love—as she deserves to be loved by any husband, and especially by me?
>
> Is it natural or reasonable at forty-five I, at least, should need, or expect to recall my youthful frenzies, before venturing upon the married condition? Is not the sort of love which we require now that which belongs rather to the deliberate consent of the mind than the warm impulses of the blood and fancy? (370)

Then, too, Porgy is sexually attracted to Widow Griffin, not to Widow Eveleigh, who is too much like him: overweight and independent, commanding and intellectual—that is, too "masculine." To be sexually aroused, Porgy must feel that he is in control. He cannot dominate Mrs. Eveleigh and that creates problems for him. The questions of gender, class, and power here transfer to the bedroom. Porgy dominates Mrs. Griffin; hence she is more sexually attractive to him. He is caught in a classic conflict of the upper-class male: being attracted to a woman of a lower class/caste, but being responsible for perpetuating class and race alliances. Since he would have no children with either woman, the drive for family security and continuity is not the issue. At stake is male authority in husband-wife relations and the need for female submission on all levels especially the physical.

Widow Eveleigh expects Porgy "naturally" to behave with a certain decorum. She wouldn't approve of Porgy's smoking or drinking or lounging about with his old army buddies. Porgy resents such restrictions on his conduct. He is more comfortable with the Widow Griffin, a yeoman class woman who would not be judgmental about his social behavior or personal habits. He could lounge about her house with his feet on the furniture without her disapproval. In effect, he could dominate her economically, intellectually, socially, and sexually—something impossible with Widow Eveleigh, and he admits as much.

> One does not want an equal, but an ally in marriage. A man ought to be wise enough for his wife and himself. To get a woman who shall best comprehend one is the sufficient secret; and no woman can properly comprehend her husband, who is not prepared to recognize his full superiority. When it is otherwise, there are constant disputes. The woman is forever setting up for herself. She is not only unwilling that you should be her master, but she sets up to be your mistress. Why, if she has the mind, should she not use it; and if she has mind enough for the household, what's the use of yours? Clearly, there can not be peace in any planet which acknowledges two masters. (374)

In short, Mrs. Eveleigh "appeared to him to be quite too masculine" (399). What Porgy wanted was a different type of woman:

> His ideas of woman were those of a period when the sex had not yet determined to set up for itself; though wielding most potent sway in society, and even in politics, particularly in Carolina. His models, accordingly, required absolute dependence in the woman, though without meaning to abridge any of her claims as a woman, or to subjugate, unjustly, her individuality. He never dreamed of denying her any of her rights, when he required that she should recognize the lordship in the hands of the man. There was something assured in the position and the endowments of Mrs. Eveleigh, that startled his sense of authority. Her very virtues had a manly air which girdled his pride; her very wealth and its importance in his own case seemed to humble him in his relations with her. (399)

As in the novel *Charlemont,* Simms is once again arguing against nineteenth-century feminists and/or self-sufficient women with their own means who "set up" for themselves and lead independent lives. Such women were threatening to Simms and to men of his time. The very effort to convince women of their "natural" destiny—marriage and children—reflects the struggle for power within the patriarchal family.

Given his needs and prejudices, one might predict that Porgy would first select Widow Griffin. But class considerations prevail, and Porgy seeks the hand of Widow Eveleigh. Mrs. Eveleigh, however, is clearly in command. If Porgy is foolish enough to overlook their basic incompatibility, despite the things which bind them, she is not. More important, she seems to be quite happy with things as they are. Assuring him of her affection she confesses:

> I am willing to trust myself to nobody again. I have been too long my own mistress to submit to authority. I have a certain spice of independence in my temper, which would argue no security for the rule which seeks to restrain me; and you, if I am to judge of men, have a certain inoperative mood which would make you very despotic, should you meet with my resistance. There would be peace and friendship between us, my dear captain—nay love—so long as we maintain our separate independence; and, in this faith, I am unwilling to risk anything by any change in our relations. Let there be peace, and friendship, and love between us, but never a word more of marriage. (513)

Her son is growing up and will be financially independent, and Widow Eveleigh is not foolish enough to allow herself again to be dominated by a man, even one from whom and for whom she feels great affection.

In a classic comic twist, Porgy then decides to marry Widow Griffin only to find that she is pledged to a minor character named only "Fordham," a man of her own class and Mrs. Eveleigh's overseer. In the end Porgy reverts to his carefree, bachelor style of life. The widows thus salvage the situation by asserting themselves, and Simms saves his favorite Porgy from the predictable domestic fate.[10]

In his portrait of Mrs. Eveleigh, Simms is arguing that there are only two possibilities: either a woman must be dominated by a man, or else he will be dominated by her. Equality in marriage as in all other social relations among "unequals" is impossible. The core issue of paternalism is thinly disguised here. A woman who allows herself to be dominated in marriage submits much as the servant does to the authority of his master. Her rights are denied, and her individuality is subjected to her husband's will, symbolized in her taking his name; because of her gender, race and class, however, the payoff for submission is greater. Simms shows paternalism as the psychological and economic base of Southern society, the dominant form of all social relationships. Above all else, the master requires the "happy submission" of his subordinates, which Simms concludes is "natural." Yet, he recognizes the fragility of the assumption of male superiority and paternalism, and pokes fun at it here. Ironically, Simms has made an excellent feminist case for the patriarchal family as an institution constructed for men's benefit in which male power is preserved and reproduced in each generation.

Porgy feels he controls his relationships with women, but in reality Widow Eveleigh and Widow Griffin determine his marital fate. Like his other supposed subordinates, they are in control and he is a spectator. This is the source of the humor in *Woodcraft*. The masterless, inept planter and the independent Widow Eveleigh mock traditional conventions and social rela-

tionships. In so doing, Simms is also reinforcing them. He exposes the coercive character of such social and economic arrangements for women, but
relieves the immediate tension by allowing both Widow Griffin and Widow
Eveleigh to escape from Porgy, and by allowing Porgy to escape from his true
responsibilities. Few men and women of the antebellum South had that
luxury.

THE IMAGES of women in this antebellum South literature conform to both
established Western literary conventions and to nineteenth-century Anglo-
American literary conventions adapted by Southern writers for their own
purposes. These Southern writers recognized that they were presenting idealized versions of men and women in their heroes and heroines, yet they
created ideals of masculinity and femininity that survived in the myth of the
Old South. Conversely, their "lowlife" characters (blacks, poor whites, and
Indians) were allegedly "realistic," even though those portraits, too, offered a
distortion of reality and betrayed the authors' racial and class prejudices.
What emerges from this conservative patriarchal literature, written by white
men who had been born into or who had married into the planter class, is a
cult of masculinity in which the superior planter inherits and maintains his
gender, racial, and class domination of society. Women are allied for better or
worse with the men of their respective races and classes, and assume their
"natural" places as the inferiors of those men. Only motherhood redeems
women of allegedly inferior races and classes. However, the authors make it
quite clear that inferiors reproduce inferiors. Hence any crossing of racial
and class lines would be especially detrimental to the social order, if not to
"civilization" itself. This planter vision of Southern society, then, is divided
between social existence on and off the plantation each dominated by the
planter master. On the plantation, women, blacks, and children know their
proper places as the planter master's inferiors, recognize his superiority, and
defer to his natural wisdom and loving guidance. Their lives are disrupted
only by his death or by the intrusion of his enemies: Indians, the British, and
poor whites, whom he dominates politically.

Unlike George Tucker, few of the post–1830 novelists portrayed planters
who failed or were corrupt. The woman who disobeyed patriarchal law was
vulnerable to abuse from inferior men, or to scorn and contempt from "polite society." Mostly she lived in poverty or died. They gave a clear message to
the woman reader: her *only* option was to submit her will and personal
ambition to the superior male's authority and to assume her role as her
father's adoring daughter, her husband's devoted and submissive wife, and
her children's loving and nurturing mother. Any attempt on her part to
liberate herself from the bonds of matrimony or the obligations and consequences of motherhood would be met by a combination of abuse and poverty, rejection and social ostracism. The adoration of the planter's mother,
wife, and daughter depicted in this literature is not to be mistaken as the

adoration of women. Instead, it is the planter's own adoration of himself as their master in a literature exclusively focused on men and on the creation of women who solve male problems. The proud patriarchal master possessed both "his" white and black families. He also possessed the land on which they lived: the possession of which transformed the frontier farmer into the socially constructed proud, patriarchal master who dominated antebellum Southern society as he mythologized it in his literature.

III

REPRESENTATIONS

OF BLACKS

THE PRIMITIVE and patriarchal, which may also be called the sacred and natural system, in which the labor is under the personal control of a fellow being endowed with the sentiments and sympathies of humanity, exists among us. It has been almost everywhere else superseded by the modern *artificial money power system,* in which man—his thews and sinews, his hopes and affections, his very being, are all subjected to the dominion of *capital*—a monster without a heart . . .
    —James H. Hammond, "Letters on Slavery"

No tribe of people have ever passed from barbarism to civilization whose middle stage of progress has been more secure from harm, more genial to their character, or better supplied with mild and beneficient guardianship, adapted to the actual state of their intellectual feebleness, than the negroes of Swallow Barn.
    —John Pendleton Kennedy, *Swallow Barn*

The term slave to this day sounds terror to my soul—a word too obnoxious to speak—a system too intolerable to be endured. . . . A slave may be bought and sold in the market like an ox. He is liable to be sold off to a distant land from his family. He is bound in chains head and foot; and his sufferings are aggravated a hundred fold, by the terrible thought, that he is not allowed to struggle against misfortune, corporal punishment, insults and outrages committed upon himself and family . . .
    —Henry Bibb, ex-slave narrative

10. Slavery: The "Patriarchal" Institution

THE ANTEBELLUM planter class understood slavery as a "patriarchal" institution; that is, as an institution where authority was vested in a patriarchal head of household who presided over a small society of women, children, and slaves. According to custom and law, he was responsible for providing his "dependents" with protection and economic security, and they returned his beneficence with their submission, respect, and grateful love. For instance, in trying to convince his Virginia friends that they should follow him to Missouri, Nathaniel Beverley Tucker argued that "like the patriarchs of old" they would depend on the women and slaves to perform the domestic work and field work while they as the natural leaders of the state would create "a great nation."[1] But of course, the relation between master and slave was not a family relationship, except when miscegenation had taken place. It was overwhelmingly a class relationship, complicated by planter racism and the fact that this slave population could be bought and sold like any commodity and were refused freedom through marriage to a free person. The racism of the planter class contributed a potent psychological dimension to the institution; and the practice of trading in human beings and selling family members off from one another gave North American chattel slavery a uniquely brutal cast.

Although one can argue that white plantation women were oppressed by gender convention, societal custom, and civil law, they were privileged by their race and class. If the whites in the plantation family forgot that members of "their black family" could be beaten and raped, separated and sold away at their master's will, the slaves never forgot it or really forgave the worse manifestations of planter brutality.

On the large plantations, especially in the East and in those Southwestern areas that emulated the Eastern planter class, the planter was taught as a young man to fulfill the duties and responsibilities of being a patriarchal husband to his wife, father to his children, and master to his slaves. Paternalism as an attitude and set of prescribed behaviors muted the violence of patriarchal rule so the master could convert his brutality to acts of compassion, his violence to acts of beneficence. Although he often referred to his "family, white and black," the cash nexus always stood between the planter and his slaves in a way it never did among his wife, his children, and himself.[2]

The following chapters analyze the fictional depiction of slavery as an institution and slaves as people. In antebellum Southern literature, the institution of slavery is defended as contributing to the "civilization" of Africans and to organic harmony and stability in a multiracial society. As with their portrayal of women, these authors construct scenes between masters and slaves in which master superiority is evident. The structural device is never to show blacks with one another or with other whites, but almost exclusively to introduce them in scenes with their master. Slaves are rarely portrayed alone, but if they are, they are usually sleeping, not thinking or working. This literature defines the slave's relationship with his or her master as the primary relationship in his or her life.

The master emerges as a commanding and resolute, but benevolent, figure who always has the slave's true interest in mind. In contrast, both male and female slaves are represented as ignorant and improvident, lazy and playful, submissive and loyal. The institution of slavery is thus redeemed as being protective and beneficial for blacks, introducing them to Christianity and teaching them the discipline of work. The implication throughout is that black men and women have neither the intelligence, self-discipline, or morality to work their own land as independent farmers. However, one sees little of the field hands, slave families, or the slave community, and for good reason. Not only did these authors know little about the private lives of slaves, because slaves kept their feelings and lives hidden from whites, but they were more interested in telling the master's story. What matters, in this literature are not the relationships of the slaves with one another, but the relationship of individual slaves with the master. By focusing on the master, these authors keep the planter as the protagonist and the dominant figure on the plantation, and structurally underscore their argument that slavery was irreducibly personal, a paternalistic relationship between masters and slaves.

In contrast, abolitionist novelists like William Wells Brown, Harriet Beecher Stowe, or Martin R. Delaney, who focus on slaves and their lives, present a completely different view of the slave and the slave community. In their hands, the slave's story emphasizes physical and psychological conflict between plantation whites and blacks, sexual abuse of women, the breakup of the slave family, and the geographic mobility of individual blacks.[3] The white Southern authors in this study emphasize the harmony, stability, and continuity of plantation society in which naturally inferior black slaves defer to their kind and generous patriarchal masters, who reward and punish them as one might discipline a child.

In concentrating on the planter and his family and setting the action of the novel in a distant and heroic past, Southern writers legitimated the origin of Southern society based on slavery and planter-class rule, but addressed the uncomfortable and embarrassing abolitionist attacks on slavery, and especially those charges of planter sexual exploitation of slave women, by omission and silence. Thus the reader's attention shifts to concern about whether the patriot planter and his (also our) revolutionary cause will prevail, whether the heroine will be rescued, and whether the plantation will be saved. Since whites and blacks on the fictional plantation cooperate to preserve the plantation, to hope for the defeat of the planter class is in effect to ally oneself with the British and their middle-class and poor-white Tory confederates. In contrast, it follows the white male planter hero symbolizes a patriarchal order and justice that must prevail if civilization is to be saved and harmony restored to this war-torn society. The planter class thus emerges as the "natural" governing elite in Southern history and politics.

What the authors omit is as revealing as what they depict.[4] They go to great lengths to describe the plantation itself, but except for Kennedy (in *Swallow Barn*) and Simms (in *The Forayers* and *Woodcraft*), they make no attempt to portray the slave's living and working conditions, family life, or community relationships. These are invisible. In proslavery fiction, blacks have had no important relationships apart from those with the master and his family, and no consciousness of themselves as more than servile inferiors. Their memories are the plantation memories; their history is the history of the planter's family. They do not dream their own dreams, recount their own stories, sing their own songs, or think their own thoughts. Instead, they are wholly responsive to the directives and feelings of the master.

These authors skirt the sensitive issue of sexuality by depicting servants as middle-aged or old, beyond courting or childbearing age. For instance, William A. Caruthers describes Old Essex (*Knights of the Golden Horse-Shoe*) as "the 'major domo' of the establishment": "He was a tall, dignified old negro, with his hair queued up behind and powdered all over, and not a little of it sprinkled upon the red collar of his otherwise scrupulously clean livery. . . . He felt himself just as much a part and parcel of the Governor's family, as if he had been related to it by blood. The manners of Essex were very far above his mental culture."[5] Similarly, in *The Scout* Simms describes Mira as "one of the staid family servants such as are to be found in every ancient household, who form an necessary part of the establishment, and are, substantially, members, from long use and habit, of the family itself. The children grow up under their watchful eyes, and learn to love them as if they were mothers, or at least grandmothers, maiden aunts, or affectionate antique cousins."[6] What the reader is supposed to see here is the stability of the black and white families and the mutual affection among "family members." In these and other fictional accounts, no slave is torn from his or her family and sold, no one is overworked or underfed, and no one is sexually abused. In fact, these fictional plantation blacks have no romantic or sexual attachments to anyone. It is very easy to be blinded to proslavery politics of these novels while one is engaged with the romantic plot and not see that the romantic plot enhances the proslavery line. One must remember that William Wells Brown, the first African American novelist, centered *Clotel; or, the President's Daughter* on concubinage and miscegenation on the plantation. Similarly, Martin R. Delaney's Maggie Holland, is subjected to the incestuous advances of her master-father.[7] There is more than a debate about "art" going on here.

Proslavery writers including William Gilmore Simms in "The Morals of Slavery" publicly acknowledge miscegenation, but argue it was a consequence of youthful indiscretion, overseer and poor-white male profligacy, or the "slave wenches'" own seductive desires. In true conservative fashion, he argues that slavery as an institution isn't at fault, individuals are. Similarly, Chancellor William Harper of the University of South Carolina went so far as to argue that although it was true that the "easy chastity" of female slaves excited young planter-class males, the system of concubinage in the South was superior to prostitution in the North: the woman involved did not lose status; any children that resulted were considered a positive contribution to the plantation economy; and it preserved the white Christian marriage bed while giving slave women life support.[8] That these authors rarely acknowledge lust as a human passion, or attribute such desire to lower-class white males who lack self-control, is an odd twist, given the colonial and post– Civil War stereotype of black males as sexually craven. In the last twenty years, social historians have taken a new look at this problem and not only concur with slave testimony that miscegenation existed as a standard feature of slavery, but agree as well that the great majority of incidents occurred as planter rape.[9] Bertram Wyatt-Brown argues that "miscegenation between a white male and a black female posed almost no ethical problems for the Southern community, so long as the rules were . . . discreetly observed."[10] The "rules" held that the woman should be light-skinned (that is, attractive), that the relationship should seem casual even if it were long-standing, and that it couldn't be another aspect of an otherwise dissolute life. "Transcendent silence was the proper policy," Wyatt Brown notes, especially in "mixed company" (307 and 308).

Plantation authors depicted the black male as a docile and content Sambo to assure themselves and Northerners that slavery was working to contain the alleged inherent barbarity of Africans. Both Ronald Takaki and Sander Gilman contend that whites projected their worst fears and fantasies onto black men and women. To confirm what they were as white men, they needed to define what they were not. The "Sambo" emerges thus as the "civilized" black male, the antithesis of both the sexual "Buck" and the rebellious "Nat," and as a testament to planter slave management.[11] However, the "Jezebel," the black seductress, doesn't appear in this literature as a type. Only the "mammy" (or "mauma," as Simms would say) is recognizable.

Part of what makes a community is common work. In plantation society that involves planting the crop, cultivating it, and taking it to market. Although slave labor is crucial to the maintenance of the plantation, work in the fields is hardly described in the literature. Most of the servants are house servants who wait on the master and his family with affection, courtesy, and deference. Kennedy describes typical plantation personnel:

A bevy of domestics, in every stage of training, attended upon the table, presenting a lively type of the progress of civilization, or the march of intellect; the veteran waiting man being well-contrasted with the rude half-monkey, half-boy, who seemed to have been for the first time admitted to the parlor: whilst between these two, were exhibited the successive degrees that mark the advance from the young savage to the sedate and sophisticated image of the old-fashioned negro nobility.[12]

Note the depiction of black children as "half-monkey" and the assumption that whites are bringing these African "savages" to civilization. The women perform general housekeeping tasks: they sew, weave, tread grain, garden, cook, and care for the sick and for the black and white children. Kennedy argues that in Virginia, black women do not work in the fields, a condition he finds shocking and deplorable in South Carolina.[13] In the fictional South, the men tend to the livestock and horses and are employed as carpenters, blacksmiths, and shoemakers. Certain male servants help with domestic chores and serve as butlers, carriage drivers, and personal servants, but most of the men work in the fields and are invisible in spite of the fact that it is the field work that produces the crops which, marketed, provide the planter with enough income to keep the plantation running.

Only Simms in *Woodcraft* betrays a faint understanding of the social relationships of production on the plantation. In *Woodcraft*, Millhouse, the boorish utilitarian yeoman overseer of Glen-Eberley, notes the economic connection between black labor and the land, and the necessity of protecting both from creditors. He says: "Ef they gits the place, thar's not much use for the niggers, and ef they gets the niggers, there's not much use for the place. The two stands together pretty much like gun and gunpowder."[14] In the division between field work and housework, field work is left undescribed, perhaps because of the planter's distance from it as a supervisor of supervisors, and because of the unpleasantness and potentially politically damaging results involved in confronting the realities of slave labor and discipline even in a fictional account. The authors try to persuade the reader that producing the crop is a community effort in which all parties reap benefits according to their respective contributions and needs. According to planter fiction, since blacks need less to live on, they get less. One is supposed to assume that they are satisfied with that arrangement. For instance, in Nathaniel Beverley Tucker's *The Partisan Leader,* Douglas Trevor argues with his Northern friend, Whiting, "It may be that what is best for me is best for my friend [slave] Jack there, and vice versa; but as long as neither of us thinks so, why not leave each to his choice? Besides, there is more room in the world for both of us than if both always wanted the same things."[15]

In an odd break with the social life of slaves, these fictional blacks are not religious. Historians agree that religion played a crucial role in giving blacks a psychological edge under slavery. It cultivated in them a sense of themselves as moral and mortal beings, and gave them faith and moral strength in believing that if they endured, life would be better here or "on the other side of the river."

Much contemporary debate in the South raged around religious issues and behavior: whether to allow rural blacks and whites to attend church together; whether in allowing black preachers they created a revolutionary class; whether slaves should be taught to read in order to read the Bible; whether slave singing and clapping in church was subversive of discipline; indeed, whether slaves had souls. If slavery were defended as a Christian institution that brought allegedly barbaric blacks to Western civilization, as Kennedy contends, then why didn't these authors, such as Nathaniel Beverley Tucker, who was himself a religious convert, portray blacks as religious people? Caruthers describes a black waiting man, Cato, looking at a brilliant sunset. "I know that he has a soul of his own, and of rare excellence, too, but it is not metaphysical in its construction," his narrator reflects. That is the closest that any of the authors come to talking about blacks as religious people.[16]

Similarly, but less surprising, recalcitrant or rebellious blacks are rarely portrayed, and those that are, are treated as exceptions. In fact, there are only three rebellious black men in all of the literature. Caesar, the slave of the villain in Caruthers's *Knights of the Golden Horse-Shoe,* runs off and joins the Indians. Inept masters, Caruthers argues, create bad servants, and Caesar would not have chosen that course had he been cared for and disciplined correctly. In a much more intriguing episode in *The Kentuckian in New York,* Caruthers creates a nameless black driver as arsonist on a South Carolinian plantation. The anonymous black slave driver had whipped the favorite servant of the young mistress, and was himself demoted and whipped. For Caruthers, the blame rested with the plantation's occupational structure: the slave driver laboring under the authority of a "degraded white," was caught between two roles: that of master with some authority and privileges, and that of slave from whom total submission is expected. Caruthers was very much the Virginian who deplored the South Carolinian custom of absentee landlordism and the institution of the black slave driver. The latter was allegedly "an odious animal," and, Caruthers notes, "it is horrible to see one slave following another at his work, with a cowskin dangling at his arm, and occasionally tying him up and flogging him when he does not get through his two tasks a day."[17]

In *Swallow Barn,* John Pendleton Kennedy described the most significant rebellious black: Abe.[18] Abe was attractive, strong, athletic, and shrewdly intellectual; as a youth "he was noted for his spirit, and his occasional bursts of passion, which, even in his boyhood, rendered him an object of fear to his older associates" (466 and 467). As an adolescent, he and his friends were "the most profligate menials" on the Swallow Barn estate and on neighboring plantations. He drank, brawled, and took food and supplies to runaway (or "outlying") blacks who lived in the swamps and hardened "into the most irreclaimable of culprits" (467). Because of his natural skill and intelligence, Abe went on to distinguish himself as a sailor, and he died a hero's death, ironically in trying to rescue white sailors run aground in a storm.

Finally, in his portraits, Kennedy not only acknowledges the fact of runaway slaves and the black slave community's connection with them but offers the premise that the rebel is more intelligent and therefore more dangerous than his less gifted fellows.[19] That all people strive for freedom and that the very fact of bondage might produce rebels one never acknowledged. Rather, Kennedy argues, the socialization of children by their parents (mostly mothers) creates character. From the planter's perspective, the rebellious slave represents the failure of individual socialization, a quirk in the system. For blacks, however, the runaway represented the assertion of their humanity, and, if male, of black masculinity.

One must remember that the goal of this fiction was to establish planter superiority. As with his relationship with the plantation mistress, planter domination of black male slaves was justified as inevitable and necessary for social order. Especially given the Revolutionary themes, which extolled patriotic masculine violence against tyranny, that black men did not often revolt indicated to the planter class that they were satisfied with their condition and need not be respected as "men." Thus planters and others engaged in stereotyping male slaves and projecting on them their worst fear: the emasculated, fawning, and dependent male. The revisionist scholarship on slavery engages this myth. For instance, John Blassingame takes as his project the viability of the slave community as a culture of resistance and makes new assertions for black masculinity under slavery. However, the trap that all these (mostly male) historians fall into is the acceptance of the conservative assertion that masculine violence is inevitable and that "true men" always meet tyranny with rebellion, or at least physical forms of subversion.[20]

The standard of living of laboring classes is always an issue of debate among historians. Traditional ruling classes maintain that rude and uneducated underclasses do not need or desire the trappings of wealth, while the bourgeoisie argues they have not earned it. For the most part, these authors steer clear of these discussions and the temptation to compare Southern slaves with Northern wageworkers. However, Kennedy's proslavery novel takes on the standard of living problem. For instance, Kennedy tells the Meriwether slaves had enough to eat with their regular food rations and produce from their own vegetable gardens) and enough to wear (the cast-off clothes from the master's family) to suit "their few and simple wants" (450–55). Similarly, after describing the unpretentious, but ample plantation house, Kennedy describes the slave cabins, near the stable and "at some distance from the main house":

These hovels, with their appurtenances, formed an exceedingly picturesque landscape. They were scattered without order, over the slope of a gentle hill. . . . The rudeness of their construction rather enhanced the attractiveness of the scene . . . green moss had gathered upon the roofs, and the coarse weatherboarding had broken, here and there, into chinks. But the more lonely of these structures, and the most numerous, were nothing more than plain log cabins. . . . Perhaps, none of these latter sort were more than twelve feet square, and not above seven in height. (449)

The cabins were "furnished according to every primitive notion of comfort." (450)

The main house suggests comfort, if not wealth and leisure. It spreads out across the yard, expands into a backyard, and is surrounded by luxurious lawns and attractive landscaping. In contrast, the humbler slave cabins, though separated from each other, are congested with people and traffic. "Decrepit old men" sit whittling on the steps, and "the prolific mothers," with their "swarms of little negroes," lazily bask in the sun, giving the impression of contented poverty (450 and 451). There is plantation harmony with each race given the necessities required to sustain life. There is no bourgeois leveling here, Kennedy asserts, the white planter class requires more, wants more from their lives than do blacks, and it gets more. Since they are dependent, slaves want less; consequently they get less.

Kennedy is particularly amused by the black children, who, under the leadership of white eleven-year-old Rip Meriwether, "dart about the bushes like untamed monkeys," each dressed only in a "long coarse shirt which reaches below the knee" (308 and 309). The crisis of slave childhood, which came with the child's realization of his or her powerlessness and poverty vis-à-vis his or her white playmates is nowhere present. Rather, the impression is conveyed of the lazy and unconscious happiness of black childhood that continues into maturity; black adults are seen as black children grown bigger.

Recreation for slave adults and children centered around traditional work (harvest), community (marriages), and religious holidays (Christmas). These were times of good eating, music, and dancing. Proslavery fiction depicted these occasions as everyday events. Pompey, from Glen-Eberley (*Woodcraft*), for instance, was "an expert violinist [who] contrived to increase the noise and the merriment . . . and to lessen the consciousness of fatigue on the part of his companions" (69). Similarly, Carey, from Swallow Barn, was "a minstrel of some repute, and, like the ancient jongeleurs [*sic*], he [sang] the inspirations of his own muse, weaving into song the past or present annals of the family" (101). Both played in the evening after work was over and blacks and whites were relaxing, and at special occasions during which people from both plantation families gathered to eat, sing, and dance. These scenes convey an impression to the reader of plantation harmony between the black and white families. The threat of the lash and the unnatural separation of families are unknown at Swallow Barn, Piney Grove, and Glen-Eberley.

In theory, the master-slave relationship was a personal as well as a work relationship, one that entailed reciprocal responsibilities and duties. Like all work relationships between unequals, it had a powerful psychological impact on both parties. For the most part it shaped a paternalistic ideology that justified patterns of dominance and submission. This ideology took a paternalistic form because the patriarchal family, the central stabilizing institution of agricultural societies, had its own psychology of dominance and submission. The planter didn't have to create a new ideology. He simply fit blacks into an old one.

As the "master," the planter was responsible for the plantation's economy and society. His wife and possibly his eldest daughter were responsible for the daily management of the "Big House." However, his paramount concern was with the efficient operation of the plantation, and he most often put his own economic interests and psychological needs ahead of his slaves. In particular, the slave marriage was in force as long as it was profitable for the slave family to be together. If the slave husband or the wife or even their children had to be sold, the planter would put his own interests first in spite of the most compelling human needs of his slaves. In the end, true plantation "harmony" was rarely achieved. Oppressed people did not overtly challenge planter authority, but they did not acquiesce to his oppression of them. The harmony that planters read in their slaves' behavior was only an illusion created to stave off enhanced planter attempts at control.

More often than not, the fictional relationships these novelists portray between planters and slaves is the stereotypical one described in proslavery tracts. The institution of slavery was a brutal and humiliating one for the slaves. It rested on the foundation of establishing white patriarchal law and authority, which sanctioned violence toward "unruly" subordinates, especially those black male slaves who sought to fulfill their own patriarchal responsibilities. The thrust of slavery was to thwart black resistance by attempting to emasculate slave men in denying them their traditional rights of manhood and by degrading slave women by subjecting them to "unfeminine" labor as well as sexual abuse. That meant all planters tolerated a certain level of brutality toward slave women and children, because psychologically they knew its impact on black men.

Whatever their critique of slavery and slaveholders, the writers in this study promulgated a consistently positive view of the institution and the planter class, while justifying the enslavement of an allegedly inferior race. Their rationalizations for the institution and their depiction of individual slaves resulted from both their privileged position in a racially and class-stratified society and the racist projections of their innermost fantasies and fears.

When we consider the individual representations of blacks, we are struck by these authors' construction of racial stereotypes which, like the gender stereotypes discussed above, justify planter-class male domination. Like the plantation mistress, an adult in her own right, adult slave men and women are depicted as naturally dependent on and in need of planter guidance and protection. Unlike the plantation belle and mistress, however, black slaves are regarded as a degraded form of humanity imported from an essentially backward and barbaric continent through the agency of the European slave trade, but according to a divine plan for the civilization of Africans. Although the planter would construct his dominion over his "family, black and white" as indivisible, in reality black slaves and white plantation women stood in essentially different and unequal positions in relation to each other.

Further, even though the plantation mistress had regular daily contact with a range of male and female house slaves as well as with some field slaves (especially on the smaller estates), with very few exceptions few plantation women are depicted alone in a scene with a slave, male or female, and there is only one plot in which the mistress-slave relationship is central to the action.[21] Instead, in the fictional South, both white plantation women and slaves share scenes with the master, not with each other.

In ignoring the mistress-slave relationship, these authors can convincingly establish the fictional planter as the dominating plantation figure. It is only when one asks about the nature of mistress-slave relationships that one realizes how these authors structure the reader's acceptance of planter domination and his depiction of plantation harmony. Instead, the master-slave relationship as an all-male affair dominates the literature, deflecting the reader's attention from the complexities of gender and race relations on the plantation. Furthermore, the portrait of the slave male as essentially effeminate, or at least "emasculated" in the patriarchal sense, underscores planter contentions about their own masculinity and virility. Again, the most critical contention of planter proslavery ideology is that the natural order is served when inherently inferior men defer to their superiors. In racial and gender terms, that means that not only are black men depicted as intellectually and morally inferior to planters and presumably to most white men but, breaking with both colonial and post–Civil War images, as less masculine as well.

11. The Master-Slave Relationship: Individual Portraits of Slaves

Q. Can you speak of any particular cases of cruelty you have seen?"
A. Yes sir; the most shocking thing I have seen was on the plantation of Mr. Farraby, on the line of the railroad. I went up to his house one morning for drinking water, and heard a woman screaming awfully in the door-yard. On going up to the fence and looking over, I saw a woman stretched out, face downwards, on the ground her hands and feet being fastened by stakes. Mr. Farraby was standing over and striking her with a leather trace belonging to his carriage harness. As he struck her the flesh of her back and legs was raised in welts and ridges by the force of the blows. Sometimes when the poor thing cried out too loud from the pain, Farraby would kick her in the mouth. After he had exhausted himself whipping her he sent to his house for sealing wax, dropped it up on the woman's lacerated back. He then got a riding whip and standing over the woman, picked off the hardened wax by switching at it. Mr. Farraby's grown daughters were looking at all this from a window of the house through the blinds. This punishment was so terrible that I was induced to ask what offense the woman had committed and was told by her fellow servants that her only crime was in burning the edges of the waffles that she had cooked for breakfast. The sight of this thing made me wild almost that day. I could not work right and I prayed the Lord to help my people out of their bondage. I felt I could not stand it much longer."

Solomon Bradley (South Carolina), testimony before the
Freedmen's Inquiry Commission, 1863

THERE WAS an enormous gulf between the planter's view of slavery and the slave's. The planter envisioned slaves as "perpetual children" who were being brought to "civilization" through slavery, without which Africans would be left in a "hopelessly savage state." Although historians have had these sources at hand, only recently has the slave's account of slavery been fully accepted. The historical studies of slavery during the last two decades have considered the institution of slavery as a socioeconomic system, and have attempted to consider slavery from the slave's point of view. The distinguished work of John Blassingame, George Rawick, Herbert Gutman, Lawrence Levine, and Eugene Genovese, among others, has attempted to portray generations of black men, women, and children as they forged a culture of resistance under the extreme conditions of chattel slavery.[1]

In antebellum Southern literature the master emerges as commanding, resolute, and benevolent in contrast to the slave who is ignorant, improvident, lazy, and playful. Moreover, Southern authors never really examine the parameters of the slave woman's life under slavery, or, for that matter the white woman as slave mistress. Thus they distort the lives of white and black plantation women in their fiction. The majority of the individual portraits from this literature then are of slave men who have no relation to the slave community. They reinforce the paternalism of planter fantasy which allows planters and their intellectual allies to justify their coercion of adult black men and women in the institution of slavery. In their bipolar conservative worldview, they create "good" characters who recognize the innate superiority of the planter and defer to him, and "bad" characters who defy planter authority and thus confront the violence inherent in planter law and order. It is not surprising that planters and their allies would portray themselves in this way. They needed to think of themselves as moral men, and to rationalize the brutality of a coercive labor and social system.

As with the stereotypes of women, the stereotypes of African American slaves involve projection. Perpetuating stereotypes of black slaves was absolutely critical for planters psychologically as they sought to convince skeptics in the South and North that slavery served the cause of civilization. In their essays and fiction, these authors drew on and contributed to Western racist thought developed since the Enlightenment. For instance, one often forgets that the term "race," as we use it, was coined in the late seventeenth century by François Bernier, a French physician who had traveled widely and decided to classify the peoples of the world into four groups he called "races": Europeans, Far Easterners, "blacks," and Lapps. Apparently Native Americans and people from the Middle East escaped his notice. "Race" emerged as a socially constructed category in the eighteenth and early nineteenth centuries for Europeans striving to distinguish themselves from the inhabitants of their colonial possessions. Enlightenment thinkers like Johann Friedrich Blumenbach of Germany and Georges Louis Leclerc, comte de Buffon, of France sought to discover and classify all the species in nature including human beings. They held European society and culture as the norm and the apex of civilization and considered all other peoples of the globe inferior in some way. Racist nationalism served as a critical ideology for Europeans and Americans during the great imperialist decades of the nineteenth and twentieth centuries.[2]

The Enlightenment was the period of the Scottish philosophical historians—Adam Ferguson, John Millar, Dugald Stewart, and David Hume—and economist Adam Smith, who followed their work and argued that society develops historically through stages and that different societies are at different stages of civilization. They thought that historical events took place when different peoples within a country (for example, Scotland) resisted progress forcefully. Then the progressive forces usually prevailed. Although they advised toleration of the "less civilized," racist imperialists used their theories to justify the genocide of Native Americans and the enslavement of Africans.[3]

Thus in the name of "civilization" and "progress," Enlightenment thinkers assert the superiority of European civilization to that of especially "tribal," polytheistic, and darker-skinned peoples. While they see themselves as "civilized," these others are "uncivilized," "savage," or "primitive." Euro-Americans are both fascinated by and horrified by the primitive; they associate it with their own uncontrolled and emotionally chaotic infancy as well as the "infancy" of the species. The only way they can defeat the primitive in themselves is to conquer the "primitive" peoples they encounter. This worldview is evident in nineteenth-century manifest destiny rhetoric, which rationalizes Euro-American conquest of Native Americans, Africans, and Mexicans.[4]

That these nineteenth-century proslavery writers were intellectually indebted to the Enlightenment racialists is as evident in their political essays as in their fiction, and their division of the world into bipolar opposites—rational/irrational, virile/effeminate, darkness/lightness, civilized/uncivilized—betrays this debt. William Gilmore Simms's "The Morals of Slavery" serves as a case in point. In this essay, Simms answers Harriet Martineau's critique of slavery in her well-regarded *Society in America* (1837) by asserting his positivist understanding of human history. Simms argues repeatedly that world history is the story of the struggle between superior and inferior peoples for dominance over the land. When inferior peoples come in contact with superior peoples as has happened with Africans and Native Americans in the United States, he argues, that conflict will inevitably result either in the subjection of these inferior peoples or in "their extermination."[5] Slavery has been the civilizing institution for Africans, he contends, and Southern chattel slavery is "one of the most essential genius, under the divine plan, for promoting the general progress of civilization, and for elevating, to a condition of humanity, a people otherwise barbarous, easily depraved, and needing the help of a superior condition—a power from without—to rescue them from a hopelessly savage state" (178). In fact, the great tragedy of life in America, he asserts, is that Native Americans successfully eluded enslavement. Had they not resisted they would have been spared extermination and "squalid poverty" fostered by idleness, "superstition and ignorance," and "degrading exhibitions which they make, in their filth and drunkenness" (265 and 283).

What marks the civilized man from the uncivilized one? What allows man to transcend his animal nature and rise to the level of "human"? Labor. Simms argues in fine Lockean fashion that by bending nature to his will, man through industry and self-discipline learns to control his own baser nature. By converting the forests to land that is then worked for sustenance, civilized man is freed from nomadism. Living in agricultural society, Simms argues, yields wealth, power, and the national state, which civilized man defends from the "wild men" who would try to take it from him (260–62).[6] Thus do social institutions—the patriarchal family, property, law, government, armies—arise among superior civilizations. Inferior peoples who are in contact with such civilizations "improve in intellectual respects" and are "lifted, by regular degrees, into the bosom of that society which has first enslaved them." For such service, the superior nation is rewarded by the labor of the other. If a nation refuses "to extend her conquests, she falls, like Rome, the victim, to the savage" (262–63). Thus Simms contends, the African, unlike the Native American, has improved under slavery, which has delivered him from his savage state and is continually stripping him of his inferior culture and replacing it with the superior Anglo-American culture (271–74).[7]

Simms's Native American, then, is a thoroughly wild and degraded being who in being removed from whites has slipped through the hands of civilization. He predicts that Native Americans will be exterminated by the advancing whites of the next generation (280 and 281). In contrast, he notes, the black slave under white tutelage is increasingly religious, industrious, and intelligent. He comments that even hostile visitors to the South like Martineau wonder at the "exceeding comfort, and great cheerfulness and contentment of the negro," his excellent treatment, and his "buoyancy" and "happy abandon." They fail to realize, Simms notes, that the African recognizes the superiority of his civilized masters and places himself in happy submission to slavery's requirements (219, 218–20).

In his preface to the 1852 edition of the "Morals of Slavery," Simms contends that when he first wrote his essay in 1839, Southern opinion on the morality of slaveholding was divided, with many Southerners only being able to justify slavery on the grounds of "mere expediency." He is pleased by his role in helping to defend the institution from abolitionist attack and in reassuring his countrymen that their peculiar institution is a morally correct one (177–79).[8]

Thus in this essay, Simms lays out the philosophical base for the creation of the "Sambo" stereotype. Like others before him, Simms imagined Sambo as his master's opposite. Where the master is a responsible, assertive, independent, intelligent, self-disciplined agent of his own destiny, the Sambo is an irresponsible, submissive, lazy dependent, incapable of self-initiated action. The Sambo needs the master's firm hand lest he decline to his former barbaric state. Simms and the other authors justify the enslavement of Africans not by the utilitarian appeal to economic expediency, but to the moral and psychological appeal of asserting that Western Christian civilization was destined to triumph over allegedly primitive peoples. Thus the planter masks what he regards as the primitive in himself by projecting it onto his "inferiors." Intellectuals like Simms and Nathaniel Beverley Tucker argued that just as the Southern belle needed the protection and assurance of the planter hero, so the irrational and uncontrolled African slave needed the stern but compassionate guidance of his or her master. It was the planter's job to learn how to govern them.[9]

At the core of this literature, then, lies a question about masculinity: Who will be "man enough" to govern Southern society? These writers never challenged the proposition that the planter class was and should continue to be the South's ruling class. Perhaps the members of the business or professional classes might marry into the planter class, but that signified their acceptance of planter-class domination and their individual acceptability to a particular family. The portraits of masters and slaves underscores the contention that only planter-class men possessed the requisite morality and intelligence that distinguished the merely successful from the "aristocratic."

These authors present a series of assumptions about planter-class masculinity. They thought that men can choose to be either leaders or followers, dominating or dominated. They held that leaders are "natural aristocrats," their superiority bred over time, not acquired. They knew that a "gentleman" commanded others by virtue of his grace and intelligence, courage and wisdom. A gentleman was honorable, never allowing any insult to himself or his family to go unanswered. He possessed a gallant regard for the women of all races and classes. Planter-class male superiority was readily acknowledged and accepted by all except imbeciles or criminals.

African American men posed a serious problem for the planter class and for all white men generally. If it were true that they were equal to whites, then they would have to have equal social, economic, and political rights and their enslavement would be immoral as well as illegal. However, if they weren't equal, indeed, if they were a subhuman species transported from a primitive continent, then their enslavement was really a progressive and Christian act. It isn't at all difficult to understand how men who profited from slave labor and slave reproduction convinced themselves of the latter. As this literature makes abundantly clear, they convinced themselves that black men were by nature docile, trusting, and naturally dependent like women and children; planters needed only to learn to master their slaves and the plantation.

Conservative myth and its interpretation of the American Revolution held that true men owned their own labor, their wives, children, and land and that they had fought British tyranny to protect this property from theft, violation, or death. The fact that African men had arrived on their shores to be bought and sold away from their families indicated to these conservatives that not only had they failed a critical test of masculinity, but that slavery did not violate the African's human spirit.

The goal of planter government was to make Africans productive and docile workers. As Frederick Douglass's autobiography makes clear, that often entailed breaking the slave's will.[10] In patriarchal terms, then, the planter sought to "emasculate" black slave men by stripping them of any respect they might garner as men within the slave community. Thus, although there were individual exceptions as a class, planters stole their labor; sexually assaulted their mothers, sisters, and wives; sold their children from them; refused to let them own land or profit much from their labor; and otherwise denied them their civil and human rights. Since black male slaves were conquered males without rights, they were considered "effeminate" according to gender and racial stereotypes. Note that in conservative patriarchal societies, when men submit their wills to other men, the most familiar metaphor is a gendered one. That does not mean that black men and plantation mistresses held the same status; only that the planter turned to the uncontested familial metaphor to describe and justify his domination of African American men. The Sambo stereotype not only made the master feel less guilty and more justified in his coercion of African American men, but was consistent with his construction of himself as the virile and benevolent patriarch of black and white families.

In one of the first proslavery novels, John Pendleton Kennedy in *Swallow Barn* offers us both the ideal planter in Frank Meriwether, "the country gentleman," and the ideal slave, in Carey, "the perfect shadow of his master."[11] Kennedy assures the reader that harmony prevails on the plantation under Meriwether's benevolent despotism. Meriwether skillfully manipulates the slaves and convinces them that what is good for him and his family is good for them as a part of his extended family.

Meriwether is described as a handsome, middle-aged man of forty-five with a tendency "to be lazy and philosophical." The "very model of landed gentlemen," he is generous and hospitable to his neighbors and acquaintances and expects that they will freely visit Swallow Barn. As a representative planter, he is anti-urban and anticapitalist, regarding merchants and bankers as "hollow-hearted and insincere." He claims for himself and his class a simple, unpretentious and virtuous country life where personal honor and the honor and longevity of the family is the plantation's most precious asset (31, 33).

As a model planter, Kennedy's Meriwether is "kind and considerate" toward his slaves and his dependents. "His slaves appreciate this," Kennedy observes, "and hold him in most affectionate reverence, and, therefore, are not only contented, but happy under his dominion" (34). Despite the realities of the whip and the auction block, there are repeated descriptions of the "air of contentment and good humor and kind family attachment" that prevails at Swallow Barn. Perhaps the most revealing portrait is that of Carey, Meriwether's special servant and family favorite. Together with Meriwether, Carey takes major responsibility for the breeding, raising, and training of Swallow Barn's famous blooded horses. They play a game in which Carey "advises" Meriwether on the care of the horses, "advice" unmistakably given with the master's indulgence. When Mark Littleton, the visitor and narrator of *Swallow Barn,* asks Meriwether why he allows Carey to be so familiar with him, Meriwether replies that Carey "has not many years left, and it does no harm to humor him!" (37). In another scene, Carey and "Old Jeff" argue about caring for a horse's sprained leg with each insisting on a different treatment. Meriwether intervened, heard out both sides, and let Carey's judgment prevail. He explained, "This old magnifico will allow no man to have an opinion but himself. Rather than disturb the peace, I must submit to his authority" (448). By seeming to defer to Carey's judgment on this issue, Meriwether gives him some responsibility and influence over the other blacks, and encouraged feelings of alliance and affection. Behind this game is the fact of Meriwether's ultimate power. It is implicit in every scene Kennedy draws.

Implied throughout as well is that blacks are taken in by this ruse and assume that they have been given power and responsibility. Eugene D. Genovese would argue that the planters and slaves feel real affection for each other, that masters needed to recognize their slaves as people in order to keep in touch with their own humanity, and that this need led the planter to surrender some power and grant slaves their "reciprocal rights."[12] However, Meriwether's power is only enhanced by having his slaves emulate his authority. What Kennedy is asking us to assume is that neither Carey nor the other slaves know that. What Genovese is asking us to assume is that only Carey and Meriwether are in on it. Black testimony revealed that everyone was in on it, but that blacks protected themselves by "puttin' on ole massa'": feigning deference and humility and assuming authority according to planter guidelines. As George Tucker shows, the ultimate contradiction of planter paternalism occurred when blacks were sold from "their white family": then the hypocrisy and brutality that governed everyday interactions lay exposed for all to recognize.[13]

Carey's skill as "a minstrel of some repute" is another source of pride for him. "Weaving into song the past or present annals of the family," he played his banjo after dinner or entertained on festive occasions. In one scene Carey first composed a ballad about Ned Hazard, Frank Meriwether's brother-in-law, and then, at Ned's insistence played more traditional country ballads and dancing tunes, and finally shared a julep with the young men before taking his leave "with a polite and gentleman-like gesture, and with a smile of the utmost benignity." Again Genovese would argue that in taking pride in his music and in having a sense of himself as an extended family member, Carey had not only carved himself out a place of self-respect, but had gained the respect of the master. Kennedy, however, comments on the "serio-comic effect the whole exhibition had upon them," and conveyed the feeling again of a slave being indulged (101–4).

The only time that Carey reverses the game with the white family is in dealing with two small female children. Kennedy notes: "He was affectionately obliging to his young mistresses and spoke to them in a tone that showed how largely he partook of the family interest in them, although it was sufficiently apparent that he deferred but little to their authority" (216 and 217). This is precisely the game that Frank Meriwether and Carey play. Like Carey in this instance, Frank Meriwether appears to defer to Carey's judgment, but they both know that the ultimate power and authority rests with Frank. The only point at which black adults seem to have any authority is when they deal with black and white children. Unfortunately, the antebellum authors are reluctant to provide any scenes that might show how black adults internalize and exercise paternalism with their own or the white children. Kennedy does not draw the parallel between Carey's relationship with and behavior toward the little girls, and Meriwether's relationship and behavior toward Carey. To Kennedy, Carey is being himself—opinionated, stubborn, and falsely deferential.

Meriwether, in a revealing passage, discusses the raising and breeding of horses and the feeling of mastery he has over them. He admires their temperament, which he claims was a testament to training. Those qualities he sought in prize horses are "patience, considerateness, discretion, long-suffering amiable obedience" (438 and 439). These are exactly the qualities sought in the "good servant," and it is a metaphor for the master-slave relationship. After all, in each instance, the goal of mastery is the same: to "domesticate" a creature of "nature" to the disciplines of "civilization."

Littleton, speaking for Kennedy in this instance, argues against slavery in the abstract and asserts that he would humanize the institution by recognizing the ties of marriage and the family, and by creating a privileged upper class of skilled slaves. Virginia's slaves, he contends are in a transitional stage from "barbarism to civilization," and their further moral and mental development rests with their white masters. "Essentially parasitical in his nature," the black is "a dependent upon the white race; dependent for guidance and direction even to the procurement of his most indispensable necessaries." Littleton asserts, "He has the helplessness of a child—without foresight, without faculty of contrivance, without thrift of any kind" (453). Unlike other laboring classes, blacks are "the most good natured, careless, light-hearted, and happily-constructed human beings" he has ever seen. In a revealing passage reminiscent of planter views of women, Meriwether notes, "he grows upward, only as the vine to which nature has supplied the sturdy tree as a support" (454). Kennedy's defense of slavery, then, takes classic form: not the economic defense based on the need for a plentiful, cheap, and tractable labor force, but on the racist one of protecting and civilizing an inferior people (452–55).

While Kennedy's black slaves are tangential to the plot, in William Gilmore Simms's fiction, what happens to the slaves is central to the fate of the plantation. Blacks serve as confessors and confidantes to the white family. Most significant, when the plantation is attacked by the British or by marauding bands of poor whites, blacks and whites stand side by side and fight.

Fictional plantation blacks, having thoroughly internalized planter racism, believe their fate depends on the good fortune of the master and his family. Hence any attack on the plantation or on the white family is an attack on them as well. Unlike their real-life revolutionary ancestors, these fictional blacks created by nineteenth-century proslavery advocates never take up arms or run to the swamps to free themselves. Instead, plantation blacks and whites constitute a peaceful and harmonious society in which slavery serves the common interest.

Simms sees blacks as being lazy, unthoughtful, faithful, lighthearted, and affectionate. The narrator in *Richard Hurdis* notes that the "grin of their mouths, the white teeth shining through the glossy black of their faces, is absolutely irresistible."[14] Like Kennedy, Simms finds them barbarians who the white man has a duty to civilize. In *Eutaw* he comments, "Ah, the dear black dirty scamps of negroes, big and little, on one of the old ante-revolutionary plantations! They acknowledge loving necessities as the flies do; are as free in their intimacies as the frogs of Egypt; will blacken the very sunshine upon your walls with the pressure of their affections; and carry real, genuine hearts, full of sympathy for all the family, in spite of their rarely washed visages—which revolt instinctively, at the unnatural application of soap and water to a skin that greatly prefers friction with oil and sunshine."[15] The essential "qualities" of blacks are restated. They can subsist on very little, are affectionate and promiscuous in their relationships, and are "instinctively" dirty. In another passage describing the flight of black families from a plantation ahead of the British, Simms explains that "a negro so relishes a change that he will even forget the charms of a first, for a second or even a third and fourth wife, and is always prepared for new lodgings. You can scarcely move him too frequently for his own satisfaction."[16] The self-serving nature of these "observations" by Simms are readily apparent. People given barely adequate food, clothing, and shelter are said to be able to subsist on very little. Their families broken up and sold off, they are charged with being promiscuous and to enjoy traveling. In short, their "nature" justifies their treatment, and in Simms's fiction, their best treatment is from their patriarchal master.

Though occasionally rambling into didacticism, Simms fictionalizes the master-slave relationship more successfully than any of the Southern writers. His views on blacks and slavery are established by these character sketches. In *The Forayers* and *Eutaw,* the heir of "The Barony" and one of Simms's heroes, is Captain William Sinclair. He has two servants: Abram Johnson ('Bram) who was his scout during the war, and Benny Bowlegs, the driver on his father's estate. When 'Bram is first introduced, he is asleep under a tree at a partisan hideout during the American Revolution. He is awakened abruptly when William Sinclair knocks him on the shoulder with a hickory stick and this exchange takes place:

"Ki! Mass Willie, da you?"

"And this is the way, you rascal, that you watch the camp when I am gone?"

"Psho, maussa, I bin see you all de time! I know he bin you from de fuss [first]."

"Then you must have a famous passion for hickory, you rascal, to receive three cuts of it before letting me know that you were awake."

"Psho! de hick'ry ain't hutt [hurt]."

"Ah! will you try a little more of it?" But the black retreated, rubbing his shoulders afresh.

"Tank you, Mass Willie; but 'scuse me, ef you please; no more dis time. Next time, maybe, I will tank you for anoder tas'e [taste]." (*The Forayers,* 15 and 16)

William warns 'Bram that he will get more than a taste of the hickory stick if he catches him napping on the lookout again. Later, 'Bram emerges as one of the finest partisan scouts, but the initial image Simms creates is that of the lazy, irresponsible black sleeping on the job. In the exchange with William, 'Bram strains to maintain his dignity while the master asserts his power, tempered with affectionate exasperation. It is clear that whatever 'Bram's army activities are and whatever the dimensions of his relationship with Sinclair, the bottom line is the master's capacity for physical coercion, and the slave's helplessness to strike back. In this literature, especially in Simms's, physical abuse of slaves is transformed into a peculiar form of Southern humor.

At one point Willie gives 'Bram a coded military message that 'Bram starts to translate, but is quickly silenced:

"I only wish you to repeat what I say, 'Bram; it is not necessary that you should comprehend it. If you have one fault, 'Bram, more than another, which I could wish you to correct, it is that of being a little too wise for your master."

"Oh! psho, Mass Willie. Git out! Don't be poking fun wid a sharp finger at you nigger." (19)

Then they parted "affectionately" with a handshake; as Willie rides off, 'Bram exclaims, "God bress he heart! God bress he heart. I lub 'em like my own chile" (19 and 20). Though now a soldier, 'Bram remains a slave in temperament and behavior; his very language is that of a child. He is beaten with a hickory stick and then upbraided; yet the relationship with his master is portrayed as loving. He is a slave by virtue of his lack of indignation toward someone who is abusive. Like a bad child, he stands corrected, is disciplined, internalizes his inferiority, and responds with affection. Such is the planter's perspective of the slave. One must remember that this is a master's description of the master-slave relationship. The ex-slave narratives suggest that 'Bram's exclamations would be anything but affectionate when his master rides off.

In *The Forayers* and *Eutaw,* the Travis family is trying to escape from the poor white outlaws who want to ransack and loot their home, and from the British who seek both the plantation and Mr. Travis so they can charge him with treason. Since William Sinclair's father is a Loyalist, the Sinclairs—Colonel Sinclair and his two daughters—are trying to escape from the patriot forces. The two families flee from their respective plantations; before leaving, however, they must dispose of their slaves. 'Bram is chosen to lead the Travis plantation blacks to safety. Before doing so, 'Bram addresses them like a kind of black Moses, but Simms, who rarely takes his black characters seriously, uses the occasion to create a seriocomic effect:

> "An' it's p'inted for me, brudderen and sisteren, 'Bram, to show you de way to dat most blessed splendiferous country ob meat and molasses. And jis' you follow me—do de ting I tell you—lie close when I say—'Nigger's, dem dam tory is about;' and push forward, quick as runner [black snake] when I say, 'Now's de time for shaking de rheumatic out ob de legs'—and I carries you safe I tell you, to dat heabben ob a country. Is you willing I axes?—brudderen and sisteren, le' me yer from you. Is you willing to eat pig? Da's de fuss question."
>
> The acclamatory and affirmative grunt was unanimous.
>
> "Meat and molasses; coon and 'possum; pork and purtatoes; hog and hom'ny; lightwood a plenty, and de beautifullest and tickest swamp in de wo'ld. Enty dese is excelling beautiful tings for sensible nigger?" (*The Forayers,* 456 and 457)

Simms comments that "the eloquence of 'Bram was irresistible." He "supplied all the deficiencies in the argument of Sinclair" (457).

Thus 'Bram's "leadership" is undercut by Simms's qualifying. Equally suggestive, the passage indicates a gap between 'Bram and "the masses" of blacks. 'Bram is imitative of whites in his speech and values, but at least he understands the seriousness of the situation; not so his "brudderen and sisteren." They are coaxed away mostly by the promise of a better life. Thus it is implied that the slaves were incapable of understanding the danger they were in and of responding to it responsibly. It is better to manipulate them with promises of material abundance and good times than to explain the nature of the threat to them. Like children they are protected from the reality of their situation. Significantly, no one tries to escape. Most of Simms's historical novels are set in the chaos of a countryside at war when the young and middle-aged white men are away fighting. Only the blacks remain to guard the women, children, and old people. Astonishingly, these fictional blacks almost never seek their freedom by fleeing to the North, to the frontier and swamps, or to the British lines. Invariably, a cadre of loyal blacks remain to defend the plantation against the British or, like 'Bram, accompany their masters as manservants.[17]

Throughout 'Bram is a brave and valued servant, yet Simms cannot allow him fully realized leadership qualities: "True Abram was faithful, and shrewd beyond the usual capacity and virtues of his race; but though a good scout, he was a poor soldier, and the only calculations which could be predicted of this trust must rest wholly on the natural cunning of the fellow, his fidelity, and perfect knowledge of the woods" (462). Much is made in these novels of young men finding their manhood in battle. If Simms allowed 'Bram to be a good soldier then, by his own standards, he would have to admit that 'Bram was a man (that is, someone who shouldn't be enslaved). For a proslavery apologist, that would be impossible.

Ben Bowlegs is the other prominent Sinclair servant. He had been an orderly sergeant to William Sinclair's father during the Cherokee War and was now the Sinclair plantation driver. Benny was sixty-two and "wifeless and childless," an unusual situation for any plantation black. He lived "in a very snug cottage" on the edge of the woods that was equidistant from the mansion house, the slave quarters, and the corncrib. He had "a profound sense of his good fortune" and was grateful to providence and his master for the small comforts he received (73 and 74). A faithful, affectionate, and trusted member of the Sinclair household, he was a driver who never spared

> himself in pushing others. Ben carried out his principles into practice. He never slept on performances *done,* as negroes and common people are very apt to do. He passed to new ones. He was a moral steam-engine, working himself, and driving everyone ahead. He pushed his master, as well as his brother-slaves; and assigned *him* his tasks with the pertinacity of one who was resolved to be something more than a counselor. His reverence for his master was never such as simply to endeavor to *please* him. Ben Bowlegs delivered the truth in spite of the consequences. (73 and 74)

Several things are striking about this passage. Simms draws someone to be admired for his dedication, his sense of pride in his work, and his not being obsequious and manipulative.

For the most part, the black male slave is portrayed as passive and cowardly. He is dependent on the white planter for direction and guidance, has minimal discretionary authority, little or no relationship to the black slave community, and no relationship with nonplantation people. Most important, he is sexually passive; he is neither husband nor father and the issue of his sexuality is a forbidden subject, as it is for all plantation people.

However, Simms, the least reticent and most willing to take risks, serialized an illuminating short story in *The Magnolia.* Entitled "The Loves of the Driver," it depicted a married black male slave driver's lust for and attempted seduction of an Indian princess. Breaking with established conventions, it introduced the "exotic primitive," or the "Buck," a type of black male who would appear in postbellum white fiction. With Mingo, the black driver; Dinah, his wife; Colonel Gillison, Mingo's master; Caloya, the Indian princess; and Enifisto, or "Richard Knuckles," her husband, Simms's comments on the moral character and social relations of Southern whites, blacks, and Indians offer a completely different picture of the slave driver.

Described as "a stout negro fellow of portly figure and not uncomely countenance," Mingo was "well made and tall and was sufficiently conscious of his personal attractions to take all pains to exhibit them in the most appropriate costume and attitude."[18] In addition to being vain and to imitating his master, Mingo was able to overestimate his importance because Gillison, his newly orphaned young master, had not fully grasped the skills and discipline of mastery.[19] Consequently, Mingo does not know his true place in the plantation hierarchy and, with his passions out of control, becomes a tyrant.

Mingo is first introduced in an argument with his master about whether the Catawba Indians should be driven off the land, which they visit annually to make the red clay pots they sell to sustain themselves as a tribe. Since the land was not cultivable, Gillison is willing to let them camp out there for a month or so as long as they don't steal from him. Internalizing white racism and referring to the Indians as "red varmints," Mingo wants them expelled from the land and does not want to have to police their activities (226 and 225). When Gillison finally decides to overrule him, Mingo is furious. He takes out his anger by kicking his dog and whipping the kitchen boy who delivered Gillison's message. Simms explains that Mingo had so lost his true sense of place that he "seemed absolutely to fancy himself the proprietor whose language of command he had habituated himself to employ" (225).

From the beginning, then, Mingo is portrayed as the worst example of what can happen when the planter fails to assert his authority over his inferiors. Although Simms's slaves display a greater range of personality than do comparable black characters in this literature, they never challenge or subvert planter authority; while they can be disagreeable, especially with each other, they never presume to argue with or contradict their masters, much less take independent action against orders. Mingo is not only a study in "lowlife," but is a warning about the consequences of planter indulgence.

Simms's Mingo is also a unique portrait of black male sexuality, albeit through planter eyes. Mingo's sexuality surfaces when he is sent to check the Indians. He starts a fight with old Enifisto by kicking his dog, and they are about to come to blows when Caloya, Enifisto's beautiful young wife, throws herself between them. Simms tells us that Caloya "was decidedly one of the comeliest squaws that had ever enchanted the eyes of the driver, and her fire-darting eyes, the emotion so visible in her face, and the boldness of her action, as she passed between their weapons, with a hand extended toward each, was such as to inspire him with any other feelings than those which possessed him toward the squatters" (226). Like Virginia Maitland (*Border Beagles*), who thrust herself between Vernon and Saxon, Caloya's courageous and self-sacrificing action establishes her as Simms's heroine and as the paradigm of feminine morality among the degraded ranks of

Southern society. Mingo also "was presumptuous enough—surely there are no white men so!—to imagine that it was scarcely possible for any of the other sex in her sober senses, to withstand him," and that he "penetrated the neighboring estates with the excursive and reckless nature of the Prince of Troy" (226; note the sexually suggestive language). Simms not only offers us one of the only portraits of black male virility; he makes an uncharacteristic allusion to masculine vanity in general.

Winthrop Jordan has discussed this white fantasy of black male sexuality as it occurs in colonial sources, and Sterling Brown and Catherine Starke explored the white creation of the black male as "exotic primitive" after the Civil War.[20] Of the authors considered here, only Simms examines black male sexuality directly. In doing so, he enlarges the racist stereotypes of the black man and also that of the Indian, in which the male is a tyrannical, lazy drunkard while his wife is attractive, hard working, self-effacing, and loyal to her husband. As Sander Gilman would observe, the planter had two main fears about himself: that he was out of control, especially sexually, and that his laziness and dissipation would render him incapable of functioning. Here in the representations of the black and Indian male, we have the planter's fears and anxiety emerging in classic stereotypes.[21]

Black women work hard and know their place as subordinates of black men, Mingo tells Caloya, but they are not so overworked as the Indian woman; moreover "a black gentleman is always more 'spectable to a woman than an Indian" (265). Mingo lectures Enifisto about his laziness and cruelty in letting Caloya do his work as well as her own. Enifisto in response observes that blacks are only good for work, and adds the ultimate insult that the "nigger man," unlike himself, "ain't free man—he must work, same like Indian Squaw" (265). Mingo brings Caloya food and helps her with some of her chores, but she remains cool and aloof, which is perceived as attraction for him.[22] When he is absent, Enifisto indulges in jealous rages and the wronged Caloya "suffered quite as much from his cruelty and injustice as if her lips had betrayed all the extravagant manifestations known to the sorrows of the civilized" (267). Simms documents what he sees as the salient traits of black and Indian men who differ from each other yet remain inferior to white men. As readers we are to conclude that Mingo, being enslaved, is less than a man; Enifisto is similarly emasculated by being a worthless drunkard. As usual in Simms's fiction, the women of inferior races of men fare better than their men do.

The conflict between Mingo and Enifisto is resolved after Caloya seeks the help of Colonel Gillison, who represents planter justice and social order. As Caloya recounts her story and tells him of Enifisto's plot to lure Mingo into a trap and kill him, she is overheard by Dinah, Mingo's termagant wife, who serves as Gillison's cook. In spite of her rage at Mingo for betraying her, she determines to help save his life. In the concluding scene, Simms creates a kind of free-for-all battle between these so-called lowlife characters, in which Enifisto hits Mingo with a hatchet and splits open his hand; Dinah starts beating Caloya, who responds by grazing her with a hatchet; Mingo turns and starts beating Dinah with his fists, and would have continued had not Gillison intervened to separate the combatants and reestablish order. In the end, then, Gillison reasserts his authority. He sends the Indians on their way and punishes Mingo for his transgressions. Mingo's unusual portrait notwithstanding, Simms asserts here and elsewhere that only white men are capable of civilizing barbaric peoples, and that order and justice will prevail in the South only through white male patriarchal authority (272–30).

While the Indian woman is portrayed by Simms as being "gentle . . . simple and unaffected" but shaped by the "severe schools of the barbarian" and thus ruined, the black woman is depicted as a strong, fearless scold who hounds her husband out of the house with her need to dominate him (319). For his part, young Gillison learns his proper place and role by taking socially necessary action to prevent bloodshed and social chaos. Although Simms's themes and characterizations in this story supported the status quo, he was criticized for portraying such immoral behavior in a family magazine. "No race is so very low, or so debased," he replied, "as to deprive them of the power of exciting interests in the breasts of men" (377). Simms went on to claim that his fictional racial stereotypes in this short story are human beings, and that whites needed to understand the true character of the peoples they sought to dominate if they were going to "civilize" the North American continent.[23]

One of the most carefully drawn master-slave relationships in this literature is that of Simms's Captain Porgy and his servants Sappho, Pompey, and Tom in the novel *Woodcraft; or, Hawks About the Dovecote.*[24] Porgy is a prime example of the Southern planter as aristocrat, aesthete, and gourmand and is Simms's most humorously drawn character. His features were thus described: "unmarked and decisive, with a large capacious nose, a mouth rather feminine and soft, and a chin well defined and masculine. But for the excessive development of his abdominal region, his figure would have been quite worthy of his face" (49).[25] Similarly Simms introduces Tom as "a fellow of flat head and tried fidelity; of enormous mouth, but famous as a cook; of a nose that scarcely pretended to elevate itself in the otherwise plain surface of an acre of a face; but of a genius for stews that commended him quite as much as any other of his virtues to the confidence and regards of his master. Tom had a reputation in camp, for his terrapin soups, which made him the admiration of the whole brigade" (51). So Porgy, true to his real interest in life, values Tom as a resourceful cook who can make any form of flora or fauna seem like a delicacy from the best tables of Europe.

Captain Porgy had had a "fast youth," "had never been taught the pains of acquisition," and in his adolescence had learned "too soon and fatally . . . the pleasures of dissipation" (101). He had served the patriot cause bravely, but like most returning planter veterans found his estate in ruin, himself deeply in debt, his slaves run off the plantation to the swamps or stolen by poor white outlaws and sold to the British for trade in the West Indies. The novel is about his attempts to ward off his creditors and reestablish himself as planter. In describing these efforts, Simms diagrams the social tensions in the plantation society as it involves gender relations within the master class, and the relationship of that class, the slaves and poor whites.

Simms argues that the critical bond is between slaves and their master, not between the slaves and his white surrogates. The basic canon is that black slaves love and respect their master and their love is reciprocated. When Porgy arrives back at Glen-Eberley after the war, the remaining blacks congregate along the tree-lined avenue leading to the plantation house and salute his arrival: "T'ank de Lord, here's maussa git to he own home at last! . . . Bress de Lord, Maussa, you come! We all berry glad for see you, Maussa—glad too much!" Simms continues: "And the same negroes who had been with him for several hours before, without so much as taking his hand, now rushed up and seized it, with loud cries, as if they were hosts, and welcoming a favorite guest. The tears stood in the eyes of our captain, though he suffered none of his companions to behold them; and he shook hands with, and spoke to them in turn" (175). In the planter imagination, "home" meant safety, shelter, privacy, the land and the Big House, the union of the black and white families. Blacks and whites were tied to the plantation in a common bond with the land and the past. They shared their history together, and it is a family history. The shared cruelty and violence goes unmentioned.

In Simms's recurring portrait of plantation society, the Revolutionary yeoman scout who serves the planter hero in war, becomes the overseer in peacetime. Thus in *Woodcraft,* Fordham becomes Mrs. Eveleigh's overseer and Millhouse serves with Porgy. In Millhouse, however, Simms creates a perfect foil for Porgy's reunion with his mammy, Sappho, which has been described above. Millhouse represents the middle-class utilitarianism Southerners hated in the Northern bourgeoisie and is the exuberant and impractical Porgy's opposite. In scene after scene, Millhouse is pitted against Porgy and the slaves, underlining the class differences between Porgy and Millhouse and the caste difference between Millhouse and the slaves.

Millhouse is caught between Porgy, the indulgent master, and the slaves whom he must work hard to produce the crop. Millhouse is portrayed as a nasty, racist bully. He is also something of a presumptuous fool in seeking to advise Porgy on how to run his personal affairs (45–47, 49–50). For example, most of the slaves had their own dogs for hunting, but the dogs often killed the pigs on the plantation. Millhouse wants the dogs destroyed and he quarrels with the slaves over the issue. He perceives the argument in terms of a power struggle between the slaves and himself. He must discipline them in this instance, he believes, in order to have more control in the fields. When Porgy learns of the problem, rather than supporting Millhouse, he postpones the decision until they can afford pigs, thus tacitly favoring the slaves and underscoring both Simms's mockery of Millhouse and the humor of the novel. Millhouse is also a strict taskmaster, which sets him against his workers, while Porgy would give them days off to hunt and relax (296–98).[26]

Another example of this conflict occurs when Porgy's slaves attend Lance Frampton's wedding. Millhouse sees the wedding as an exclusive whites-only social event. He orders the slaves to continue working on the plantation; when they appear, he accuses them of "treachery and insubordination." Millhouse is disturbed, for two reasons: first, the presence of slaves dancing and celebrating makes the fact of being an "invited guest" meaningless; second, if they frolic all day and night, no one will work for two days (396). Porgy, casual as ever, totally misunderstands the necessity of tilling the fields and intercedes by giving everyone the day off. Tom has the last word: "He don't comprehend nigger nater 't al! He's always a-talking 'bout wuk, as ef der's no play in de worl'; and always a-talking 'bout hick'ries, as ef de airth was nebber mek' to raise any better t'ings! Da's always de way wid dem poor buckrah, wha's got no nigger ob he own. He always a-wantin' to wuk de niggers ob udder gempleman's tell he bones come out ob he skin" (397). In letting the slave participate in the wedding festivities, Porgy recognizes them as significant members of the plantation community, and apparently uses that connection to bind the blacks to him. Although Simms portrays Porgy as "inefficient," he obviously favors inefficient but humane planter paternalism to the utilitarian callousness of the middling overseer. In having Porgy prevail, Simms both portrays such paternalism at its best and answers the antislavery critics who charged planters with overworking their labor force.

In Simms's vision, then, the master is a gentleman, and as a gentleman "always duly considered the claims of the inferior, and anticipated their reasonable desire" (105). In the planter view that is the key to mastery: to win the respect and confidence of one's dependents so that they believed that the measures you take are in their best interest. In *Woodcraft,* Simms contends, an overseer like Millhouse failed to understand the needs of the master or the slaves. "A utilitarian" who thinks only of working hard to make a crop, he is representative of his acquisitive class of overseers and of the capitalist class in the North who, unable to enjoy life, drive themselves to work and to make money. Within plantation society, therefore, although he is white, Millhouse is not part of the extended planter family. He is a hired hand. His labor will be used on the plantation, just as his vote is used off of it, but he is an outsider whose fate will be to gaze longingly down the tree-lined avenue that leads to the Big House.

Of all the authors, Simms is the most sensitive to the caste-class division of plantation society. Most emphasize the class differences between whites; he alone is sensitive to the way in which the division between poor whites and blacks works to the advantage of the planter class.[27] In all of Simms's historical novels, blacks defend the besieged plantation not only from the British, but from the marauding bands of poor white outlaws. In fact, blacks are armed in many instances, and actually shoot poor whites.[28] In Simms's *Mellichampe,* for example, the black slave Scipio defends Ernest Mellichampe, the fiancé of his mistress, by bashing in the head of Mellichampe's would-be assassin, Loyalist Captain Barsfield.[29]

Usually, the poor-white–black relationships are less violent. They involve the black's identification with the planter family and the exclusion of the poor white from plantation society. *The Forayers* is typical. Pete Blodgit, a poor-white squatter on Sinclair's plantation, comes to speak to Colonel Sinclair about the alleged abduction of Sinclair's patriot son, William, or "Willie." He is greeted at the front door of "The Barony" by Benny Bowlegs, who makes him go around to the rear. "Like the servants of the most lordly planters of that day," Simms explains, "Benny Bowlegs had but small esteem for the class he described as 'poor buckrah.' For Pete Blodgit, as a sample of this class in particular, his disgust was without limit" (182). In this scene, Benny also upbraids Blodgit for unmannerly behavior and slovenliness, thus clearly identifying with the prejudices of the master class.

However, in planter fiction the reverse is also true: poor whites loathe black slaves. Earlier, Blodgit has had another unsuccessful interview with Colonel Sinclair. In reporting back to his cronies Blodgit angrily declared that Sinclair "talked to me jest as ef I was no better than a nigger"; and moreover, he had "niggers" protecting him. The outlaw chief, Hell-Fire Dick, was infuriated: "I ain't afeared of him; and I never seed the nigger yit that had the impidence to look into my eyes" (118–20). The climax occurred when the poor white outlaws attacked The Barony, which was defended by William Sinclair and the loyal black slaves (182–99). Simms is acutely aware that black–poor-white antagonism benefited the planter class. The planter nightmare was unity between them.[30]

Of the authors considered here, Kennedy and Simms create the most memorable master-slave relationships, although it is, for obvious reasons of propriety, always a relationship between men. Simms's counterpart to the Meriwether-Carey relationship is the Porgy-Tom partnership albeit with a critical difference: Porgy is always a humorous Falstaffian figure in Simms's work and thus the Porgy-Tom relationship exaggerates for comic effect certain aspects of the master-slave bond. However, for the contemporary reader, sensitive to gender and racial stereotypes, Simms's representation of the relationship, especially in *Woodcraft,* lends itself to alternative readings.

By Simms's standards, Porgy is an indulgent master who allows his subordinates an unusual amount of freedom. Porgy not only asks Tom's advice in picking out the proper clothes, but even what he thinks about Porgy's taking a wife (327–29, 176). Though Porgy is at times sharp and abusive with Tom, the initial impression is that Tom has slightly more personal freedom than one customarily finds in a master-slave relationship. To be sure, Porgy can be demanding of Tom. Witness, for instance, their first night at home. Porgy is impatient because in the abandoned plantation, which has been stripped of its kitchen equipment and supplies, Tom is a little slow in producing dinner. Porgy exclaims: "Supper we must have. I am famishing. Tom! Tom! where the d—l is that fellow! Does he think he's free of me, because he is free of the army?—Tom! Tom!" Tom answers him: "Sah! yer maussa! Wha' de debbil mek' [makes] you holler so loud, maussa, when I's jis' [just] at your elbow? You tink I hard o' hearing, 'cause I got hard maussa, I 'spose!" And Porgy's response: "Hard maussa, you impertinent scamp! Another master would have roasted you alive long before this. See, and let us have something, in the twinkling of an eye" (176).

In being so extraordinarily demanding of Tom, Porgy is unreasonable in his demands and shows none of the "kind and courteous" behavior that Frank Meriwether manages with his slaves. Further, there is always an implied warning in these "good-humored" exchanges between Simms's masters and slaves. William Sinclair threatens to whip 'Bram more, and Porgy tells Tom that another master would have him "roasted alive" for similar behavior. Intimidation, thinly disguised, is implicit in each exchange in which the master asserts his power by playing on the slave's fears of being mistreated. The very tone of the language reinforces the qualities of dominance and submission in the master-slave relationship, and daily encounters of this kind serve as constant reminders to the reader (and of course to the slave) of the slave's servile status.[31]

Like Kennedy, Simms notes that the treatment a slave receives from his master is often carried over to his relationships with other slaves. Just as Carey imitates the mannerisms and repeats the opinions of his master when he deals with other plantation blacks, so Tom does the same with other servants, especially Pompey. Porgy has been portrayed as an indulged and demanding master who often expects the impossible, especially when his appetite is involved. Similarly, Tom treats Pompey, "a great favorite" and "an expert violinist," with exasperation if not contempt. The following scene between them appears as a humorous interlude in the action. Again, the subject is supper:

> "Why you no spread de table-clot', Pomp?" was the snappish demand of Tom, seeing the other hesitate.
> "I no see no clot', uncle Tom," replied the bewildered fiddler.
> "Enty blanket is clot', you son ob a skunk! Is you lib so long in de worl' dat you neber l'arn wha' one t'ing is, and wha'nodder t'ing is— wha' is wood, and wha' is clot'! I reckon, boy, when we calls you to eat you' own supper, you wunt ax ef it's dut [dirt] you mus' eat, or hom'ny."
> (179)

Pompey is humbled by this rebuke, and goes and gets one of the blankets their neighbor, Mrs. Eveleigh, has sent over to them. But he is puzzled, unable to understand this sort of improvisation on the looted plantation. He is the classic "stupid nigger," standing there staring vacantly at the empty room. Again Tom is angry at him:

> "Well," quoth our major domo, "wha' you 'tan' [stand] for, sucking in de whole room wid your eyes?"
> "I no see any table, uncle Tom!"
> "Don't you uncle me, you chucklehead! Lay de table on de floor! Who could b'lieb dat a pusson could lib so long and grow so big, and nebber l'arn nuttin! Ha! boy, you bin in de army, you'd ha' l'arn all sort of t'ing at de sharp p'int ob de baggnet! De army's de place for mek' man ob sense out ob fool. Ax de gempleman's to git out ob de way, so you kin spread de table-clot'; dough genplemans ought to hab sense 'nough, hese'f for moob [move] widout axing!" (179)

Porgy is amused by this exchange, realizing that Tom is as much imitating him as asserting himself. Indeed, these exchanges raise the whole question of the planter perception of the black personality under slavery. Even when Tom is intelligent and assertive and not fawning like Pompey, he is thought to be imitating his master, just as the intellectual woman is perceived as "masculine." Any deviation from gender and racial convention threatens planter hegemony. Such then, is the master's view of the slave. Simms was a planter, it should be remembered, as well as one of the most vociferous defenders of both slavery and the African American's basic inferiority.[32]

However, he was also a skillful storyteller, with a sharp ear for dialect, and it is easy to believe that he is accurately describing slave dialogue and a particular slave personality. Two things are important to note: blacks *were* different when they were with their masters; that is, they had dual personalities; and house servants may have emerged from slavery with fundamentally different experiences and attitudes than field slaves.

Porgy is deeply in debt and must mortgage his whole plantation to raise sufficient capital to continue. Hence, his slaves, being property, would be mortgaged with the rest of the estate. In this context, the question of Tom's fate arises. Earlier Porgy has confessed to Lance, "I love Tom. Tom is virtually a free man. It is true, being a debtor, I can not confer freedom upon him. But let the sheriff touch him, and I'll put a bullet through his diaphragm." Then like a jealous lover he exclaims that he will shoot Tom "in order to save him" (113). Later, Porgy raises the subject with Tom. Porgy declares: "I will neither give you nor sell you, nor suffer you to be taken from me in any way, by Saint Shadrach! who was your blessed father in the flesh, and from whom you inherit your particular genius for the kitchen! Nothing but death shall ever part us, and even death shall not if I can help it. When I die, you shall be buried with me. We have fought and fed too long together, Tom, and I trust we love each other quite too well, to submit to separation" (183).

Tom concurs in these sentiments. Porgy then launches into a diatribe against the creditor class and their lackies, including the sheriff who might carry Tom off, and proposes a novel solution: "Tom! sooner than have you taken off by these vermin, I will shoot you! . . . Yes, Tom! You shall never leave me. I will put a brace of bullets through your abdomen, Tom, sooner than lose you" (184). The thought next occurs to Porgy that Tom might be stolen and that prospect prompts another "solution": "If they should do so, Tom, I rely upon you to put *yourself* to death, sooner than abandon me and become a slave of another!" (184). Tom is equally unenthusiastic about these solutions, yet Porgy continues: "I thought you were more of a man—that you had more affection for me. Is it possible that you could wish to live, if separated from me? Impossible, Tom! I will never believe it. No, boy, you shall never leave me. We shall never part. You should be my cook, after death, in future worlds, even as you are here. Should you suffer yourself to survive me, Tom—should you be so hard-hearted—I will haunt you at mealtime always" (185).

The last two sentences are indication enough, that Porgy is putting Tom on in this exchange, and that Simms is putting us on as readers. In the proslavery defense, emphasis is always on the bonds of affection between master and slave. Simms does as much. Unlike the marital relationship to which Simms alludes, the master and slave are not bound until death, and can live without each other. Simms may humorously exaggerate the degree of loyalty between them, but he also carefully defines the true bounds of the relationship.

The final scene in the novel finds Porgy reigning supreme over his household of slaves and war buddies. While Millhouse is still in favor of his marrying, Tom thinks, "Maussa better widout 'em [women] and they would never be happy in a house 'whar woman's is de maussa'" (518). Porgy dramatically announces he is "determined to live a bachelor for your sakes. I sacrifice my happiness for your own. I renounce temptations of the flesh . . . dear comrades, there shall be no mistress, while I live, at Glen-Eberley" (518). This form of humor—the imagining of the perfect world of male buddies without women—is an American staple. In fact, Leslie A. Fiedler would argue seriously it is *the* American love story. Fiedler observes interracial male buddies in American classical literature of the nineteenth century: Cooper's Natty and Chinachgook, Melville's Ishmael and Queequeg, Mark Twain's Huck and Jim. He notes that the "Sacred Marriage" represents repressed homoerotic impulses and a longing for innocent love without sexual passion among men living in nature away from the (patriarchal) responsibilities of civilization.[33] Has Simms created male "buddies" in Porgy and Tom, Southern style?

Although it is a tempting reading, one should avoid it. Fiedler, writing three decades before gay liberation, assumes that all male bonding is latently homoerotic and that those who would deny it are being squeamish and naive ("homophobic," we'd say now). But homosocial bonding is not necessarily repressed sexuality and it certainly did not have that meaning for nineteenth-century men and women (though it did have that meaning in the homophobic 1950s).[34] Although Fiedler bypasses an in-depth discussion of miscegenation fears, he notes that interracial marriage is the most logical choice for solving racial conflict and binding the nation. Because American authors find that solution psychologically and socially impossible, they come up with interracial male buddies, not lovers.

In the case of Porgy and Simms, one reacts to Tom's deference and domesticity as "feminine." However, even though he is a cook, Tom is no plantation mistress. Southern planters sought to emasculate the male slave by stripping him of his patriarchal rights and responsibilities, but the slave is not to be confused with either the mistress or a homosexual. Porgy renounces "temptations of the flesh," clearly making that heterosexual equation of women with sex, and camaraderie and freedom with male buddies. The humor of this tale derives from Simms's reversals of those conventions that he spent a lifetime establishing. As his essay "The Morals of Slavery" demonstrates, Simms in the 1850s was anxious about certain aspects of plantation life: planter profligacy, unscientific farming methods, overindulgence of slaves, slave violence and licentiousness. The humor of this tale derives from Simms's reversals of planter power and female and slave submission. Paradoxically, however, Simms undermines the planter's case for female, black, and yeoman deference to planter government in portraying Porgy's (and most planters') dependence on these "inferiors" in providing plantation wealth.

Like Simms, Nathaniel Beverley Tucker defended slavery and shared his vision of the master-slave relationship. In Tucker's futuristic novel *The Partisan Leader,* Bernard Trevor's family is in danger because of Trevor's secessionist political activities. President Martin Van Buren has dispatched troops to the Trevor plantation in an effort to prevent Trevor from escaping. Since the Trevor family is under siege, the plantation blacks are armed to protect them.[35] The problem becomes how to overcome the federal guard, which has surrounded the plantation, to allow the Trevors to escape. They do it through the game of "puttin' on de ol' massa."

Bernard Trevor's "faithful servant," Jack, is praised as "the man I would wish to have beside me in the hour of danger." He approaches the federal troops in the interest of diverting them, singing, apparently oblivious to their presence. The sentry stops him and then tells him to advance. Seeing the rifles, Jack falls prostrate before the guards, and begs for mercy (216). Believing they have subdued him, the soldiers ask him what is happening in the Big House. Jack tells them that dinner is being served, which prompts discontent since they haven't as yet eaten, and they demand food and whiskey. Still somewhat suspicious, they ask him whether he loves his master. Jack answers: "Who?—I, Massa? My name Jack, sir. Lord, no sir! What I love him for? Hard work and little bread, and no meat? No, Massa; I love soldier, cause I hear 'em say soldier come after a while, set poor nigur free" (219). Jack returns with food and brandy. They eat and drink, ignoring Jack. Suddenly their torches are extinguished. The slaves led by Jack have surrounded them and have taken their weapons. The Northern soldiers are now prisoners.

Nathaniel Beverley Tucker clearly and didactically conveys the planter vision of slavery and his understanding of the nature of his mastery. The protagonist of his novel *George Balcombe* is a middle-aged planter removed from Virginia to Missouri. Discussing blacks and slavery with his young traveling companion, William Napier, he makes a case for slavery as a hereditary institution that has bound the black and white families for generations. In one of the clearest statements in this literature, Tucker, speaking through his character Balcombe, lays out the psychological foundation of paternalism: "But, right or wrong, they feel themselves inferior in point of fact, and there is nothing to prevent the formation of that strong tie which is spun out of the interchange of service and protection. . . . So long as the inferiority is actual, and felt to be so, none but affectionate and loyal feelings grow out of it. Whether the negro *race* is inferior to the white is not the question. The inferiority of the individual is the thing, and this inferiority, left to himself, he will never question" (164 and 165). The bargain the master struck between master and slave had a material basis: the slave's labor was exchanged for decent treatment, food, clothing, shelter, and minimal health care. At least such is the theory.

In reality, court records, slave narratives, traveler reports, Southern biographies and diaries indicate that neither party to the "contract" honored it. Masters mistreated their slaves; slaves stole from and lied to their masters. The problem lies in the conceptualization of this economic and social arrangement as a "deal" or as a "contract." Slaves never gave their consent to their condition. They were captives held on plantations by the organized force of the society: the planter, the county, the state, and the federal government. Force underlay every exchange between master and slave, as any investigation of the restraining and "disciplinary" plantation hardware will reveal. That the planter envisioned himself as a benevolent patriarch should not suggest that he was or that that was how his slaves viewed him. Rather, the benevolent patriarchal planter was a creation of the proslavery defense of slavery, and was replicated in antebellum Southern literature. The portrait of Tucker's Jack and the Balcombe–Napier conversation indicate that Tucker, a member of the planter class, like Simms, knew exactly what the game of "puttin' on ole massa'" was. Planters were aware of the game their slaves were playing and colluded with them in it.

The fictional images of antebellum blacks for the most part stay monotonously the same. Although George Tucker and James Ewell Heath offered a critique of slavery and a positive view of the black slave character, after 1831–32 writers such as Caruthers, Kennedy, N. B. Tucker, and Simms sought to justify slavery as an institution by arguing that blacks were a barbaric and inferior people who were in need of white civilization and were thus well served by the institution of slavery. Further, they portrayed the patriarchal master as a kind, generous, and benevolent patriarch who balanced his concern with making a crop and turning a profit with a genuine regard for the welfare of "his people." Most important, especially in the historical romance, the fictional master was not only family head and the leader of his black workforce, but he figured among the "natural" leaders of Southern society. Through his experience in gender and racial governance on the plantation, the master allegedly learned the civic lessons of self-assurance, graciousness, moderation, temperance, compassion, patience, and self-control that antebellum Southerners prized as the values and attributes of their statesmen. What was left out of these fictional accounts of slavery are the true accounts of black life under slavery.

At the same time this antebellum Southern literature was being produced, abolitionist blacks—Frederick Douglass, William Wells Brown, and Martin Delaney—produced a counterhegemonic literature that celebrated heroic and rebellious African American men and women who thwarted their masters and slavery either by "stealing themselves" (that is, running away) or by inciting rebellion. All of them start their indictment of slavery with planter crimes against women. The denial to blacks of the rights and privileges of citizenship, after they had fought valiantly in the American Revolution; the lack of adequate food, clothing, shelter, and medical care; the forced labor at menial agricultural tasks under the threat of the whip were not the ultimate cruelties of slavery. The unforgivable cruelties (and they received no notice in antebellum literature) were the master class's sexual exploitation of black women and the forcible separation of black families. The other assaults on their humanity might have been rationalized or even excused but not these, regardless of the estimable qualities of a particular master.

Because of the sexual abuse of black women and the forcible separation of members of the black family, including the planter's own mulatto children, black people as a whole could never trust or accept the white planter and his family.[36] Their natural feelings of affection for a young child or a kind master or mistress, these accounts reveal, were always tempered by feelings of contempt and anger at the daily incivilities and humiliation they experienced in the Big House. As Eugene D. Genovese and legions of other historians have noted, not all planters sexually abused their female slaves; indeed, some relationships between masters and their female slaves were mutual seductions that led to lifelong relationships, but these are the exceptions. To find otherwise is to justify racist violence against the black community, as well as against black women. Finally, it should be clear to anyone who cares to examine black accounts of slavery, that white racism, rather than "undermining the slave's sense of worth as black people" and "reinforcing their dependence on white masters," relieved blacks of any tendency to love and trust their white captors, and instead enabled them to find in Christianity, in their own African American culture, and in their family and kinship networks the hope and strength to form a subculture of resistance.[37]

IV

REPRESENTATIONS OF
POOR WHITES

To WORK industriously and steadily, especially under directions from another man is, in the Southern tongue, to "work like a nigger"; and, from childhood, the one thing in their condition which has made life valuable to the mass of whites has been the niggers are yet their inferiors.
                    —Frederick Law Olmsted, *The Cotton Kingdom*

There is as yet no settled population. The country is uncleared, and thoroughly wild; settled by squatters chiefly without means, tastes, education, or sensibility; rude rough people; a people particularly fitted for the conquest of savages and savage lands, but utterly incapable of appreciating an art so exquisite and intellectual as that of the legitimate drama.
                    —William Gilmore Simms, *Border Beagles*

. . . a densely ignorant, morally degraded lawless being, despised alike by planter and slave. He lives in a dilapidated log cabin and ekes out a wretched existence by the half-hearted cultivation of a few corn rows, by hunting squirrels in the pine woods, and by fishing for catfish around the cypress stumps of sluggish streams. There is something wrong with him, something inferior, possibly in his blood.
                    —A. J. N. Hollander, "The Tradition of the Poor Whites"

12. The Problem of Class in Southern Society and Southern Literature

IN TRAVELERS' ACCOUNTS, fiction, and histories, there has been surprising agreement about the poor whites. Known under such contemptuous terms as "hillbillies," "peckerwoods," "dirt eaters," "clay eaters," "poor white trash," "po' buckra," "tackies," "piney woods folk," and "crackers," they have been pitied, scorned, hated, and condescended to by both their contemporaries and by later generations of historians who find their lives sad, amusing, and even disgusting.[1] From the publication of Augustus Baldwin Longstreet's *Georgia Scenes* (1835) and Johnson Jones Hooper's *Adventures of Captain Simon Suggs* (1845) to William Faulkner's development of the Snopes family and Erskine Caldwell's *Tobacco Road,* the poor white has been equally a subject of ribald humor and outright contempt.[2]

No one really agrees about the origins of the poor-white class although it constituted some 15 to 20 percent of the non-slaveholding white population in the antebellum period.[3] Some writers have suggested that poor whites were the descendants of the colonial indentured servants.[4] Others have suggested they were just part of any unfit, lazy, and degenerate population.[5] A few have suggested that they were only a figment of anti-Southern abolitionist and neo-abolitionist fantasy.[6]

The most convincing explanation, however, comes from contemporary social historians who have studied the socioeconomic development of individual states. Their conclusions are similar to those of James G. Bonner, who found that in Hancock County, Georgia, in the 1850s, large planters with surplus capital started buying up the mortgages of small farmers and forced squatters and tenants off their land in order to plant cotton there. This process began when "the more affluent planters were buying up the land of small farmers, acquiring more slaves and closing up the avenues by which landless farmers might acquire small landholdings. Many small farmers, thus thwarted in their efforts to become planters, or even landowners, were moving to new counties in the northern and western parts of the state, or to the southwest."[7] These small farmers had a limited range of choices: they could remain in their home counties living on the fringes of plantation society as low-paid landless agricultural workers; become semiskilled workers or wageworkers in the relatively few Southern factories; head for the least desirable land in the sand hills and pine barrens; or move their families to the frontier where, repeating a familiar Southern pattern, they were forced into guerrilla warfare with Native Americans. Similarly, in a more recent study, Steven Hahn notes that slavery provided an advantage to the yeoman in allowing him to be left alone by the planter class as an "independent, non-market oriented freeholder," who formed his own kinship networks and country culture.[8]

Poor whites, then, should not be confused with mountain whites, who had their own history and pattern of settlement, traditions, and culture. Nor were they yeoman farmers, who owned few or no slaves and/or hired those hands needed for planting and harvest, and who aspired to planter status and values. Rather, poor whites were tenant farmers or squatters who lived on the back acres of plantation estates; or they were non-slaveholding small farmers who lived on the sandy ridges of plantation districts, in the pine barrens, on the sand hills of the fall lines, or on the fringes of the frontier. They were nonplantation whites—self-sufficient farmers and traders—who supplemented their diets of cornmeal and corn products by hunting, fishing, and raising livestock; and they traded the surplus of what they caught or grew for staples and tools. The very poorest of them barely had enough to subsist on, much less to trade.

The nineteenth-century position in regard to poor whites swung between two extremes: (1) that they suffered from poverty and malnutrition because they were lazy and would not work, especially at tasks they considered "nigger work" or (2) that despite their industriousness, they had been pushed off the best land owing to planter greed. In any case, they crowded into one- or possibly two-room wood cabins with dirt floors and little furniture. Although everyone worked in the fields, like most agricultural people they reflected a sharp division between men's work—hunting, fishing, field work, trading, fighting—and women's work, which was child care and domestic tasks. Worn down by years of poverty, pregnancy, and childbirth, by all accounts women grew old before their time. And for these women, the tyranny of gender was as great as the tyranny of class. Their husbands were perceived by the outside world as well as by themselves as their superiors. Significantly, these poor whites lived in their own isolated communities. They had no schools, churches, libraries, townhalls, or stores. If they were sick, a family member, usually a woman or a neighbor who knew something about herbal remedies, would attend them. It does seem that they were always seriously ill with rickets, hookworm, and malaria, all of which went untreated. They couldn't write, or even read the Bible if they had one, and they got their fundamentalist religion from lay preachers who visited them, or they went to Baptist and Methodist camp meetings. In spite of their ignorance and poverty, they were a proud people with a sense of racial superiority.

Planters knew they resented their despised and impoverished lower-class condition, but trusted that their acceptance of the principle of white supremacy motivated them to accept slavery (and thus planter power) as an institution for the exploitation and control of African Americans. In comparison to blacks, poor whites, mountain whites, and upwardly mobile yeoman farmers—the so-called plain folk of the South—considered themselves "freemen" since they regulated their day pretty much as nature and necessity demanded. Unlike slaves or women, they did not have "superiors" watching over their work and regulating their leisure activities. In what appears to be a persistent Southern interpretation of "individualism," the nonplantation white insisted upon regulating his life as he saw fit, with no planter interference. It was this pre-industrial capitalist sense of "freedom," combined with the institution of slavery that enhanced this sense of their racial superiority, for which they fought during the Civil War.[9]

James L. Roark notes, "thinking in terms of classes came naturally to planters."[10] Planters thought of themselves in patriarchal terms as the guardians of inferior black and white men and at the same time as the guardians of "civilization" against the immorality and criminality of those classes. Since they had greater daily control over blacks, it was easier for planters to use paternalistic ideology in rationalizing their system of exploitation. Poor whites lived away from the plantation and were not under the planters' direct control; thus they appeared to be a constant threat. Planters were deeply troubled by the egalitarian thrust of bourgeois democratic ideology and the concomitant move to grant Northern wageworkers equal political rights. Egalitarianism in any form represented to them "an erosion of traditional restraints and a rejection of traditional authority," all of which, they thought, undermined the steady progress of Western civilization—*their* civilization—and hence their power.[11] Southern reaction to both the Denmark Vesey conspiracy (1822) and the Nat Turner rebellion (1831) would indicate that below the surface of planter rhetoric and manners, planters recognized the facts of daily black oppression, and feared the possibility of black revenge. For the "literary South," however, the social order was not threatened by rebellious African American slaves, but by degenerate poor whites. What is initially surprising about these Southern novels, then, written as they were in the egalitarian "Age of Jackson," is the unabashed class hatred expressed toward poor whites. Whether the setting was in the colonial, Revolutionary, or antebellum period, the gravest threat to peaceful social relations derived from the criminal acts of an allegedly lazy, illiterate, and poverty-stricken lower class against the master class.

This characterization of poor whites makes sense only if one remembers that the plantation novels were written to defend and glorify the planter class and the institution of slavery that was the economic and social base of its power. In the literary South, the plantation is the central location for social activity. Antebellum Southern writers created a fictional region where the plantation, under the control of the patriarch-master, was the site of "Southern civilization." They sought to create the impression that the plantation's black and white families lived harmoniously, accepting both white supremacy and planter rule. The plantation is considered "safe space," in contrast to the threat from outsiders, whether British, Native Americans, Yankees, or poor whites. When members of plantation society (especially women) left the security of the plantation compound, they were depicted as being in the most danger from poor whites. The degraded poor whites thus provided a convenient counterpoint for the mannered and attractive upper-class plantation family.

Whether one is reading a Caruthers novel set in the seventeenth century or a Simms novel set in the nineteenth century, women and blacks are portrayed as the loyal and passive dependents of white male planters, while poor whites are portrayed as vicious criminals who menace them and the social order. Even more remarkable, given the historical period in which they were written, the yeoman farmer—the pioneer who becomes a national hero in these years—is depicted as superior to the poor white but completely inferior to the planter. In the Revolutionary War romances, he is the faithful "scout" for the planter hero, and in peacetime he becomes a "neighborly" (that is, deferential) small farmer or an overseer. However, unlike characters in the Northern novels of the period, the yeoman farmer manifests ignorance and lack of "breeding" that prevent him from achieving true heroism. Often men of this class fall into crime with the poor white when they lose control of their passions. When a fictional crisis occurred, the common man is unable to command the respect of his fellows that would enable him to lead and govern them with the same "natural" ease possessed by the planter and his son. Unlike the poor white, the yeoman is depicted as brave, resourceful, religious, and industrious. He has a kind of commonsense intelligence that came from living a conservative and virtuous life. Such qualities help the fictional yeoman to realize that superior planter-class males should lead in war and govern in peace.

Not only did this Southern literature denigrate the poor-white class, but it denied the fundamental assumption of liberal thought, which held out the promise of social mobility and political democracy. While the popular Northern literature of this period celebrated the honest yeoman farmer as the heroic conqueror of Native Americans and the humble and virtuous defender of his nation in the American Revolution; while writers like Melville and Hawthorne were exploring the nature of human nature and human evil regardless of class; while the Northern middle class was beginning to form and attain economic and political power; while social mobility was increasingly perceived as an American ideal, Southern literature continued to celebrate the elitist values of an earlier generation that assumed the best government was founded on the superiority of a landed ruling class. The defense of slavery, then, became not only an assertion of white supremacy but of class domination as well.[12]

Since the class attitudes of these authors are deeply embedded in the novels, it is important to understand the three standard ways class conflict plays itself out in this literature. First, the authors portray conflict within the planter class. Typically the hero and the heroine come from different strata within the planter class and one father or another objects to their union for reasons of class. Love eventually triumphs over these kinds of class considerations.[13] In the Revolutionary novels, the novelists equate that new egalitarianism—defined by them as the erosion of class prejudice between old planter families and "new" planter families—as one of the positive effects of the Revolution. Simms's depiction of the upper-class schism is perhaps the most vivid in his novel sequence *The Forayers* and *Eutaw,* where he most clearly connects these changing mores to the new republic. Second, class conflict is portrayed as an overt clash between law-abiding planters and poor-white criminals. Third, class is embodied in the virtuous and deferential yeoman farmer who is denied social mobility and political leadership. Although blacks make up another strata of the laboring class, both their communities and their field labor are ignored in this literature, and they are subsumed into the planter household; consequently, they are not treated as a separate class. Unlike planters or criminal poor whites, fictional blacks do not display class consciousness; that is, though they are a class in themselves, they are not depicted as a class for themselves.

Marriage in a patriarchal and aristocratic society is a family and social affair and not simply a compact between individuals. Families are paired with each other to preserve wealth and power. The problem for Simms and the men of his generation, as for the generations before them, was to interpret the democratic thrust of the American Revolution in their political and personal lives. Did the fact of the Revolution mean that the class was open to any man who could own slaves or get himself elected, or would substantial men of merit and "breeding" continue to govern?

In *The Forayers* and *Eutaw,* the hero, William Sinclair, is pitted not only against the British but against his father, who represents the "old way." The discussion among the Sinclair family members over class issues is representative of the generational struggle and of the nature of the debate over democracy that Southerners conducted after the 1780s. In their talk about Bertha Travis, William and his sister Carrie argue about class and the nature of democratic society. William claims that in seeking Bertha Travis, he would marry her as an individual and was not marrying her family. He recognizes that one way to ensure excellence in society is to continue the governance by the "very best people," who are "most often found in the upper classes."[14] But "class" is not something that can be purchased with money as Bertha Travis's father has tried to do. William Sinclair, speaking for Simms, declares that "caste and class properly pride themselves upon the habitual refinements of mind and moral, acquired in long periods of time. This constitutes their just claim to authority; and they rightly hold themselves aloof from association with other classes, who do not know, and do not properly value these refinements" (*The Forayers,* 86). However, William, cast in the role of the "democrat" by Simms, argues from his class position that there exists "a natural nobility in individuals, which overrides the law and demands recognition. There are persons to whom refinement is *native*—who are *born* nobles—delicate and just in sentiment, magnanimous in soul, generous in courage, endowed with noble talents, and devoted in noble purposes. It is the duty of an aristocracy to acknowledge all such persons, as soon as found, and take them lovingly into their embrace, and seek to do them honor; and here is a twofold wisdom in doing so, since we thus add to our own resources of society, and increase our influence upon manhood at large" (86 and 87). He concludes by affirming his faith in the "claims of social caste" and by arguing that Bertha Travis is worthy of membership in such a class (87).

Simms here is speaking for himself as well as for a more generous planter view of class. Born the son of an impoverished but not penniless Charleston merchant who immigrated to the Mississippi frontier when his wife died and his business collapsed, Simms, however talented, was on the periphery of South Carolinian planter social circles until he married into the planter class. Democracy for Simms, then, was part of that social fluidity that allowed men and women of merit to move into the planter class, but that did not challenge the base of planter economic or political power.[15] In spite of Simms's assertions, the only mobility that occurred in his novels (or any of the others) was between strata of the planter class and not between the classes themselves.

Class conflict occurred when a "new man" believed himself worthy of the planter's daughter. Again, in Simms's *The Forayers* and *Eutaw,* this class plot forms the tension in the romantic plot and intersects with the military-political plot. The British ally "naturally" with the very richest aristocratic planters of Virginia and South Carolina. They are called "Loyalists" by Simms (and Kennedy) to distinguish them from the "Tories," or the aspiring yeoman farmers, overseers, and poor whites who join with the British more from self-interest and immediate personal gain, it was alleged, than from political principle. In *The Forayers* and *Eutaw,* the villain is Richard Inglehardt, the son of the Travis family's overseer who is a British officer in charge of contraband. Inglehardt "was a new man; an ambitious man, anxious to shake off old and inferior associations, anxious to bring himself into constant communication with persons of whose social rank there could be no question. . . . [He] had abandoned his caste, an unforgiveable offense."[16] Inglehardt lusts after the plantation belle, Bertha Travis, more for her wealth and social status than because of any deep feeling he has about her. Simms goes to great lengths to describe Inglehardt. Beneath a pleasant exterior, he was "savage, selfish, of a bloody reckless mold," at once "shrewd, quick, keen and thoughtful, but imperfectly educated" (292). Furthermore, Inglehardt was a "common sense man" whose cunning allowed him to succeed in "small operations among small people," but who lacked "enthusiasm," "generous self-sacrifice," "ardent adventure," and "eager impetuous zeal" (294). The admirable masculine qualities are realized in the hero, William Sinclair, who rescues Bertha Travis and her brother from Inglehardt and his men, after Inglehardt abducts them when Bertha refuses his advances. Inglehardt's great mistake, Simms tells the reader, was his belief that he could overcome "the almost immeasurable space which, in a society like South Carolina, separates the overseer's family from that of his employer" (295).[17]

These authors must reconcile a seeming contradiction in creating popular patriotic leaders out of this alleged "superior" planter class, in making a "natural aristocrat" into a revolutionary. One way they solve this problem is to create a "generation gap." That is, planters' families were divided by generations on the issue of the Revolution, with Loyalist fathers opposing patriot sons. Their standard romantic plot meshed with both the military plot and class imperatives. In the narrative, a planter's son is a patriot hero who wants to marry another planter's daughter. They cannot marry because the war interferes or because their families have conflicting loyalties. To further complicate the plot—especially in Simms's work—a British officer wants to marry the heroine but she will not have him. Driven to desperation, the officer plans to abduct her and/or kill the hero. Usually, he enlists poor whites in his cause. The latter thus emerge as unprincipled mercenaries willing to sell out their country and commit any atrocity for money. Poor whites are depicted as living on the edge of respectable society, as shiftless woodsmen and hunters. In war, their antisocial impulses and vicious class hatreds lead them to serve the British or to roam the countryside in criminal gangs that loot, rape, and rob. For Simms their reckless passions, more than poverty or Southern social injustice, are the cause of their criminal behavior.

The narrative and characters present the planter worldview. His son and daughter are hero and heroine; his slaves are faithful family retainers who live in harmony with whites on the plantation. Relative to their actual social positions on the plantation, blacks are generally minor characters who scarcely figure in the plot. In contrast, poor-white males are vital to the storyline since their behavior provides a dramatic foil to that of the planter family. Specifically, their criminal behavior contrasts with the planter's self-discipline; and it offers up a villain whom the planter hero can defeat, thereby saving the heroine and proving himself as a man. In so doing the planter legitimizes his own class power and his masculinity.

The conflict between these two classes of white men, as well as between British and American soldiers, confirms the patriarchal "cult of masculinity" that serves as the mythical base of this literature. These authors depict Southern planters who have demonstrated their virility and "toughness" by conquering Native Americans and black men, defeating the British, and subduing a reckless and immoral poor-white class, and thus "winning" the pure heroine. Physical skill, courage, and honor are the values of this conservative literature. As ever, the purpose of these portraits is to demonstrate how the planter-class male is superior to all other men and why he alone is capable of bringing order to the chaos of Southern society.

13. Representations of Poor Whites

THE ACTUAL IMAGE of the poor white is drawn through a variety of comparisons and contrasts between allegedly inferior male members of the poor-white class and superior male members of the planter class. As in all patriarchal literature, men represent their class and/or race, and women are attached to them as their social inferiors, even though as mothers they may exhibit socially redeeming qualities.[1] In contrast, the men of the lower classes are represented as being loathsome and vicious not because they are economically stifled in Southern society, but because they are intemperate and lack self-discipline, which leads them to give in to their allegedly vicious passions.

The poor white is contrasted both to the planter and to the poor, virtuous, and disciplined yeomen farmer, who "knows his place" in Southern society and serves as a patriot soldier in war and as a solid citizen in peace. In comparison, then, poor whites are life's losers. They have capitulated to vice, corruption, and licentiousness early in life and have fallen into a criminal web from which there is no escape. Possessing an exaggerated sense of their talents and worth, they are allegedly jealous of the natural aristocratic leaders of the society and are inspired by the demagoguery of planter enemies who convince them that they are the social and political equals of the men of the planter class. In portraying the poor-white man in this manner and in giving the yeoman farmer a limited role in the leadership of plantation society, this literature mirrors the antebellum planter's conservative worldview by rejecting the ideals of liberalism and the social goals of the bourgeois democratic North.

Throughout this literature, the poor-white male is described as a "dark and swarthy" ruffian who lives in a dilapidated hovel without furniture, curtains, or a neat garden plot, thereby reflecting his lack of industriousness and a lack of self-esteem. A coarse and brutal man, he abuses his wife and children and is unable to make lasting bonds based on respect even with his criminal comrades. In both war and peace, in both the Old South and the new Southwest, he is a constant threat to the "plantation family," including black slaves whom he detests and who detest him. Like the black slave and the planter's daughter, the poor white is contrasted to the planter's son—the hero, who is everything he is not. In their depiction of agrarian-class conflict, these conservative Southern writers explain why Northern democracy will not work for the masses of men, and why Northern "utopian schemes" based on the equality of community members are doomed to fail. For them a just society is one that recognizes the "natural" inequalities among people and that structures orderly democratic government between equals; that is, between the natural aristocrats of the planter class.[2]

This Southern portrait of the dissolute poor white is in marked contrast to Northern and Northwestern literature, which allows the poor white to find salvation if not heroism as the frontier woodsman and pioneer. But the Southern poor white is by definition not a slaveholder; hence he is socially and politically suspect. Kennedy and Simms of these Southern authors are most insistent on the assessment of the poor white as criminal and as threat to planter hegemony. Kennedy developed the type in his revolutionary romance *Horse-Shoe Robinson* and his domestic novel *Swallow Barn,* and Simms depicted the type in his Revolutionary romances *The Forayers, Eutaw,* and *Woodcraft,* and in his border romance, *Richard Hurdis.*

Kennedy's Wat Adair (*Horse-Shoe Robinson*) offers the typical description of a poor white in this literature:

> A thin, dark, weather-beaten countenance, animated by a bright restless eye, expressed courage rather than hardihood, and seemed habitually to alternate between the manifestations of waggish vivacity and distrust. The person of this individual might be said, from its want of symmetry and from a certain slovenly and ungraceful stoop in the head and shoulders, to have been protracted rather than tall. It better deserved the description of sinewy than muscular, and communicated the idea of toughness in a greater degree than strength.[3]

Dressed in a "coarse and short hunting shirt of dingy green, trimmed with a profusion of fringe," Adair wore a black leather belt that supported a hunting knife and wallet. His rifle stood in a nearby corner of the hovel that was his home. Adair is menacing and violent, intemperate and unpredictable (155).

Moreover, he is as brutal to his family as he is rude to his guests—patriot soldiers, Horse-Shoe Robinson, and Arthur Butler. In contrast, Butler is a gentleman, something obvious to Adair's niece, Mary Musgrove, who easily sees through his woodsman's disguise (155 and 161).[4] Adair treats his wife, Peggy, with disdain and contempt, and thinks of her more as a degraded servant than anything else. He never calls her by name, but refers to her either as "wife" or "woman." At one point he admonishes her, "Hold your tongue. . . . Boil your kettle, and give us none of your tinkling brass, the Bible calls it" (159). Thus asserting himself as the patriarch, Adair goes on to discuss the British and the war with his guests. Adair supports his family by supplying them with game and selling animal pelts at a profit. He is also in British pay as a mercenary.

In one of the most sickening passages in this literature, Adair skins a she-wolf alive while he jokes about her pain. In contrast to Butler, who is too sickened to watch, Horse-Shoe Robinson, the yeoman, stays behind and berates Adair for his cruelty (182–87).[5] Kennedy makes the point, then, that the poor white is not only crude and vulgar, but also without understanding or compassion. Living on the edge of civilization, he has become as wild and dangerous as the wilderness he would conquer. He knows no rules and abides by no laws. Walter Adair leads Robinson and Butler into a trap set by a British allied poor-white gang. Lacking political principles, he merely chooses the side that will pay him the most money (168).

Like Simms, Kennedy is fascinated by the poor-white gang: that is, bands of poor-white men who rob the planter aristocracy and serve as British mercenaries.[6] Adair's gang is led by Hugh Habershaw, "a bluff, red-visaged, corpulent man, with a face of gross, unmitigated sensuality." He had a "pale blood-shot eye," a "sinister glance," and a "wiry, almost white beard, a low forehead, a bold crown, and meagre reddish whiskers (193). He was the captain of a "band of ruffians" who make their living by stealing from local farmers and trading with the British. Their current assignment is to capture Butler and turn him over to the British (198). The gang includes such notables as Pimple, Longshanks, Black Jack, Red Mug (Shad Green), Planter Breech (Andy Clapper), Marrow Bone (Dick Waters), Five Nose, Screech Owl (Tom Dobbs), Clapper Claw (Roger Bell), Bow Legs, and Moonface Bugger (Gideon Blake). These aggressively humorous epithets identify them as brothers in crime. When they are not kidnapping, robbing, and killing, they play cards, drink, and fight among themselves. What Kennedy creates here is a group who in peacetime lack ambition and live in poverty on the margins of society, but profit by crime in the chaos of war. They are poor because they are immoral, not the other way around (see chaps. 16 and 17).

In Kennedy's *Swallow Barn* poor whites are not so vividly drawn as Wat Adair in *Horse-Shoe Robinson,* but they are nonetheless recognizable types. Jemmy Smith, "a mad-cap ragamuffin," made his appearance on Court Day "for disturbing the peace of a camp meeting by drinking whiskey and breeding a riot wither the confines of the conventicle." He appears as an "indescribably swaggering saucy blade" who presents a "wild, grinning disorderly countenance to his peers."[7] He is freed in a humorous way and appears as a comic character.

Similarly, Kennedy portrays Haffen Blok as a former Hessian soldier in the American Revolution who defected to the American side as soon as possible. And "being one of those mortals whose carelessness of accommodation is mathematically proportioned to their aversion to labor, Haffen was equally idle, and ragged, and contrived generally, by a shrewd and droll humor, to keep himself in good quarters" (255). A fiddler of some repute, he plays and tells stories at most social gatherings. He had been a tinker before the war, and did odd jobs and served as Bel Tracy's "minstrel." Haffen, then, "was universally regarded as a well-meaning, worthless, idle stroller, who, if he could not make himself useful, was at least in nobody's way" (256).

Finally, in Miles Rutherford, Kennedy creates the poor white as fallen yeoman. Rutherford had been liberally educated and had a promising career (in what it is not clear), but he never learned self-discipline, and considered virtue and self-control "a tax which only men of inferior parts pay for success" (361). This delusion, Kennedy explains, has led him to debauchery. As a consequence, Rutherford is penniless, but he is known for his "domineering temper, a boastful spirit, a supreme hatred of those in better circumstances than himself" (361). True to character, he picks a fight with the planter hero, Ned Hazard, by insulting Bel Tracy. Hazard soundly thrashes him, demonstrating again which of these two classes of men is the fitter and more "masculine."

Thus are poverty and crime seamlessly wedded in this ruling-class literature. The poor are undisciplined, immoral, and vicious; they choose to steal rather than work. In contrast, the planter emerges as industrious and self-disciplined with a well-developed sense of justice and the courage to defend what is right. According to the planter code of honor, it would have been permissible and expected for Hazard merely to horsewhip Rutherford for his impudent challenge. By consenting to fight, Hazard has put himself on an equal level with Rutherford. Although Kennedy is not an egalitarian, he rejects the chivalric pretensions of the antebellum South. However, he does support the role of superior men. They will prevail regardless of the code of conduct that governs their lives.[8]

William Gilmore Simms has offered at once the most complete and the most stereotypical range of "lowlife" characters. Although heralded in its time, his "realism" was that of an upper class that sought to indulge its prejudices and class hatred in images of a semicivilized barbaric black race with "uncivilized impulses" and a profligate poor-white class. Simms's work reflects the enormous class differences between plantation and nonplantation whites, especially in the Eastern states. Moreover, he conveys the planter rationale for those differences.

Two of Simms's revolutionary romances, *The Forayers* and *Eutaw,* offer a class picture of the South's social and political forces during the American Revolution. The romantic plot, the Revolutionary plot, and the class plot complement each other as Simms describes a region convulsed by both revolutionary and civil war. The action of the novel centers around the fate of members of two planter families, the Travises and the Sinclairs. The plot of these sequential novels is as convoluted as one can imagine, with a series of twists and turns that mesh the actions of the principal characters. Because the antebellum Southern hero and heroine cannot act as "individuals" in the bourgeois sense, by working out their fate alone, but are the creatures of their family and class, members of both families figure significantly in the romantic and revolutionary plots.

Furthermore, generational differences over the Revolution are laced with class differences that parallel political divisions.[9] For Simms, "poor white" was synonymous with "criminal"; and in these two novels, the poor whites join the British and, under British protection, plunder the countryside. They hate the planter class, a feeling that was reciprocated. For example, in *The Forayers* and *Eutaw,* as we have seen, the gender theme and class theme are realized in the Sinclair–Travis–Inglehardt triangle.[10] In rescuing Bertha Travis from the control of Tory Captain Richard Inglehardt, William Sinclair establishes his virility and superiority.

Additionally, the intricate plot of both *The Forayers* and *Eutaw* serves at several points to illustrate the degraded condition of the poor-white class. For instance, the Jeff Rhodes gang, which captures Bertha and her mother, is unaffiliated with the British or Inglehardt, but is involved in various forms of criminal activities that depended for their success on the chaos of revolution. It is described as:

> Rude, irregular, untrained, and lawless, the swarthy outlaws grouped about the lowly cabin where we find them, were, at least, a fearless gang of blackguards. They could fight better than pray; could more easily strike than serve; their laws readily yielded to their moods; and, in this respect, they had very little advantage of their leader. [Rhodes] was recognized as a chief only because of his stalwart frame and superior audacity.[11]

> War then—the cause of the crown—was simply a pretext for these marauders. They were nothing less than plunderers under the sanction of the war. (11)

The gang plans to ransom Bertha and her mother to the British, and go on to other business. When the British come upon them, they kill the members of the gang, and they free the mother and her daughter and escort them to the Sinclair plantation where they are all temporarily safe. Note that in Simms's view, British officers as gentlemen can be expected to act honorably toward women. Women are safest when they are on the plantation even if it isn't their own home.

Pete Blodgit, introduced in *The Forayers,* and Joel Andrews (or "Hell-Fire Dick," as he is called) appear in both *The Forayers* and *Eutaw* and emerge as representative of Simms's poor-white criminals. Blodgit is a member of Hell-Fire Dick's gang, a band of robbers who victimize the patriot families who have sent their young men to war. They trade the "contraband," including stolen slaves, with the British. They are described as: "a haggard, wretched, scowling reckless set, the whole of them, branded with lust and murder, gaming, drinking, cheating, lying without even the rogue's virtue of keeping faith with one another" (184). In *The Forayers,* "dark" and "swarthy" Pete Blodgit lives with his despicable mother as a squatter on William Sinclair's land. In his depiction of Mary Blodgit, as we have seen, Simms makes his case for the inherited inferiority of the poor whites. Blodgit has been commissioned by William to sell the plantation grain to the British to support the Sinclair family and to supply the patriots with arms.

Blodgit and his mother have been pocketing some of the money, and she berates her short, lame son for being "unmanly" when he is unwilling to kill Sinclair when he discovers their theft. Sinclair is more masculine and virile; Blodgit is weak and deformed. Hence, Sinclair is "tougher" and more of a "man" in addition to being of a superior class. Sinclair notes the Blodgits' ingratitude: "And these are people for whom I have found shelter and protection—whom I have kept from starvation—whom I shall feed, and to whom I have given the very servant to whom they look for help and water!" (36). In the planter worldview, then, poor whites are so degraded they cannot make an honest living even when it is handed to them.

Joel Andrews, or "Hell-Fire Dick," was one of Simms's most memorable characters, recalled not only for his brutality, animal magnetism, and despicable character, but also for his remarkable Christian redemption. Simms introduces Dick as he bullies his functionary, Pete Blodgit:

> his visage, scarred and savage, fully justifying the title which he bore. His eyes were great and rolling, owl-like, in a broad but degraded forehead. The black hair came down over cheeks and neck, worn long to conceal some horrid scars. His lips had been split by stroke of sabre. His teeth projected, very white, like enormous spades. . . . He was a stout and swarthy giant—short, thick, with a bull-dog figure and figure-head, and a neck, as he himself was apt to boast, quite too short for a rope. (54)

He demonstrated an uncontrollable passion for drinking and gambling, robbery and murder. He loathed William Sinclair, the hero, because Sinclair was a gentleman. At one point when he is treated with contempt by Sinclair's father, he angrily exclaims:

> "You're one of them bloody, proud, heathen harrystocrats, that look upon a poor man, without edication, as no better than a sort of two-legged dog, that you kin lay the lash on whenever you see him lying in the doorway. And your son is just another sich a tyrant heathen! And you've had a long swing between you, living on the fat of the land, and riding roughshod over poor men's backs . . . and the good time for the poor man's come at last!—and, now, we've got a-top of the wheel! We've got the chance at the good things of this life; and we kin pay off old scores." (140 and 141)

In addition to description and narrative devices, Simms, as with his black characters, creates a poor-white dialect that conveys their intemperateness, their lack of education, and their hatred of the planter class. Poor whites are depicted as superior to blacks, however. Simms permits Dick to escape after being captured and imprisoned in the Sinclair mansion's cellar because of the stupidity and gullibility (but not the treachery) of a black female slave. More significant, Simms implicitly argues in this portrait for educating poor whites and thus possibly turning them from crime.

Interestingly, in one of the few depictions of religious experience in this literature, Simms decides to redeem Dick. Dick's redemption starts from his jealousy of Inglehardt, who is as evil as himself, but far richer. His wealth, Dick reasons, is owed to his education. Inglehardt's education alone has made the difference between them. As he explains to his confederates: "Now what makes the difference twixt us and all these rich people. How's it that whatever we does turns out nothing, and they seem to get at every turning in the road. We works more than they, and we has all the resks, and trouble, and danger; yet nothing comes from it, and by blazes, I'm jest as poor a critter this day, as the day I begun, and something poorer; and I'm now past forty" (*Eutaw*, 189). Because the rich have been educated, he concludes, they have a great advantage over the poor. Even though he observes "them harrystrocrats keep all the books to themselves," Dick decides to have the captured Henry Travis teach him to read. Henry Travis reads Bunyan's *Pilgrim's Progress* to him and both of them are converted by the Pilgrim (248).[12] In the end, therefore, this most vivid of poor-white villains is redeemed by a little "book l'arnin" and a little Christian kindness. It is Simms's message to his fellow planters; although Dick would never have been one of them, he is capable of moral regeneration.

Simms's portrait is most interesting, but atypical for a number of reasons. First, Dick is the only character who undergoes a religious conversion. Second, it articulates one of Simms's criticisms of the planter class; namely, that in their failure to support basic education, they contributed to many of their own problems and hamper the development of Southern letters.

In the concluding pages, Simms restores order to the lives of his protagonists and to Southern society. The Americans win their battle with the British at Nelson's Ferry. The new democracy and order is served when old Colonel Sinclair gives his blessing for William and Bertha to marry. Goodness has triumphed over evil with the deaths of the duplicitous Travis and the evil Inglehardt and his poor-white confederate, Hell-Fire Dick. The leadership of the post-Revolutionary South will pass to men like Colonel William Sinclair and his son, "the natural aristocrats" of the planter class.

In Samuel Bostwick, a squatter on Widow Eveleigh's land (*Woodcraft*, 1854), Simms introduces one of the most pathetic and despicable poor-white characters in this literature. Bostwick and his accomplices kidnap slaves from the plantations and sell them to the British, who in turn sell them in the West Indies at great profit. Bostwick's contact is a man named M'Kewn, an apparently respectable Scottish merchant who has gotten wealthy from the war. Bostwick is stereotypically dark and swarthy. His "slight form, sidelong gait, low, swarthy features, and long black hair which hung down heavily upon his cheeks and shoulders" suggest stealth and deceit.[13] Bostwick's family live in a hovel: "one of the meanest sort of long-houses, not more than sixteen by twenty feet—built of slender pine poles, which were already greatly decayed. . . . Much of the roofing had decayed and the openings were thatched with broom-grass and pure straw" (215). Everyone sleeps in the same room, and the only furniture is a pine bed, a table, and four chairs. The reader learns that Bostwick had been a simple farmer until he met up with Dick Jeffords who persuaded him to indulge his passions in drinking, gambling, and stealing (220). While Rachel Bostwick blames Jeffords for Bostwick's crimes, Simms finds Bostwick culpable for yielding to his passions.

Bostwick's visits home are moments of terror for his family. Rachel Bostwick serves as one of the ideal poor-white wives and mothers who is the moral representative of her class (see Chapter 8). She passively accepts her lot, raising her children without adequate food, clothing, and shelter and without complaint, and tries to dissuade her profligate husband from his criminal ways. For his part, Bostwick only thinks of his wife "as the creature from whom he might find service." He returns home if he needs food, dry clothes, or shelter (214). Dory, his sixteen-year-old daughter, is his one love. He is "cold and truculent" to all of the others, especially to his wife. But he sees in Dory "that higher phase of society to which he felt that he himself could never aspire, and to which, as is commonly the case with the class to which he belonged, he looked over with feelings of envy and desire" (217). However, he never shares his ill-gotten loot, being "too selfish and too wary for that" (221).

Bostwick, a man trapped by his passions and greed, has also lost his self-respect. Arguing with M'Kewn over money, Bostwick complains that his efforts have brought them wealth but he (M'Kewn) received an unfair percentage, considering the risks involved in kidnapping slaves from the plantations. He says to M'Kewn: "You've got rich by my labors. You and he . . . got all the niggers—more than two hundred, I reckon. If I had got for them niggers—all of my bringing—what they focht, or will fetch, to you—I'd ha' been as rich as any" (16). M'Kewn admits that Bostwick may have done the most dangerous labor, but reminds Bostwick that without M'Kewn's business connections and Moncrieff's cover of British respectability and access to ships, he "wouldn't have had the price of the hair of a negro for your pains" (16). White supremacy, Simms recognizes, binds the poor white to the merchant and planter class. In one scene after a fight with M'Kewn over money, Bostwick declares to his confederates: "Well, I'm about as poor a dog as ever gnaw'd a bone;': but, by Jiminy! I'm not so poor a dog as to let any man say whether I shill bark or not jest as it pleased him! . . . In some things, I knows I'm worse than a nigger, but bad as I am, I reckon I'll never let any man put his collar round my neck" (248). Bostwick, unlike the black slave, labors for no man and is owned by no man. As bad as he is, though wretched and despised by the planter class, he knows he is free.

Bostwick's attitude toward Mrs. Eveleigh, who has let his family live on her land and has given Rachel and Dory paid sewing to do, is one of unsuppressed anger. After Mrs. Eveleigh gave them a Bible, Rachel taught Dory how to read it. Bostwick stops Dory from reading; he demands to know why she was spending her money on such "trash." Dory replied the Bible was a present, and Bostwick angrily declared: "Well, she might hev' given you something to be more useful to you. She's rich; she might hev' given you some good clothes, I'm a-thinking, ef she'd ha' wanted to do a good thing for you. But these great rich folks are all as mean as h—ll!" (222). When Dory explains that Mrs. Eveleigh had given her nice clothes that serve as her Sunday best, Bostwick retorts that there was never Sunday for a poor man. Rejecting "good books and good women," he says they are fools for believing all of the religious lies which the rich teach them: "Blast all the gifts of your rich people. They only burn the heart out. What's good you kin get out of them, is what you kin take!" (224).

In contrast to her father, Dory is a model of lower-class purity, simplicity, and piety: "She was very fair. . . . She was tall, and, moving to and fro about the spinning wheel, she exhibited a natural grace such as a humble life like hers seldom displays. Her hair, a rich auburn, curled and floated free in long silken tresses" (216). Beautiful and innocent, she displays a "lively flashing of her eye, and the clear silvery flute-like accents of her voice" (475). Most important, she knows her place as a woman and as a member of the lower class.

One day Bostwick watches as young Arthur Eveleigh tries to help her carry a bucket of water to the cabin, insisting that as a man he is "the ablest (and) the strongest" (476). She declined, noting that he was a gentleman and such hard labor was "unworthy" of him. Bostwick, watching the scene, immediately seizes the class dimensions of their relationship: "She's beautiful and sweet enough to be the wife of any man. But 'tain't possible that sich a thing could happen. His mother would be agin it. When he grow'd a little older and more knowing, he'd be agin it. People would talk. He'd hear 'em speak of the Squatter Bostwick. He'd hear 'em tell of how she was the child of a poor man, that lived in a cabin; and who was, altogether, a most bad man, a rascal" (477). Bostwick also notes that if Arthur Eveleigh is up "to any mischief" he'll "put a knife in him" as quickly as he would "stick a pig" (477).[14] Bostwick hopes that by betraying M'Kewn to Mrs. Eveleigh and the law, he will be able to obtain enough money to purchase slaves and a small farm for Dory. He harbors the illusion, which Simms indicates is common among the poor, that property and slaves would make her socially acceptable to Arthur Eveleigh, his mother, and the members of the planter elite.

Thus have Bostwick and his family become vehicles for Simms's view of the contradictions of planter society: that a poor man can choose humble squalor or a life of crime; that wholly redeemable people like Dory Bostwick and her mother are born into the lower classes and are unable to work or marry their way out because of class prejudice; that even the most depraved father would not let his daughter be shamed by a planter's son. In the end, after Bostwick dies of a fever, Captain Porgy and Widow Eveleigh, in true paternalistic spirit, come to Rachel's help by giving her two black slaves and providing for her comfort. Her mobility now rests on the oppression of African Americans. Widow Eveleigh also takes Dory into her home to raise her "in a superior society, and with proper education," where "the natural talents and genius of the child" could bloom and develop until she matured into "a marvelous woman" (507).

In this Southern fairy tale, then, one is led to admire and accept the moral position of Rachel Bostwick who prays and passively accepts her oppression. Unlike her debauched and degraded husband, who hates the rich and makes war on them while coveting their wealth, she is grateful to them and teaches her children to be grateful for the little kindnesses bestowed upon them by the charitable impulses of the planter class. She eventually escapes the worst deprivations of poverty by accepting and profiting by the enslavement of a race allegedly inferior to hers. Charity masks the reality of class power as it protects and reinforces class relationships. The poor white is an ungrateful, atheistic, drunken criminal; the planter emerges as the benevolent stabilizing force of moral order. In this novel, then, Simms telegraphs the ways in which planter-class men relied on religion, racism, and paternalism to assure themselves of their own humanity and rectitude and to stifle the resistance of poor whites to their lack of opportunity and political rights.

In his border romances, Simms plays out these masculine conflicts in another setting. Set on the Southwestern frontier, these romances serve as precursors to the Western genre.[15] Like the poor whites in his Revolutionary tales, the frontier whites who first settle in unchartered territory are "rude, rough people . . . particularly fitted for the conquest of savages and savage lands" (*Border Beagles,* 159). Social order is brought to the frontier by members of the planter and yeoman class, the new Southwestern planters who will learn their new social role "over generations."

Simms argues that "the wandering habits of our people are the great obstacles to their perfect civilization." They become diseased by the license of the wilderness," which is far removed from the influence of civilization. Though he sees their work as critical for eventual Southern prosperity and thinks these poor yeoman whites are superior to the "savage" North Americans, he contends they are not the best representatives of American Civilization (*Border Beagles,* 159, 66).

As if to underscore that point, he populates his frontier with poor-white gangs that, like his colonial gangs, terrorize the law-abiding citizens in frontier communities. For instance, in his border novel *Richard Hurdis,* Clement Foster leads a criminal poor-white gang that terrorizes the people of newly settled Alabama. Simms likes Foster so well that he allows him to escape and reappear as Mississippi's archcriminal, "Edward Saxon," in *Border Beagles.* Like Kennedy's Hugh Habershaw (*Horse-Shoe Robinson*), Saxon is surrounded by a ruthless and bizarre set of social misfits.[16]

Richard Stillyards, Saxon's trusted confidante, is a dwarf. This "chunky little imp" is guarding naive Thomas Horsey, a youth who has been spirited to the outlaws hideout to set a trap for the hero, Harry Vernon. Simms relishes his description of Stillyards, noting his "arms were long like those of an ape; his ears of corresponding dimensions; his lips, pursed into a point like two bits of shrivelled coonskin, were covered with a thick furze [*sic*], not unlike that of the hair upon the same animal; and with a short, pug-like nose, and little, quick, staring gray eyes, that peeped out from under a shaggy white pent-house of hair" (*Border Beagles,* 303). This portrait is meant to be humorous, the dwarf as animal, drawn to emphasize the uncivilized nature of frontier society. In this particular scene, Horsey, the protypical "country bumpkin," doesn't even realize he has been captured by an outlaw gang. An enthusiastic backwoods actor, he thinks he has been brought to entertain a serious theater audience. Again, his self-centeredness coupled with his nonsensical rendering of Shakespeare to an audience that hasn't the faintest idea of what he is doing underscores Simms's contention that these unsophisticated frontier whites are so uncivilized they are "utterly incapable of appreciating an art so exquisite and intellectual as that of the legitimate drama" (*Richard Hurdis,* 159).

For his part, Stillyards is as much a grotesque comic character as he is a criminal. Noting that he "seemed almost entirely without flesh" and his "lower limbs were not merely short and deformed, but slender" while his shoulders were "broad and strong," Simms has him scare a horse as he emerges from the woods to beguile Horsey into following him. For Simms, then, anything goes on the frontier—semiliterate boys with theatrical pretensions; outlaw poor-white gangs who ravish innocent women and rob the law-abiding; deformed dwarfs who join the socially unfit in the woods; Negroes who are taught to read (*Border Beagles,* 303–8). The only corrective to such wildness is the emigration of members of the Eastern planter class who will bring order and civilization to the frontier chaos.

In *Border Beagles* that role is played by Harry Vernon; in *Richard Hurdis* a similar service is performed by Richard Hurdis and Colonel Grafton. As seen above, Harry Vernon and Richard Hurdis are two of Simms's classic young heroes. They defeat the outlaws and rescue the heroine.[17] In Colonel Grafton, a gentleman planter, Simms presents the best representative of an emerging Southwestern planter class. Grafton "wants for nothing that he has not, he is beloved by his family, and has acquired so happily the arts of the household . . . that he can not but be happy. Everything is snug, and everything seems to fit about him. Nothing is out of place; and wife, children, servants—all, not only seem to know their several places, but to delight in them" (*Richard Hurdis,* 158). Love of order and self-restraint are Grafton's abiding virtues and are the critical qualities that will lead men like Grafton to "civilize" the West. Simms's hostility to the West might be understood not only in biographical terms, but in the context of increasing rancor with the Southern planter class about how best to defend slavery. If James Oakes is correct, the small planters of the Southwest did not necessarily regard the

Eastern planters as their spokesmen, maintaining their own more acquisitive orientation toward slavery. Simms's vision of Eastern planter values and culture being transplanted to the new Southwest might be nothing more than wishful thinking on his part.[18]

On Simms's frontier, everyone was a little cruder and rougher than in the East. His representations of frontier whites were totally at odds with the developing ideology of Northern bourgeois society, which began to clamor for the free, heroic average man defeating "wild savages" in the name of civilization and settling free homesteads in the West. While Northerners shared Southern racist nationalism and did their part to advance the cause of "manifest destiny," their best writers began to create a mythical literature in this period that celebrated the honesty, sobriety, and piety of the very pioneers who in Southern literature were being depicted as degraded and naturally inferior. Granted, the bourgeois hero—Natty Bumppo, Ishmael, Huck Finn—arrives with his own set of problems, not the least of which is the positing of a virile freedom-seeking masculinity against the allegedly stultifying effects of "feminine" civilization. Nonetheless, in portraying the "common man" as hero, Northern writers of the period emerge as more democratic than their Southern counterparts. The social pretensions and elitism of the Southern planter "aristocracy" is insulting to the average middle-class Northern reader. While antebellum Northern readers would accept the stereotypes of women, Native Americans, and African Americans, they rejected this conservative vision of class relationships. During the Civil War when Abraham Lincoln, prototypical "common man," and the common men of the Union Army "saved the Union," the poor, honest frontier farmer reemerged as the embodiment of the "New American." The representations of poor yeoman whites among these Southern writers stands in direct contrast with the emerging liberal ideology of their own period and that which would follow at the end of the nineteenth and the beginning of the twentieth century. One of the continuing mysteries, which I shall discuss in the Conclusion, is *why* the American public continues to cherish these conservative plantation stereotypes.

14. The Problem of the Yeoman Farmer

IN THEIR CONSERVATIVE depiction of the yeoman farmer, antebellum Southern writers were completely out of step with both the progressive trend of Jacksonian republicanism and popular literary characters and themes. In this period, the yeoman farmer/Indian fighter was increasingly becoming a national hero, but in Southern literature he remained the social and economic subordinate of the planter. While planter-class prejudice might be overlooked in the "realistic" portrayal of the lowly poor whites, an emerging Northern middle-class reading public would not sanction aristocratic pretension in their literature. Indeed, yeoman farmers and small planters of the Southwest played a considerably larger role in the territorial and state government and economy than did their Eastern peers. However, antebellum Southern literature was written by Easterners who upheld planter dominion and an elitist vision of the social contract.

In their historical romances, William Alexander Caruthers, John Pendleton Kennedy, and William Gilmore Simms describe a "civilized" colonial and antebellum South comprising an interrelated web of patriarchal families. Each family was governed by its own male head of household who ruled "naturally inferior" women and children as well as black slaves. Social order in public and private spheres was maintained when natural inferiors deferred to natural superiors. Planter-class males propounded the myth that they possessed "masculine qualities" essential for leadership. Warfare offered the ultimate test of masculinity, and thus fictive planters and their sons served as the officers in the Revolutionary militias and proved themselves on the battlefield, surpassing all other races and classes of men. Through their heroic deeds, they earn the right to lead in peace as well as in war. In the literary South, then, the patriot yeoman takes his direction from his social better, the planter, who guides him intelligently, compassionately, and fearlessly. Caruthers in *Knights of the Golden Horse-Shoe* (1842), Kennedy in *Horse-Shoe Robinson* (1835), and Simms in *The Partisan* (1835) and *Mellichampe* (1836) created a series of gentleman military commanders and yeoman scouts, to answer the egalitarianism of the Northern middle class and to assert the natural superiority of the planter class.[1] At the core of these stereotypical stories lies a conservative vision of masculinity and an argument about what makes the planter-class male superior to all others.

William A. Caruthers's *Knights of the Golden Horse-Shoe* is set in eigh-

teenth-century Virginia where Alexander Spotswood gathered the leading young colonists for his Tramontaine expedition across the Blue Ridge
Mountains. In a proclamation to the planters' sons ("the young gentry")
he called for volunteers to enlist fifty men from their respective parishes
to go on a perilous campaign. Their objective was to learn if white settlers could survive in the fabled Shenandoah Valley. It would take them "beyond the reach of civilized resources—among savage tribes—over mountains, hitherto considered impassible—and through trackless wilderness."[2]
They would march into Indian territory and would probably have to do
some fighting. Thus Caruthers sets up a twofold test of masculinity: these
troopers would have to prove themselves superior to nature and to the "alien
race" that lived in the Shenandoah Valley. The "Tramontaine Order" was
composed of a group of planters' sons who as officers would lead others on
the expedition. Caruthers does his best to evoke a sense of pageantry, so-
lemnity, and adventure, as he describes the "gay young cavaliers," their
"rude followers," and the "more disciplined Rangers" who knelt next to their
horses and prayed for God's guidance in their mission into the wilderness
(2:174).[3] In spite of their breeding and high birth, however, they had to be
guided through the wilderness by Joe ("Red") Jarvis, the son of a fisherman
who was himself a hunter and a scout.

Caruthers describes Jarvis as being six feet tall with red whiskers and
sandy hair. In contrast to the smartly uniformed young officers, he wore a
coonskin cap, "buckskin leggings and moccasins," homespun breeches, and
hunting shirt held together by a "broad leather strap, into which were stuck
various utensils of the woman's craft," including a deadly looking hunting
knife (2:175). He also carried a rifle on his shoulder and rode a pony for
traveling over the rocky, mountainous terrain. Displaying self-confidence,
common sense, and a droll sense of humor, Jarvis's reply to Governor Spotswood, when asked why he had a pony rather than a horse, was simple and
pointed: "Hoses is like men, Governor—it is not always the smoothest coats
has the bravest hearts inside on 'em" (2:176). This observation came in the
course of laughing at a young soldier's new boots and "gaudy attire in gold
lace." Jarvis, then, was a man without formal schooling. An American original
like Natty Bumppo, he had been educated by nature; and his experience
would guide the troops through their wilderness adventure.

Thus, Jarvis showed them how to live off the land by killing and preparing
game; how to tell if they were being followed by Native Americans, and how
to fight and beat them with their own tactics (2:181 and 182, 188). His most
valuable service, however, was neither in woodcraft nor in warfare, but in a
commonsense solution to the problem of lame horses which had been taken
to the highlands without horseshoes. At a meeting of the officer corps, Jarvis
explained that their horses were accustomed to the sandy and soft lands of
the Tidewater and that they needed horseshoes in the craggy mountains or

else they would go lame. Without horses, they would have to turn back. Jarvis joined with Spotswood in proposing that they shoe the horses themselves. Since Jarvis had once been apprenticed to a blacksmith, he went to work melting and shaping into horseshoes as much metal (including the planter's gold) as could be found for horseshoes. In this and countless other ways, Jarvis proved himself to be indispensable. However, as a nonplantation white, he was given qualities and traits that made him unfit for true leadership. His speech betrayed his ignorance and his hatred of Native Americans made him dangerously intemperate.

In this latter attribute, Caruthers casts Jarvis in the role of the classic "Indian Hater."[4] In a conversation with Frank Lee, the novel's hero, he commented that "no good kin come out of an Ingin. I've hearn tell of all the grand talk about their native gifts, and all that, but if you listen to my racket, you may build a college over every son of a gun of 'em, and clap a church on the tip top o' that, and after all he will have a turkey buzzard's heart in him. God never made an Ingin for a human critter" (2:183). Like many, Jarvis had gone westward to the mountains as land in the eastern counties was appropriated by the planter class. He made his living from hunting; consequently he had had bloody contact with Native Americans and had come to hate them. Paradoxically, however, he wanted to marry Wingina, a Native American princess, who had been impregnated by the Governor's dissolute son. When Frank Lee asked him about this contradiction, he replied, "Well, now, it does beat all natur', that's a fact. How it ever came about, was jist a little touch above my larnin'" (2:183).[5] Jarvis thus gave voice to the Southerner's dilemma over miscegenation. His attraction to Wingina is not against "nature" but against Southern cultural prohibitions. Because he is a poor white and a hunter living off "wild land" with "wild people," he is allowed to express feelings and attitudes deemed totally improper for a "gentleman." Significantly, he is depicted as suitable for an Indian princess, who rejects him as too lowborn. Caruthers sketches the only instance of miscegenation in antebellum Southern literature, one that has class as well as racial connotations. Only intemperate and dissolute members of the planter classes or crude, intemperate poor whites, Caruthers appears to be asserting, would be interested in women of other races. Jarvis and Spotswood also gave voice to two dominating antebellum attitudes toward Native Americans: they were "yaller niggers" fit only for killing; and they were human beings who needed to be brought to "civilization."[6]

"Red" Jarvis is a classic nonplantation type. He is intelligent, resourceful, multiskilled at artisanal tasks. Yet his ignorance and his lack of "breeding" keep him from assuming political leadership in the South. At a crucial point in their expedition, Frank Lee devised a plan for surprising their Native American foes. When Jarvis learns of the plan, he remarks, "the very *idee,* I was going to propose to you, and I'll tell you what it is, Governor, as fine a scout was spiled when Squire Frank was made a gentleman of, as ever wore a moccasin" (2:223). The "young cavaliers" laughed heartily because this comment emphasized the social gulf between them. While Lee could readily use his natural intelligence to learn the arts of woodcraft and Indian warfare, Jarvis could no more become a gentleman than could his pony. That distinction is underscored toward the conclusion, when the young gentlemen of the Tramontaine Order are recognized at a special ceremony in the Virginia Hall of the House of Burgesses and "invested in due form with the insignia of the "Knights of the Golden Horse-Shoe." According to the values of the plantation South, a man like Jarvis might guide men through the wilderness, risk his life fighting Native Americans, and provide critical skills and expertise, but he is not a gentleman hero. He may make the golden horseshoes, but will never wear one.

In *Horse-Shoe Robinson,* John Pendleton Kennedy comes as close as is possible in this literature to creating a genuine plebeian hero. Galbraith Robinson is the scout of planter Major Arthur Butler of South Carolina. Robinson was nicknamed "Horse-Shoe" because he had been a blacksmith and small farmer before the war. Although Butler is supposed to be the gentleman hero of the novel, until the final battle at King's Mountain, he spends most of the novel getting himself captured by the British and rescued by Robinson. Kennedy describes Butler:

> His frame was well proportioned, light and active. His face, though distinguished by a smooth and almost beardless cheek, still presented an outline of decided manly beauty . . . a rich volume of black hair upon his brow had preserved the original fairness of a high, broad forehead. A hazel eye sparkled under the shade of a dark lash, and indicated, by its alternate playfulness and decision, an adventurous as well as a cheerful spirit. His whole bearing, visage and figure, seemed to speak of one familiar with enterprise and fond of danger; they denoted gentle breeding predominating over a life of toil and privation.[7]

In spite of the privations of war, Butler is still discernibly a gentleman.

In contrast, Robinson, who was seven years Butler's senior, "was a man of altogether rough mold" (15). A striking physical specimen, one of America's "natural noblemen," he sported "a shock of yellow hair terminating in a luxuriant queue":

> Every lineament of his body indicated strength. His stature was rather above six feet; his chest broad; his limbs sinewy, and remarkable for their symmetry. There seemed to be no useless flesh upon his frame to soften the prominent surface of his muscles. . . . With all these advantages of person, there was a radiant, broad, good nature on his face; and the glance of a large, clear blue eye told of arch thoughts and of shrewd, homely wisdom. A ruddy complexion accorded will with his sprightly but massive features, of which the prevailing expression was such as silently invited friendship and trust. (15)

Hence their very appearance and physical attributes distinguished Butler and Robinson respectively as gentleman and common man. Kennedy invests Robinson with "cheeful, confident" qualities that allowed him to give Butler unsolicited advice on several occasions. In permitting such freedom, Kennedy creates a structural situation where the common man eclipses the gentleman in importance.

Although Kennedy introduces a common complication—namely, the patriot planter hero in love with the daughter of a Loyalist father—the primary heroic action of the novel is provided by Robinson.[8] The difference in their class is indicated by their different reactions to events and by their speech. For instance, as seen earlier, when poor white Mat Adair is skinning a she-wolf alive and cursing at it, Robinson not Butler deals with him. In terms of pleasing his Western and Northern audiences, Kennedy has another problem with the Butler–Robinson duo. By the mid-1840s, the emerging Northern middle-class audience was far more appreciative of the rough-hewn masculinity of Robinson than the effete, aloof masculinity of Butler. Masculine aggression and violence, not aristocratic disdain for competition and aggression, were admired. In class terms, then, Robinson appealed more to the Northern middle-class reading public than did Butler, who even to the modern reader seems to be "a wimp."[9]

Their respective use of language provides the clearest distinction between Butler and Robinson. In one early conversation, for example, Robinson relates his experience at the siege of Charleston, South Carolina. Butler, portrayed as the cool aristocrat, listens and smokes his pipe and adds occasional encouragement, or comments on the events in an amused and detached fashion especially as Robinson gets increasingly passionate in his storytelling. At one point Butler condescendingly comments, "It wasn't a bad repartee, Galbraith. . . . But go on with your siege" (21). Robinson relates how the British tried to convince the captured troops that their planter colonel, Charles Cotesworth Pinckney, had deserted to the British side, but Robinson reassures Butler, "that was too onprobable a piece of rascality—we didn't believe one word on't" (19). Pinckney, he continues, addressed his men in front of the British officers and persuaded them that the news of his desertion was, in Robinson's words, an "infamous, audacious calumny [*sic*]" (22). Like his earlier reaction, Butler's response is poised and measured. Although Robinson had related a dramatic if sentimental story, Butler was not much drawn into its passion.

In contrast to Robinson, Butler speaks precisely; he never mispronounces words or creates malapropisms. Furthermore, being educated and knowledgeable, he doesn't have to resort to homespun aphorisms to make a point. Robinson's commonsense folk wisdom is underscored by a number of appropriate adages that lace his conversations. For example, in describing his hunger after he has escaped from the Charleston garrison, he says, "The first bread of freedom, no matter how coarse, a man eats after his escape from

prison, is the sweetest morsel in nature" (25). Or again, cheering a disconso-
late Butler: "Drop thinking and chawing overy your troubles, and take them
with a light heart, and things that's not to be mended by a solemnically long-
facedness. A good victual's meal and a fair night's rest would make another
man of you" (57). In establishing his faith in and deference to his superiors,
Robinson's goodness is also established. Notwithstanding Robinson's inherent abilities and talents, he remains a variation on the faithful-retainer caricature. He is a passionate man; he accepts the cruelty of degraded men and
the brutalities of war; he conducts himself honorably and fairly with other
men; he performs one heroic feat after another. But his intelligence and
limitations owe to a lack of "breeding" and education, and his actions were
largely directed to saving the life of his superior, Major Arthur Butler, not in
leading other men in battle. To emphasize the "place" of the loyal yeoman,
Kennedy has Robinson return to his old occupation of blacksmith and small
farmer, rather than seek election to public office in the new republic. Governance in war and peace is clearly left to the "superior" planters.

Kennedy draws out the differences among poor whites, the yeoman
farmer, and the aristocrat in a scene at Walter Adair's cabin. At this meeting
of Arthur Butler, Horse-Shoe Robinson and Mary Musgrove, Mary appears as
"a sylvan Hebe, just merging upon womanhood, with a round, active and
graceful figure, which was adorned with that zealous attention to neatness
and becoming ornament which, in every station of life, to a certain extent,
distinguishes those of the sex who are gifted with beauty" (150). Her temperament and demeanor seems as distant from the Adairs as Butler seems from
her. Her manner "was altogether different from that of the mistress of the
house," who, though scarcely middle-aged, had "wan and somewhat haggard features" and a "surly, discontented expression of face" (149 and 150).

Mary instantly realized that Butler was a gentleman, someone different
from her. Though posing as a common man, Butler displayed "more gallan-
try than belonged to the station he affected," and his manners and speech
were not those of a common man" (157). Similarly, Butler notes Mary's natural piety, and her "modest and natural courtesy" (160). Mary warns Butler
and Robinson of a plot against them by Wat Adair, in conjunction with other
poor white Tories. Later Mary testifies in Butler's court-martial on his behalf,
and carries messages back and forth to him when he is in jail. When her
fiancé, John Ramsay, is killed on a mission, Butler consoles Mary and the
Ramsay family.

As soon as she meets Butler's fiancé (actually his wife) Mildred Lindsey,
Mary defers to her as a "lady"; she "warmly and fervently attache[s] herself to
Mildred and wins her way into [the] lady's esteem by the most amiable
assiduities" (538). In Kennedy's view, Mary was to be admired for her piety,
honesty, and courage, and her deference to superiors. Unable to marry the
man she has loved, Mary is rewarded by becoming a kind of lady-in-waiting
to Mildred Lindsey at the end of the novel. In class terms, then, like Horse-

Shoe Robinson, she is expected to serve her superiors, not lead them at the end of the war. As a woman, she is allowed only one "true love"; without that man, her predestined life of service can be dedicated to the upper class.

Kennedy's picture of Mary Musgrove's and John Ramsay's families further emphasize the role of deference between the two classes. Allen Musgrove is a miller who farms a few acres on the side, and David Ramsay is a plain yeoman farmer who owns a family or two of slaves. Neither is rich or affluent. Their oldest children, Mary and John, are engaged to be married. In both homes the wife and mother is compassionate, pietistic, fecund, and hardworking; a woman who takes pride in her domestic skills and achievements. Allen Musgrove provides an important contact for patriot soldiers because he grinds both rebel and Loyalist wheat, and thus is privy to information about British troop movements. Both he and Ramsay are benevolent patriarchs who expect their children's attendance at evening prayer and who expect to make the important family decisions. Neither family lives extravagantly, and neither seems unable to meet their basic needs in wartime.

Allen Musgrove and David Ramsay, like Horse-Shoe Robinson, have the requisite traits of the Southern yeoman class. For example, Musgrove has the capacity to restrain his emotions. When his mill is "visited" by British soldiers, "the habitual control of his temper, which his religious habits inculcated, kept him silent; and considerations of prudence again swayed him from surrendering to the impulse, which would have led him to declare himself openly against the cause of the royal government and its supporters in the district where he lived" (249). David Ramsay had matching virtues: a "man of sturdy frame—now only in the prime of life—brave, thoughtful and intelligent and firmly resolved to stand by his principles through whatever adverse changes" (274). Both men, then, serve as respectable representatives of their class; unlike the degenerate, unreligious, and intemperate poor whites, they are staunch patriots and are willing to make great sacrifices for the American cause. Unlike the poor whites who seek after personal gain, the yeoman farmer was engaged in a revolutionary war against British exploitation and not in a civil war against the planter class. Furthermore, he would readily and dutifully resume his humble station at the war's conclusion.

Similarly, William Gilmore Simms offered a range of loyal yeoman farmers and scouts in his Revolutionary and border novels. While these characters achieve a measure of heroism, they are clearly subordinate to the planter hero. In *The Partisan* and *Mellichampe,* Simms describes the class warfare that South Carolina experienced during the Revolution.[10] For Simms, Loyalists were wealthy planters who shared with the British a common temperament and who were faulted for their indolence and love of luxury.[11] In contrast to the "malignant tories" (who are always poor white criminals in Simms's sociology of the Revolution), Loyalists, like some of the British officers, conducted themselves honorably during the war.

Simms is most comfortable with the planters, who even if they are Loyalists are gentlemen and men of honor. His portraits of yeoman farmers and
poor whites are more complex. On the whole, he mistrusted poor whites and
believed yeoman farmers were divided in their loyalties. In *The Partisan,*
Simms compared and contrasted two yeoman types: Walter Griffin, a "stout
yeoman" patriot, and Amos Gaskins, "a notorious wretch and tory." Griffin
had been "an industrious farmer" and "a sober, quiet man, who had long
been married, and found his chief enjoyment in the bosom of his family"
(383). He had no slaves, and his home "was a poor cabin of logs, with but two
rooms, such as was common enough about the country. The tract of land,
consisting of two hundred acres, was ample for so small a family."[12] In contrast, Gaskins, an overseer before the war, "loved the race-turf and the cock-
pit, and his soul was full of their associations" (383). Although he had made
overtures of friendship to Griffin and wanted to court his daughter, Ellen,
Griffin refused to associate with him. When the British came to power in
South Carolina in 1780, Griffin immediately joined the patriot cause, while
Gaskins became the leader of a "marauding and malignant" Tory band. Griffin's motives, Simms explains, were the natural and virtuous response of a
man who defended his wife and family from the enemies of his country;
while Gaskins became a Tory "with thousands of others, to whom all considerations were as nothing, weighed against the love of low indulgence, unrestrained power, and a profligate lust for plunder" (384; see also 370 and 371).
In a critical scene that joins issues of class and masculinity, Lance Frampton
fires the fatal shot that kills Gaskins as he is about to hang Griffin.[13]

From one of the country's "poorest class of farmers," Frampton is "a tall
fine-looking lad of sixteen" who joined Major Robert Singleton's band of
partisans—a troop of Francis Marion's men—when the Tories terrorized his
country and murdered his pregnant mother. Singleton, the planter hero,
guides him and trains him in the "manly art" of war. For his part, Lance

> listened to every word he uttered, watched every movement, and care-
> fully analyzed, so far as his immature capacities would admit, every
> feeling and thought of his superior. . . . Singleton became one and the
> same with his mind's ideal and a lively imagination, and warm sen-
> sibilities, identified his captain, in his thought, with his only notion of
> a genuine hero. . . . The lofty, symmetrical strong person—the high but
> easy carriage—the grace of movement and attitude—the studious deli-
> cacy of speech, mingled, at the same time, with that simple adherence
> to propriety, which illustrates genuine manliness, were all attributes of
> Singleton and all obvious enough to his admirer. (*The Partisan,* 373–74)

Singleton takes time with the boy and calms his fears about not being able to
do his duty and kill a man. He instills Lance with courage and self-reliance.
When the time comes, he places Lance in a position to take the first shot and
thus Frampton "with a determined coolness" raises his rifle, take aim, and

pulls the trigger. Seconds later the hated Amos Gaskins lay dead and the patriots routed the Tory band, taking many prisoners and killing the rest. After the fight, Singleton congratulated Frampton: he had "behaved like a man" (390).

Frampton is a little dazed by the whole experience and questions the morality of such behavior, especially since his mother had taught him that the Bible forbids killing. But, as Simms commented, "The boy was a boy no longer; he had realized one of the capacities of manhood; he had slain his man; he had taken one step in revenging the murder of his mother; he had destroyed one of the murderers; but, more than all—he had taken human life," (398). Thus does Simms join the themes of masculinity and class. In his conservative view, the planter class was the most capable of producing superior men who could lead their inferiors into battle and who would display those qualities of masculinity absolutely necessary for the survival of Western civilization. A true man, like Singleton or Griffin, is passionately tied to his land and his family, which he will defend violently if he must. The conservative creed holds that a boy becomes a man, then, when he is willing to kill another man in defense of his land, his family, and his country.

In contrast, "true women" like Singleton's dying sister, Emily, are physically and morally incapable of any form of violence, even in self-defense. That is why women need men to protect them. They will never be "equal" with men in any meaningful way, being incapable of any kind of violence against the life they have created. The "feminine" woman is "naturally" nurturant and always seeks to preserve life, while "masculine" men understand that the taking of life is sometimes necessary to its maintenance. "True men," like the temperate and sturdy yeoman Walter Griffin and the patrician planter Robert Singleton, know that their higher obligations to family and country at times compel killing, but only in compliance with self-preservation, allegedly the first law of nature. However, immoral cowards like Amos Gaskins take human life for the mere sport of it. Thus, for Simms, men and women may be differentiated by their relation to violence, and classes of men are distinguished by their understanding and acceptance of their masculine responsibilities. Poor men like Lance Frampton must learn the meaning of masculinity from their natural superiors like Singleton, who show them respect for life as well as the capacity for masculine patriotic murder.

When it seems that young Frampton is beginning to enjoy killing, Singleton urges him to remember that "war is not a sport, but a duty, and we should not love it. It is a cruel necessity, and only to be resorted to as it protects from cruelty; and must be a tyranny even though it shields us from a greater" (401). Frampton is astonished by this admonition and stands uncomprehending while his hero discusses the need for restraint and justice as well as revenge. In the end, the superior Singleton has to recognize that in the lesser man he had awakened "courage to desperation and love of the fight—that rapture of strife, which was the Hun's passion" (403; see also 398–

403). Although those are qualities that would make Frampton a fine soldier, he lacks the intellect, moral understanding, or emotional restraint to be a leader of men. In Simms's worldview, Frampton's deficient morality and understanding are not only the result of individual failure, but underscore the contention that even the very best men of the poor-white class needed the example and leadership of the planter class to restrain them on the battlefield and as well as in peace time.[14]

In addition to Frampton and Griffin, Simms introduces two scouts in *The Partisan* and *Mellichampe*. Bill Humphries rides with Singleton in Francis Marion's Revolutionary guerrilla troop; John Witherspoon or "Thumbscrew" rides with Ernest Mellichampe. Both are introduced in *The Partisan*. In *Mellichampe* Humphries plays a minor but significant role, while Thumbscrew is a major figure who achieves a measure of heroism. Both scouts are highly skilled at woodcraft and betray the same kind of native intelligence and commonsense wisdom of Horse-Shoe Robinson. Of the two, Thumbscrew comes the closest to replicating Horse-Shoe Robinson's heroism.

Humphries is described as

> a stout able-bodied person, of thirty years, or perhaps more—a rough-looking man, one seemingly born and bred entirely in the humble life of the country. He was powerful in physical development, rather stout than high, with a short thick neck—a head round and large, with eyes small and settled, and piercing—and features even solemn in their general expression of severity . . . no one who looked in his face could doubt that he was full of settled purpose, firm in his resolve, and reckless, having once determined, in the prosecution of the most desperate enterprises. (*The Partisan,* 45 and 46)

His assignment is to pass as a nonbelligerent and to report his findings about British and Tory movements in the country, popular resistance to the British, and the general political climate in South Carolina. Additionally, he serves as a recruiting officer for the partisans. In an early adventure, as they are tracking a Tory band, Humphries acts as a decoy to draw enemy fire and then leads them back into the trap which Singleton has waiting. He "found no difficulty in misleading his pursuers," Simms notes, and was "cool and confident" in luring them to the ambush (90). Humphries also gathers information on the local people so that Singleton can decide whom to trust and whom to avoid. Singleton, a planter, does not know the common people in his district, and so Humphries, the son of a tavernkeeper in Dorchester provides him with critical information.

One of Humphries' principal antagonists is a mixed-blood poor white named Ned Blonay, or "Goggle" because of his blear eyes. The Humphries–Blonay contrast lets the reader draw the distinction between a sturdy yeoman/villager type and a degenerate poor white. Humphries tells Singleton that Blonay is bad because he had "bad blood" in him. According to Humphries, Blonay's father was a horse thief and, worse, "a mulatto or an Indian"

(97).[15] No one knows how he supported himself and his mother, but everyone in the county suspected that he was dishonest. Singleton, being naive, is inclined to trust Blonay, Humphries's objections to the contrary.

The Humphries–Blonay conflict carries over into *Mellichampe,* Simms's next novel. Hating Humphries for his complicity in his court-martial and for killing his mother, however inadvertently (she fell under Humphries's horse's hooves and was trampled to death), Blonay decides to seek bloody revenge. He would hunt Humphries down like an animal and kill him. In a climactic scene of the subplot, one illustrating Humphries's cunning, his rough yeoman sense of justice, and his tolerance of brutality, he finds Blonay hiding from him in a hollow tree after he and Blonay have been pursuing each other like animals. Simms draws a clear distinction between Humphries and his cowardly and thus unmanly poor-white adversary. Humphries is enraged that Blonay wouldn't "come out like a man" and face him in a fair fight, and decides to fill up the hollow tree with wood and trap Blonay there until he starved to death. Humphries exclaims: "You took to the hollow like a beast. You shall die like one. It's a fit death for one like you. You've been hunting after my blood quite too long. I won't spill yours, but I'll leave it to dry up in your heart, and you should feel it freezing and crying all the time."[16] While engaged in his task, Humphries feels a "malicious joy," and when he has finished entrapping Blonay, he marks his success by a "tumultuous and unmitigated laughter" that fills the woods until he has disappeared (380). Although Humphries returns to free Blonay, Simms makes his point: in the moral world of the yeoman and the poor white, disputes are not settled by either formalized duelling rituals or expensive lawsuits. Instead, justice was swift, brutal, and primitive. Humphries, to be sure, is portrayed as honest and reliable, but he is also a coarse, ignorant, and brutal man. He is a capable soldier, but incapable of either wartime or peacetime leadership because his ignorance and passion compromise his ability to make intelligent and moral decisions under pressure.

In Jack Witherspoon or "Thumbscrew," Simms creates a comparable rural man. He is different, however, in having more of Horse-Shoe Robinson's self-possession, creativity, and commonsense intelligence, and less of Humphries's brutality. He is first introduced in *The Partisan* as a scout for Francis Marion, carrying a message from Marion to Singleton. He has been captured by some of Singleton's men and plays a dissembling comic character until he is sure he has met up with his man. The interrogation by Singleton's men discloses Simms's play with the language and character of these middling types:

> "You say your name is Thumbscrew?"
> "Yes, my boy-name; but at the christening they gin me another that ain't so easy to mention. The true name is John Wetherspoon, at your sarvice; but Thumbscrew comes more handy, you see, and them that knows me thinks it suits me better."
> "And what are you? Are you a whig or a tory?"

"Neither, thank God, for all his civilities and marcies. I'm a gentleman, and not a soldier, no how, I'll hev you to know."

"And where do you live when you're at home?"

"In the Big Bend, by Red Stone Hollow, close to the Clay Church,
and right side of Black Heifer Swamp. My farm is called Hickory Head
Place; and the parson who does our preaching is named Broadcast—he
preaches through his nose, and has a way with him."

"What way?"

"Margery Way, what does his mending; all the parish knows her."[17]

This exchange conveys a sample of Southern humor with the parodic directions and the pun at the end. Witherspoon's nickname (no fictional planter
gentlemen have nicknames), speech, and style reveal him to be one of the
clever, independent yeoman types more comfortable on his farm or in the
woods than in any drawing room.

The reader meets Witherspoon again in *Mellichampe,* but this time as the
companion/protector of young Ernest Mellichampe, whose father has been
murdered by Tories. Witherspoon is described as being between thirty and
forty years old: "His face, however, had an expression of its own; and the sanguine flush which overspread the full cheeks and the quick restless movement of his blue eye spoke of an active spirit, and one prompt enough at all
times to govern and set in motion the huge bulk of that body, now so inert
and sluggish" (32).[18] He dresses in "the common blue and white homespun of the country," wears a hunting shirt over his breeches, and a "cone-
crowned hat" with part of the rim torn away. He has moccasins on his feet,
which indicates his connection with woodcraft and underscores his independent "wildness" and social distance from the plantation (32).

In contrast, Witherspoon's young aristocratic companion, scarcely "more
than twenty years of age," differed greatly in appearance. Young Mellichampe's "eye was black and fiery, his cheek brown and thin, his hair of a
raven black like his eye, his chin full, his nose finely Roman, and his forehead imposingly high. His person was slender, of middle height, and seemed
to indicate great activity" (32). Further, "there was more of pretension in his
dress," which was made of the finest materials (32 and 33). Mellichampe's
delicacy and elegance is supposed to convey immediately his highborn
state. Mellichampe, however, unlike other Simms heroes, was a hot-blooded
planter's son bent upon avenging his father's murder and rejoining Janet
Berkeley, his fiancée, at whose plantation, Piney Grove, the detested British
have bivouacked.

In contrast to the passionate Humphries (yeoman)–cool Singleton (planter) model, Simms offers the passionate Mellichampe (planter)–cool Witherspoon (yeoman) model. The yeoman scout is always the opposite of the
planter captain. Yet this is the only instance of Simms's representing the
planter as being in need of supervision and fatherly counsel. In a surprising
and uncharacteristic twist, the passionate, hot-blooded planter is incapable
of true heroism, and his social inferiors have to rescue him from the British.

Hence Witherspoon is permitted to achieve a measure of heroism denied the other yeomen scouts. He is also older than Mellichampe and his protection of him has a kind of paternal quality to it. In fact, after an argument with Mellichampe, he confesses: "Dang my button, you know, boy, I love you the same as if you was my own blood and bone, though I knows my place to you, and know you're come of better kin, and are better taught in book-larning; but, by God! Airnest, you hav'n't larned, in all your larning, to love anybody better than I love you" (35). While Northern writers of this period like Cooper and Melville portray male bonding between men of different races, Southern writers like Kennedy and Simms describe similar relationships between men of the same race but of different classes. Because black men located on the plantation are assumed to be planter dependents and part of their extended families, the crucial unresolved difference is that of class. Witherspoon's confession of love for young Mellichampe gives salience to Simms's point that simple God-fearing men understand their "place" in society and accept deference toward their betters with love. Ernest is moved to tears by this simple expression of affection, and returns it with a gesture rather than words, since as "Thumby" notes, it is "onbecoming" for them to cry. Witherspoon, then, also teaches Mellichampe his lessons in masculinity, and in that way does take the place of his deceased father.

Mellichampe is an angry young man; and well he might be. His father has been "cruelly murdered," his mother "has been driven away from the home of his ancestors—that home confiscated, given to the murderer," Captain Barsfield, while he, an aristocratic planter, is hiding, a "hunted" man (36). "My blood boils, my brain burns," he exclaims melodramatically, "I can not think, and when I do it is only to madden." He wants immediate revenge even if it means ambushing Barsfield and killing him in cold blood (36).[19] Witherspoon cautions restraint and talks to him about the savagery of war: "My idee is, that fighting is the part of a beast-brute, and not for a true born man, that has a respect for himself, and knows what's good breeding; and I only fights when there's brutes standing waiting for it" (34). He advises Ernest to defend himself but he should never start a fight. However, Mellichampe is unpersuaded. Witherspoon cautions him, "No good comes of submission, except to make tyrants and slaves" (33 and 34). Witherspoon urges restraint on Mellichampe and advises him that it's "onbecoming to be cast down like a woman because trouble presses on the heart" (37).

By such exchanges between these two men, Simms in an early novel establishes more subtly what it means to be a man. A man doesn't cry, doesn't give in to despair like a woman; he doesn't submit like a slave. Notwithstanding the praise Simms and indeed all Southern writers lavish on women and blacks "in their place," these subtle comparisons, hidden in the middle of paragraphs or buried in the discussion of other topics, disclose their true contempt for both women and blacks and their corresponding feelings of their own superiority.

Furthermore, like Horse-Shoe Robinson who devotes his tour of duty to protecting planter Arthur Butler, Witherspoon dedicates himself to the service of Mellichampe. He held for Mellichampe, Simms tells us, "a sentiment of respect a little short of awe: the natural sentiment of one brought up, as he had been, to regard the family of his wealthy neighbors as superior beings in many respects" (128). Witherspoon's love, it follows, is not that found between equals, but the self-effacing love that conservative patriarchal ideology celebrates as "naturally" occurring between inferior and superiors. Witherspoon tries to restrain Mellichampe against his own impetuous behavior; Mellichampe abuses him for his interfering; Witherspoon gets hurt and withdraws; they then apologize and make up because of the love they bear for each other.[20] In the climactic scene in the novel, Witherspoon makes the ultimate sacrifice for Mellichampe, dying in an effort to protect him from one of Barsfield's men.

Witherspoon's death represents the noble sacrifice of an inferior for his beloved superior, friend, and companion. Mellichampe, however, does not seem worthy of his sacrifice. In not protecting Janet Berkeley, but in endangering her life with his recklessness; in being an ineffectual opponent of Barsfield and relying upon a black slave to "kill his man"; and in displaying a consistent impetuosity and rashness, Mellichampe fails as hero. His personality may come closer to the real planter than is usual in this fiction, but it violated those standards of masculinity and heroism that Simms would develop consistently in his other novels. However, this failed hero enables us to see how gender, racial, and class distinctions are reinforced. When the alleged inferiors of the planter hero are allowed to step out of their stereotypical roles and to assert themselves with a measure of individuality and courage, the hero, in becoming more human, is therefore diminished and is shown realistically to be dependent on those very people he claims as dependents.

Such realism, however, did not serve the planter cause very well and Simms himself thought of *Mellichampe* as one of his early failures. But this "failure" enables today's reader to see that the carefully constructed plantation novel with its dashing planter heroes and their passive and swooning ladies, its loyal and yeoman farmers, only served to reinforce the sexual, racial, and class superiority of the white male planter.

In his border novels, Simms describes the yeoman in peacetime.[21] Simms, who formed his opinions from reading travelers' accounts and from his visits to the Southwest as a young man, thought that each successive wave of settlers brought a better kind of person to the frontier. The Southwest, he believed, would not attain a desirable level of "civilization" until it could support a planter class. His border novels, like the first "Westerns," celebrate justice and social order transported to the Southwest by men like Ralph Colleton (*Guy Rivers*) and Harry Vernon (*Border Beagles*). As noted, these planter heroes organize and lead the sturdy yeomen against poor-white criminal gangs who rob, steal, and otherwise terrorize them.[22] Walter Rawlins (*Border Beagles*), for instance, is honest, intelligent, and just but also an ignorant and crude woodsman who simply needs a little direction and leadership from a superior planter. Although not educated himself, Rawlins will make certain that his children are and through them and the generations that follow "civilization" will be achieved gradually.[23] Similarly, William Hinkley (*Charlemont* and *Beauchampe*) is of only average intellect and ability; nonetheless he will prosper as a backwoods lawyer and politician because his competition is inferior to that in the East (*Charlemont,* 129–34, 138–48, 276–89). Owing to the absence of an established planter class, Simms tells us, Westerners misperceive their abilities and talents. Such absence also leads to "a single and unreserved freedom among the people" (*Charlemont,* 8).

While Simms believed that providence had destined Anglo-Saxons to settle the continent, he is convinced (in contrast to the Jacksonian mythmakers) that the vanguard of expansionism was the "poor and vulgar classes" who had failed to establish themselves in the East. The "American hero" emerging from this period would be the plebeian white male yeoman farmer, Indian fighter, and military hero: Daniel Boone, Davy Crockett, and Andrew Jackson. For Simms and other Southern writers the simple, law-abiding but unsophisticated yeoman farmers and frontier woodsmen were superior to both African Americans and degenerate poor whites, though inferior to the members of the planter class. In the antebellum planter worldview as described in these novels, and especially in the work of Simms, the middle class was fit to govern only the "uncivilized" frontier counties and territories. It could never be allowed to achieve national political power. For this proud and haughty planter class, Abraham Lincoln's crime was not simply that he belonged to an antislavery party, but to an inferior class as well.[24]

Thus does Simms link conservative ideals of masculinity to class, finding that the most virile men—that is, those who are skillful and courageous, compassionate, and just—are to be found in the planter class from which is drawn the South's "natural" leadership. In this conservative patriarchal planter worldview, human nature is evil, and men are especially prone to violence in order to get what they desire. Such violence can be curbed only by the ability of the superior men of the planter class to accept their social responsibility to assume military and political leadership, and to create and maintain a society based on patriarchal law and order.

The allegedly natural hierarchical relations between "natural superiors" and "natural inferiors," between men and women, and between whites and blacks are thus intertwined and mutually reinforcing in this literature, which creates the planter as the embodiment of the highest ideals of "humanity." While honorable men like planter Singleton take human life only in self-defense or in defense of their family, land, or nation, dishonorable men like Hell-Fire Dick, Ned Blonay, and Samuel Bostwick wage civil war against their countrymen to obtain illegally, in a time of turmoil, what they cannot earn through their own efforts because they are naturally inferior. According to this conservative literature, men commit crimes not because they have been wronged or are victims of injustice, but because as innately inferior men they have not learned self-discipline and prefer the easy path of crime to the hard road of honest labor. Although poor whites are degraded, they still possess their own women and children, and some even have squatters' rights to land.

As a class subordinate even to poor whites, black men in this literature are, in patriarchal terms, "emasculated." That is, in spite of the historical record of their active participation in the American Revolution on both sides of the conflict, the black men described in this literature do not fulfill the patriarchal ideal of masculinity by owning their wives, children, and land and defending them against British and poor white attack. Rather, they themselves are owned and are protected by the planters and/or serve in essentially noncombative roles.[25] Writers like Kennedy, Caruthers, N. B. Tucker, and Simms, all of whom had family ties to the planter class, which had a monopoly on education, literacy, and the production of ideas in the antebellum South, sustained the conservative patriarchal "masculine mystique" in their fiction.

Conclusion

AT NO OTHER TIME in the history of the United States has such a small ruling class held so commanding an influence over the economic, political, and intellectual life of a region as did the antebellum planter class. While slaveholding was comparatively widespread among Southerners, the great majority of slaves lived on the largest Eastern and Southwestern cotton plantations and those estates that dotted the Mississippi River. Gavin Wright notes that between 1850 and 1860, "slaveholders controlled between 90 and 95 percent of agricultural wealth."[1] In a region where industrial and commercial wealth was negligible, planters (those owning twenty or more slaves) dominated officeholding in the state and in the Congressional delegations. What is remarkable about the antebellum planter class is not that they defended their class position articulately and effectively—after all, that is what ruling classes do—it is the power they commanded to suppress legitimate debate of slavery as an institution.

It was in this climate of authoritarian suppression that Caruthers, Kennedy, N. B. Tucker, and Simms lived and produced their proslavery novels. Although Tucker and Simms were more vociferous in their proslavery politics than Caruthers and Kennedy, these latter writers agreed with the racial and class prejudices of the planter class and Kennedy produced one of the classic proslavery novels. They used familiar literary conventions formulated by European writers as well as that of the new historical romance developed by Sir Walter Scott to make a Southern contribution to American literature and to formulate the literary proslavery defense for the planter class. What these authors offer, then, is a unique perspective on the planter worldview as it emerged in their fiction. However, had they written from the contradictions and complexities of their own lives, the literature they produced might have been more compelling.

For instance, John Pendleton Kennedy, a lawyer, is the only one of the authors to work in the commercial sector and the only one who refused to own slaves. He held the post of secretary of the navy in the Polk administration and opposed secession. Except for humorous jibes at his countrymen and women, who imagine themselves a neo-aristocracy, his more liberal politics never appear in his work. Similarly, Caruthers, for all his liberalism, married into a wealthy Georgian slaveholding family and celebrated white Christian America's "manifest destiny" to conquer Native Americans and inhabit the continent. And Simms, who was the most talented and prolific of the group, married into the planter class, abandoning his early democratic politics. Only Nathaniel Beverley Tucker was born into the planter class and consistently defended its gender, race, and class politics his whole life.

The social world of the Southern antebellum novel bears little resemblance to the multiethnic and class antagonisms that pervaded antebellum Southern society. Indeed, this literature seeks to convey a Southern society far more stratified, harmonious, and orderly than it really was. When one realizes, for example, that Southerners sought to defeat the Seminole and Cherokee tribes not only because they wanted their land and material resources, but because runaway slaves were either given sanctuary or enslaved by them, one begins to appreciate the kind of "disorder" that confronted the planter class. After reading this literature, one cannot imagine a greater contradiction in planter terms than Native American slaveholders, yet before Removal (1832–38), the Creek, the Cherokees, and the Seminoles held slaves and prospered.[2]

The proslavery defense seeks to convince the reader that the South, unlike the North, is a racially ordered society free from class struggle. These authors, in spite of their political differences, create a uniform fictional world in which the white males of the planter class had long defeated disruptive and uncivilized Native Americans and maintained authority and power over women, blacks, and poor whites, who recognize their superiority and therefore assent to their domination. The exceptions to that pattern—Simms's *Mellichampe* or Kennedy's *Horse-Shoe Robinson*—derive more from the two authors' faulty execution of the plot than from a shift in their worldview.

The Southern planter hero emerges, then, not only as the ideal representative of his race and class, but as a masculine ideal. The hero's physical domination of other men underscores the planters' contention that they as superior men are the most fit to govern and their superiority is recognized by their natural inferiors. The planter hero is not only respected by his subordinates, but adored with an abasing selflessness. George and Bet Balcombe, Porgy and Tom, Mellichampe and Witherspoon represent the planter's desire and even expectation that he will be loved by his subordinates. In these extreme portraits, one perceives the master's view that he is the center of the subordinate's life. Although Simms jokes about that expectation in his portrayal of Porgy and Tom, self-sacrifice and the merging of an individual's identity in the interest of the master is the primary expectation of the patriarchal planter. What distinguishes the proslavery defense, however, is that it explained such deference not in terms of the relations of power within the social structure of slavery, but as the "natural" psychology of inferiors (women, blacks, and poor whites) who recognize in the planter a superior. Patriarchal rule, then, rather than being recognized as coercive and violent, is defended by these writers and others as bringing social inferiors to their own true nature and thus establishing true social order and harmony in the South.

While the Northern fictional hero of this period is a seeker, an explorer, and a visionary who leaves "civilization" to take his chances in the uncorrupted world of the wilderness or the sea, the Southern hero is a conservative, patriarchal planter who strives to defend his society against internal class conflict and external threat (that is, from the British) and seeks to export the Southern political economy to the frontier. An embodiment of ideal masculinity, he stands for loyalty to family and country, respect for age and women, care for one's subordinates, generosity to one's friends and neighbors, honesty in business and politics, courage in combat, and personal integrity matched by an overwhelming sense of honor that leads him to defend any real or imagined insult to himself, his family, or his country.[3]

In contrast, Cooper, Melville, and Hawthorne, while not without gender and racial biases, create heroes and heroines who find themselves in active struggle with the innocence and optimism of nineteenth-century America and the reality of human evil. Unlike plantation novels, their novels shift settings as their heroes set out into the world. Nothing about their plots is predictable. One is always unsure about what will challenge the protagonist and what choices he or she will make. Consequently, their work presents contradictory social relationships between men of different races and classes. Although Mark Twain has been proved correct in his criticism of Cooper's mishandling of Native Americans, in comparison to the antebellum Southern writer who was incapable of imagining interracial friendship in any form in any setting, Cooper's Natty Bumppo and Chinachgook hold out for the reader's imagination possibilities that Simms's Gabriel Harrison (Lord Craven) and Sanutee (*The Yemassee*) never approach. Additionally, all of these authors actively resist the specter of black masculinity realized in Melville's "Benito Cereno," a slave revolt at sea based on the Amistad revolt. The classic Northern literature of the period, then, is more psychologically and symbolically layered than the Southern novel. In the Southern novel the hero and heroine are ideal types who are never fraught with guilt or doubt about their social responsibilities or moral choices. Consequently, there are no unexpected conclusions to these Southern novels. The heroes are virtually interchangeable with each other. They never struggle as individuals with questions of good and evil, or confront a chaotic and unpredictable society. These writers' patriarchal and conservative worldview structures their heroes' choices and chances. Thus these novels are historically interesting only for the insight they give into the class that produced them.

Significantly, in this context, the romance reveals itself as a profoundly conservative form. It is predicated on the assumption of innate and immutable male sexual aggressiveness toward "unprotected" women, and violence toward men perceived as essentially "different" from ruling-class men (and therefore presumed inferior). In antebellum Southern literature, only superior males are bred to protect the weak; most other men are predators on them. The major concession this literature makes to chance and luck is the existence of male strangers who arrive unexpectedly in a woman's life as

either evil villains or heroic saviors. In a convention that created some problems for Southern writers, it is possible in this New World romance for young
people to break free of patriarchal control and "fall in love" with a stranger.[4]
The romantic gaze in which the newly beloved is "seen" for the first time
becomes a cliché of this literature, but these Southern authors consistently
make both "strangers" the same race and class, so they are eventually
"known" to each other through the same patriarchal institutions that appear
to be initially undermined. Witness, for instance, the courtship of Virginia
Fairfax and Nathaniel Bacon (*Cavaliers of Virginia*). Bacon, though an orphan raised with Virginia, is unacceptable as a mate until it is confirmed that
he was born of respected English gentry. Thus Virginia's noble instincts are
confirmed. In this antebellum Southern fiction, the romantic moment becomes a vehicle for establishing the most conservative gender, race, and
class lines, not for exploring new possibilities. However, no matter how one
rearranges the scene and changes the actors, the basic romantic form is
predicated on conservative assumptions that turn on the inevitability of
male violence and female helplessness.

Inevitably, we come to a question that has captured the attention of many
scholars: Why have these myths of the Old South persisted so long after the
defeat of the planter class?[5] Certainly the persistence of white racism contributes to the acceptance of Southern mythology. As others have noted, the
Northern construction of the antebellum South as virulently and irredeem-
ably racist allows Northerners to avoid responsibility for their historic complicity in underwriting slavery and for their own institutionalized racism.[6]
The denial of African American suffering in slavery and the refusal to consider reparations for their stolen labor; the persistent refusal to include the
history and literature of African Americans as part of the standard secondary
and college curricula; the denial of African Americans as intellectual, social,
and political equals, which results in employment discrimination and tangi-
ble, documented human suffering—this institutionalization of racism makes
individuals more inclined to accept the myths of the plantation South rooted
as they are on notions of white supremacy. But racism alone does not explain
the myth's persistence.

The Civil War was a true watershed in United States history. It marked the
birth of industrial America and the triumph of the capitalist class. From
the Civil War on, America's ruling class became industrialists and finan-
ciers; although the country would not become fully industrialized until after
World War I, the defeat of the planter class removed the primary obstacle to
industrialization in the South and West.

The mythical plantation with its stately manor house, its lush and well-
tended grounds, its aristocratic and beneficent master, its charming and
gracious mistress, and its deferential and controlled labor force stands in
sharp contrast to the "dark Satanic mills," labor and ethnic conflict, and
mean streets of urban America. On the mythical plantation no one wakes to

the alarm clock, gobbles down coffee and doughnuts and plunges into rush-hour traffic. No one worries about drugs or crime. Everyone is employed and no one starves. The American myth of a simpler and more virtuous agrarian past, where people lived nestled in nurturing and protective families in small and cooperative communities, makes the plantation myth a powerful one even for (especially for) contemporary Americans. Additionally, the plantation myth appeals to the most conservative impulses among those threatened by the liberation movements of the last twenty years. There are no liberated blacks and women on the fictional plantation. The criminals are swiftly brought to justice and external enemies are defeated. Everyone knows his and her place and recognizes white males as the natural superiors.

This literature offers order in place of chaos, harmony for discord, community for alienation. Yet is is also antidemocratic to the core. One must remember that conservative Southerners like Nathaniel Beverley Tucker and William Gilmore Simms argued against the new liberalism of the industrial North. They argued against universal suffrage and the market economy as being inimical to the natural order. Freedom to these Southerners was "the right to fill that place in society to which the merit of the individual entitles him."[7] Thus the planter, who daily demonstrates his superiority to women, blacks, and poor whites, governs Southern society. Tucker and Simms contend it is only when inferiors, filled with false notions of their own abilities and drunk with ambition, forget their proper places, and aspire to conditions beyond their capabilities, that chaos reigns.

In an 1844 address to the National Institute, Tucker assured his white, ruling-class male audience that they had "been chosen as the instrument of God, for accomplishing the great purpose of his benevolence, according to a plan devised by his wisdom, and proclaimed in his word."[8] And what was that plan? To conquer the Indians; tame the wilderness; bring Africans from barbarism to civilization; and to raise their families according to divine law. He urged them to have confidence in themselves in spite of Northern criticism and to join with him "in perpetuating a form of government under which all are free, and none so free as those the world calls slaves."[9]

In celebrating the values of patriarchal conservativism, these authors align themselves with the ruling planter class. In an age where they were threatened by Native American warfare within their borders and on the frontier, a multiethnic working class in the North, and the promised assault of both a strident women's-rights movement and a militant abolitionist crusade, they retreated to the security of the plantation and tried to write the world into order.

As a literature, then, antebellum Southern literature neither speaks to the complexities and contradictions of Southern society nor depicts adequately the lives of women, blacks, and poor whites. Instead, adapting the form of the historical novel for its own use, it supports the hegemony of the planter class and must be viewed as the literary component of the proslavery argument, embodying a conservative theory not only of race, but of gender and class as well. That it failed to survive as "American literature," however, was not necessarily because of its offensive gender and racial stereotypes; many in the North, then and afterward, shared those biases. Nor was it because Southern writers lacked talent. Simms's work can at least be entertaining, though rarely enlightening. It did not prevail because it dodged the harsh realities of slavery and defended the values of a pre-industrial capitalist, deferential society openly antagonistic to the liberal vision of an emerging American society based on individualism, social mobility, and political democracy. Northern victory in the Civil War was more than a military, political, and economic victory; it was an ideological victory as well.

APPENDIX
MAJOR FIGURES

Author	Title	Hero/Heroine	Indians/African Americans	Poor Whites	Yeomen/Scouts
William Alexander Caruthers (1802-1846)	*The Kentuckian in New York* (1834) epistolary novel	August Lamar Isabel Hazelhurst Victor Chevillere Francis St. Clair Damon Montgomery Betsey (no last name) Beverley Randolph Virginia Bell Chevillere	Cato, slave unnamed driver, arsonist		
	Cavaliers of Virginia (1835) historical romance	Nathaniel Bacon Virginia Fairfax	Wyanokee, Indian Red Feather Jack, Indian Pompey slave		Joe ("Red") Jarvis, scout
	Knights of the Golden Horse-Shoe (1841) historical romance	Frank Lee Ellen Evylin Bernard Moore Ann Catherine Spotswood	Old Essex, slave Caesar, rebellious slave Chunuluskee, Indian chief Wingina, Chunuluskee's sister		
James Ewell Heath (1792-1862)	*Edge-Hill* (1828) historical romance	Charles Fitzroyal Ruth Elmore	Alice, nurse James, Alice's son		
John Pendleton Kennedy (1795-1870)	*Swallow Barn* (1832) picaresque novel	Ned Hazard Bel Tracy Frank Meriwether Lucretia Meriwether	Luke, slave Lucy, Luke's wife Abe, their rebellious son Carey, slave	Jemmy Smith Miles Rutherford Hafen Blok	
	Horse-Shoe Robinson (1835) historical romance	Arthur Butler Mildred Lindsey		Walter Adair Peggy Adair Hugh Habershaw, gang leader	Galbraith ("Horse-Shoe") Robinson Allen Musgrove and family David Ramsey and family
	Rob of the Bowl (1838) historical romance	Albert Verheyden Blanche Warden	Pamesack Nalta		Richard Cocklescraft, criminal
William Gilmore Simms (1806-1870)	*Guy Rivers* (1834) border romance	Ralph Colleton Edith Colleton	Caesar, slave		Mark Forrester Guy Rivers

Work				
The Yemassee (1835) historical romance	Gabriel Harrison / Elizabeth Matthews	Sanutee, chief / Matiwan, Sanutee's wife / Occonestoga, their son / Ishiagaska / Hector, slave		Walter Grayson / Hugh Grayson
The Partisan (1835) historical romance	Robert Singleton / Katherine Walton	Ned Blonay, half-breed / Tom, Porgy's slave	Polly Blonay (Ned Blonay is her son) / Lance Frampton / Amos Gaskens	Bella Humphries / Bill Humphries / Captain Huch / John Davis / Walter Griffin
Mellichampe (1836) historical romance	Ernest Mellichampe / Janet Berkeley	Scipio, slave / Blonay, half breed		Jack Witherspoon
Richard Hurdis (1838) border romance	Richard Hurdis / Mary Easterby		Ben Pickett / Betsy Pickett, Ben's wife	Mat Webber, former overseer; criminal
Border Beagles (1840) border romance	Harry Vernon / Virginia Maitland	Cudjo, slave	Florence Marbois / Richard Stillyards	Walter Rawlins, woodsman / William Badger, Walter's uncle / Gideon Badger, William's son / Rachel Morrison, niece
The Kinsmen (1841) (rpt. *The Scout* [1845]) historical romance	Clarence Conway / Flora Middleton	Mira, slave		Jack Bannister / Mary Clarkson
Beauchampe (1842) border romance	Orville Beauchampe / Anna Cooke (a.k.a. Margaret Cooper)			Mrs. Cooper / Margaret Cooper / William Hinkley
Katherine Walton (1851) historical romance	Robert Singleton / Katherine Walton		Lance Frampton	Walter Griffin
The Sword & the Distaff (1852) (rpt. *Woodcraft* [1854]) historical romance	Porgy / Widow Eveleigh / Widow Griffin / Lance Frampton / Ellen Griffin	Tom, Porgy's slave / Pompey / Sappho / Jenny	Samuel Bostwick / Rachel Bostwick, Samuel's wife / Dory Bostwick, their daughter	Millhouse, Porgy's overseer / Fordham, Eveleigh's overseer

Author	Title	Hero/Heroine	Indians/African Americans	Poor Whites	Yeomen/Scouts
William Gilmore Simms (continued)	The Forayers (1855) historical romance	William Sinclair Bertha Travis	Abram (Bram) Johnson Ben Bowlegs	Pete Blodgit Jenny Blodgit, Pete's mother Joel Andrews, "Hellfire Dick," gang leader	Richard Inglehardt, overseer's son
	Eutaw (1856) historical romance (sequel to The Forayers)	William Sinclair Bertha Travis	Abram (Bram) Johnson Ben Bowlegs	Ellen Floyd ("Hurricane Nell") Jeff Rhodes, gang leader	Richard Inglehardt, overseer's son
	Charlemont (1856) border romance	Margaret Cooper William Hinkley			
George Tucker (1775-1861)	The Valley of Shenandoah (1824) sentimental novel	Edward Grayson Matilda Fawkner	Old Phill Old Jeffrey Granny Mott Bristow Peter	Jacob Scryder	M'Culloch, Irish Mrs. M'Culloch Frederick Steener Susan Tidball
Nathaniel Beverly Tucker (1784-1851)	George Balcombe (1836) border romance	William Napier Ann Howard George Balcombe Bet Balcombe	Charles		Mary Scott
	The Partisan Leader (1836)	Douglas Trevor Delia Trevor	Jack		
	Gertrude (1844/45) sentimental novel	Gertrude Courtney Henry Austin			

Notes

INTRODUCTION

1. Richard Beale Davis, "The 'Virginia Novel' before *Swallow Barn*," *Virginia Magazine of History and Biography* 71 (July 1963): 278–93.

2. Vernon L. Parrington, *Main Currents in American Thought*, vol. 2, 1800–1860, *The Romantic Revolution in America* (New York: Harcourt, Brace, and World, 1954); Henry Nash Smith, *The Virgin Land* (New York: Vintage, 1950); Henry Steele Commager, *The American Mind: An Interpretation of American Thought and Character since the 1880s* (New Haven: Yale University Press, 1950); Leo Marx, *The Machine in the Garden: Technology and the Pastoral Ideal in America* (New York: Oxford University Press, 1964). Although I have various differences with their formulations, these classical American intellectual historians provide a good starting point and a method.

3. Karl Marx, *The German Ideology* (1846; New York: International Publishers, 1965), 39.

4. Antonio Gramsci, *Selections from the Prison Notebooks*, ed. Quintin Hoare and Geoffrey Nowell Smith (New York: International Publishers, 1973); Raymond Williams, "Base and Superstructure in Marxist Cultural Theory," *New Left Review* 82 (November–December 1973): 3–16; Raymond Williams, *Marxism and Literature* (London: Oxford University Press, 1977).

5. See for example Ian Angus and Sut Jhally eds., *Cultural Politics in Contemporary America* (New York: Routledge, Chapman, and Hall, 1989); Chandra Mukerji and Michael Schudson, *Rethinking Popular Culture: Contemporary Perspectives in Cultural Studies* (Berkeley and Los Angeles: University of California Press, 1991); Andrew Parker et al., *Nationalisms and Sexualities* (New York: Routledge, Chapman, and Hall, 1992); Lawrence Grossberg et al., *Cultural Studies* (New York: Routledge, Chapman, and Hall, 1992).

6. Lucien Goldmann notes that when analyzing a literary text one needs to remember "what is true of the whole is also true for each of the parts taken separately; though none of these is a primary element, each is a relative whole taken by itself" (6). He then asserts: "Ideas are only a partial aspect of a less abstract reality: that of the whole, living man. And in his turn, this man is only an element in a whole made up of the social group to which he belongs. An idea which he expresses or a book which he writes can acquire their full meaning for us, and can be fully understood, only when they are seen as integral parts of his life and mode of behavior. Moreover, it often happens that the mode of behavior which enables us to understand a particular work is not that of the author himself, but that of a whole social group; and, when the work with which we are concerned is of particular importance, this behavior is that of a whole social class" (7).

I am arguing that these Southern historical romances are important historically and offer us a way to comprehend the "worldview" of the planter class. I realize that Goldmann is thinking about works of "art" with transhistorical importance, but I am adapting his method to examine these texts. See Lucien Goldmann, *The Hidden God:*

A Study of Tragic Vision in the "Pensées" of Pascal and the Tragedies of Racine (1964; reprint, London: Routledge and Kegan Paul, 1976), 3–21. Terry Eagleton's *Marxism and Literary Criticism* (Berkeley and Los Angeles: University of California Press, 1976) also influenced my method.

7. Anne Firor Scott, *The Southern Lady* (Chicago: University of Chicago Press, 1970); Catherine Clinton, *The Plantation Mistress: Woman's World in the Old South* (New York: Pantheon, 1982). I initially used Clinton's dissertation (Princeton, 1980) for my dissertation; although her book is based on her dissertation, she has added sections and chapters, dropped material, and moved some sections in her book. As much as possible, I have tried to convert my original endnotes to correspond with her book. See as well Robert Shalhope, "Race, Class, Slavery and the Antebellum Southern Mind," *Journal of Southern History* 37 (November 1971): 557–74; Angela Davis, "Reflections on the Black Woman's Role in the Community of Slaves," *Black Scholar* 3 (December 1971): 3–15; John W. Blassingame, *The Slave Community: Plantation Life in the Antebellum South* (New York: Oxford University Press, 1972) and *Slave Testimony: Two Centuries of Letters, Speeches, Interviews and Autobiographies,* ed. Blassingame (Baton Rouge: Louisiana State University Press, 1977); George P. Rawick, *From Sundown to Sunup: The Making of the Black Community* (Westport, Conn.: Greenwood, 1972); Herbert G. Gutman, *The Black Family in Slavery and Freedom, 1750–1925* (New York: Vintage, 1977); Lawrence W. Levine, *Black Culture and Black Consciousness: Afro-American Folk Thought from Slavery to Freedom* (New York: Oxford University Press, 1977); Bertram Wyatt-Brown, *Southern Honor: Ethics and Behavior in the Old South* (New York: Oxford University Press, 1982); Deborah Gray White, *Ar'n't I a Woman? Female Slaves in the Plantation South* (New York: Norton, 1985); Sterling Stuckey, *Slave Culture: Nationalist Theory and the Foundations of Black America* (New York: Oxford University Press, 1987).

8. Eugene Genovese, *The Political Economy of Slavery: Studies in the Economy and Society of the Slave South* (New York: Vintage, 1965), and *The World the Slaveholders Made* (New York: Vintage, 1971). Genovese's *Roll, Jordan, Roll: The World the Slaves Made* (New York: Pantheon, 1974) is beset by a number of problems that stem from his hostility toward both feminism and industrial capitalism. I think he so hates industrial capitalism that he is blind to the terror and violence of fully realized patriarchal power in pre-industrial society. Furthermore, his early hostility to feminism (which, it is to be hoped, has abated since he wrote the book) ignored feminist analysis of patriarchy and patriarchal relations and thus distorted his analysis of the master-slave relationship. In this text, he does not appear to understand rape. The tip-off is his section on miscegenation. He denies widespread planter rape and incomprehensively asserts that "But most men, even most free-wheeling, gambling, whoring young aristocrats, do not readily indulge their sadistic impulses" and "the tragedy of miscegenation lay, not in its collapse into lust and sexual exploitation, but in that terrible pressure to deny the delight, affection, and love that so often grew from tawdry beginnings" (417, 419, 413–31). My argument developed in Part III and the Conclusion is that one cannot read long in the slavery sources without concluding that precisely this kind of sadism and violence lay at the core of slavery. Although I substantially agree with Elizabeth Fox-Genovese's analysis of the race and class relations on the plantation and believe she goes much further than her husband in recognizing and delineating planter violence, she still retains his attachment to the unity of the "black and white families" joined in difficult but ultimately preferable social relationships than that of capitalist and wageworker. See Elizabeth Fox-Genovese, *Within the Plantation Household: Black and White Women of the Old South* (Chapel Hill: University of North Carolina Press, 1988). An important critique of *Roll, Jordan, Roll* is offered by Martin A. Kilian and E. Lynn Tatom, "Marx, Hegel, and the Marxian of the Master Class: Eugene D. Genovese on Slavery," *Journal of Negro History* 66 (Fall 1981): 189–208.

9. Simone de Beauvoir, *The Second Sex* (New York: Knopf, 1949), see chapter 9: "Dreams, Fears, and Idols." In *Difference and Pathology: Stereotypes of Sexuality, Race and Madness* (Ithaca: Cornell University Press, 1985), Sander Gilman lays out his theory of stereotyping based on projection.

10. Sheila Rowbotham, *Woman's Consciousness, Man's World* (London: Penguin, 1976); Adrienne Rich, *Of Woman Born: Motherhood as Experience and Institution* (New York: Bantam, 1977; Cynthia Griffen Wolff, "A Mirror for Men: Stereotypes of Women in Literature," in *Woman: An Issue,* edited by Lee Edwards, Mary Heath, and Lisa Baskin; special issue of *Massachusetts Review* 13 (Winter–Spring 1972): 205–18.

11. Jean Fagan Yellin, *The Intricate Knot: Black Figures in American Literature, 1776–1863* (New York: New York University Press, 1972); and William Rogers Taylor, *Cavalier and Yankee: The Old South and the American National Character* (New York: Harper and Row, 1961).

12. See Minrose C. Gwin, *Black and White Women in the Old South: The Peculiar Sisterhood in American Literature* (Knoxville: University of Tennessee Press, 1985); and Hazel V. Carby, *Reconstructing Womanhood: The Emergence of the Afro-American Woman Novelist* (New York: Oxford University Press, 1987). I am thinking of the work of Henry Louis Gates and Houston Baker in particular, but I have also enjoyed reading the essays in the following anthologies: Roseann P. Bell, Bettye J. Parker, and Beverly Guy-Sheftell, eds., *Sturdy Black Bridges: Visions of Black Women in Literature* (Garden City, N.Y.: Anchor, 1979); Barbara Christian, *Black Women Novelists: The Development of a Tradition, 1892–1976* (Westport, Conn.: Greenwood, 1980) and *Black Feminist Criticism: Perspectives on Black Women Writers* (New York: Pergamon, 1985); Barbara Smith, *Home Girls: A Black Feminist Anthology* (New York: Kitchen Table: Women of Color Press, 1983); Alice Walker, *In Search of Our Mothers' Gardens* (New York: Harcourt Brace Jovanovich, 1983); Mari Evans, ed., *Black Women Writers (1950–1980): A Cultural Evaluation* (Garden City, N.Y.: Anchor, 1984); and Marjorie Pryse and Hortense Spillers, eds., *Conjuring: Blacks, Women, Fiction, and Literary Tradition* (Bloomington: Indiana University Press, 1985).

13. See for instance, Constance Rourke's *American Humor: A Study of the National Character* (New York: Harcourt, Brace, 1931) and Louis D. Rubin, *The Comic Imagination in American Literature* (New Brunswick: Rutgers University Press, 1973). A more complete listing of sources appears after Chapter 12.

14. At my last count, there were 31 titles cited by various scholars including Carolyn Lee Hentz's *The Planter's Northern Bride* (1854). See Jeanette Reid Tandy, "Pro-Slavery Propaganda in American Fiction of the Fifties," *South Atlantic Quarterly,* part 1, 21 (1922): 41–50; part 2, 21 (1922): 170–78; Francis Pendleton Gaines, *The Southern Plantation: A Study in the Development and the Accuracy of a Tradition* (New York: Columbia University Press, 1924); Thomas F. Fossett, *"Uncle Tom's Cabin" and American Culture* (Dallas: Southern Methodist University Press, 1985): 185–238.

William Gilmore Simms responded directly to Stowe three times in one year. He chose Louisa S. McCord to review Stowe's *Uncle Tom's Cabin* in the *Southern Quarterly Review* 23 (January 1853): 81–120. In the same journal, he responded in an article that reviewed Mrs. Mary H. Eastman's *Aunt Phillis' Cabin, or Southern Life As It Is,* 23 (April 1853): 523; and, since Stowe had entered the "masculine" fields of history and politics, he reviewed her *Key to "Uncle Tom's Cabin"* (1853) in vol. 24 (July 1853): 214–54. There are also scholars who think that Simms's novel, *Woodcraft, or Hawks About the Dovecote* (1854) responds to Stowe. See S. P. C. DuVall, "W. G. Simms's Review of Mrs. Stowe," *American Literature* 30 (March 1958): 107–17; Joseph V. Ridgely, "*Woodcraft:* Simms's First Answer to *Uncle Tom's Cabin,*" *American Literature* 31 (January 1960): 420–33; John R. Welsh, "William Gilmore Simms, Critic of the South," *Journal of Southern History* 26 (May 1960): 201–14; Hugh W. Hetherington, *Cavalier of Old South Carolina: William Gilmore Simms's Captain Porgy* (Chapel Hill: University of North Carolina

Press, 1966), 38–50; Jean Fagan Yellin, *The Intricate Knot,* 72–78; Charles S. Watson, "Simms's Answer to *Uncle Tom's Cabin:* Criticism of the South in *Woodcraft,*" *Southern Literary Journal* 9 (Fall 1976): 78–90, and "Simms's Review of *Uncle Tom's Cabin,*" *American Literature* 48 (1976): 365–68. Most recently, John Caldwell Guilds notes publishing discrepancies that suggest that Simms's *Woodcraft* could not be a direct planned response. See his *Simms: A Literary Life* (Fayetteville: University of Arkansas Press, 1992): 206–8.

1. THE ANTEBELLUM SOUTH

1. Getting the "exact figures" on the slave and planter population is something of an art as the following representative sources reveal. A fairly standard enumeration is 12 million people: 4 million blacks; 8 million whites, 46,274 of whom are "planters" with twenty slaves or more; see Clement Eaton, *Growth of Southern Civilization* (New York: Harper and Row, 1961), 83. Kenneth Stampp, *The Peculiar Institution.* Slavery in the Ante-Bellum South (New York: Vintage, 1956), cites 12,302,000 people; 8,098,000 whites; 3,954,000 slaves; 250,000 free blacks. James Oakes, *The Ruling Race: A History of American Slaveholders* (New York: Knopf, 1982), 37–41, defines a "typical slave-holder" as someone who owns five slaves or fewer and a "planter" as someone who owns twenty slaves or more. He argues therefore that planters aren't typical slaveholders. Leslie Howard Owens, *This Species of Property: Slave Life and Culture in the Old South* (New York: Oxford University Press, 1977) notes that by 1860, "one tenth of the planter community of 385,000 slaveholders held half of the existing human property" and that only 3,000 individuals throughout the antebellum South owned 100 or more slaves, 72% of the slaveholders owning 10 slaves or fewer (9).

2. Clement Eaton, *A History of the Old South* (New York: Collier, 1966), 401; Amy Mittleman, "A Perceptual Study of the Ante-Bellum Yeomanry, 1820–1860" (M.A. thesis, Columbia University, 1978), 15 and 16; James Oakes, *The Ruling Race,* ix.

3. Oakes, *The Ruling Race,* 58–61.

4. Gavin Wright, *The Political Economy of the Cotton South* (New York: Norton, 1978), 35.

5. Kenneth Stampp, *The Peculiar Institution,* 30; Leslie Howard Owens, *This Species of Property,* 8; Oakes, *The Ruling Race,* 41.

6. The transition of American society from mercantile capitalism to industrial capitalism is one of the more contested areas of historical research. Among the books that have most influenced my thinking in this connection are: Edward Pessen, *Riches, Class, and Power Before the Civil War* (Lexington, Mass.: Heath, 1973); Alan Dawley, *Class and Community: The Industrial Revolution in Lynn* (Cambridge: Harvard University Press, 1976); Anthony F. C. Wallace, *Rockdale: The Growth of an American Village in the Early Industrial Revolution* (New York: Knopf, 1970); Burton J. Bledstein, *The Culture of Professionalism: The Middle Class and the Development of Higher Education in America* (New York: Norton, 1978); Mary P. Ryan, *Cradle of the Middle Class: The Family in Oneida County, New York, 1790–1865* (New York: Cambridge University Press, 1981). Two textbooks by Leonard Richards, *The Advent of American Democracy, 1815–1848* (Glenview, Ill.: Scott, Foresman, 1977) and Mary Beth Norton, et al., in *A People and a Nation: A History of the United States,* 3d ed. (Boston: Houghton Mifflin, 1991) offer this interpretation of the antebellum period.

7. See Catherine Clinton, *The Plantation Mistress: Woman's World in the Old South* (New York: Pantheon, 1982).

8. Gordon Wood, *The Creation of the American Republic, 1776–1787* (New York: Norton, 1972), 478.

9. Ibid., 50–52, 63–65.

10. Linda K. Kerber, *Women of the Republic: Intellect and Ideology in Revolutionary America* (Chapel Hill: University of North Carolina Press, 1980), 281.

11. See Ronald Takaki, *Iron Cages: Race and Culture in Nineteenth-Century America* (New York: Knopf, 1979; 2d ed., New York: Oxford University Press, 1990), 5. Gordon Wood's text is of course replete with these kinds of gendered quotations. For a discussion of how this language and these antiwoman sentiments played themselves out in the French Revolution, see Joan B. Landes's compelling study *Women and the Public Sphere in the Age of the French Revolution* (Ithaca: Cornell University Press, 1988).

12. Gordon Wood, *The Creation of the American Republic,* 471–518; David Hackett Fischer, *The Revolution of American Conservatism: The Federalist Party in the Era of Jeffersonian Democracy* (New York: Harper and Row, 1965), esp. 1–49.

13. George Tucker, *The Valley of Shenandoah; or, Memoirs of the Graysons* (1824; reprint, Chapel Hill: University of North Carolina Press, 1970), 2:206.

14. Quoted in Jessie Bernard, "George Tucker: Liberal Southern Social Scientist," *Social Forces* 25 (1946–47): 141, from George Tucker, *The History of the United States: From their Colonization to the End of the Twenty-Sixth Congress, in 1841* (Philadelphia: J. B. Lippincott, 1856–57), 4:431.

15. See Linda K. Kerber, *Women of the Republic,* 139–55, for a discussion of "femme couverture." See as well Clinton, *The Plantation Mistress,* and Suzanne Lebsock, *The Free Women of Petersburg: Status and Culture in a Southern Town, 1784–1860* (New York: Norton, 1984), for a discussion of how Southern women struggled with economic and legal limitations. Susan Moller Okin, *Women in Western Political Thought* (Princeton: Princeton University Press, 1979), 247–73, discusses the "feme covert" and the history of married women's struggle to own themselves.

16. George Fitzhugh, "Cannibals All!" 122, in *Ante-Bellum,* ed. Harvey Wish (1857; reprint, New York: Capricorn Books, 1960).

17. Nathaniel Beverley Tucker, "The Caucasian Master and the African Slave," 10 (June 1844) *Southern Literary Messenger,* 331.

18. William Gilmore Simms, "The Morals of Slavery," in *The Proslavery Argument As Maintained by the Most Distinguished Writers of the Southern States* (1852; reprint, New York: Negro Universities Press, 1968), 246–50.

19. Another influential essay of the day was T. R. Dew's, "On the Characteristic Differences Between the Sexes," *Southern Literary Messenger* 1 (August 1834): 493–512; 621–32; 672–91. For a provocative and enlightening discussion of the relationship among William Gilmore Simms, Nathaniel Beverley Tucker, James Henry Hammond, Edmund Ruffin, and George Frederick Holmes, see Drew Gilpin Faust, *A Sacred Circle: The Dilemma of the Intellectual in the Old South, 1840–1860* (Baltimore: Johns Hopkins University Press, 1977).

20. See John Ehle, *Trail of Tears: The Rise and Fall of the Cherokee Nation* (New York: Doubleday, 1988). At the time of their removal from the South, the Cherokees were governed by a constitution and had their own newspaper. They lived in towns and raised cattle, horses, pigs, and sheep. They owned as well sawmills and grist-mills and plied the usual complement of nineteenth-century artisanal trades. Similarly, although they practiced slavery very differently from whites, Creeks and Seminoles owned slaves. Indeed, rather than their being unable to "live in contact with a civilized community and prosper" as Andrew Jackson claimed, they may have prospered too well. See as well Theda Perdue, *Slavery and the Evolution of Cherokee Society, 1540–1866* (Knoxville: University of Tennessee Press, 1979); and Daniel F. Littlefield, Jr., *Africans and Creeks from the Colonial Period to the Civil War* (Westport, Conn.: Greenwood, 1976) and *Africans and Seminoles: From Removal to Emancipation* (Westport, Conn.: Greenwood, 1977).

21. William Gilmore Simms, "The Morals of Slavery," 276.

22. Ibid., 260–63, 276–85. For a more thorough discussion of manifest destiny in this period, see Frederick Merk, *Manifest Destiny and Mission in American History* (New York: Random House, 1963); Robert F. Berkhofer, Jr., *The White Man's Indian: Images of the American Indian from Columbus to the Present* (New York: Knopf, 1978); Reginald Horsman, *Race and Manifest Destiny: The Origins of American Racial Anglo-Saxonism* (Cambridge: Harvard University Press, 1981).

23. Simms, "The Morals of Slavery," 266. Similarly, Nathaniel Beverley Tucker notes, "We have but to think of the African as he appeared at first to the European, hardly bearing the lineaments of humanity, in intellect scarcely superior to the brutes, and mainly distinguishable from them by the greater variety of his evil propensities, and by a something answering the purposes of speech better—though not much better—than the chattering of monkeys" ("The Caucasian Master and the African Slave," 333).

24. Tucker, "The Caucasian Master and the African Slave," 336.

25. Nathaniel Beverley Tucker, *Slavery in the United States* (1836), by James K. Paulding, *Southern Literary Messenger* 2 (1835–36): 338.

26. Ibid. The full quote is "They grow in the habitual use of the word 'my,' used as the language of affectionate appropriation, long before any idea of value mixes with it. It is a term of endearment." This defense of slavery as a patriarchal institution, which avoids the alienation of capitalist-wage work relation, is adopted by both Eugene D. Genovese and Elizabeth Fox-Genovese who, like Tucker, make much of the planter's phrase, "My family, black and white." The astute reader should not be swayed by such paternalist obfuscation. See Eugene D. Genovese, *Roll, Jordan Roll: The World the Slaves Made* (New York: Pantheon, 1974); and Elizabeth Fox-Genovese, *Within the Plantation Household: Black and White Women of the Old South* (Chapel Hill: University of North Carolina Press, 1988).

27. Michael Wallace notes that paternalism "is at root despotic; and if much good is done in its name, much that is odious goes unchecked, even unrecognized precisely because its name is such a good one." See his essay, "Paternalism and Violence" in Philip P. Wiener and John Fisher, eds., *Violence and Aggression in the History of Ideas* (New Brunswick: Rutgers University Press, 1972), 203–20. George Fitzhugh, Eugene Genovese's planter spokesman in *The World the Slaveholders Made* is completely frank about his understanding of patriarchal relationships. He says that women and children have only one right, protection; that the husband and father who is their "lord and master" has the right to "abuse" them if they disobey. See Fitzhugh, *Sociology for the South; or, the Failure of Free Society* (1854; reprint, New York: Burt Franklin, 1964), 215. For the full Fitzhugh quote, see the opening of Part 3.

I am arguing against Eugene Genovese's characterization of the master-slave relationship and his sympathetic characterization of paternalism in *Roll, Jordan Roll*, 3–49; 70–97. Catherine Clinton and Bertram Wyatt-Brown have discussed planters' brutality toward their wives and children as well as their slaves. See Clinton, *The Plantation Mistress*, and Wyatt-Brown, *Southern Honor: Ethics and Behavior in the Old South* (New York: Oxford University Press, 1982), 272–91. For similar critiques of Genovese's analysis, see Angela Davis, *Women, Race, and Class* (New York: Vintage, 1981): 24–27; Martin A. Killian and E. Lynn Tatom, "Marx, Hegel, and the Marxian of the Master Class: Eugene D. Genovese on Slavery," *Journal of Negro History* 66 (Fall 1981): 189–208.

28. Edmund S. Morgan, *American Slavery: American Freedom* (New York: Norton, 1975).

29. See for example, John W. Blassingame, *The Slave Community: Plantation Life in the Antebellum South* (New York: Oxford University Press, 1972); George P. Rawick, *From Sundown to Sunup: The Making of the Black Community* (Westport, Conn.: Greenwood, 1972); Herbert G. Gutman, *The Black Family in Slavery and Freedom, 1750–1925*

(New York: Vintage, 1977); Lawrence W. Levine, *Black Culture and Black Consciousness: Afro-American Folk Thought from Slavery to Freedom* (New York: Oxford University Press, 1977); Jacqueline Jones, *Labor of Love, Labor of Sorrow* (New York: Basic Books, 1985); Deborah Gray White, *Ar'n't I A Woman? Female Slaves in the Plantation South* (New York: Norton, 1985).

30. Bertram Wyatt-Brown, *Southern Honor,* 277–96; 331–61; see Wilbur J. Cash, on the "hell of a fellow," in his *The Mind of the South* (New York: Knopf, 1991), 29–58; Drew Gilpin Faust, *James Henry Hammond and the Old South: A Design for Mastery* (Baton Rouge: Louisiana State University Press, 1982); Catherine Clinton, *The Plantation Mistress;* and Deborah Gray White, *Ar'n't I a Woman?*

2. THE PRODUCTION OF SOUTHERN LITERATURE

1. William Charvat, *Literary Publishing in America, 1790–1850* 2nd ed. (Amherst: University of Massachusetts Press, 1993), 76; Clement Eaton, *The Freedom of Thought Struggle in the Old South* (Durham: Duke University Press, 1940), 32–63; Drew Gilpin Faust, *A Sacred Circle: The Dilemma of the Intellectual in the Old South, 1840–1860,* "Bald and Sterile Fields: The Context of Intellectual Discontent," 7–14.

2. When I use the term "middle class," I use it in the sense that Burton J. Bledstein develops in *The Culture of Professionalism: The Middle Class and the Development of Higher Education in America* (New York: Norton, 1978). I see it as a historical and structural phenomenon brought about by the requirements of industrial capitalism for an educated, managerial, and technically skilled elite who were paid salaries. I would argue that in the South one might find middle-class small businessmen, but I prefer the term "yeoman" to indicate non-slaveholding farmers because I think it is more precise than to call these people "middle class."

3. Matthew J. Bruccoli, ed., *The Profession of Authorship in America, 1800–1870: The Papers of William Charvat* (Columbus: Ohio State University Press, 1968), 304, and 305; Eaton, *The Freedom of Thought Struggle,* 66, and 67; Faust, *A Sacred Circle,* 8; Merle Eugene Curti, *The Growth of American Thought* (New York: Harper and Row, 1943); see notes to pages 48 and 449.

4. Faust, *A Sacred Circle,* 8–10; Eaton, *The Freedom of Thought Struggle,* 58–63.

5. Charvat, *Literary Publishing in America,* 44 and 45; John Tebbell, *A History of Book Publishing in the United States,* vol. 1, *The Creation of an Industry, 1630–1865* (New York: Bowker, 1972), 229.

6. Charvat, *Literary Publishing in America,* 38–60.

7. John Tebbell, *Between Covers: The Rise and Transformation of Book Publishing in America* (New York: Oxford University Press, 1987), 14 and 15.

8. Tebbell, *A History of Book Publishing,* 1:207–11; Charvat, *Literary Publishing in America,* 40–44; Charles A. Madison, *Book Publishing in America* (New York: McGraw-Hill, 1966), 44–46; Curti, *The Growth of American Thought,* 346–47. From 1839 to 1843 until the Post Office shut them down, some printer/publishers began bootlegging European novels in weekly periodicals they called "newspapers." In reality they were selling pirated British novels on newsprint for as little as 25 cents when book publishers had to sell books for between one to two dollars to cover their costs. This practice proved ruinous for Northern and Southern writers. See Tebbell, *Between Covers,* 68–71; Madison, *Book Publishing in America,* 24–32; Bruccoli, *The Profession of Authorship in America,* 30–32.

9. Charvat, *Literary Publishing in America,* 55–60.

10. Henry Nash Smith, *Democracy and the Novel: Popular Resistance to Classic American Authors* (New York: Oxford University Press, 1978), 8–10; Ann Douglas, *The Feminization of American Culture* (New York: Knopf, 1977); see esp. her chap. 7: "The Peri-

odical Press," 273–309; Leo Lowenthal, *Literature, Popular Culture, and Society* (Palo Alto, Calif.: Pacific Books, 1961); Dwight MacDonald, "Masscult and Midcult," in his *Against the American Grain* (New York: Vintage, 1962), 3–75.

11. Susan Warner, Fannie Fern, E.D.E.N. Southworth, and Maria Cummins were among the more successful novelists of the period. Their work has been denigrated as "sentimental," but when one discovers the themes of the sentimental novel with its critique of masculinity—the primacy of feeling over intellect, the centrality of women's life experiences and problems, the perfidy of male friendship and protection, and the threat of male passion and sexuality—it is not difficult to see why they were dismissed by their male cohorts. Ann Douglas traces this debate and is critical of these women writers for being anti-intellectual; see Douglas, *The Feminization of American Culture*, 4–12; 354–56; and her epilogue on anti-intellectualism in American life. Her argument was initially challenged by Nina Baym, *Women's Fiction: A Guide to Novels By and About Women in America, 1820–1870* (Ithaca: Cornell University Press, 1987), 11–21, who argues that this fiction has real merit and should not be so easily dismissed. See as well studies by Cathy Davidson and Jane Tompkins, who challenge Douglas's assertions: Cathy Davidson, *Revolution and the Word: The Rise of the Novel in America* (New York: Oxford University Press, 1986), and Jane Tomkins, *Sensational Designs: The Cultural Work of American Fiction, 1790–1860* (New York: Oxford University Press, 1985).

12. For Northerners, see Douglas, *The Feminization of American Culture*, 349–99; Bruccoli, *The Profession of Authorship in America*, 32, 57–70, Madison, *Book Publishing in America*, 24–30; for Southerners, see Faust, *A Sacred Circle*, 21 and 22.

13. On Kennedy see J. V. Ridgely, *John Pendleton Kennedy* (New York: Twayne, 1966), 27, 57–90. Bohner reports that while Kennedy thought that only gentlemen should pursue literature, he also thought it was an "effeminate" occupation for a man. Charles H. Bohner, *John Pendleton Kennedy: Gentleman from Baltimore* (Baltimore: Johns Hopkins University Press, 1961), 114, 178–204. On this problem in American society in general at this time, see Douglas, *The Feminization of American Culture*, 273–309.

14. Robert Colin McLean, *George Tucker: Moral Philosopher and Man of Letters* (Chapel Hill: University of North Carolina Press, 1961), 3–40; Tipton R. Snavely, *George Tucker as Political Economist* (Charlottesville: University of Virginia Press, 1964), 1–6. For more on Tucker, see Chapter 4.

15. Carroll Curtis Davis, *Chronicler of the Cavaliers* (Richmond, Va.: Dietz Press, 1953). Almost everything that has been written about Caruthers has been written by Davis, who apparently devoted his life to the study of Caruthers.

16. Although Simms complained about having started his life with few material advantages and complained of financial difficulties his whole life, there is considerable evidence to suggest that his father left him financially secure and that he was a wealthy man. For Simms's paternal inheritance see Edd Winfield Parks, *William Gilmore Simms as Literary Critic* (Athens: University of Georgia Press, 1961), 1–5; Jay B. Hubbell, *The South in American Literature* (Durham: Duke University Press, 1954), 572–75; A. S. Salley, "William Gilmore Simms," *The Letters of William Gilmore Simms*, ed. Mary C. Simms Oliphant, Alfred Taylor O'Dell, and T. C. Duncan Fines (Columbia: University of South Carolina Press, 1952–56), 1:lix–lxii.

17. One should note that "Robert Singleton" (*The Partisan*, 1835; and *Katherine Walton*, 1953) is one of Simms leading planter heroes. For excellent biographical information on Simms, see Edd Winfield Parks, *William Gilmore Simms;* and introduction to William Gilmore Simms, *Views and Reviews in American Literature, History and Fiction*, ed. C. Hugh Holman (Cambridge: The Belknap Press of Harvard University Press, 1962). The standard Simms biographers are William R. Trent, *William Gilmore*

Simms (New York: Greenwood, 1892); J. V. Ridgely, *William Gilmore Simms* (New York: Twayne, 1962); and Jon L. Wakelyn, *The Politics of a Literary Man: William Gilmore Simms* (Westport, Conn.: Greenwood, 1973). Drew Gilpin Faust's *A Sacred Circle* is indispensable in placing Simms in his social and literary milieu. See also John Caldwell Guilds, *Simms: A Literary Life* (Fayetteville: University of Arkansas Press, 1992), 3–22; 69–75.

18. See "James Ewell Heath," *Dictionary of American Biography,* 8:489; and Robert D. Jacobs, "Campaign for a Southern Literature," *Southern Literary Journal* 2 (Fall 1969): 66–75.

19. See Robert Brugger, *Beverley Tucker: Heart Over Head in the Old South* (Baltimore: Johns Hopkins University Press, 1978); and Beverley D. Tucker and Percy Winfield Turrentine, *Nathaniel Beverley Tucker: Prophet of the Confederacy, 1784–1851* (Tokyo, Japan: Nan' Un-Do Co., 1979).

20. See for example Vernon L. Parrington, *Main Currents in American Thought,* vol. 2, 1800–1860, *The Romantic Revolution in America* (1927; New York: Harcourt, Brace, and World, 1954), 33–54; 119–30; William Rogers Taylor, *Cavalier and Yankee: The Old South and the American National Character* (New York: Harper and Row, 1961), see chaps. 5–7; Jessie Bernard, "George Tucker: Liberal Southern Social Scientist," *Social Forces* 25 (1946–47): 131–45; 406–16.

21. Faust, *A Sacred Circle,* x; The others in that circle included George Holmes, Edmund Ruffin, and James Henry Hammond.

22. Antonio Gramsci, *Selections from the Prison Notebooks,* ed. Quintin Hoare and Geoffrey Nowell Smith (New York: International Publishers, 1973), 5.

23. Ibid., 5 and 6. I am suggesting that these antebellum Southern intellectuals would be similar to but not identical with the European "noblesse de robe," nonecclesiastical intellectuals. See ibid., 7 and 14. I am also obviously supporting Karl Marx's initial observation in his "Thesis on Feurbach" that "the ideas of the ruling class are in every epoch the ruling ideas; i.e., the class, which is the ruling material force of society, is at the same time its ruling intellectual force." Karl Marx, *The German Ideology* (New York: International Publishers, 1965), 39.

24. Ridgely, *John Pendleton Kennedy,* 27.

25. Bohner, *John Pendleton Kennedy,* 179.

26. See Henry Nash Smith, *Democracy and the Novel,* 8–15.

27. See Drew Gilpin Faust, *A Sacred Circle,* 7–14; 21–22, 112–31. For instance, Faust notes, "Justifying slavery became for the intellectual an evangelical act, a defense of morality and truth, a 'sacred duty' for men who regarded themselves as a 'sacred circle' " (115); Mary Ann Wimsatt, *The Major Fiction of William Gilmore Simms: Cultural Traditions and Literary Form* (Baton Rouge: Louisiana State University Press, 1989), 136–55; John Caldwell Guilds, *Simms: A Literary Life,* 130–84. On Simms as a literary rationalist, see William Gilmore Simms, *Views and Reviews in American Literature.*

28. Michael Wallace, "Changing Concepts of Party in the United States: New York, 1815–1828," *American Historical Review* 74 (1968): 471.

29. Gordon S. Wood, *The Creation of the American Republic, 1776–1787* (Chapel Hill: University of North Carolina Press, 1969), 508. See as well David Hackett Fischer, *The Revolution of American Conservatism: The Federalist Party in the Era of Jeffersonian Democracy* (New York: Harper and Row, 1965).

30. Wood, *Creation of the American Republic,* 50–59.

31. Ronald Takaki, *Iron Cages: Race and Culture in Nineteenth-Century America* (Seattle: University of Washington Press, 1979), p. 5. Note as well the dichotomy between virile, manly Republicans and "effeminate" aristocrats. Republicans also found themselves as men by contrasting themselves to women whom they denigrated while they praised them as "Republican Mothers." See Mary Beth Norton, *Liberty's Daugh-*

ters: The Revolutionary Experience of Women (Boston: Little, Brown, 1980); Linda Kerber, *Women of the Republic: Intellect and Ideology in Revolutionary America* (Chapel Hill: University of North Carolina Press, 1980). For a view of a similar phenomenon from the French Revolution, see Joan B. Landes, *Women and the Public Sphere in the Age of the French Revolution* (Ithaca: Cornell University Press, 1988.)

32. Other states that gave blacks with property the vote were Maryland, North Carolina, Tennessee, New York, Connecticut, and New Jersey. See Leon Litwack, *North of Slavery: The Negro in the Free States, 1790–1860* (Chicago: University of Chicago Press, 1961), 74–93.

33. There is an enormous literature on Jacksonian politics. Sean Wilentz's "On Class and Politics in Jacksonian America," *Reviews in American History* 10 (December 1982): 45–63, provides an excellent review of Jacksonian politics historiography. It supersedes Ronald P. Formisano's, "Toward a Reorientation of Jacksonian Politics: A Review of the Literature, 1959–1975," *Journal of American History* 63 (1976): 42–65, and precedes his own award-winning study of New York City, *Chants Democratic: New York City and The Rise of the American Working Class, 1788–1850* (New York: Oxford University Press, 1984).

Among the works that I have found helpful in thinking through this problem for the South are Charles Grier Sellers, "Who Were the Southern Whigs?" *American Historical Review* 59 (1954): 335–46; Richard H. Brown, "The Missouri Crisis, Slavery, and the Politics of Jacksonianism," *South Atlantic Quarterly* 65 (Winter 1966): 55–72; Lynn Marshall, "The Strange Stillbirth of the Whig Party," *American Historical Review* 72 (1967): 445–68; Michael Wallace, "Changing Concepts of Party in the United States: New York, 1815–1828," *American Historical Review* 74 (1968): 453–91; and B. W. Folsom II, "Party Formation and Development in Jacksonian America: The Old South," *Journal of American Studies* 7 (1973): 217–29; William J. Cooper, Jr., *The South and the Politics of Slavery, 1828–1856* (Baton Rouge: Louisiana State University Press, 1978); James Oakes, *The Ruling Race: A History of American Slaveholders* (New York: Knopf, 1982; 2d ed., New York: Vintage, 1983). Oakes's evidence does not really challenge Eugene Genovese's argument so much as he thinks it does. One can still make a distinction between the large and the small planters.

Among the books that have influenced my thinking about the political economy of the period, excluding books specifically about slavery, are: Marvin Meyers, *The Jacksonian Persuasion: Politics and Belief* (1957; reprint, Stanford: Stanford University Press, 1957); Lee Benson, *The Concept of Jacksonian Democracy* (Princeton: Princeton University Press, 1961); Richard P. McCormick, *The Second American Party System* (Chapel Hill: University of North Carolina Press, 1966); Edward Pessen, *Jacksonian America: Society, Personality, and Politics* (Homewood, Ill.: Dorsey, 1969), and *Riches, Class, and Power Before the Civil War* (Lexington, Mass.: Heath, 1973); Alan Dawley, *Class and Community: The Industrial Revolution in Lynn* (Cambridge: Harvard University Press, 1976); and Bruce Laurie, *Working People of Philadelphia, 1800–1850* (Philadelphia: Temple University Press, 1980).

34. Takaki, *Iron Cages,* 9–13. See also his chap. 6: "The Metaphysics of Civilization: 'The Black Race Within Our Bosom,'" 108–44. See Edmund S. Morgan, *American Slavery/American Freedom: The Ordeal of Colonial Virginia* (New York: Norton, 1975), 295–387.

35. Litwack, *North of Slavery,* 74–93.

36. William W. Freehling, *Prelude to Civil War: The Nullification Controversy in South Carolina, 1816–1836* (New York: Harper and Row, 1968), 240–42. C. Hugh Holman sees Simms as a democrat, but I think Simms's elitist position on poor whites and yeoman farmers precludes that conclusion; see Holman's introduction to Simms's *Views and Reviews,* xii–xvii.

37. Bohner, *John Pendleton Kennedy,* 48 and 131.

38. I am arguing that the planter class is struggling to keep the South in its mercantile capitalist phase where they hold economic and political power. Some of them think that the South could industrialize without dislodging the planter class but that is a debate within the class. See Eugene D. Genovese, *The Political Economy of Slavery: Studies in the Economy and Society of the Slave South* (New York: Vintage, 1965), and *The World the Slaveholders Made* (New York: Vintage, 1971).

39. This reference as found in Kenneth S. Greenberg's excellent article, "Revolutionary Ideology and the Proslavery Argument: The Abolition of Slavery in Antebellum South Carolina," *Journal of Southern History* 42 (August 1976): 365–84. He cites his source as the *Southern Quarterly Review* 2 (October 1842): 364–65 and *Southern Quarterly Review* 14 (July 1848): 164. See also Louisa S. Cheves McCord's review of *Uncle Tom's Cabin,* in *Southern Quarterly Review* 23 (January 1853): 87, 106, 109, 111; and Betty L. Mitchell, *Edmund Ruffin: A Biography* (Bloomington: Indiana University Press, 1981), 114 and 115.

40. See John W. Blassingame, ed., *Slave Testimony: Two Centuries of Letters, Speeches, Interviews, and Autobiographies* (Baton Rouge: Louisiana State University Press, 1977); Gilbert Osofsky, ed., *Puttin' On Ole Massa* (New York: Harper and Row, 1969); William Wells Brown, *Clotel, or The President's Daughter* (1853; reprint, New York: Arno Press, 1969); Martin R. Delaney, *Blake, or The Huts of America,* (1857; reprint, Boston: Beacon, 1970).

41. See William Sumner Jenkins, *Pro-Slavery Thought in the Old South* (Gloucester, Mass.: Peter Smith, 1960). Three helpful collections of proslavery articles and essays are Eric L. McKitrick, ed., *Slavery Defended: The Views of the Old South* (Englewood Cliffs, N.J.: Prentice-Hall, 1963); *The Proslavery Argument, As Maintained by the Most Distinguished Writers of the Southern States* (1852; reprint, New York: Negro Universities Press, 1968) includes essays by Simms, Dew, Hammond and Harper; E. N. Elliott, ed., *Cotton Is King and Proslavery Arguments* (1860; reprint, New York: Negro Universities Press, 1969), essays by Hammond, Harper, Christy, Stringfellow, Hodge, Bledsoe, and Cartwright.

42. See Betty L. Mitchell, *Edmund Ruffin, A Biography,* chaps. 3 and 8; William Gilmore Simms, "The Morals of Slavery," in *The Proslavery Argument,* 181–285; Robert S. Starobin, *Industrial Slavery in the Old South* (New York: Oxford University Press, 1970), chap. 6; James D. B. DeBow's views are best found in *DeBow's Review.*

43. Catherine Clinton makes this point in her fine "The Plantation Mistress: Another Side of Southern Slavery, 1780–1835" (Ph.D. diss., Princeton University, 1980), 12–16, 248, 254–89. Her book, *The Plantation Mistress: Woman's World in the Old South* (New York: Pantheon, 1982) considerably revises the thesis by rearranging the chapters and toning down some of the former's more strident assertions. Still, she seems to make similar observations on pages 16 and 17, 96 and 97, 109, and 179 of her book. For instance she notes, "southern slaveowners required obedience without question; if women undermined the planters' absolute authority, the entire network of power relations might be challenged" (179).

44. See Karl Marx, "Feurbach, Opposition of the Materialistic and Idealistic Outlook," *The German Ideology,* 1–78; Lucien Goldmann, "The Whole and the Parts" *The Hidden God: A Study of Tragic Vision in the "Pensées" of Pascal and the Tragedies of Racine* (1964; reprint, London: Routledge and Kegan Paul, 1976), 3–21; Antonio Gramsci, "The Intellectuals," in *Selections from the Prison Notebooks,* 3–23; Walter Benjamin, "The Author as Producer," in *Reflections: Essays, Aphorisms, Autobiographical Writings,* ed. Peter Demetz (New York: Harcourt Brace Jovanovich, 1978), 220–38.

45. U. B. Phillips, "The Central Theme of Southern History," *American Historical Review* 34 (October 1928): 34–43; James M. McPherson, "Slavery and Race," *Perspectives*

in American History 3 (1969): 460–73; Kenneth S. Greenburg, "Revolutionary Ideology and the Proslavery Argument.

46. Charles Grier Sellers, Jr., chap. 3: "The Travail of Slavery," in *The Southerner as American* (Chapel Hill: University of North Carolina Press, 1960), 40–71; Ralph E. Morrow, "The Pro-Slavery Argument Revisited," *Mississippi Valley Historical Review* 48 (June 1961): 79–84; William W. Freehling, *Prelude to Civil War,* argues that South Carolinian planters were afraid of the Denmark Vesey uprising, felt guilty about slavery, and were angry at having to cope with blacks and slavery and having to defend slavery to its critics. William Rogers Taylor in his admirable *Cavalier and Yankee* arrives at a psychological interpretation in arguing that the proslavery literature derived from a response to the women's rights movement and abolitionist movements as well as an "uneasy sense that slavery is a wretched, insupportable, human condition"; see 174 and 175; 297; 303.

47. William B. Hesseltine, "Some New Aspects of the Pro-Slavery Argument," *Journal of Negro History* 21 (January 1936), 1–14, 12; Kenneth Stampp, "An Analysis of T. R. Dew's *Review of the Debates in the Virginia Legislature," Journal of Negro History* 27 (October 1942): 380–87; Eugene Genovese, "Race and Class in Southern History: An Appraisal of the Work of Ulrich Bonnell Phillips," *Agricultural History* 41 (October 1967): 345–58 and *The World the Slaveholders Made.* He argues here that questions of class take precedence over questions of race. David Donald, "The Proslavery Argument Reconsidered," *Journal of Southern History* 37 (February 1971): 3–18, in which he argues that "status anxiety" caused Southern professionals to defend slavery.

48. Robert E. Shalhope, "Race, Class, Slavery, and the Antebellum Southern Mind," *Journal of Southern History* 37 (November 1971): 571, 573; George M. Fredrickson argues: "many 'poor whites' in the North and the South were ready to respond violently to apparent threats to social value of their single claim to status—the white skin that guaranteed that they were better than someone else and not at the rock bottom of society"; see *The Black Image in the White Mind* (New York: Harper and Row, 1971), 95. Wilbur J. Cash, in his controversial masterpiece *The Mind of the South* (New York: Alfred A. Knopf, 1941), argues that racism and slavery precluded class conflict and provided the hook in the system for non-slaveholding whites.

49. Larry E. Tise, *Proslavery: A History of the Defense of Slavery in America, 1701–1840* (Athens: University of Georgia Press, 1987), 285.

50. It is difficult to do justice to Tise's carefully documented study in a few short paragraphs. I think he has succeeded in demonstrating that there is a continuous conservative tradition in the United States from the American Revolution onward and has very skillfully laid out its premises. Additionally, he has proven that Northern anti-abolitionist clergy and educators played a critical role in fashioning the proslavery argument, although I cannot agree that Southerners were completely liberal before that. The biographies of Nathaniel Beverley Tucker, his cousin John Randolph, and John Pendleton Kennedy refute Tise's contention. At any rate, Tise needs to test his thesis with a similar study of literary men, college professors, newspapers editors and book editors. Any study of the impact of the French and Haitian revolutions on American political life would also test his thesis.

51. Genovese, *The Political Economy of Slavery* and *The World the Slaveholders Made;* and Eric Foner, *Free Soil, Free Labor, Free Men* (London: Oxford University Press, 1970).

3. THE FORM OF SOUTHERN LITERATURE

1. Ralph Waldo Emerson, "American Scholar Address," in *Selections from Ralph Waldo Emerson,* ed. Stephen Whicher (Boston: Houghton-Mifflin, 1960), 63–80.

2. For nineteenth-century American themes see Henry Nash Smith, *The Virgin*

Land (New York: Vintage, 1950); Perry Miller, *Nature's Nation* (Cambridge: The Belknap Press of Harvard University Press, 1967), 197–201; Vernon L. Parrington, *Main Currents in American Thought,* vol. 2, *The Romantic Revolution in America* (New York: Harcourt, Brace, and World, 1954); R. W. B. Lewis, *The American Adam: Innocence, Tragedy, and Tradition in the Nineteenth Century* (Chicago: University of Chicago Press, 1955); D. H. Lawrence, *Studies in Classic American Literature* 1923; (New York: Viking, 1972); David W. Noble, *The Eternal Adam and the New World Garden: The Central Myth in the American Novel Since 1830* (New York: George Braziller, 1968).

3. William Gilmore Simms produced a third kind of romance, which I think was probably the precursor to the "Western": the "border romance." It combined the heroic rescue of the virginal heroine from a poor white criminal, this time in a contemporary setting. The hero in each case is an Easterner who has business on the frontier. He is of the planter class himself or he represents planters who are trying to restore "law and order" to their territory. See Simms's *Guy Rivers* (1834); *Richard Hurdis* (1838); *Border Beagles* (1840). Mary Ann Wimsatt develops this idea skillfully in chapter 4 of *The Major Fiction of William Gilmore Simms: Cultural Traditions and Literary Form* (Baton Rouge: Louisiana State University Press, 1989), 85–119.

4. See Ian Watt, *The Rise of the Novel: Studies in Defoe, Richardson, and Fielding* (Berkeley and Los Angeles: University of California Press, 1974); Herbert Ross Brown, *The Sentimental Novel in America, 1789–1860* (Durham: Duke University Press, 1940); Leslie A. Fiedler, *Love and Death in the American Novel,* rev. ed. (New York: Stein and Day, 1966). See also Dale Spender, *Mothers of the Novel* (London: Pandora, 1986) and Margaret Doody, *A Natural Passion: A Study of the Novels of Samuel Richardson* (Oxford: Clarendon Press, 1974), esp. 139–53 on Richardson's "debt" to Eliza Haywood.

5. Watt, *Rise of the Novel,* 157–64; 176 and 177.

6. Ibid., 231; Fiedler, *Love and Death in the American Novel,* 65–73.

7. Watt, *Rise of the Novel,* 222.

8. Ibid., p. 222. Her father demands that Clarissa give up the aristocratic Lovelace and marry the "upstart Solmes"; see 220–23. As previously noted there has been much disagreement with Watt's assertions about the origins of the novel. Additionally, critics have criticized his analysis of the actual rape of Clarissa, arguing that he is embedded in the novel's alleged realism, or "mimetic allusion" as the deconstructionists would have it and that his ideas about Clarissa's rape are sexist. Yet no one has really shaken his assertions about the connections among the advent of industrial capitalism, the rise of the novel, and the centrality of gender and class tensions in the new form. Among the scholars who concede these socioeconomic points to Watt and then take a different approach to *Clarissa* are Mark Kinkead-Weekes, *Samuel Richardson: Dramatic Novelist* (London: Methuen, 1972); Margaret Doody, *A Natural Passion*; Nancy K. Miller, *The Heroine's Text* (New York: Columbia University Press, 1980), 83–95; Terry Eagleton, *The Rape of Clarissa: Writing, Sexuality, and Class Struggle in Samuel Richardson* (Minneapolis: University of Minnesota Press, 1982), 3–10, 89–94; Rita Goldberg, *Sex and the Enlightenment: Women in Richardson and Diderot* (Cambridge: Cambridge University Press, 1984). Goldberg, like Doody, thinks Richardson is a spokesman for middle-class Protestantism and the emergent middle-class morality.

Clarissa has also offered the deconstructionists a fertile field in which to work out their theories; see William Beatty Warner, *Reading Clarissa: The Struggles of Interpretation* (New Haven: Yale University Press, 1979); and Terry Castle, *Clarissa's Ciphers: Meaning and Disruption in Richardson's "Clarissa"* (Ithaca: Cornell University Press, 1982). However much they disagree with each other, they are more concerned with the epistemological questions the text raises than with questions of biography and history. They are interested in the form of the novel, the problem of the actual writing of the text, and the issue of reader response to the novel. In criticizing Warner's reading of the novel, Castle asserts that the principal problem of the text is that Clarissa is subjugated by Lovelace's writing and that she is "an exemplary victim of hermeneutic violence" in being silenced, which culminates in her actual physical rape, both acts of colonization. Therefore, Castle is justifiably critical of Warner's, Watt's, and Fiedler's dismissal of Lovelace's sexual violence (Castle, 22–25, 90–98, 183–85).

9. Cathy Davidson, *Revolution and the Word: The Rise of the Novel in America* (New York: Oxford University Press, 1986), 11. Jane Tompkins makes a similar case in her early chapters on Charles Brockden Brown's *Wieland* and *Arthur Mervyn;* see Jane Tompkins, *Sensational Designs: The Cultural Work of American Fiction, 1790–1860* (New York: Oxford University Press, 1985).

10. Tompkins, *Sensational Designs,* 139–49. Tompkins takes on Ann Douglas's assessment of these writers as being self-indulgent narcissists who produce inferior, oversentimentalized popular pap that appealed to the most reactionary and anti-intellectual strata in American society; see Ann Douglas, *The Feminization of American Culture* (New York: Knopf, 1977).

Other informative and provocative recent studies of these novelists include: Nina Baym, *Women's Fiction: A Guide to Novels By and About Women in America, 1820–1970* (Ithaca: Cornell University Press, 1978); Terry Lovell, *Consuming Fiction* (London: Vergo, 1987); Shirley Samuels, ed. *The Culture of Sentiment: Race, Gender and Sentimentality in Nineteenth-Century America* (New York: Oxford University Press, 1992).

11. It should not be surprising then that American female novelists of the 1850s returned to this form and argue that woman as wife and mother embodied Christian virtue and was God's emissary to "refine men and spiritualize men through their soft influence on him, to ennoble civilization itself"; H. R. Brown, *The Sentimental Novel,* 113. See also Frederick Lewis Pattee, *The Feminine Fifties* (New York: Appleton-Century, 1940) for a sexist analysis of this literature; and Baym, *Women's Fiction,* for a feminist analysis. Jane Tompkins develops this idea the most completely.

12. George Tucker's rake is a Northern merchant's son whose dishonorable behavior is avenged by the fallen planter heroine's brother. Tucker makes Louisa Grayson an avid novel reader, which he claims influenced her judgment. James Ewell Heath stays with the poor heroine and the upper-class male seducer but employs the romantic construction, which requires a male-hero rescuer; see Tucker, *The Valley of Shenandoah* (1824) and Heath, *Edge-Hill; or, the Family of the Fitzroyals* (1828). See also chapter 4 for a discussion of these novels.

13. Irving Babbitt, *Rousseau and Romanticism* (Austin: University of Texas Press, 1977), 16–38.

14. Ibid., 18–20.

15. Arnold Hauser, *The Social History of Art* (New York: Pocket Book, 1972), 3:33–35, 152–57. Perry Miller, *Nature's Nation,* 197–207; Nathaniel Hawthorne, Preface to *The House of the Seven Gables, A Romance* (1851; reprint, Boston: Houghton Mifflin, 1960), xxi. William H. Gilman, "The Hero and the Heroic in American Literature: An Essay in Definition" in *Patterns of Commitment in American Literature,* ed. Marston La France (Toronto: University of Toronto Press, 1967), 3–18.

16. See Scott's *Waverley* (1814), *Rob Roy* (1818), and *Redgauntlet* (1824).

17. Georg Lukács, *The Historical Novel,* trans. Hannah Mitchell and Stanley Mitchell (Boston: Beacon, 1962), 39. Of the antebellum Southern authors, John Pendleton Kennedy's background and professional life as a lawyer and politician were most like Scott's. See Thomas Crawford, *Scott* (Oliver and Bond: Edinburg, 1965), 1–3; and David Daiches, "Literature and Social Mobility" in *Aspects of History and Class Consciousness,* ed. Istvan Meszavos (New York: Herder and Herder, 1971), 162 and 163.

18. Lukács, *The Historical Novel,* 34; Graham McMaster, *Scott and Society* (Cam-

bridge: Cambridge University Press, 1981), 92 and 93; D. D. Devlin, *The Author of Waverley: A Critical Study of Walter Scott* (London: Macmillan, 1971), notes Scott "follows a complex middle way between an Enlightenment view of history, with human nature as the great and totally fixed point, and an historicist approach to the past" (47); see also Marian H. Cusac, *Narrative Structure in the Novels of Sir Walter Scott,* (Paris: Mouton, 1969), 74.

19. Lukács, *The Historical Novel,* 54.

20. See especially Scott's *Rob Roy* (1818). Avrom Fleishman, *The English Historical Novel: Walter Scott to Virginia Woolf* (Baltimore: Johns Hopkins Press, 1971), 49; David Daiches, "Scott's Achievement As a Novelist," in his *Literary Essays* (1956; reprint, London: Oliver and Boyd, 1967), 91–94, 113; David Brown, *Walter Scott and the Historical Imagination* (London: Routledge and Kegan Paul, 1979), 6–30; 202 and 203.

21. Lukács, *The Historical Novel,* 35; Daiches, "Scott's Achievements," 93; Devlin, *Author of Waverly,* 52; Cusac, *Narrative Structure,* 70.

22. See Duncan Forbes, "The Rationalism of Sir Walter Scott," *Cambridge Journal* 7 (1953): 20–35; Peter D. Garside, "Scott and the 'Philosophical' Historians," *Journal of the History of Ideas* 36, no. 3 (1975): 497–512. Using the insights of Forbes and Garside, David Brown has argued that Scott's historical imagination was limited to society "in which the clan (the Scottish patriarchal system), the feudal aristocracy, and the commercial classes held sway with all the complexities of the interface between these three great social systems in Scottish history"; David Brown, *Walter Scott and the Historical Imagination,* 184 and 197–203. See also Daiches, "Scott's Achievement," 88 and Cusac, *Narrative Structure,* 80, who discuss the rationalist influence on Scott.

23. Lukács, *The Historical Novel,* 33–35.

24. William Gilmore Simms's *The Yemassee* (1835) and William Alexander Caruthers's *Knights of the Golden Horse-Shoe* (1841) come the closest to the "American" manifest destiny tradition described in Richard Slotkin's *Regeneration Through Violence: The Mythology of the American Frontier, 1600–1860* (Middleton: Wesleyan University Press, 1973).

25. See William Gilmore Simms, preface to *The Yemassee: A Romance of Carolina* (1835; reprint, Boston: Houghton Mifflin, 1961), 3–7; Mary C. Simms Oliphant, Alfred Taylor O'Dell, T. C. Duncan Fines, eds. *The Letters of William Gilmore Simms* (Columbia: University of South Carolina Press, 1952–56), 3:388 and 389. Simms writes: "The Yemassee, & in fact most of my works are *romances,* not novels. They involve sundry of the elements of heroic poetry. They are imaginative, passionate, metaphysical; they deal chiefly in trying situation, bold characterization, & elevating moral. They exhibit *invention* in large degree & their progress is dramatic; the action being bold salient, & with a regularly advancing convergence to the catastrophe. They exhibit frequent new situations, which are effective, & exercise large ingenuity in the extrication of the *dram. pers*" (Simms's emphasis). For a similar discussion, see Simms, *Views and Reviews in American Literature, History and Fiction,* ed. C. Hugh Holman (Cambridge: The Belknap Press of Harvard University Press, 1962), 7–29. See as well Hawthorne's preface to *The House of the Seven Gables* where he makes a similar distinction. Georg Lukács has argued that the epic hero is never an "individual" in the usual sense since his quest and his destiny is collective, not personal; see Lukács, *The Theory of the Novel: A Historic-Philosophical Essay on the Forms of Great Epic Literature,* trans. Anna Bostock (1920; reprint, Cambridge: MIT Press, 1971), 60–69. Mary Ann Wimsatt, *Major Fiction of William Gilmore Simms,* 9–11, 34–42, makes similar distinctions in her thoughtful comments about Simms's work.

For other studies that discuss this issue, see Perry Miller, *Nature's Nation,* 241–78; and George Dekker, *The American Historical Romance* (New York: Cambridge University Press, 1987), 14–28. Dekker argues that the historical romance was for nineteenth-century authors a modern version of the epic, "hence a heroic and masculine genre preoccupied with the fate of entire societies and but little concerned with individualistic introspection or, reversing the mirror cosmic questionings" (28). The "masculine" nature of the historical romance and the "feminine" nature of the sentimental novel emerges from the work of literary scholars of the period.

26. A. N. Kaul, *The American Vision: Actual and Ideal in Nineteenth-Century Fiction* (New Haven: Yale University Press, 1963), 51–70. This description could have easily come from any of the other innumerable studies on nineteenth-century "American" fiction. For example, the following sample of classic studies of the "American novel" not only either omit Southern writers or treat them perfunctorily, but also propose themes and character types as "American" that are completely incompatible with those found in this antebellum Southern literature: D. H. Lawrence, *Studies in Classic American Literature* (1923); Lewis Mumford, *The Golden Day* (1926); Carl Van Doren, *The American Novel* (1931); Howard Mumford Jones, *The Theory of American Literature* (1948); R. W. B. Lewis, *The American Adam* (1955); Leo Marx, *The Machine in the Garden* (1964); David W. Noble, *The Eternal Adam and the New World Garden* (1968); Theodore L. Gross, *The Heroic Ideal in American Literature* (1971). In addition to Vernon Parrington, notable exceptions to this tendency include: Henry Nash Smith, *The Virgin Land* (1950); Richard Slotkin, *Regeneration through Violence* (1973); Annette Kolodny, *The Lay of the Land* (1975).

27. Although Leslie A. Fiedler has argued that these relationships between men of different races are homoerotic, I think it is more accurate to see them as fantasies of racial reconciliation to heal "the nation." The only way true racial reconciliation could take place is through miscegenation when men of different ethnicities become "brothers" in the traditional patriarchal way. The fact that Southerners could not imagine interracial friendship except within relations of white supremacy and that Northerners could only imagine interracial friendship between men in a world without women indicates the depth of the racism in nineteenth-century America. See Leslie A. Fiedler, *Love and Death in the American Novel,* 192–214, 370–90, and "Come Back to the Raft Ag'in, Huck Honey," in his *An End to Innocence: Essays on Culture and Politics* (Boston: Beacon, 1955), 142–51.

28. See Eric Foner, *Free Soil, Free Labor, Free Men* (London: Oxford University Press, 1970); Marvin Meyers, *The Jacksonian Persuasion: Politics and Belief* 1957; reprint, (Stanford: Stanford University Press, 1960); and Leo Marx, *The Machine in the Garden: Technology and the Pastoral Ideal in America* (New York: Oxford University Press, 1964), for different descriptions of the new bourgeois ideology and the way it played itself out in American political life and culture. See also Sean Wilentz, *Chants Democratic: New York City and the Rise of the American Working Class, 1788–1850* (New York: Oxford University Press, 1984).

29. According to the *Oxford English Dictionary,* the modern term "stereotype" originated from a late eighteenth-century printing process "in which a solid plate or type-metal, cast from a papier-maché or plaster mould taken from the surface of a form of type, is used for printing from instead of the form itself." That plate is called a stereotype and was named by the French printer Didot in 1798.

30. *The Colored American,* 4 March 1837 (my emphasis). My thanks to Sidney Kaplan, professor emeritus of English and African American Studies at the University of Massachusetts, Amherst, for sharing his notes with me on this topic. He uncovered the material on Cornish and did the critical research on the Tilton article and the Child letter that follow. Further, he convinced me that Lippmann and Allport who follow were still relevant to this discussion.

31. Theodore Tilton review, *The Independent,* 27 March 1862.

32. Milton Meltzer and Patricia G. Holland, eds., *Lydia Maria Child: Selected Letters, 1817–1880* (Amherst: University of Massachusetts Press, 1982), 408.

33. For a parallel discussion of the "real Indian," see Roy Harvey Pearce, *Savagism and Civilization: A Study of the Indian and the American Mind* (Baltimore: Johns Hopkins University Press, 1965), and Robert F. Berkhofer, Jr., *The White Man's Indian: Images of the American Indian from Columbus to the Present* (New York: Knopf, 1978). For an introductory discussion of "domestic feminism" and the opposing women's rights position, see Mary P. Ryan, *Womanhood in America from Colonial Times to the Present* (New York: New Viewpoints, 1975); Barbara Berg, *The Remembered Gate: Origins of American Feminism—The Woman and the City 1800–1860* (New York: Oxford University Press, 1978); Nancy Woloch, *Women and the American Experience,* 2d ed. (New York: McGraw-Hill, 1994); Sara Evans, *Born for Liberty: A History of Women in America* (New York: Free Press, 1989); Mary Beth Norton, *Major Problems in American Women's History: Documents and Essays* (Lexington, Mass.: Heath, 1989).

34. Walter Lippmann, *Public Opinion* (New York: Free Press, 1922), 55.

35. Gordon Allport, *The Nature of Prejudice* (Cambridge, Mass.: Addison-Wesley, 1954), 191.

36. Sander L. Gilman, *Difference and Pathology: Stereotypes of Sexuality, Race, and Madness* (Ithaca: Cornell University Press, 1985), 27. He uses the language and methodology of semiotics to convey his ideas. That approach is of course missing from Beauvoir.

37. Ibid., 17. Gilman is not without his problems. First, most psychological theory presupposes the bourgeois nuclear family that was only created by industrial capitalism. In spite of that, I thought his theory of stereotyping had value for my understanding of Southern literature. Second, as the object-relations theorists have demonstrated, "the world" here is actually the mother, and Gilman doesn't distinguish between the weaning and nurturing of girls and boys as they do. They also point out that the first object of infant anger is the mother. Third, white male planters were nursed and weaned by black nurses, a fact that Lillian Smith finds pivotal in the development of the forms of Southern racism, but that Gilman doesn't address because of the different French experience. See Melanie Klein, *Contributions to Psycho-Analysis, 1921–1945* (London: Hogarth, 1948); and Nancy Chodorow, *The Reproduction of Mothering: Psychoanalysis and the Sociology of Gender* (Berkeley and Los Angeles: University of California Press, 1978). See Lillian Smith, *Killers of the Dream* (New York: Norton, 1949).

38. Gilman, *Difference and Pathology,* 20. Other scholars who use the concept of "projection" to describe the phenomenon are Allport, *Nature of Prejudice,* 360–68; Frantz Fanon, *Black Skins, White Masks* (New York: Grove, 1967), 17–40; and Ronald Takaki, *Iron Cages: Race and Culture in Nineteenth-Century America* (Seattle: University of Washington Press, 1979).

39. George Levine, ed., *Realism and Representation: Essays on the Problem of Realism in Relation to Science, Literature, and Culture* (Madison: University of Wisconsin Press, 1993), 3 and 4. In the same volume, J. Hollis Miller argues that a "representation" is literally a "re-presentation" of a person or object by a storyteller or novelist. That means that there is a reality that exists and the observer/narrator changes how we view that object by the story he or she tells about it. I think that Miller would say because language itself is representational, we are never dealing with reality; language limits our perception of what is supposed to exist outside ourselves. As one who believes that there is a reality that exists outside myself in the past as well as in the present (however ineptly I describe it), I find in the concept of representation a dynamic that draws attention to the writer as an active agent in shaping how we view nature and society; see J. Hollis Miller, "Is Literary Theory a Science," 155–68.

40. In addition to George Levine cited in the previous note and the initial volumes of the journal *Representations,* other texts I have found useful are W. J. T. Mitchell, "Representations," in *Critical Terms for Literary Study,* ed. Frank Lentricchia and

Thomas McLaughlin (Chicago: University of Chicago Press, 1990), 11–22; Philip Fisher, ed., *The New American Studies: Essays from "Representations"* (Berkeley and Los Angeles: University of California Press, 1991).

The idea of the "cultural work" of literature springs from two sources: Philip Fisher, *Hard Facts: Setting and Form in the American Novel* (New York: Oxford University Press, 1985), and Jane Tompkins, *Sensational Designs*. I am not so sanguine as Tompkins is about the political effect of stereotypes and am not convinced that the sentimental writers offer exceptional examples of writing at its best. For instance, I do not think she made her case in her last chapter, "But Is It Any Good? . . . " With Ann Douglas, I would answer no, but I think it is still worth reading. Nevertheless, Tompkins's concept of cultural work is very helpful for understanding these Northern and Southern didactic novels. See Laura Wexler's brilliant essay on Native American boarding schools, which reveals the elitist and coercive side to the nineteenth-century female Christianizing project: "Tender Violence: Literary Eavesdropping, Domestic Fiction, and Educational Reform," in Samuels, *The Culture of Sentiment*.

4. THE GENESIS OF THE "PLANTATION NOVEL"

1. See Chapter 2 for a discussion of this issue.

2. Robert Colin McLean, *George Tucker: Moral Philsopher and Man of Letters* (Chapel Hill: University of North Carolina Press, 1961), 3–40; Tipton R. Snavely, *George Tucker as Political Economist* (Charlottesville: University of Virginia Press, 1964), 1–6.

3. Jessie Bernard, "George Tucker: Liberal Southern Social Scientist," *Social Forces* 25 (1946–47): 131–45; 406–16; Leonard C. Helderman, "A Social Scientist of the Old South," *Journal of Southern History* 2 (1936): 148–74; McLean, *George Tucker;* and Snavely, *George Tucker*.

4. McLean, *George Tucker,* 179–202.

5. Ibid., 199–201.

6. See "James Ewell Heath," *Dictionary of American Biography,* 8:489; Frank Luther Mott, *A History of American Magazines,* 5 vols. (Cambridge: Harvard University Press, 1938–1968), 1:631–33; Robert D. Jacobs, "Campaign for a Southern Literature," *Southern Literary Journal* 2 (Fall 1969): 66–75. To date there has been no biography of Heath although he was an influential Southern literary man. Material about him may be gleaned from the papers of more prominent literary people. For that reason, my conclusions about Heath are tentative.

7. See the *Southern Literary Messenger* 1 (August 1834): 1–3 and also note his use of the word "vassalage": when colonial and antebellum Southerners wanted to describe extremely oppressive treatment, they often referred to "vassalage" or "slavery." These same people would turn right around, then, and defend Southern slavery as "mild" bondage.

8. See Tucker's subsequent commentary in the *Southern Literary Messenger* 1 (January 1835): 230. In his commentary Heath had noted, "we regard it [slavery], on the contrary, as a great evil, which society sooner or later will find it not only to its interest to remove or mitigate, but will seek its gradual abolition, or amelioration, under the influence of those high obligations imposed by an enlightened Christian morality." For Heath's response, see *Southern Literary Messenger* 1 (January 1835): 254.

9. John Pendleton Kennedy's *Swallow Barn* and Nathaniel Beverley Tucker's *Gertrude* are the only other novels in the literature that are not "romances" of some kind.

10. See Clement C. Eaton, *The Freedom of Thought Struggle in the Old South* (Durham: Duke University Press, 1940); and Carl N. Degler, *The Other South* (New York: Harper and Row, 1974). Eaton argues that this period in the South was marked by "a dramatic struggle" between "the forces of conservatism and liberalism," where people

"fought over the gradual removal of human bondage, civil liberties, adoption of a democratic system of education, and freedom from religious orthodoxy" in which "the liberals were defeated on almost all fronts" (v).

11. See George M. Frederickson, *White Supremacy: A Comparative Study in American and South African History* (New York: Oxford University Press, 1981).

12. See Anne Firor Scott, *The Southern Lady* (Chicago: University of Chicago Press, 1970); Catherine Clinton, *The Plantation Mistress: Woman's World in the Old South* (New York: Pantheon, 1982); Elizabeth Fox-Genovese, *Within the Plantation Household: Black and White Women of the Old South* (Chapel Hill: University of North Carolina Press, 1988) for a discussion of the lives of these women.

13. Tucker, *The Valley of Shenandoah,* 1:1, 13, 14; 2:138–43.

14. Tucker notes that although Gildon was "as much attached to her as he was capable of being," he had "lost some portion of the high respect he had previously entertained for her" (2:265); 130–133.

15. James Ewell Heath, *Edge-Hill; or, The Family of the Fitzroyals. A Novel. By A Virginian* (Richmond, Va.: T. White, 1828), 1:45.

16. I am indebted to Cynthia Griffen Wolff's article, "A Mirror for Men: Stereotypes of Women in Literature," in *Women: An Issue,* special issue of *Massachusetts Review* 13 (Winter–Spring 1972): 205–18, for discussing this phenomenon so clearly and intelligently.

17. McLean, *George Tucker,* 179–202. McLean argues convincingly that Tucker wasn't a "liberal" opponent of slavery.

18. For a discussion of the "Virginian" or "plantation novel," see Jay B. Hubbell, *Southern Life in Fiction* (Athens: University of Georgia Press, 1960); Alexander Cowie, *The Rise of the American Novel* (New York: American Book, 1948), 228–80; Francis Pendleton Gaines, *The Southern Plantation: A Study in the Development and the Accuracy of a Tradition* (New York: Columbia University Press, 1924). Perhaps the most important essay in this regard is Richard Beale Davis, "The 'Virginia Novel' Before *Swallow Barn,*" *Virginia Magazine of History and Biography* 71 (1963): 278–93. In it he summarizes the scholarship to date and argues that although John Esten Cooke popularized the idea of the "Virginia novel" because he was a Virginian, the most accomplished writer of the form was William Gilmore Simms from South Carolina. Therefore, Davis prefers "plantation novel" as a more accurate description of a certain type of antebellum fiction. In this essay, Davis also argues that there were at least five plantation novels before *Swallow Barn* that should be recognized, among them the novels of Tucker and Heath considered in this study.

19. *The Valley of Shenandoah,* 1:59–73. Tucker tells us through Edward Grayson's commentary to his friend, Gildon, that "on a well-regulated estate, on which the slaves *have been properly brought up and managed,* their labour, when they are actually engaged, differs little from that of free men. They have, too, their feelings of pride and their emulation with the neighboring farms, and with one another, which, though so operating so generally, or so steadily as self-interest, operates at sometimes, and on some individuals, quite as efficiently. I am sure there are several men in that race who as completely identify themselves with our family as if the crop was their own; 1:67 and 68 (my emphasis).

20. James Ewell Heath, *Edge-Hill,* 1:103.

21. See John Pendleton Kennedy, *Swallow Barn, or A Sojourn in the Old Dominion* (1832; reprint, 1853 edition, New York: Hafner, 1971), 465, 465–90.

22. Compared with the other novelists considered in this study, Heath is scarcely mentioned in any standard discussions of antebellum Southern literature and his novel has never been reprinted. Heath's work is available only on microfilm. Interestingly, Heath's "James" may have been modeled on a real-life counterpart in James

Armistead Lafayette, who was emancipated by the General Assembly of Virginia in 1786 at Lafayette's and Washington's request. For a discussion of James Armistead Lafayette's life and his portrait, see Sidney Kaplan and Emma Nogrady Kaplan, *The Black Presence in the Era of the American Revolution* (Amherst: University of Massachusetts Press, 1989), 37–44.

23. See William Alexander Caruthers's discussion in *The Kentuckian in New York; or, The Adventures of Three Southerners* (New York: Harper, 1834), 1:115–19.

24. Historians have disagreed about whether fidelity or infidelity was more common in the slave quarters. For instance, Phillips and Stampp think that black men and women were promiscuous; Genovese and Blassingame argue that neither fidelity nor infidelity dominated as a pattern; and Rawick and Gutman argue that fidelity rather than infidelity was the choice of blacks though they were often coerced in other directions. See Ulrich Bonnell Phillips, *Life and Labor in the Old South* (Boston: Little, Brown, 1929), 203–5; Kenneth M. Stampp, *The Peculiar Institution* (New York: Vintage, 1956), 245–51; John W. Blassingame, *The Slave Community: Plantation Life in the Antebellum South* (New York: Oxford University Press, 1972), 77–103; Eugene D. Genovese, *Roll, Jordan, Roll: The World the Slaves Made* (New York: Vintage, 1971), 450–501; Herbert G. Gutman, *The Black Family in Slavery and Freedom, 1750–1925* (New York: Vintage, 1977), 75–87; and George P. Rawick, *From Sundown to Sunup: The Making of the Black Community* (Westport, Conn.: Greenwood, 1972), 77–94.

25. McLean, *George Tucker,* 38–40, 223–29.

5. REPRESENTING SOUTHERN WOMEN'S LIVES

1. See Anne Firor Scott, *The Southern Lady* (Chicago: University of Chicago Press, 1970), chap. 2; Catherine Clinton, *The Plantation Mistress: Woman's World in the Old South* (New York: Pantheon, 1982), chap. 2; and Elizabeth Fox-Genovese, *Within the Plantation Household: Black and White Women of the Old South* (Chapel Hill: University of North Carolina Press, 1988).

2. Scott, *Southern Lady,* chap. 2; Clinton, *Plantation Mistress,* esp. chap. 6. Clinton and Fox-Genovese disagree about the degree of participation of plantation mistresses in the actual hands-on labor. Fox-Genovese contends that when a Southern woman wrote in her diary that "we" put up pickles or made clothes, she was writing of supervising black women who did the hard work (Fox-Genovese, *Within the Plantation Household,* 112, 117–29). Clinton's opening vignette of chap. 2 in *The Plantation Mistress* belies that contention, as does the rest of her second chapter. Deborah Gray White agrees with Clinton; see *Arn't I a Woman? Female Slaves in the Plantation South* (New York: Norton, 1987), 51–53.

3. Scott, *Southern Lady,* chap. 2; Clinton, *Plantation Mistress,* chap. 5; Fox-Genovese, *Within the Plantation Household,* chap. 2.

4. On the ever-present danger of death, see Clinton, *Plantation Mistress,* chaps. 6 and 7; D. G. White, *Arn't I a Woman?* chap. 2; Elizabeth Fox-Genovese, *Within the Plantation Household,* 129–32. On slaves and health, see Kenneth M. Stampp, *The Peculiar Institution* (New York: Vintage, 1956), chap. 7; Leslie Howard Owens, *This Species of Property: Slave Life and Culture in the Old South* (New York: Oxford University Press, 1976), chap. 2.

5. On the physical abuse of black slave women, see Angela Davis, "Reflections on the Black Woman's Role in the Community of Slaves," *Black Scholar* 3 (December 1971): 3–15; Stampp, *The Peculiar Institution,* 139–91, 245–56, 350–61; John W. Blassingame, *The Slave Community: Plantation Life in the Antebellum South* (New York: Oxford University Press, 1972), 77–103; and John W. Blassingame, ed., *Slave Testimony: Two Centuries of Letters, Speeches, Interviews, and Autobiographies* (Baton Rouge: Loui-

siana State University Press, 1977), passim (see 372 for a description of an especially gruesome torture of a black woman); Leslie H. Owens, *This Species of Property,* 50–69, 182–213; Eugene D. Genovese, *Roll, Jordan, Roll: The World the Slaves Made* (New York: Pantheon, 1974), 413–31, 450–75, 494–501; Herbert G. Gutman, *The Black Family in Slavery and Freedom, 1750–1925* (New York: Vintage, 1977), 3–100, 257–376. Jacqueline Jones, *Labor of Love, Labor of Sorrow* (New York: Basic Books, 1985), 18–21; D. G. White, *Arn't I a Woman?*34–42; Fox-Genovese, *Within the Plantation Household,* 34, 43, 135, 139 and 140, 154–56, 164 and 165, 309–15.

6. Blassingame, *Slave Testimony;* Frederic Bancroft, *Slave Trading in the Old South* (New York: Ungar, 1959).

7. For the transition from the sentimental heroine to the romantic heroine, see Ian Watt, *The Rise of the Novel: Studies in Defoe, Richardson, and Fielding* (Berkeley and Los Angeles: University of California Press, 1974); Leslie A. Fiedler, *Love and Death in the American Novel,* rev. ed. (New York: Stein and Day, 1966); Cynthia Griffin Wolff, "A Mirror for Men: Stereotypes of Women in Literature," in *Women: An Issue;* special issue of *Massachusetts Review* 13 (Winter–Spring 1972): 205–18; Ralph P. Boas, "The Romantic Lady," in *Romanticism in America,* ed. George Boas (Baltimore: Johns Hopkins University Press, 1940), 62–88; Herbert Ross Brown, *The Sentimental Novel in America, 1789–1860* (Durham: Duke University Press, 1940). On the Victorian heroine who is essentially the middle-class heroine, see Walter E. Houghton, *The Victorian Frame of Mind, 1830–1870* (New Haven: Yale University Press, 1957); Barbara Welter, *Dimity Convictions: The American Woman in the Nineteenth Century* (Athens: Ohio University Press, 1976); Katharine M. Rogers, *The Troublesome Helpmate: A History of Misogyny in Literature* (Seattle: University of Washington Press, 1966); Nina Baym, in her *Women's Fiction: A Guide to Novels By and About Women in America, 1820–1970* (Ithaca: Cornell University Press, 1978), notes that the sentimental novel gave the heroine more dignity, independence, and ability to act, and so was the choice of the "scribbling women in the 1850's."

8. Richard Slotkin, *Regeneration Through Violence: The Mythology of the American Frontier, 1600–1860* (Middletown, Conn.: Wesleyan University Press, 1973), chap. 13, describes this difference.

9. Rogers, *Troublesome Helpmate;* Welter, *Dimity Convictions;* Houghton, *The Victorian Frame of Mind;* Clinton, *Plantation Mistress,* 123–38. In her discussion of the Southern "lady," Fox-Genovese makes a distinction between Northern and Southern gender conventions, though her argument that Southerners actually adopted Roman forms of patriarchy is unconvincing and stems from the planter class's illusions about itself. However, given the violence and lechery of the Romans maybe she has a point. See Fox-Genovese, *Within the Plantation Household,* 60–68, 107–10.

10. Rogers, *Troublesome Helpmate,* 209. Catherine Clinton notes that plantation women were overworked and emotionally drained. Plantation mistresses who were supposed to guard the health of everyone else after themselves had the worst health, but nevertheless mothers often encouraged their daughters about maintaining their health by building their bodies through vigorous exercise; see Clinton, *Plantation Mistress,* chaps. 6, 8, and 210–13.

11. D. G. White, *Arn't I a Woman?* chap. 1. Mary Boykin Chesnut has noted: "Under slavery, we live surrounded by prostitutes, yet an abandoned woman is sent out of any decent house. . . . Like the patriarchs of old, our men live all in one house with their wives and their concubines; and the mulattoes one sees in every family partly resemble the white children"; *A Diary from Dixie,* ed. Ben A. Williams (1905; Boston: Houghton Mifflin, 1961), 21. See C. Clinton, *Plantation Mistress,* chap. 11; and Fox-Genovese, *Within the Plantation Household,* 50–52.

12. For white planter miscegenation activities and fantasies see Winthrop Jordan,

White Over Black: American Attitudes Toward the Negro, 1550–1812 (Baltimore: Penguin, 1968); George M. Fredrickson, *The Black Image in the White Mind* (New York: Harper and Row, 1972); Herbert G. Gutman, *The Black Family;* Bancroft, *Slave Trading;* Blassingame, *Slave Community;* James Hugo Johnston, *Race Relations in Virginia and Miscegenation in the South, 1776–1860* (Amherst: University of Massachusetts Press, 1970); Joel Kovel, *White Racism: A Psychohistory* (New York: Pantheon, 1970); Angela Davis, "Reflections on the Black Woman's Role"; Carl N. Degler, *Neither Black Nor White* (New York: Macmillan, 1971). Among the historians who discount either the existence of planter miscegenation or its seriousness for the black woman and her family include Ulrich Bonnell Phillips, *Life and Labor in the Old South* (Boston: Little, Brown, 1929); Edward B. Reuter, *The Mulatto in the United States* (New York: Negro Universities Press, 1969). In his otherwise admirable *The Problem of Slavery in Western Culture* (Ithaca: Cornell University Press, 1966), David Brian Davis asserts: "Bondwomen have always been the victims of sexual exploitation, which was perhaps the dearest recognition of their humanity" (59). Earl E. Thorpe, *Eros and Freedom in Southern Life and Thought* (Durham, N.C.: Seeman Printery, 1967); and Eugene D. Genovese, *Roll, Jordan, Roll* think that black women and white men were the victims of racial jealousy and bigotry in being unable to mate more freely. In a breathtaking passage that not only distorts plantation relations but that minimizes the suffering that white male sexual aggression caused white women, black men, and, most important, black women, Genovese asserts: "The tragedy of miscegenation lay, not in its collapse into lust and sexual exploitation, but in that terrible pressure to deny the delight, affection and love that so often grew from tawdry beginnings" (419).

13. See Bertram Wyatt-Brown, *Southern Honor: Ethics and Behavior in the Old South* (New York: Oxford, 1982), 292–98, 307–9; Catherine Clinton, *The Plantation Mistress,* 199–219; Elizabeth Fox-Genovese, *Within the Plantation Household,* 196–201.

14. Eleanor Flexner, *A Century of Struggle: The Woman's Rights Struggle in the United States* (New York: Atheneum, 1973); Leo Kanowitz, *Woman and the Law: The Unfinished Revolution,* (Albuquerque: University of New Mexico Press, 1969); Carl N. Degler, *At Odds: Women and the Family in America from the Revolution to the Present* (New York: Oxford University Press, 1980). For women who act against convention see Victoria E. Bynum, *Unruly Women: The Politics of Social and Sexual Control in the Old South* (Chapel Hill: University of North Carolina Press, 1992).

15. Simone de Beauvoir, "Dreams, Fears, Idols," in *The Second Sex* (New York: Knopf, 1949), 129–85.

16. Beauvoir, *The Second Sex,* Susan Brownmiller, *Femininity* (New York: Simon and Schuster, 1984), 53 and 54; Sander Gilman, *Difference and Pathology: Stereotypes, of Sexuality, Race and Madness,* (Ithaca: Cornell University Press, 1985): 15–35.

17. The reclamation of women's history that has taken place over the last twenty years has addressed these issues of lived female existence and female political consciousness. The following anthologies of women's history and theory provide a starting point for anyone interested in these issues and certainly informed my thinking on this topic: Mary S. Hartman and Lois Banner, eds., *Clio's Consciousness Raised* (New York: Harper and Row, 1974); Bernice A. Carroll, ed., *Liberating Women's History: Theoretical and Critical Essays* (Urbana: University of Illinois Press, 1976); Renate Bridenthal and Claudia Koontz, eds., *Becoming Visible: Women in European History* (Boston: Houghton Mifflin, 1977); Gerda Lerner, *The Majority Finds Its Past: Placing Women in History* (New York: Oxford University Press, 1979); and Joan Kelly, *Women, History, and Theory: The Essays of Joan Kelly* (Chicago: University of Chicago Press, 1984). Although there have been extensive discussions of African American literature and the images of and production of literature by women and a lively debate on black feminism, historiographical discussion of African American women's history is rarer. Gerda Lerner offers two essays in *The Majority Finds Its Past,* but that is an exception. See bell

hooks, *Ain't I a Woman: Black Women and Feminism* (Boston: South End Press, 1981); and Angela Davis, *Women, Race, and Class* (New York: Vintage, 1981) for two different approaches to this issue. One of the latest attempts to provide an inclusive women's history is Ellen C. DuBois and Vicki L. Ruiz, eds., *Unequal Sisters: A Multi-Cultural Reader in U.S. Women's History* (New York: Random House, 1990).

18. For mistresses' consciousness about their oppression, see Clinton, *Plantation Mistress,* and Scott, *The Southern Lady.* Scott notes that women were psychologically and economically threatened: "Be a lady and you will be loved and respected and supported. If you defy the pattern and behave in ways considered unladylike you will be unsexed, rejected, unloved, and you will probably starve" (21). Clinton notes also that mistresses' psychological, social, and economic oppression made them physically ill (see her chapter 8) and states that many Southern women became addicted to laudanum (143–46).

19. On the viability of slave culture, see especially George P. Rawick, *From Sundown to Sunup: The Making of the Black Community* (Westport, Conn.: Greenwood, 1972); Blassingame, *Slave Community* and *Slave Testimony;* Owens, *This Species of Property;* Lawrence W. Levine, *Black Culture and Black Consciousness: Afro-American Folk Thought from Slavery to Freedom* (New York: Oxford University Press, 1977); Gutman, *The Black Family.* Although he would argue that black-white relations on the plantation were more mutually beneficial than would the above authors, Genovese's *Roll, Jordan, Roll* provides enough evidence, especially in the religion section, for one to argue against his thesis about the master-slave relationship.

6. THE "BELLE"

1. See Appendix for a list of heroes and heroines considered in this study. The passive heroines include: Virginia Maitland, Gertrude Austin, Bet Balcombe, Delia Trevor, Kate Spotswood, Ann Howard, Edith Colleton, Elizabeth Matthews, Mary Easterby, Flora Middleton, Bertha Travis. The assertive heroines are: Katherine Walton, Janet Berkeley, Ellen Evylin, Virginia Fairfax, Bel Tracy, Margaret Cooper. Of Tucker's and Heath's characters, Louisa Grayson would be clearly passive while Ruth Elmore would be clearly active. Matilda Fawkner displays aspects of both types. Note as well the number of heroes and heroines whose mothers are absent.

2. Nathaniel Beverley Tucker, *Gertrude, Southern Literary Messenger* 10 and 11 (1844–45): 10:515.

3. Gerda Lerner, *The Grimké Sisters from South Carolina* (New York: Schocken, 1971) presents information about the Grimkés' reaction to slave beatings on the plantation. Bertram Wyatt-Brown, *Southern Honor: Ethics and Behavior in the Old South* (New York: Oxford University Press, 1982), discusses the implications of patriarchy for planters and mistresses, their children and slaves.

4. In 1819 Tucker set out for Missouri with his family and two of his best friends and their families to create "a slave-holder's Valhalla." Tucker loathed Irish immigrants and had nothing but contempt for non-slaveowners. Tucker notes that Southern society had solved the problem of social control in its patriarchal institutions in which "power is gentle and obedience liberal, and the will of the superior prevails"; see Robert J. Brugger, *Beverley Tucker: Heart Over Head in the Old South* (Baltimore: Johns Hopkins University Press, 1978), 60, 146. James Oakes argues that the small slaveholders in the new Southwest had a much more utilitarian and less paternalistic attitude toward their slaves than those large planters in the East; see *The Ruling Race: A History of American Slaveholders* (New York: Knopf, 1982).

5. Nathaniel Beverley Tucker, *George Balcombe. A Novel,* 2 vols. (New York: Harper, 1836) 1:278.

6. I am grateful to William Rogers Taylor for revealing this quote in his *Cavalier*

and Yankee: The Old South and the American National Character (New York: Harper and Row, 1961), 174; this quote inspired this study. See William Gilmore Simms, "The Morals of Slavery," and Thomas R. Dew, "Review of the Debate in the Virginia Legislature, 1831–1832," in *The Pro-Slavery Argument, As Maintained by the Most Distinguished Writers of the Southern States* (1852, reprint; New York: Negro Universities Press, 1968), 175–285 and 286–490 respectively. The Simms essay first appeared as a review of Harriet Martineau's *Society in America,* which was critical of slavery. Simms's criticism of "intellectual women" is as telling as his diatribe against African Americans. See as well Nathaniel Beverley Tucker, "The Caucasian Master and the African Slave," *Southern Literary Messenger* 10 (June 1844): 329–39, 470–80, and "Slavery," *Southern Literary Messenger* 2 (1835–36): 336–39. Another important article on women from this group of conservative Southerners is Thomas R. Dew's "On the Characteristic Differences Between the Sexes, and the Position and Influence of Women in Society," *Southern Literary Messenger* 1, nos. 11 and 12 (May–August 1835): 493–512, 620–32, 672–91.

7. See C. Hugh Holman's scholarship on Simms's treatment of the South in the Revolutionary War: "William Gilmore Simms' Picture of the Revolutionary War as a Civil War," *Journal of Southern History* 15 (November 1949): 441–62, and "Simms's Changing View of the Loyalists During the Revolution," *Mississippi Quarterly* 29 (Fall 1976), 501–72; introduction to *Views and Reviews in American Literature and History,* ed. William Gilmore Simms (Cambridge: The Belknap Press of Harvard University Press, 1962): vii–xxvii. See as well Roger J. Bresnahan, "William Gilmore Simms's Revolutionary War: A Romantic View of Southern History" *Studies in Romanticism* 15 (Fall 1976): 573–87; and Charles S. Watson, "Simms and the American Revolution," *Mississippi Quarterly* 29 (Fall 1976): 498–500. In his revolutionary romances, Simms neglects to mention Native Americans, thereby implying they are not present in Southern society when in fact they play a critical disruptive role.

8. William Gilmore Simms, *The Forayers; or, the Raid of the Dog Days* (1855; reprint, New York: A. C. Armstrong and Son, 1882), 84–88, 125, 158–60, 282–87.

9. See Frederick I. Carpenter, "Puritans Prefer Blondes: The Heroines of Melville and Hawthorne," *New England Quarterly* 9 (June 1936): 253–72; and Leslie A. Fiedler, *Love and Death in the American Novel* (New York: Stein and Day, 1966), 291–336. Since these authors rarely mention sexuality at all, it is even difficult to say that black women represent sensuality. The most one can assert about the color politics of the novelists is that all of the villains are dark or swarthy with dark hair. The fair-complexioned, light-haired heroines include Bel Tracy, Mildren Lindsey, Virginia Fairfax, Kate Spotswood; dark-haired heroines (all Simms heroines) include Katherine Walton, Janet Berkeley, Bertha Travis, Carrie Sinclair, Mary Esterby, Virginia Maitland. Although Simms heroines had dark hair and eyes, all of them had pale complexions— the true test in the South. See Appendix for a chart on the heroines.

10. Chapter 12 addresses the issue of class in these novels and specifically takes up the case of the characters in these two novels. William Gilmore Simms, *Eutaw* (1856; reprint, New York: A. C. Armstrong and Son, 1882), 495–97, 565–78.

11. See Simms's introductions to *Richard Hurdis* (1838), *Guy Rivers* (1835), *Beauchampe* (1842), and *Border Beagles* (1840). For instance, he describes the frontier settlement Mississippi in *Border Beagles: A Tale of Mississippi* (1840; reprint, New York: A. C. Armstrong and Son, 1882) as follows: "There is as yet no settled population. The country is uncleared and thoroughly wild; settled by squatters chiefly without means, tastes, education, or sensibility; rude rough people; a people particularly fitted for the conquest of savages and savage Indians" (159).

12. *Border Beagles,* 25.

13. William Gilmore Simms, preface to *Katherine Walton* (1851; reprint, New York: J. S. Redfield, 1854), 4.

14. William Gilmore Simms, *The Partisan: A Romance of the Revolution* (1835; reprint, New York: Belford, Clarke, 1885), 133 and 134.

15. See discussion in Chapter 8 of *Margaret Cooper*. Also Flora Middleton of *The Scout; or, The Black Riders of Congaree* (1841; reprint, New York: A. C. Armstrong and Son, 1882) is another strong Simms heroine.

16. Simms's mother, Harriet Ann August Singleton, was descended from the wealthy low-country Singleton family, which migrated to South Carolina from Virginia before the American Revolution. Her grandfather, Thomas Singleton, was involved in the defense of Charleston (subject of *The Partisan* and, to some extent, *Katharine Walton*) and her uncle John rode with Francis Marion, the legendary Swamp Fox (like Willie Sinclair and Robert Singleton). Simms's maternal grandmother, who raised him, told him family stories that Simms later worked into these novels. See William P. Trent, *William Gilmore Simms* (New York: Greenwood, 1892), 8 and 9; Jay B. Hubbell, *The South in American Literature* (Durham: Duke University Press, 1954), 572 and 573; J. V. Ridgely, *William Gilmore Simms* (New York: Twayne, 1962), 17–22; Jon L. Wakelyn, *The Politics of a Literary Man: William G. Simms* (Westport, Conn.: Greenwood, 1973); A. S. Salley, "William Gilmore Simms," in *The Letters of William Gilmore Simms*, ed. Mary C. Simms Oliphant, Alfred Taylor O'Dell, and T. C. Duncan Forbes, 5 vols. (Columbia: University of South Carolina Press, 1952–56), 1:lix–lxiii.

17. William Gilmore Simms, *The Partisan: A Romance of the Revolution* (1835; reprint, New York: Belford, Clarke, 1885), 152–56, 275–92. Victorian women are "true Christians" who, unlike men who go to war and take life, are allegedly too fragile and pure for the real world. In additon, men become moral beings as they heroically bear their grief in seeing such beauty, youth, and innocence depart from their lives. See Ann Douglas's able discussion of this issue in *The Feminization of American Culture* (New York: Knopf, 1977).

18. William Gilmore Simms, *Mellichampe: A Legend of the Santez* (1836; reprint, New York: A. C. Armstrong and Son, 1882), 71 and 72.

19. See Ronald Takaki's *Iron Cages: Race and Culture in Nineteenth-Century America* (Seattle: University of Washington Press, 1979) for a discussion of what this dichotomy means in political terms.

20. See chap. 25, pp. 224–34 and chap. 27, pp. 235–42 in which Simms describes Janet's selflessness as a womanly instinct. ("Indeed the instinct of love is woman's best reason," 238). See E. P. Thompson, "Eighteenth-Century English Society: Class Struggle Without Class?" *Social History* 3 (May 1978): 133–65.

21. When Mellichampe is first introduced, John Witherspoon ("Thumbscrew"), his older companion and confidante, is trying to convince him to be more patient and temperate in his dealings with Barsfield. Ernest wants to hunt Barsfield down and shoot him as one would hunt a wild beast. Witherspoon tries to convince him that given the guerrilla nature of the war they are fighting, Mellichampe will be able to confront him on the battlefield and confront him honorably. In one incident, when Witherspoon tells Mellichampe that he had had a chance to murder Barsfield but didn't, Mellichampe "leaped to his feet in a convulsion of passion, that seemed to set at defiance all restraint." Although Witherspoon brings Mellichampe to his senses and apologizes to him for doubting his loyalty, it is clear that Mellichampe's temper is too volatile to be trusted. Mellichampe is similarly foolhardy in his behavior toward Janet. In spite of Janet's and Witherspoon's admonitions to him about danger, Mellichampe insists on visiting her at her house even when Barsfield is there and he runs a real risk of being caught. Simms, *Mellichampe*, 83 and 84, 94–103, 121–31. For a more thorough discussion of the Witherspoon-Mellichampe relationship, see Chapter 14.

22. See discussion of Butler and Robinson in Chapter 14 below.

23. John Pendleton Kennedy, *Horse-Shoe Robinson: A Tale of the Tory Ascendancy* (1835; reprint, New York: Hurd and Houghton, 1866), 405.

24. Pp. 371, 405, and 370. For descriptions of Mildred, see 89 and 90, 369–71, 404 and 405.

25. John Pendleton Kennedy, *Swallow Barn; or, A Sojourn in the Old Dominion* (1832; reprint, New York: Hafner, 1971); see 109 and 110, 225–37; 351–58, 374–85.

26. William Alexander Caruthers, *The Cavaliers of Virginia; or, The Recluse of James-town: An Historical Romance* (New York: Harper, 1834), 1:14 and 15.

27. The historical Nathaniel Bacon was born in England and was forced to the Virginia frontier with other yeomen when he couldn't afford land in the Tidewater region. He had no known association by marriage with the Virginia tidewater aristocracy; see Edmund S. Morgan, *American Slavery American Freedom: The Ordeal of Colonial Virginia* (New York: Norton, 1975), 250–70.

28. Others are Ruth Elmore and Harriet Wilton in *Edge-Hill;* Bertha and Carrie from Simms's *The Forayers* and *Eutaw* are not really developed as female friends. See Carroll Smith-Rosenberg, "The Female World of Love and Ritual: Relations Between Women in Nineteenth-Century America," *Signs* 1 (Autumn 1975): 1–29, reprinted in her *Disorderly Conduct: Visions of Gender in America* (New York: Oxford, 1985), 53–76; Lillian Faderman, *Surpassing the Love of Men: Romantic Friendship and Love Between Women from the Renaissance to the Present* (New York: William Morrow, 1981): 157–203; and Catherine Clinton, *The Plantation Mistress: Woman's World in the Old South* (New York: Pantheon, 1982): 174–76.

29. William Alexander Caruthers, *The Knights of the Golden Horse-Shoe: A Traditionary Tale of the Cocked Hat Gentry in the Old Dominion,* 2 vols. (1842; reprint, Chapel Hill: University of North Carolina Press, 1970), 1:95. The setting of the *Knights of the Golden Horse-Shoe* is Governor John Spotswood's seventeenth-century Virginia when Spotswood formed a band of soldier-explorers to cross the Blue Ridge Mountains in search of the fabled Mississippi River Valley. The romantic subplot involves Kate Spotswood's courtship with two rather dull planters' sons, Bernard Moore and Kit Carter, and Ellen Evylin's sad affair with her stepbrother, Frank Lee. Ellen had promised Lee that she would wait for him to return from Scotland to be married. When news of his heroic death reached Virginia, Ellen was heartbroken and refused to believe that he had died. She refused to consider courting anyone else and instead began to lose her health in mourning for Frank. News of Frank's death was followed by the arrival in Virginia of a talented and gallant young man, Henry Hall, who is the Spotswood children's tutor. In the end, Hall reveals himself as Frank Lee who has a special mission in the New World. Although Kate Spotswood has far more status than Ellen, the Ellen–Frank courtship dominates the romantic plot, which consumes the first volume of the novel.

30. This problem will be taken up again in Part III. Since Deborah Gray White and others have argued for the persistence of the "Jezebel" as an antebellum stereotype, it is important to note that while it is an important component of the proslavery argument, it is not a component of this proslavery literature. See White, *Ar'n't I A Woman? Female Slaves in the Plantation South* (New York: Norton, 1987), 27–61. However, Stowe's *Uncle Tom's Cabin* elicited more than thirty proslavery novels that need to be studied along these lines.

7. THE "SPINSTER" AND THE "FALLEN WOMAN"

1. See Catherine Clinton, "The Plantation Mistress: Another Side of Southern Slavery, 1780–1835" (Ph.D. diss., Princeton University, 1980), 4. In *The Plantation Mistress: Woman's World in the Old South* (New York: Pantheon, 1982) Clinton seems to have

moved this information somewhere else. Chap. 5 of the dissertation and chap. 6 in the book discuss courtship and marriage. Another helpful source in understanding the reality of Southern women's lives has been Anne Firor Scott, *The Southern Lady* (Chicago: University of Chicago Press, 1970). See Suzanne Lebsock, "The Political Economy of Marriage," in *The Free Women of Petersburg: Status and Culture in a Southern Town, 1784–1860* (New York: Norton, 1984), 15–53. For a similar study of Northern women's lives during the same period see Nancy F. Cott, *The Bonds of Womanhood: Women's Sphere in New England, 1780–1835* (New Haven: Yale University Press, 1977).

2. Clinton, "The Plantation Mistress," 133–35. Her dissertation offers a more spirited discussion of this problem than the book. See the book, chap. 4, (59–86), in which she devotes only one page (85) to spinsters.

3. William Alexander Caruthers, *The Knights of the Golden Horse-Shoe: A Traditionary Tale of the Cocked Hat Gentry in the Old Dominion* (1842; reprint, Chapel Hill: University of North Carolina Press, 1970), 1:84.

4. John Pendleton Kennedy, *Swallow Barn; or, A Sojourn in the Old Dominion* (1832; reprint, 1853 edition. New York: Hafner, 1971), 47 and 48.

5. Kennedy reflects the enduring prejudice that women who got involved in antebellum reform were frustrated old maids who turned their pent-up sexual energies to "good works" in the absence of a "normal" life. The tendency to charge reformers with being emotionally disturbed has also become a way of discrediting their political activity. See as an example of this kind of modern critique David Herbert Donald's treatment of the abolitionists in "Toward a Reconsideration of the Abolitionists," in his *Lincoln Reconsidered* (New York: Knopf, 1959 [© 1956], David Herbert Donald's "Toward a Reconsideration of Abolitionists," *Journal of Southern History* 25 (August 1959): 356–65; Betty Fladeland's "Who Were the Abolitionists?" *Journal of Southern History* 30 (April 1964): 99–115; and Larry Gara's "Who Were the Abolitionists?" in *The Anti-Slavery Vanguard* ed. Martin B. Duberman (Princeton: Princeton University Press, 1965), 32–51: all answered Donald.

6. Recent work on female networks in the nineteenth century suggests that women were neither heartbroken nor resourceless without men, unless their families rejected them. See Clinton, "The Plantation Mistress," 151–53, 241–44; Carroll Smith-Rosenberg, "The Female World of Love and Ritual: Relations Between Women in Nineteenth-Century America," *Signs* 1 (Autumn 1975): 1–29, reprinted in her *Disorderly Conduct: Visions of Gender in America* (New York: Oxford: 1985): 53–76; Lillian Faderman, *Surpassing the Love of Men: Romantic Friendship and Love Between Women from the Renaissance to the Present* (New York: William Morrow, 1981).

7. William Gilmore Simms, *Eutaw* (1856; reprint, New York: A. C. Armstrong and Son, 1882). Nell and her younger sister, Molly, and brother, Mat, were orphaned and were brought up by a kind widow, Mother Ford. Mrs. Landgreve Nelson, a rich plantation mistress, who was impressed with Nelly's natural grace and intelligence, decided to take her into her home as a playmate for her daughter, Bettie. Nell left the Nelson home because she fell in love with Sherrod Nelson, Bettie's older brother, and knew the match to be impossible because of their class differences. Mat Floyd became a criminal and joined Jeff Rhodes's gang from Florida, one of Simms's marauding poor white gangs and the gang that captured Bertha and Mrs. Travis. Nell spends most of the novel tracking her brother and trying to keep him alive and out of trouble—a task at which she finally fails. In her adventures, then, she encounters all of the principals in the novel and is allowed by Simms considerable freedom for a woman.

8. Some of these women include Katherine Walton (*The Partisan* and *Katherine Walton*); Janet Berkeley (*Mellichampe*); Widow Eveleigh (*Woodcraft*); and Margaret Cooper (*Charlemont* and *Beauchampe*). Hurricane Nell dies in the end, and Mrs. Eveleigh rejects the hero Porgy, and is rejected by him because she is too independent and

would never accept him as her master. In Margaret Cooper, Simms creates an ambitious and intelligent woman who thinks she is superior to other women. See Chapter 6 for a discussion of Katherine Walton and Janet Berkeley, and Chapter 9 for a discussion of Mrs. Eveleigh. Margaret Cooper will be discussed below.

9. William Gilmore Simms, *Border Beagles: A Tale of Mississippi* (1840; reprint, New York: A. C. Armstrong and Son, 1882), 342.

10. "Edward Saxon" in *Border Beagles* is the same criminal as "Clement Foster in *Richard Hurdis* who is the leader of the "Mystic Confederacy." See *Border Beagles*, 84, 86–88. There is some confusion about his name. Simms calls him "Ellis" Saxon early in the novel and has Florence call him "Edward" at the end. See *Border Beagles*, 60 and 400.

11. Simms tells us that when Virginia dashed forward to help Vernon, "All apprehension for herself departed when she feared for her lover; and that living grace of form and movement, which speaks out when the mother mood prevails, revived, at the same moment, with a sense of equal admiration, the souls of Vernon and the outlaw." (482) The "true woman" is never "truer" than when she is self-sacrificing.

12. For a good discussion of the phenomenon in Western literature and myth, see Adrienne Rich, *Of Woman Born: Motherhood as Experience and Institution* (New York: Bantam, 1977), esp. chaps. 4 and 5.

13. "Amalgamation" was the preferred nineteenth-century term for interracial sexual relations. "Miscegenation" is a curious word that derives from the Latin, "miscere," to mix, and "genus," race. The term was first used by David Goodman and George Wakeman in their "pro-miscegenation" pamphlet during the election of 1864. Their pamphlet was a ruse designed to arouse the most virulent racist hatred against Abraham Lincoln and the Republican Party, which were depicted as supporting racial mixing. For the full story of this bizarre incident in American presidential politics, see Sidney Kaplan's important "The Miscegenation Issue in the Election of 1864," *Journal of Negro History* 34 (July 1949): 274–343; reprinted in Kaplan, *American Studies in Black and White* (Amherst: University of Massachusetts Press, 1991), 47–100.

14. Nathaniel Beverley Tucker, *George Balcombe: A Novel*, 2 vols. (New York: Harper, 1836), 1:47.

15. Simms has only one other planter's son who is a criminal, John Hurdis, of the novel *Richard Hurdis*. Only John Spotswood (*Knights of the Golden Horse-Shoe*) is a similarly dissolute failure among upper-class men. See William Gilmore Simms, *The Scout; or, The Black Riders of Congaree* (1841; reprint, New York: A. C. Armstrong and Son, 1882), 317.

16. These authors are extraordinarily silent about the most common upper-class male–lower-class female alliance: master and slave. See discussion of this issue in Part Three.

17. Simms is quite pleased with his vine and tree metaphor for female-male relationships. He repeats it again in this passage when he has Mary declare to Conway, "I cling to you because I can cling nowhere else; and you have yourself said that a woman is a dependent—she must cling somewhere!" (178). The woman in love in Simms's depiction, then, is a born victim of male treachery. This is the condition against which the "sentimental" novelists were protesting.

18. William Gilmore Simms, *Charlemont; or, The Pride of the Village* (1856; reprint, New York: A. C. Armstrong and Son, 1882), 28.

19. Simms's full quote on nineteenth-century feminists and intellectual women is in the following passage from the introduction to *Charlemont*. Had Margaret Cooper been Simms's only intelligent and spirited woman character, one could argue persuasively that he was completely hostile to intellectual development in women. However, since some of his other heroines possess both intellect and "female" nurturing

qualities, Simms emerges as more ambivalent about the intellectual woman than one might expect:

> In those days of "strong-minded women," even more certainly than when the portrait was first taken, the identity of the sketch with its original will be sure of recognition. Her character and career will illustrate most of the mistakes which are made by that ambitious class, among the gentler sex, who are now seeking so earnestly to pass from that province of humiliation to which the sex has been circumscribed from the first moment of recorded history. What she will gain by the motion, if successful, might well be left to time, were it not that the proposed change in her condition threatens fatally some of her own and the best securities of humanity. . . . The first great duty of woman is in her becoming the mother of men; and this duty implies her proper capacity for the education and training of the young. To fit her properly for this duty, her education should become more elevated, and more severe in degree with its elevation. . . . To train fully the feminine mind, without in any degree impairing her susceptibilities and sensibilities, seems at once the necessity and the difficulty of the subject. Her very influence over man lies in her sensibilities. It will be to her perilous fall from pride of place, and power, when goaded by an insane ambition, in the extreme development of her mere intellect, she shall forfeit a single one of these securities of her sex. (11 and 12)

20. Simms has Margaret exclaim against the sexist oppression in her life: "If, forgetful of earth, and trees, and the human stocks around me, I pour forth the language of the great song-masters, they grin at my insanity—they hold me incapable of reason, and declare their ideas of what that is, by asking who knows most of the dairy, the cabbage-patch, the spinning-wheel, the darning-needle—who can best wash Polly's or Patty's face and comb its head—can chop up sausage-meat the finest—make the lightest paste, and more economically dispense the sugar in serving up the tea! and these are what is expected of woman! These duties of the meanest slave! From her mind nothing is expected. Her enthusiasm terrifies, her energy offends, and if her taste is ever challenged, it is to the figures on the quilt or in a flower-garden, where the passion seems to be to make flowers grow in stars, to hearts, and crescents. What has woman to expect where such are the laws; where such are the expectations from her?" (176 and 177).

21. For a discussion of plantation mistresses with their slaves see Catherine Clinton, *The Plantation Mistress,* chap. 2. Elizabeth Fox-Genovese thinks this is the dominant attitude of plantation women; see *Within the Plantation Household: Black and White Women of the Old South* (Chapel Hill: University of North Carolina Press, 1988), chaps. 3 and 5. William Gilmore Simms, *Beauchampe; or, The Kentucky Tragedy* (1842; reprint, New York: A. C. Armstrong and Son, 1882), 26. One should note that *Beauchampe,* though the thematic sequel to *Charlemont,* was actually written more than ten years before it, and that "The Kentucky Tragedy" captured the imaginations of Southerners and Westerners alike and was celebrated in songs, poems, and plays as well as Simms's novel: see Loren J. Kallsen, *The Kentucky Tragedy: A Problem in Romantic Attitudes* (New York: Bobbs-Merrill, 1963).

22. Simms, *Beauchampe,* 26, 285. See chapter 2: "The Unexpected Meeting," 26–34, for Margaret Cooper's rebirth as "Anna Cooke."

23. Simms argues, "Give us, say I, Kentucky practice, like that of Beauchampe, as a social law, rather than that which prevails in some of our pattern cities, where women are, in three-fourths the number of instances, the victims—violated, mangled, murdered—where men are the criminals—and where (Heaven kindly having withdrawn the sense of shame) there is no one guilty—at least none brave enough or manly enough to bring the guilty to punishment! What is said is not meant to defend or

encourage the shedding of blood. We may not defend the taking of life, even by the laws. We regard life as an express trust from Heaven, of which as we should not divest ourselves, no act but that of Heaven should divest us: but there is a crime beyond it, in the shedding of that vital soul-blood, its heart of hearts, life of all life, the fair fame, the untainted reputation; and the one offence which provokes the other should be placed in the opposing balance, as an offset, in some degree, to the crime by which it is avenged" (*Beauchampe,* 342 and 343).

24. Catherine Clinton notes that planters were not oblivious to their wives' complaints, but refused to allow their wives to challenge their authority for fear of the repercussions for their other dependents, most important, slaves. In a passage that reminds me of Charlotte Perkins Gilman's horrific "The Yellow Wallpaper," Clinton quotes planter David Campbell's writing to his wife who had complained that she was as sheltered "like a canary bird": "I know you are shut up like the canary bird, but you sing so sweetly, that to make you sing seems more justification for the tyranny exercised." See Clinton, *The Plantation Mistress,* 179. Clinton's dissertation offers a more pointed discussion; see 247–48. The point is not that plantation mistresses and slaves are in the same position, but that their master—the planter—understands his authority over them as being indivisible.

8. MOTHERS

1. For the lives of "real" Southern women see Anne Firor Scott, *The Southern Lady* (Chicago: University of Chicago Press, 1970); Catherine Clinton, *The Plantation Mistress: Woman's World in the Old South* (New York: Pantheon, 1982); Suzanne Lebsock, *The Free Women of Petersburg: Status and Culture in a Southern Town, 1784–1860* (New York: Norton, 1984); and Elizabeth Fox-Genovese, *Within the Plantation Household: Black and White Women of the Old South* (Chapel Hill: University of North Carolina Press, 1988).

2. Interestingly, the misery of Southern women's lives as a result of these very conditions has been the subject for the "sentimental" novels of the so-called Southern scribbling women. See Nina Baym, *Woman's Fiction: A Guide to Novels By and About Women in America, 1820–1870* (Ithaca: Cornell University Press, 1978), 110–39.

3. See Adrienne Rich, *Of Woman Born: Motherhood as Experience and Institution* (New York: Bantam, 1977).

4. One should understand that the myth of individualism for the so-called self-made man is based on gender, racial, and class prejudices that work in his favor, and that even the most independent man exists within a network of relationships that support his activity and give him the illusion of independence. The "free man" of this period was "free" from his father and/or a patriarchal master. Most likely the work and care of a woman—his mother or his wife—prepared him for work each day. Still, the male characters in Southern and Northern antebellum literature have hopes, dreams, and fears that are articulated as their own, while the female characters only repeat what they have been told to think by their fathers or suitors. Social historians like Anne Firor Scott, Catherine Clinton, Carroll Smith-Rosenberg, and Nancy F. Cott have demonstrated that women not only had their own interior lives, but they had relationships—bonds—with each other, which are ignored in this literature.

5. John Pendleton Kennedy, *Swallow Barn; or, A Sojourn in the Old Dominion* (1832; reprint, 1853 ed., New York: Hafner 1971), 38–40.

6. Clinton, *The Plantation Mistress,* chaps. 2 and 8; Scott, *The Southern Lady,* chap. 2; Fox-Genovese, *Within the Plantation Household,* chap. 2. As noted at Chap. 5 n.2, Clinton and Fox-Genovese disagree about the plantation mistress's workload. Clinton contends that plantation women did many if not all domestic chores themselves, while

Fox-Genovese argues these women were the privileged supervisors of slave women. D. Harland Hagler would agree with Clinton. See "The Ideal Woman in the Antebellum South: Lady or Farmwife?" *Journal of Southern History* 46 (August 1980): 405–18.

7. William Alexander Caruthers, *The Cavaliers of Virginia; or, The Recluse of Jamestown: An Historical Romance,* 2 vols. (New York: Harper, 1835) 1:24.

8. William Gilmore Simms, *The Forayers; or, The Raid of the Dog Days* (1855; reprint. New York: A. C. Armstrong and Son, 1882), 282.

9. William Gilmore Simms, *Eutaw* (1856; reprint, New York: A. C. Armstrong and Son, 1882), 157 and 158.

10. They include: Bel Tracy, *Swallow Barn;* Mildred Lindsey, *Horse-Shoe Robinson;* Virginia Fairfax, *Cavaliers of Virginia;* Ellen Evylin, *Knights of the Golden Horse-Shoe;* Katherine Walton, *The Partisan* and *Katherine Walton;* Janet Berkeley, *Mellichampe;* Ellen Floyd ("Hurricane Nell"), *The Forayers* and *Eutaw.*

11. See Nina Baym, *Women's Fiction;* Herbert Ross Brown, *The Sentimental Novel in America, 1789–1860* (Durham: Duke University Press, 1940); Frederick Lewis Pattee, *The Feminine Fifties* (New York: Appleton-Century, 1940); Cathy N. Davidson, *Revolution and the Word: The Rise of the Novel in America* (New York: Oxford University Press, 1986); Patricia Stubbs, *Women and Fiction: Feminism and the Novel, 1880–1920* (New York: Barnes and Noble, 1979).

12. Women who are more involved with their husbands than with their children include the wives of Bernard and Hugh Trevor in N. B. Tucker's *The Partisan Leader* and Bet Balcombe in his *George Balcombe.* Husbands and wives who are involved in taunting and teasing each other for comic effect include the Weasals, in Kennedy's *Rob of the Bowl,* and the Horseys in Simms's *Border Beagles.*

13. They include Charles Fitzroyal, *Edge-Hill;* Nathaniel Bacon, *Cavaliers of Virginia;* Frank Lee, *Knights of the Golden Horse-Shoe;* Ned Hazard, *Swallow Barn;* Robert Singleton, *The Partisan* and *Katherine Walton;* Ernest Mellichampe, *Mellichampe;* William Sinclair, *The Forayers* and *Eutaw;* Edward Conway, *The Scout;* Ralph Colleton, *Guy Rivers;* Henry Vernon, *Border Beagles.*

14. See Simms's biographies: William P. Trent, *William Gilmore Simms* (New York: Greenwood, 1892); J. V. Ridgely, *William Gilmore Simms* (New York: Twayne, 1962); Jon L. Wakelyn, *The Politics of a Literary Man: William Gilmore Simms* (Westport, Conn.: Greenwood, 1973); C. Hugh Holman, Introduction to *Views and Reviews in American Literature, History, and Fiction,* ed. C. Hugh Holman (Cambridge: The Belknap Press of Harvard University Press, 1962), xii–xxxvii; and Edd Winfield Parks, ed., *The Antebellum Southern Literary Critics* Athens: University of Georgia Press, 1962), 83–135; Mary Ann Wimsatt, *The Major Fiction of William Gilmore Simms: Cultural Traditions and Literary Form* (Baton Rouge: Louisiana State University Press, 1989), 12–32, 85–119; John Caldwell Guilds, *Simms: A Literary Life* (Fayetteville: University of Arkansas Press, 1992), 3–14.

15. John Pendleton Kennedy, *Horse-Shoe Robinson: A Tale of the Tory Ascendancy* (1835; reprint, New York: Hurd and Houghton, 1866), 264.

16. The modern fascist aesthetic exhibits "a preoccupation with situations of control, submissive behavior, extravagant effort, and the endurance of pain," which celebrates the glorification of surrender and the glamorization of death, and finally revels in "the exhibition of physical skill and courage and victory of stronger men over the weaker." This cult reflects the conservative patriarchal insistence on the indissoluble division between men and women, masculinity and femininity, Anglo-Saxon purity and rationality and Native American and African American corruption and irrationality. See Susan Sontag's brilliant essay, "Fascinating Fascism," which first appeared in the *New York Review of Books* 27 (6 February 1975), and is now published as part of a

collection of essays in her *Under the Sign of Saturn* (New York: Farrar, Straus and Giroux, 1980). See as well Renate Bridenthal, Atina Grossman, and Marion Kaplan, eds., *When Biology Became Destiny: Women in Weimer and Nazi Germany* (New York: Monthly Review Press, 1984) and Claudia Koonz, *Mothers in the Fatherland: Women, the Family, and Nazi Politics* (New York: St. Martin's Press, 1987).

17. The transformation of the man's world to a more nurturant and supportive arena (the so-called feminizing of society) threatens the power of ruling-class males who achieve power not only through the failure of other men, but through their ability to marshal the legal institutions of the society to do their violent work for them. In these Southern novels, poor white men are characterized as being as tough as ruling-class planters, but they are depicted as not so intelligent, and they let their passions dominate their actions, so they make stupid mistakes. However, at every point at which a planter fought a poor white, the planter, with the force of law behind him, "won," underscoring the fact that although gentlemen were bred for polite society, they knew how to fight when they had to, and in the end they were as tough and as fit as any poor white male. Their victory established them as the superiors of poor white men in terms of both masculinity and class standards. See Chapter 13. Also see Dorothy Dinnerstein's *The Mermaid and the Minotaur: Sexual Arrangements and Human Malaise* (New York: Harper and Row, 1976), in which she makes many of these points and others about the price we have paid and will continue to pay for the patriarchal cult of masculine violence. An old standard among conservatives is the naturalness of human evil and the necessity of institutions that curb antisocial human behavior. William Gilmore Simms's defense of slavery as a system rests on this theoretical base, and he argues against abolitionists like Harriet Beecher Stowe who, he contended, labeled as evils of slavery those wrongs that were actually attributable to the personal weaknesses of individual masters. Simms argues that "evil is everywhere inseparable from humanity. It is only another of its imperfections." William Gilmore Simms, "Stowe's *Key to Uncle Tom's Cabin*," *Southern Quarterly Review* 24 (July 1853): 249; 214–54.

18. The heroes of the border novels are difficult to classify by class, and thus are a bit truer to being "American" types. Planters by definition own twenty slaves or more. The only one who would qualify as a planter under these terms is Richard Hurdis (*Richard Hurdis*), but his older brother John will inherit these slaves and his father's estate even though Richard has put the time into managing the slaves and the estate. Harry Vernon (*Border Beagles*) is a lawyer, but is of "noble stock"; he represents planters' interests in the West. Ralph Colleton (*Guy Rivers*) is from a prominent South Carolinian family but his father has married beneath him and has moved to the Southwest. Ralph has "noble blood," however, and will marry his first cousin Edith Colleton. Simms was prejudiced against the people who lived in the Southwest, which he took to be a wild, uncivilized place initially settled by the worst of the white population. He thought that with time "the better elements" from the South would immigrate there, and his heroes in these border romances represent that kind of better Eastern stock. One could argue that Simms has stumbled onto the formula for the American "Western," in which the good guy from the East wins the hand of the helpless maiden by rescuing her from poor white outlaws and making the West safe for decent people.

19. William Gilmore Simms, *Charlemont; or, the Pride of the Village* (1856; reprint, New York: A. C. Armstrong and Son, 1882), 242.

20. Hurdis's class as well as the family relationships are revealed when Simms has Richard complain to his mother, "and then, mother, we will see whether John Hurdis is a better man with thirty negroes than Richard Hurdis with three." William Gilmore Simms, *Richard Hurdis: A Tale of Alabama* (1838; reprint, New York: A. C. Armstrong

and Son, 1882), 18. John Hurdis is one of only two Simms planter sons who is a villain. The other is Edward Conway in *The Scout.*

21. For a discussion of the origins of the Western, see Henry Nash Smith, *The Virgin Land: The American West as Symbol and Myth* (New York: Vintage, 1950).

22. See Simms' "Stowe's *Key*," in which he argues that "It is fondness for change, in part, that reconciles the negro to be sold away from his family, his parents, his children and all his old associates." And to those whites who would object to that aspect of slavery, he contends that black slaves didn't really mind being separated from their families; "to escape from all sorts of bonds—(is) a natural passion with all inferior and savage races" (252).

23. Simms begins *Richard Hurdis* comparing and contrasting "the hardihood of the American character" with the "silk shodden and sleek citizens" of Europe, and notes in the voice of the protagonist, "with manhood . . . comes the desire to range" (13 and 14).

24. For a discussion of American racism in this period see Richard Slotkin, *Regeneration Through Violence: The Mythology of the American Frontier, 1600–1860* (Middletown: Wesleyan University Press, 1973); Ronald T. Takaki, *Iron Cages: Race and Culture in Nineteenth-Century America* (New York: Knopf, 1979; 2d ed., New York: Oxford University Press, 1990); George M. Fredrickson, *The Black Image in the White Mind* (New York: Harper and Row, 1972); Robert F. Berkhofer, Jr., *The White Man's Indian: Images of the American Indian from Columbus to the Present* (New York: Knopf, 1978); and Reginald Horsman, *Race and Manifest Destiny: The Origins of American Racial Anglo-Saxonism* (Cambridge: Harvard University Press, 1981).

25. Simms, *Richard Hurdis,* 13–15; *Charlemont,* 14–16, 17–20. Simms has Hurdis exclaim, "The man who lives by measuring tape and pins by the sixpence worth, may make money by his vocation—but, God help him! he is scarce a man. His veins expand not with generous ardor; his muscles wither and vanish, as they are unemployed; and his soul—it has no emotions which prompt him to noble restlessness, and high and generous exertion" (15). Southern intellectuals like Simms were in a bind similar to that of the man who lives by "measuring tapes and pins," as they spent a large part of their day behind a desk writing. However, they were also the masters of male slaves, and enjoyed plantation recreation like hunting and fishing, and so saw themselves as active men.

26. For a discussion of the treatment of the black family in this literature see Part III.

27. William Gilmore Simms, *Woodcraft; or, Hawks About the Dovecote: A Story of the South at the Close of the Revolution* (1854; reprint, New York: A. C. Armstrong and Son, 1882), 308.

28. See Deborah Gray White, "Jezebel and Mammy: The Mythology of Female Slavery," *Ar'n't I A Woman: Female Slaves in the Plantation South,* (New York: Norton, 1985), 27–61. This literature supports her contention about the mammy. Also see Catherine Clinton, *The Plantation Mistress,* 199–222.

29. Most obviously, this connection occurred in cases of the birth of mulatto children fathered by planters. Miscegenation between the planter class and their slaves is a well-known fact of the antebellum period that is undepicted in this fiction even by Simms because of its potential to be used by antislavery activists, because it was considered unmentionable in polite society, and because it could only cause trouble with plantation mistresses to admit what was private and shameful in public. See the discussion of this issue in Part IV.

30. One should note that ruling-class men have always claimed that "inferior" men treat their wives brutally. See the discussion of the characterization of poor-white men in Chapter 13.

31. For instance, Arthur Eveleigh, a planter's son, tries to help Dory carry water from the well. First Simms tells us Dory warns him off: " 'Not you, Arthur,' said the child, keeping always in mind the superior social position of her companion." And later Simms has Dory argue, "Oh! You mustn't, Arthur; mother will be vexed if she sees you doing such work."

32. This depiction of the poor white family is discussed in much more detail in Chapter 13.

33. This is one of those few instances in this literature where a man of the allegedly superior class is sexually abusing an incompetent young woman from a lower class. In fact, the novel as a middle-class form defended middle-class and poor-white female chastity against aristocratic male lust. For a discussion of this phenomenon, see Ian Watt, *The Rise of the North: Studies in Defoe, Richardson and Fielding* (Berkeley and Los Angeles: University of California Press, 1974), and Leslie A. Fiedler, *Love and Death in the American Novel* (New York: Stein and Day, 1966).

34. William Rogers Taylor, *Cavalier and Yankee: The Old South and the American National Character* (New York: Harper and Row, 1961), 167.

35. Judy Grahn, "VII. Vera, from My Childhood," in *The Work of A Common Woman: The Collected Poetry of Judy Grahn, 1964–1977,* with an introduction by Adrienne Rich (Trumansburg, N.Y.: Crossing Press, 1978), 73.

36. Simms tells us that "Hitherto Margaret Cooper had been a girl of strong will; nursed in solitude and by the wrong-headed indulgence of a vain and foolish mother" (*Charlemont,* 306).

37. William Gilmore Simms, *Guy Rivers: A Tale of Georgia* (1834; reprint, New York: A. C. Armstrong and Son, 1882), 453.

38. William Gilmore Simms, *The Partisan: A Romance of the Revolution* (1835; reprint, New York: Belford, Clarke, 1885), 180 and 181.

9. WIDOWS

1. John Pendleton Kennedy, *Horse-Shoe Robinson: A Tale of the Tory Ascendancy* (1835; reprint, New York: Hurd and Houghton, 1866), 448–50.

2. The story of *Woodcraft* is simply told. It is set at the end of the Revolutionary War when the South was in chaos. The British were evacuating America, taking with them some Loyalists and whatever property and cash they could. The most valuable property were black slaves, which they could sell to British and French planters in the West Indies. In the meantime, the patriot soldiers were returning in large numbers to find themselves numbered in the debtor class, their farms destroyed, and their slaves run off to the swamps or stolen by the British and their allies. Additionally, widows and orphans had to find a way to turn out a crop and subsist on the land. In *Woodcraft* the British officer in charge of South Carolina is Colonel Moncrief and his Loyalist subordinate, M'Kewn, who has designs on both Widow Eveleigh's and Captain Porgy's plantations. M'Kewn is the son of Porgy's former overseer. Captain Porgy is a returning veteran who finds himself in debt to M'Kewn, his home in shambles, and his slaves run off or confiscated by the British. He returns from the war with three friends: Lance Frampton, his junior aide; Sergeant Millhouse, who will be his overseer; and his loyal black slave Tom. His neighbors are Widow Griffin, whose husband Walter was in Porgy's unit, and her daughter, Ellen, who marries Lance Frampton. Widow Eveleigh's plantation borders his on the other side; her husband had been a British officer, but she is sympathetic to Porgy because they are "neighbors." The narrative of the novel describes Mrs. Eveleigh's effort to secure Porgy's and her own human property from the British and their poor-white allies, Porgy's attempts to reestablish himself as a planter, and the social relationships between Porgy and the two widows. It is clear

from this novel how marriage, family, and class are intertwined with the concepts of the plantation and community in the antebellum South.

3. Charles S. Watson, "Simms' Answer to *Uncle Tom's Cabin:* Criticism of the South in *Woodcraft," Southern Literary Journal* 9 (Fall 1976): 85.

4. For a discussion of Simms's identification with Porgy, see Hugh Hetherington, *Cavalier of Old South Carolina: William Gillmore Simms' Captain Porgy* (Chapel Hill: University of North Carolina Press, 1966), 51–69.

5. William Gilmore Simms, *Katherine Walton* (1851; reprint, New York: Lovell, Coryell, n.d.), 375.

6. William Gilmore Simms, *Woodcraft; or, Hawks about the Dovecote: A Story of the South at the Close of the Revolution* (1854; reprint, New York: A. C. Armstrong and Son, 1882), 12.

7. Simms notes in *Woodcraft:* "Widow Eveleigh was no ordinary woman. She was a good whist player, and when you find a good whist player among women, be sure that she knows how to keep a secret" (41).

8. On this aspect of the proslavery argument see the following examples from Eric L. McKitrick, ed., *Slavery Defended: The Views of the Old South* (Englewood Cliffs, N.J.: Prentice-Hall, 1963), 34–50, 51–56, 69–85; and William Sumner Jenkins, *Pro-Slavery Thought in the Old South* (Gloucester, Mass.: Peter Smith, 1960).

9. In fact, George Fitzhugh has argued quite baldly that government of all kinds is "a thing of force, not of consent." He notes that "the women, the children, the negroes, and but a few of the non-property holders were consulted, or consented to the Revolution or the governments that ensued from its success," and that "fathers do not derive their authority, as heads of families, from the consent of wife and children, nor do they govern their families by consent." Fitzhugh continues to argue that slaves do not vote for their masters' power but all as weaker dependents recognize the masters' force in their government and realize that ultimately they all have the same self-interest. See George Fitzhugh, "Cannibals All! or Slaves Without Masters," in *Ante-Bellum,* ed. Harvey Wish (1857; reprint, New York: Capricorn Books, 1960), 150–52.

10. Simms includes Porgy in almost all of his Revolutionary War romances. See *The Partisan, Mellichampe, Katherine Walton, The Forayers,* and *Eutaw.* See also the study of Porgy as a character by Hugh Hetherington, *Cavalier of the Old South.*

10. SLAVERY

1. Robert J. Brugger, *Beverley Tucker: Heart Over Head in the Old South* (Baltimore: Johns Hopkins University Press, 1978), 55–59.

2. While I think Elizabeth Fox-Genovese, like Eugene Genovese, is too sentimental about the actual reality of the planter's vision of his "white and black families," her discussion of the gender, race, and class relationships on the plantation is thoughtfully and comprehensively drawn; see *Within the Plantation Household: Black and White Women of the Old South* (Chapel Hill: University of North Carolina Press, 1988.)

3. See William Wells Brown, *Clotel; or, the President's Daughter* (1853; reprint, New York: Arno, 1969) and Harriet Beecher Stowe, *Uncle Tom's Cabin; or, Life Among the Lowly* (1852; reprint, New York: Washington Square Press, 1963; Martin R. Delany, *Blake; or, the Huts of America* (1857, reprint, Boston: Beacon, 1970).

4. In his *A Theory of Literary Production* (London: Routledge and Kegan Paul, 1978), Pierre Macherey has argued that all texts have silences that are necessary for the author to be able to make his or her argument, but those silences have meaning and need to be interpreted. He notes, "meaning is in the *relation* between the implicit and the explicit. . . . What is important in the work is what it does not say" (87). Similarly, Robert E. Scholes, a semiotician argues, that the analyst can legitimately speculate

about "what is excluded as well as what was included" in a text; see Scholes, *Semiotics and Interpretation* (New Haven: Yale University Press, 1982), 16.

5. William Alexander Caruthers, *The Knights of the Golden Horse-Shoe: A Traditionary Tale of the Cocked-Hat Gentry in the Old Dominion* (1842; reprint, Chapel Hill: University of North Carolina Press, 1970), 14.

6. William Gilmore Simms, *The Scout; or, The Black Riders of Congaree* (1841; reprint, New York: A. C. Armstrong and Son, 1882), 332–33. This novel's original title was *The Kinsmen.*

7. See William Wells Brown, *Clotel; or, the President's Daughter,* and Martin R. Delaney's *Blake, or the Huts of America.*

8. W. G. Simms, "The Morals of Slavery," in *The Proslavery Argument, As Maintained by the Most Distinguished Writers of the Southern States* (Philadelphia: Lippincott, Grambo, 1852; reprint, New York: Negro Universities Press, 1968), 181–285; Chancellor Harper, "Memoirs of Slavery," in *The Proslavery Argument,* 40–46, 1–98 passim; James Henry Hammond, "Letters on Slavery," *The Proslavery Argument,* 117–20, 99–174 passim; Hammond was forced from political office by his brother-in-law, Wade Hampton, for sexually abusing his nieces, Hampton's daughters. Hammond rationalizes the existence of mulattoes by blaming poor whites and foreigners and says it doesn't occur often. He recommends silence "on this disgusting topic." See Drew Gilpin Faust, *James Henry Hammond and the Old South: A Design for Mastery* (Baton Rouge: Louisiana State University Press, 1982).

9. See Catherine Clinton, *The Plantation Mistress: Woman's World in the Old South* (New York: Pantheon, 1982), 90–92, 188 and 187, 223–31; Jacqueline Jones, *Labor of Love, Labor of Sorrow* (New York: Basic Books, 1985), 11–43; Deborah Gray White, *Ar'n't I a Woman? Female Slaves in the Plantation South* (New York: Norton, 1987), 27–61, 68–78, 146–48, 152; Elizabeth Fox-Genovese, *Within the Plantation Household,* 271, 294–99.

10. Bertram Wyatt-Brown, *Southern Honor: Ethics and Behavior in the Old South* (New York: Oxford University Press, 1982), 307.

11. Ronald Takaki, *Iron Cages: Race and Culture in Nineteenth-Century America,* (New York: Knopf, 1979; 2d ed., New York: Oxford University Press, 1990), 108–55; Sander L. Gilman, *Difference and Pathology: Stereotypes of Sexuality, Race, and Madness,* (Ithaca: Cornell University Press, 1985), 15–38; John W. Blassingame, *The Slave Community: Plantation Life in the Antebellum South,* (New York: Oxford University Press, 1972), 184–216.

12. John Pendleton Kennedy, *Swallow Barn; or, A Sojourn in the Old Dominion,* (1832; reprint, New York: Hafner, 1971), 327. Kennedy in this text and Simms in *Eutaw, The Forayers,* and *Woodcraft* describe plantation work. In most of the other texts, work by slaves is not mentioned.

13. There is no actual historical evidence for this assertion. It is one of the myths that Virginians propounded about themselves. If one checks any of the references in the slave histories written over the last twenty-five years, he or she will find references to female slaves working in the fields in Virginia. For female slave labor see Jacqueline Jones, *Labor of Love, Labor of Sorrow,* chap. 1; Deborah Gray White, *Ar'n't I a Woman?* chap. 2; Elizabeth Fox-Genovese, *Within the Plantation Household,* chap. 2. Although her focus is the plantation mistress in this chapter, she consistently refers to female slave labor as she argues that slave women did most of the heaviest and most disagreeable work. In chap. 3 she addresses female slave labor directly.

14. William Gilmore Simms, *Woodcraft; or, Hawks About the Dovecote: A Story of the South at the Close of the Revolution* (1854; reprint, New York: A. C. Armstrong and Son, 1882), 417.

15. Nathaniel Beverley Tucker, *The Partisan Leader: A Tale of the Future* (1836; reprint, Chapel Hill: University of North Carolina Press, 1971), 224 and 225.

16. For the importance of religion for black slaves see Eugene D. Genovese, *Roll, Jordan, Roll: The World the Slaves Made* (New York: Pantheon, 1974), 159–284; Lawrence W. Levine, *Black Culture and Black Consciousness: Afro-American Folk Thought from Slavery to Freedom* (New York: Oxford University Press, 1977), esp. chaps. 1 and 3; John Blassingame, *The Slave Community*, chap. 2; George P. Rawick, *From Sundown to Sunup: The Making of the Black Community* (Westport, Conn.: Greenwood, 1972), chap. 3; Albert J. Raboteau, *Slave Religion: The "Invisible Institution" in the Antebellum South* (New York: Oxford University Press, 1978).

17. William Alexander Caruthers, *The Knights of the Golden Horse-Shoe,* 119–203; also *The Kentuckians in New York; or, the Adventures of Three Southerners,* 2 vols. (New York: Harper, 1834) 2:116. This image must be compared with blacks' own testimony and the portraits of the plantation and plantation people in such antislavery novels as Stowe's *Uncle Tom's Cabin,* Richard Hildreth's *Archy Moore: The White Slave, or Memoirs of a Fugitive* (1836; reprint New York: Negro Universities Press, 1969); Brown's *Clotel,* and Delany's *Blake.*

18. See Chapter 8 for a discussion of Abe's parents and history.

19. The topic of slave rebellion and the personalities of slaves who resisted by running away or by being physically violent has long interested historians. Most of the major histories of slavery have discussions of rebellion and resistance. See the work of Kenneth Stampp, George Rawick, Eugene Genovese, Leslie Owens, and John Blassingame cited above as well as the following more specialized studies: Herbert Aptheker, *American Negro Slave Revolts* (New York: International Publishers, 1969); Gerald W. Mullin, *Flight and Rebellion: Slave Resistance in Eighteenth-Century Virginia* (New York: Oxford University Press, 1972) and Eugene D. Genovese's helpful "Rebelliousness and Docility in the Negro Slave: A Critique of the Elkins Thesis," *Civil War History* 13 (December 1967): 293–314. Of course the ex-slave narratives themselves provide the primary sources for these historians.

20. Though his argument offered a necessary corrective to Stanley Elkins's depiction of the slave personality, Blassingame's "stereotyped slaves" are males. Jacqueline Jones, Deborah Gray White, and Elizabeth Fox-Genovese have corrected that omission from the literature. Similarly, historians like Herbert Aptheker or Gerald Mullin have as a subtext black masculinity. They are showing that black male slaves were "men" in the traditional sense. In a different context, Benjamin Quarles and Sidney and Emma Kaplan discuss black male soldiers in the American Revolution and the Civil War. Proving their manhood for the nation and thus earning their civil rights was one of the chief incentives for blacks to enroll in the Civil War regiments. See Gerald W. Mullin, *Flight and Rebellion;* Herbert Aptheker, *American Negro Slave Revolts;* Benjamin Quarles, *The Negro in the Civil War* (Boston: Little, Brown, 1953), and *The Negro in the American Revolution* (1961; reprint, New York: Norton, Inc., 1973); Sidney Kaplan and Emma Nogrady Kaplan, *The Black Presence in the Era of the American Revolution* (Amherst: University of Massachusetts Press, 1989).

21. The exceptions are Kate Spotswood's visiting sick slaves in Caruthers's, *Knights of the Golden Horse-Shoe;* and Widow Eveleigh's (*Woodcraft*) and Katherine Walton's shoring up hysterical female servants when they are under attack from the British. The Janet Berkeley–Scipio alliance (*Mellichampe*) is the only instance where the relationship and actions of the belle and the slave male made a difference to the outcome of the plot.

11. THE MASTER-SLAVE RELATIONSHIP

1. Other important histories of slavery that consider slave culture but that are not nineteenth-century studies include Peter H. Wood, *Black Majority: Negroes in South*

Carolina From 1670 Through the Stono Rebellion (New York: Knopf, 1971); Edmund S. Morgan, *American Slavery American Freedom: The Ordeal of Colonial Virginia* (New York: Norton, 1975); and Gerald W. Mullin, *Flight and Rebellion: Slave Resistance in Eighteenth-Century Virginia* (New York: Oxford University Press, 1972); Eugene D. Genovese's *Roll, Jordan, Roll: The World the Slaves Made* (New York: Pantheon, 1974). takes as his subject the slave community, but his thesis that blacks as a group are ultimately prevented from forming a culture of resistance by their internalization of white racism distinguishes him from these other historians.

See John W. Blassingame, *The Slave Community: Plantation Life in the Antebellum South* (New York: Oxford University Press, 1972); Herbert G. Gutman, *The Black Family in Slavery and Freedom, 1750–1925* (New York: Vintage, 1977); Lawrence W. Levine, *Black Culture and Black Consciousness: Afro-American Folk Thought from Slavery to Freedom* (New York: Oxford University Press, 1977); Leon Litwack, *Been in the Storm So Long: The Aftermath of Slavery* (New York: Vintage, 1980). These historians work in the same tradition as that established by the great black historians W. E. B. DuBois and G. Carter Woodson.

2. See Thomas F. Gossett, *Race: The History of an Idea in America* (New York: Schocken Books, 1965), for Bernier (32–33), Blumenbach (37–39), and Buffon (35–37). For other books on early racial thought, see Winthrop Jordan, *White Over Black: American Attitudes Toward the Negro, 1550–1812* (Baltimore: Penguin Books, 1968); George M. Fredrickson, *The Black Image in the White Mind* (New York: Harper and Row, 1972); Reginald Horsman, *Race and Manifest Destiny: The Origins of American Racial Anglo-Saxonism* (Cambridge: Harvard University Press, 1971); Ronald Takaki, *Iron Cages: Race and Culture in Nineteenth-Century America* (Seattle: University of Washington Press, 1979).

For books specifically on Native Americans see Roy Harvey Pearce *Savagism and Civilization: A Study of the Indian and the American Mind* (Baltimore: Johns Hopkins University Press, 1967); Robert F. Berkhofer, Jr., *The White Man's Indian: Images of the American Indian from Columbus to the Present* (New York: Knopf, 1978); Francis Jennings, *The Invasion of America: Indians, Colonialism, and the Cant of Conquest* (New York: Norton, 1976). Ronald Takaki (cited above) and Richard Slotkin have investigated the white settler's ambivalent attitudes toward Nature and Native Americans; see Slotkin's *Regeneration through Violence: The Mythology of the American Frontier, 1600–1800* (Middletown: Wesleyan University Press, 1973).

3. See David Brown, *Walter Scott and the Historical Imagination* (London: Routledge and Kegan Paul, 1979), 195–209; Duncan Forbes, "The Rationalism of Sir Walter Scott," *Cambridge Journal* 7 (1953): 20–35; Peter D. Garside, "Scott and the 'Philosophical' Historians," *Journal of the History of Ideas* 36, no. 3 (1975): 497–512; Duncan Forbes, "Scientific Whiggism: Adam Smith and John Millar," *Cambridge Journal* 7 (August 1954): 643–70.

4. The anthropolgist Ashley Montague challenged the whole concept of race almost fifty years ago. He argues that geneticists have discovered that we are all closely related and there is as much variation within so-called racial groups as between allegedly different groups. He favors the term *ethnicity.* However, given the vested interests in current racialist politics, it does not seem likely that we will be able to abandon the concept in the near future. See his *Man's Most Dangerous Myth: The Fallacy of Race* (1942; reprint, New York: World Publishing, 1965) and *The Concept of Race* (1964; reprint, New York: Collier, 1972). I am grateful to my colleague Alan Goodman for reminding me about Montagu and for suggesting other anthropological race theorists.

For manifest destiny ideas see Reginald Horsman, *Race and Manifest Destiny;* Robert Berkhofer, *The White Man's Indian;* and Frederick Merk, *Manifest Destiny and Mis-*

sion in American History (New York: Random House, 1963). Projection theory may be found in the work of Gordan Allport, *The Nature of Prejudice* (Cambridge, Mass.: Addison-Wesley, 1954), 360–68; Ronald Takaki, *Iron Cages;* and Sander L. Gilman, *Difference and Pathology: Stereotypes of Sexuality, Race, and Madness* (Ithaca: Cornell University Press, 1985), 15–35.

5. William Gilmore Simms, "The Morals of Slavery," in *The Proslavery Argument, As Maintained by the Most Distinguished Writers of the Southern States* (Philadelphia: Lippincott, Grambo, 1852; reprint, New York: Negro Universities Press, 1968).

6. This is also very Lockean. See John Locke, "Property," in "The Second Treatise of Government."

7. Simms notes, "Providence has placed him in our hands, for his good, and has paid us from his labor for our guardianship" (274).

8. See John Blassingame, *The Slave Community,* 184–216 for a discussion of "slave personality" and stereotypes. Unfortunately, he only deals with stereotypes of men here.

9. For an interesting discussion of the derivation of the name "Sambo" and his emergence as an antebellum stereotype, see Joseph Boskin, *Sambo: The Rise and Demise of An American Jester* (New York: Oxford University Press, 1986), 3–85. Boskin locates the character of Sambo in plantation entertainment and in minstrel shows.

10. Frederick Douglass, *Narrative of the Life of Frederick Douglass: An American Slave* (New York: Doubleday, 1963). See chap. 10 on his life with the slave breaker Edward Covey.

11. John Pendleton Kennedy, *Swallow Barn; or, A Sojourn in the Old Dominion* (1832; reprint 1853 ed., New York: Hafner, 1971), 36.

12. See Genovese, *Roll, Jordan, Roll,* 5, 7, 49.

13. Among the printed sources of slave testimony that are available to the public, in addition to the nineteen volumes of slave testimony that George P. Rawick has edited from the Federal Writers' Project of the Works Progress Administration, are numbers of collections of slave narratives. They include John Blassingame, ed., *Slave Testimony: Two Centuries of Letters, Speeches, Interviews, and Autobiographies* (Baton Rouge: Louisiana State University Press, 1977); Gilbert Osofsky, ed., *Puttin' On Ole Massa'* (New York: Harper and Row, 1969); John F. Bayliss, ed., *Black Slave Narratives* (London: Collier Books, 1970); William Loren Katz, ed., *Five Slave Narratives* (New York: Arno, 1969); Robert S. Starobin, ed., *Blacks in Bondage: Letters of American Slaves* (New York: New Viewpoints, 1974); Bert James Lowenberg and Ruth Bogin, eds., *Black Women in Nineteenth-Century American Life: Their Words, Their Thoughts, Their Feelings* (University Park: Pennsylvania State University Press, 1976); Arna Wendell Bontemps, comp., *Great Slave Narratives* (Boston: Beacon Press, 1969). Important autobiographies by exslave include those of Charles Ball, Henry Bibb, Frederick Douglass, Moses Grandy, William Wells Brown, Josiah Henson, Harriet Jacobs, Solomon Northrop, Sojourner Truth, and Harriet Tubman.

14. William Gilmore Simms, *Richard Hurdis: A Tale of Alabama* (1838; reprint, New York: A. C. Armstrong and Son, 1882), 69.

15. William Gilmore Simms, *Eutaw* (1856; reprint, New York: A. C. Armstrong and Son, 1882), 291.

16. William Gilmore Simms, *The Forayers; or, The Raid of the Dog Days* (1855; reprint, New York: A. C. Armstrong and Son, 1882), 455.

17. On conditions for blacks during the American Revolution see Benjamin Quarles, *The Negro in the American Revolution* (1961; New York: Norton, 1973) and Sidney Kaplan and Emma Nogrady Kaplan, *The Black Presence in the Era of the American Revolution, 1770–1800* (Amherst: University of Massachusetts Press, 1989).

18. William Gilmore Simms, "The Loves of the Driver: A Story of the Wigwam," *The*

Magnolia 3 (May 1841): 223. One of the problems with the copy is that it is misnumbered as "122" instead of 222 for the 220s. These page numbers correct that mistake. This novella was serialized in *Magnolia* 3 in *Wigwam and the Cabin* (May 1841): 222–29 (June 1841): 264–73; and (July 1841): 317–24.

19. Simms notes, "Few persons of any race, color or condition could have had a more elevated idea of their own pretensions than our present subject" (223).

20. See Tremaine McDowell, "The Negro in the Southern Novel Prior to 1850" in Seymour L. Gross and John Edward Hardy, eds., *Images of the Negro in American Literature* (Chicago: University of Chicago Press, 1966), 54–70; Sterling Brown, "A Century of Negro Portraiture in American Literature," in *Black and White in American Culture: An Anthology from "The Massachusetts Review,"* ed. Jules Chametzky and Sidney Kaplan, (Amherst: University of Massachusetts Press, 1969), 333–59; Catherine Starke, *Black Portraiture in American Fiction: Stock Characters, Archetypes, and Individuals* (New York: Basic Books, 1971), 137–51. Winthrop Jordan has noted "white men anxious over their own sexual inadequacy were touched by a racking fear and jealousy" of black men that we now see led them to project vicious racial stereotypes about black men and women, engage in sexual violence against black women, and forbid white women any sexual contact with black men; see Jordan, *White Over Black,* 152 and passim.

21. In addition to Gilman, *Difference and Pathology,* see Ronald Takaki, *Iron Cages,* chaps. 5 and 6.

22. Simms has Mingo mutter to himself that "a woman is never so near won as when she seems least willing" (267). This is of course an old patriarchal attitude as well as an established convention.

23. For Simms's reply see *The Magnolia* 3 (August 1841): 376–79.

24. *Woodcraft* (1854) is actually the revised title of Simms's original work, *The Sword and the Distaff, or "Fair, Fat and Forty,"* written by Simms in 1852.

25. See discussion of Porgy and Mrs. Eveleigh in Chapter 9.

26. One can easily imagine "resourceful" slaves destroying the evidence of their dogs' nighttime forays into the pig pen.

27. For a discussion of these authors' treatment of the yeoman farmer and poor-white class, see Chapters 13 and 14.

28. Other examples of poor white–black antagonism in Simms's work include *The Forayers,* 171–73, 187, 211; and *Eutaw,* chaps. 2–5. In Kennedy's *Swallow Barn,* Abe dies saving white sailors (478–83); and in Tucker's *The Partisan Leader,* blacks defend their master against federal troops (chap. 34).

29. Simms, *Mellichampe: A Legend of the Santez* (1836; reprint, New York: A. C. Armstrong and Son, 1882), 423–24.

30. For a discussion of the planter's attitude toward poor whites see James L. Roark, *Masters Without Slaves: Southern Planters in the Civil War and Reconstruction* (New York: Norton, 1977), esp. chap. 2; and Clement Eaton, *A History of the Old South* (New York: Collier, 1966), 158, 170–73. See also Chapter 13.

31. For a fine discussion of this kind of spontaneous violence as the particular nemesis of the house slave, see Blassingame, *Slave Testimony,* 372; and Elizabeth Fox-Genovese's *Within the Plantation Household: Black and White Women of the Old South* (Chapel Hill: University of North Carolina Press, 1988), 34, 43, 135, 139 and 140, 154–56, 164 and 165, 309–15.

32. For instance, in his preface to "The Morals of Slavery," in *The Proslavery Argument,* which was a revised edition of his 1837 review of Harriet Martineau's *Society in America,* Simms notes that he is republishing the review: "in defense of a domestic institution, which we hold to be not simply within the sanctions of justice and propriety, but as constituting one of the most essential agencies under the divine plan for

promoting the general progress of civilization, and for elevating, to a condition of humanity, a people otherwise barbarous, easily depraved, and needing the help of a superior condition—a power from without—to rescue them from a hopelessly savage state." In this brief passage, then, Simms notes that slavery is a patriarchal, "domestic" institution designed by God to bring an inferior and "barbaric" people to a "condition of humanity" within civilized society.

33. Leslie Fiedler, "Come Back to the Raft Ag'in, Huck Honey," in *An End to Innocence: Essays on Culture and Politics* (Boston: Beacon Press, 1955), 142–51. Fiedler notes the forest, the sea, a river all remove the barriers to male love between the "outcast, ragged woodsman, or despised sailor . . . or unregenerate boy" who "turn to the love of a colored man" (150).

34. See Eve Kosofsky Sedgwick, *Between Men: English Literature and Male Homosocial Desire* (New York: Columbia University Press, 1985); John D'Emilio and Estelle Freedman, *Intimate Matters: A History of Sexuality in America* (New York: Harper and Row, 1988); Lillian Faderman, *Surpassing the Love of Men Romantic Friendship and Love Between Women from the Renaissance to the Present* (New York: William Morrow, 1981); Carroll Smith-Rosenberg, "The Female World of Love and Ritual: Relations Between Women in Nineteenth-Century America," *Signs* 1 (Autumn 1975): 1–29; reprinted in her *Disorderly Conduct: Visions of Gender in Victorian America* (New York: Knopf, 1985), 53–76. The irony is that Fiedler did open up this question in a very gutsy way for his time; nonetheless, I think he misread it. Now that we have more freedom to examine a range of sexualities, we can be more precise about the distinctions between homosocial and homosexual behavior. Although Faderman and Smith-Rosenberg concentrate on women, their research sheds some light on gender relations and attitudes during the nineteenth century.

35. Nathaniel Beverley Tucker, *The Partisan Leader: A Tale of the Future* (1836; reprint, Chapel Hill: University of North Carolina Press, 1971), 215.

36. W. E. B. DuBois has written in *Darkwater: Voices from Within the Veil* (1920; reprint, New York: AMS, 1969): "I shall forgive the white South much in its final judgment day: I shall forgive its slavery, for slavery is a world-old habit; I shall forgive its fighting for a well-lost cause, and for remembering that struggle with tender tears; I shall forgive its so-called "pride of race," the passion of its hot blood, and even its dear old laughable strutting and posing; but one thing I shall never forgive, neither in this world nor the world to come: its wanton and continued persistent insulting of the black womanhood which it sought and seeks to prostitute its lust" (172). See as well, Frederick Douglass's short story, "The Heroic Slave" (1853); William Wells Brown's, *Clotel; or, the President's Daughter* (1853); and Martin R. Delany's *Blake; or, The Huts of America* (1859).

37. Genovese, *Roll, Jordan, Roll,* 5–7, 87–97, 417–19. See especially his distorted view of miscegenation, 413–31.

12. THE PROBLEM OF CLASS

1. A. N. J. Hollander, "The Tradition of 'Poor Whites,'" in *Culture in the South,* ed. W. T. Couch (1934; reprint, Westport, Conn.: Negro Universities Press, 1970), 403–31. Hollander defines the "planter" as a slaveholder owning twenty or more slaves. He estimates that the planter class constituted approximately 3 percent of the population of the slave states. Hollander uses the 1860 census to argue that non-slaveholders constituted three-fourths of the Southern population as a whole, four-fifths of the border state population and two-thirds of the cotton state population. That would mean that 75 percent of the antebellum Southern population was non-slaveholding, but that the majority of that 75 percent is not of the poor-white category. In con-

trast, in the literary South, non-slaveholders are almost always characterized as poor whites, while "yeoman" farmers, contradictory to social reality, own at least one family of slaves. Avery O. Craven thinks the term "crackers" came from the cracking of snake whips or from the Gaelic word meaning "boaster"; see his "Poor Whites and Negroes in the Antebellum South," *Journal of Negro History* 15 (January 1930): 14–25. Hollander's data is substantiated by later demographic profiles of the South. See Clement Eaton, *The Growth of Southern Civilization* (New York: Harper and Row, 1961) and *A History of the Old South* (New York: Collier, 1966); Fabian Linden, "Economic Democracy in the Slave South: An Appraisal of Some Recent Views," *Journal of Negro History* 31 (April 1946): 140–89; Amy Mittleman, "A Perceptual Study of the Ante-Bellum Yeomanry, 1820–1860" (M.A. thesis, Columbia University, 1978); Robert R. Russell, "The Effects of Slavery Upon Nonslaveholders in the Antebellum South," *Agricultural History* 15 (April 1941): 112–26; William N. Parker, ed., *The Structure of the Cotton Economy of the Antebellum South* (Washington, D.C.: Agricultural History Society, 1970), 63–85; Gavin Wright, *The Political Economy of the Cotton South* (New York: Norton, 1978); James Oakes, *The Ruling Race: A History of American Slaveholders* (New York: Knopf, 1982), 37–68; Steven Hahn, *The Roots of Southern Populism: Yeoman Farmers and the Transformation of the Georgia Upcountry, 1850–1890* (New York: Oxford University Press, 1983), 1–85.

2. A distinguished study of American humor that treats Southern and Southwestern humor is Constance Rourke's *American Humor: A Study of the National Character* (1931; reprint, New York: Harcourt Brace Jovanovich, 1959); see also Louis D. Rubin, Jr., ed., *The Comic Imagination in American Literature* (New Brunswick: Rutgers University Press, 1973). Longstreet and Hooper celebrate the violence and ignorance of mountain people and poor whites who descend into Southern towns on market days for shopping as well as "entertainment," which included drunken brawls, cockfighting, eye gouging, and wrestling. The implication throughout their work is that these people are congenitally inferior and are best left hidden away from "civilization" in their mountain retreats. See Longstreet, *Georgia Scenes: Characters, Incidents, Etc., in the First Half Century of the Republic,* intro. B. R. McElderry, Jr. (1835; New York: Sagamore, 1957) and Johnson James Hooper, *Adventures of Captain Simon Suggs: Late of the Tallapoosa Volunteers,* intro. Manly Wade Wellman (1845; reprint, Chapel Hill: University of North Carolina Press, 1969). See also in this tradition, William Faulkner's Snopes trilogy: *The Hamlet, The Mansion,* and *The Town.*

3. Hollander, "The Tradition of 'Poor Whites,' " 403–31, makes the distinction between yeomen, mountaineers, and poor whites; Mittleman, "A Perceptual Study," 7–28; and Eaton, *A History of the Old South,* 207–26.

4. Shields McIlwaine, *The Southern Poor-White from Lubberland to Tobacco Road* (Norman: University of Oklahoma Press, 1939), 10–21. He attributes this "fact" to William Byrd's observations in his *History of the Dividing Line* (1738) and his *Secret History of the Dividing Line* (1841). William Byrd II surveyed the line in 1728 and 1734. His findings were published in the *Westover Manuscripts;* see Byrd, *The Westover Manuscripts,* in *The Prose Works of William Byrd of Westover: Narratives of a Colonial Virginian,* ed. Louis B. Wright (1841; Cambridge: The Belknap Press of Harvard University Press, 1966).

5. David Bertelson, *The Lazy South* (New York: Oxford University Press, 1967) and Merrill Maguire Skaggs, *The Folk of Southern Fiction* (Athens: University of Georgia Press, 1972).

6. This idea was propounded by the "Owsley School" led by Frank L. Owsley; see Frank L. Owsley and Harriet C. Owsley, "The Economic Basis of Society in the Late Antebellum South," *Journal of Southern History* 6 (1940): 24–45, and "The Economic Structure of Rural Tennessee, 1850–1860," *Journal of Southern History* 8 (1942): 161–82;

and Frank L. Owsley, *The Plain Folk of the Old South* (Baton Rouge: Louisiana State University Press, 1949). The school inspired the following people and studies: Chase C. Mooney, "Some Industrial and Statistical Aspects of Slavery in Tennessee," *Tennessee Historical Quarterly* 1 (1942): 195–228; Harry L. Coles, Jr., "Some Notes on Slaveownership and Landownership in Louisiana, 1850–1860," *Journal of Southern History* 9 (1943): 381–94; Blanche Henry Clark, *The Tennessee Yeoman, 1840–1860* (New York: Octagon, 1971); and Herbert Weaver, *Mississippi Farmers, 1850–1860* (Nashville: Vanderbilt University Press, 1945). The people who responded to the assertions of the Owsley School include Fabian Linden, "Economic Democracy in the Slave South"; and Robert R. Russell, "The Effects of Slavery." Roger Wallace Shugg, *Origins of Class Struggle in Louisiana* (Baton Rouge: Louisiana State University Press, 1939) substantially refutes the Owsley thesis.

7. James G. Bonner, "Profile of a Late Antebellum Community," *American Historical Review* 50 (July 1944): 663–80, reprinted in Elinor Miller and Eugene D. Genovese, eds., *Plantation, Town, and Country* (Urbana: University of Illinois Press, 1974), an excellent anthology of articles on the political economy of the antebellum South. See also Robert E. Gallman, "Self-Sufficiency in the Cotton Economy of the Antebellum South," *Agricultural History* 44 (January 1970): 5–24; Eugene D. Genovese, "Yeomen Farmers in a Slaveholders' Democracy?" *Agricultural History* 49 (April 1975): 331–42; Philip G. Davidson, "Industrialism in the Antebellum South," *South Atlantic Quarterly* 27 (October 1928): 405–25; Amy Mittleman, "A Perceptual Study," 7–28. Paul H. Buck, similarly to Bonner, has noted that "the plantation system, by virtually monopolizing industry, rendered superfluous the potential labor contribution of the poor white, consigning him to a life of uselessness so far as productive society was concerned. Economically, the class was not directly exploited by others, but its unutilized capacities presented a serious indictment"; see his "Poor Whites of the Old South," *American Historical Review* 31 (October 1925): 41–54. See also Roger W. Shugg, *Origins of Class Struggle in Louisiana,* for an early study of this problem; and Raimondo Luraghi, *The Rise and Fall of the Plantation South* (New York: New Viewpoints, 1978), for an unusual and controversial analysis of the political economy of the antebellum South. See also Oakes, *The Ruling Race.*

8. Steven Hahn, *The Roots of Southern Populism,* 84; see also 15–133. Buck, "Poor Whites, 47 and 48, notes that planters would not hire whites to work with whites because of their need to preserve their racial hegemony. Gary Nash, Edmund Morgan, and Peter Wood have documented the ways in which white planters played poor white, blacks, and Native Americans off against each other. See Gary B. Nash, *Red, White, and Black: The Peoples of Early America* (Englewood Cliffs, N.J.: Prentice-Hall, 1974); Edmund S. Morgan, *American Slavery, American Freedom* (New York: Norton, 1975); and Peter H. Wood, *Black Majority: Negroes in South Carolina from 1670 through the Stono Rebellion* (New York: Knopf, 1971).

9. See Amy Mittleman, "A Perceptual Study"; Robert E. Shalhope, "Race, Class, Slavery, and the Antebellum Southern Mind, *Journal of Southern History* 3 (November 1971): 557–74; James L. Roark, *Masters Without Slaves: Southern Planters in the Civil War and Reconstruction* (New York: Norton, 1977); George M. Fredrickson, *The Black Image in the White Mind* (New York: Harper and Row, 1972), 71–96; and Eugene D. Genovese, "Yeoman Farmers," 331–42; *The Political Economy of Slavery: Studies in the Economy and Society of the Slave South* (New York: Vintage, 165); and *The World the Slaveholders Made* (New York: Vintage, 1971; see also Steven Hahn, *The Roots of Southern Populism.*

10. James L. Roark, *Masters Without Slaves,* 58. As Roark explains, "Thinking in terms of class came naturally to planters. They had been raised in an environment in which class distinctions were in the air, taken for granted as reflections of the established social order. The tendency was more pronounced among the older, eastern

lowland aristocracy perhaps, but planters everywhere exhibited a self-conscious elitism. They were the legitimate guardians of the lesser classes, black and white, the arbiters of the economy, culture and government of the South."

11. Ibid., 15. See also Nathaniel Beverley Tucker, "The Caucasian Master and the African Slave," *Southern Literary Messenger* 10 (June 1844): 470–80; William Gilmore Simms, "The Morals of Slavery," in *The Proslavery Argument, As Maintained by the Most Distinguished Writers of the Southern States* (Philadelphia: Lippincott, Grambo, 1852; reprint, New York: Negro Universities Press, 1968): 250–59.

12. For a discussion of the themes of popular and "high" literature of this period see Henry Nash Smith, *The Virgin Land: The American West as Symbol and Myth* (New York: Vintage, 1950) and *Democracy and the Novel* (New York: Oxford University Press, 1978); Richard Slotkin, *Regeneration Through Violence: The Mythology of the American Frontier, 1600–1860* (Middletown: Wesleyan University Press, 1973); Alexander Cowie, *The Rise of the American Novel* (New York: American Book, 1948); Carl Van Doren, *The American Novel* (New York: Macmillan, 1931); Richard Chase, *The American Novel and Its Tradition* (New York: Doubleday, 1957); Vernon L. Parrington, *Main Currents in American Thought,* vol. 2: *The Romantic Revolution in America, 1800–1860* (New York: Harcourt, Brace, and World, 1954). See discussion of this issue in Chapter 2. Larry E. Tise argues that indeed through the aegis of conservative clergy, both Southerners trained in the North and Northerners who migrated, the antebellum South renewed and developed further its conservative tendencies. Whether or not one agrees with Tise's conservative clerical–conspiracy thesis or not, it is clear that these elitist, antidemocratic ideas were developed earlier in American political life by the Federalists and were kept alive by their ideological descendants until the Civil War; see Tise, *Proslavery: A History of the Defense of Slavery in America, 1701–1840* (Athens: University of Georgia Press, 1987).

13. See John Pendleton Kennedy's *Rob of the Bowl: A Legend of St. Indioes* (1838; reprint, New Haven: Yale University Press, 1965); William Alexander Caruthers's *Cavaliers of Virginia; or, The Recluse of Jamestown: An Historical Romance,* 2 vols. (New York: Harper, 1835) and *The Kentuckian in New York; or, The Adventures of Three Southerners* (New York: Harper, 1834); Nathaniel Beverley Tucker, *Gertrude, Southern Literary Messenger* 10 (1844): 513–647, 705–13; 11 (1845): 178–86, 219–23, 251–60, 276–80, 380–44, 690–712. *Gertrude* is an exception since "true love" was defeated.

14. William Gilmore Simms, *The Forayers; or The Raid of the Dog Days* (1855; reprint, New York: A. C. Armstrong & Son, 1882), 86.

15. For these details about Simms's life, see Edd Winfield Parks, *William Gilmore Simms as Literary Critic* (Athens: University of Georgia Press, 1961), 19; William Gilmore Simms, *Views and Reviews in American Literature, History, and Fiction,* ed. C. Hugh Holman (Cambridge: The Belknap Press of Harvard University Press, 1962), i–xxv; John Caldwell Guilds, *"Long Years of Neglect": The Work and Reputation of William Gilmore Simms* (Fayetteville: University of Arkansas Press, 1992), 3–22; Mary Ann Wimsatt, *The Major Fiction of William Gilmore Simms: Cultural Traditions and Literary Form* (Baton Rouge: Louisiana State University Press, 1989), 12–32.

16. Simms was known to be a sloppy and hasty writer with some impatience for detail. Inglehardt's origins are a case in point. In *The Forayers* we are told on page 90 that Inglehardt's father was "a small Dutch farmer in the same neighborhood as the Travis Holly-Dale plantation." However, Simms tells us on page 292 that "the widow Bruce was compelled to recognize the claims of the loyalist captain, in a lawless period, . . . the son of an obscure overseer, of no good character . . ."; see 292–98 on Inglehardt.

17. Among Inglehardt's sins, we are told, was that "he had abandoned his *caste,* an unforgiveable offense which moved the dislike of all its members."

13. REPRESENTATIONS OF POOR WHITES

1. See Chapter 8.

2. In Simms's work this tendency is the most pronounced. Most of his major poor-white characters are discussed below. Caruthers with Brian O'Reilly (*Cavaliers of Virginia*) and Kennedy with Jemmy Smith and Haffen Block (*Swallow Barn*) portray the dissolute lives and irresponsible behavior of poor-white men as comical. However, in his characterization of Mat Adair and the Hugh Habershaw gang (*Horse-Shoe Robinson*) discussed below, Kennedy matches Simms's portrayal of the criminal poor white. Finally, N. B. Tucker, who had little respect or compassion for the poor, described a poor white, John Kiezer, converted to a useful scout type by planter hero, George Balcombe: "John, in Balcombe's hands, was the wild dog, retaining his courage, his rapacity, and his hardihood, but fitted to the uses of his master by having her ferocity subdued, his sagacity trained, and his courage directed against the denizens of his native forest." Nathaniel B. Tucker, *George Balcombe. A Novel* (New York: Harper, 1836), 71. Caruthers and George Tucker rarely portray the poor white in stereotypical terms, although they do create a frontier character who will be discussed later as a type: the scout. In war against the British or the Indians, the scout knows the woods and how to handle a gun, but as the above example illustrates he recognizes the planter as his leader and natural superior. His peacetime equivalent is the overseer, the planter's hired man who disciplines another refractory racial group.

3. John Pendleton Kennedy, *Horse-Shoe Robinson: A Tale of the Tory Ascendancy* (1835; reprint, New York: Hurd and Houghton, 1866), 156.

4. Mary watches Butler carefully. We are told, "In truth there was some incongruity between his manners and the peasant dress he wore" (155). Later, she confronts him with her suspicions that he is a gentleman. She tells him he talks differently from other people and he doesn't "look and walk and behave" as if he were a yeoman (161). She noticed he was contemplative, and he didn't swear, and he was kind and courteous. Finally, she saw that he carried a picture of a woman on a blue ribbon around his neck. Only "gentlemen of quality" carry these (161).

5. After Adair has skinned the wolf alive he is angry that she didn't suffer as much as he had wanted her to. Kennedy comments that Adair acted "with that stoicism which belongs to uncivilized life."

6. Because American historians have been only sporadically interested in issues of class, there is a dearth of historical research about the existence of these Southern poor-white gangs. One exception to the general trends is Ronald Hoffman's "The 'Disaffected' in the Revolutionary South," in *The American Revolution: Explorations in the History of American Radicalism,* ed. Alfred F. Young (DeKalb: Northern Illinois University Press, 1976), 275–316.

7. John Pendleton Kennedy, *Swallow Barn; or, a Sojourn in the Old Dominion* (1832; reprint, 1853 ed., New York: Hafner, 1971), 171 and 172.

8. Although Kennedy demurred from the feudal pretensions of some of his more zealous contemporaries, he was far from being a democrat. He believed in public education and thought that the average man was capable of being a useful citizen, yet he allied himself against the "leveling tendencies" of the Jacksonian Democrats and argued that it "was the responsibility of a gentleman to take the lead in public affairs." See Charles H. Bohner, *John Pendleton Kennedy: Gentleman from Baltimore* (Baltimore: Johns Hopkins University Press, 1961), 115. See also J. V. Ridgely, *John Pendleton Kennedy* (New York: Twayne, 1966), 30 and 31, 54–56.

9. As we have seen in Kennedy's *Horse-Shoe Robinson,* Arthur Butler, a patriot officer, is engaged to Mildred Lindsey, the daughter of Loyalist Philip Lindsey. In Kennedy's work, as in Simms's, upper-class planters who ally with Britain are dubbed

"Loyalists," while poor whites and middling whites who ally with Britain are labeled "Tories." In *The Forayers* and *Eutaw*, Colonel Sinclair, "The Baron" and father of hero William Sinclair, is a Loyalist, "a natural aristocrat," and a "gentleman among gentlemen," who believed in the absolutist state and the hereditary right of the aristocracy to rule. (See William Gilmore Simms, *The Forayers; or, The Raid of the Dog Days* [1855; reprint, New York: A. C. Armstrong and Son, 1882], 123, 109, 147). In contrast, poorwhite Hell-Fire Dick and middle-class Inglehardt are derogatorily labeled "Tories" and are presented as dishonest criminals who take advantage of the chaos of war to steal what they cannot earn for themselves. See Chapter 12 above.

10. See Chapters 3 and 6. Again one should stress that Simms had reversed the tradition of the sentimental novel in having an aristocrat rescue the virgin-heroine from the rapacious middle-caste villain.

11. William Gilmore Simms, *Eutaw* (1856; reprint, New York: A. C. Armstrong and Son, 1882), 10.

12. This theme is developed in two chapters (246–57; 258–75). Vernon L. Parrington notes what he sees as Simms's more egalitarian impulses, "And so in spite of the fact that his every instinct was democratic, and every natural impulse generous and manly, he fought the battles of the peculiar institution as stoutly as if he had been born to his three hundred slaves; and he suffered in consequence the loss of pretty nearly everything, including his art." See Parrington, *Main Currents in American Thought*, vol. 2: *The Romantic Revolution in America* (1927; reprint, New York: Harcourt, Brace and World, 1954), 120, 119–30. I think there is a marked difference between the young and the mature Simms on this score. His essays and fiction do not reveal him as a "democrat" even as it was understood in Jacksonian America.

13. William Gilmore Simms, *Woodcraft; or, Hawks About the Dovecote: A Story of the South at the Close of the Revolution* (1854; reprint New York: A. C. Armstrong and Son, 1882), 13.

14. Simms depicts two other poor whites who defend their daughters; see Watson Gray in *The Scout* and Betsy Pickett in *Richard Hurdis*.

15. Simms's border romances are *Guy Rivers: A Tale of Georgia* (1834); *Richard Hurdis: A Tale of Alabama* (1838); *Border Beagles: A Tale of Mississippi* (1840); *Beauchampe; or, The Kentucky Tragedy* (1842), which in plot is the sequel to *Charlemont; or, The Pride of the Village* (1856). Mary Ann Wimsatt makes this point in *The Major Fiction of William Gilmore Simms: Cultural Traditions and Literary Form* (Baton Rouge: Louisiana State University Press, 1989), 120–35.

16. Simms, *Richard Hurdis*, 401–2; *Border Beagles*, 87–88, 227–33. See Mary Ann Wimsatt, *The Major Fiction of William Gilmore Simms: Cultural Traditions and Literary Form* (Baton Rouge: Louisiana State University Press, 1989), 85–119, 120–35 for her argument about these "border romances" as our first Westerns and for her discussion of the John Murrin gang, on which the "Saxon Gang" was based.

17. See Chapters 6 and 8 for a discussion of these characters.

18. James Oakes, *The Ruling Race: A History of American Slaveholders* (New York: Knopf, 1982; 2d ed., New York: Vintage, 1983).

14. THE PROBLEM OF THE YEOMAN FARMER

1. Because plantation mistresses as women exist only in the private, allegedly natural and pre-political sphere, they never appear as heroic individuals or leaders as their sons, husbands, and fathers do. Instead, women of all classes reflect the positive and negative characteristics and qualities of their men, and plantation mistresses and their daughters serve as helpless victims who need the men of their class to protect them. See discussion of this issue in Chapters 6, 8, 9, and 13.

2. William Alexander Caruthers, *The Knights of the Golden Horse-Shoe: A Traditionary Tale of the Cocked Hat Gentry in the Old Dominion* (1842; reprint, Chapel Hill: University of North Carolina Press, 1970), 1:59.

3. 2:174. Caruthers was a true believer in the Anglo-Saxon Christian "manifest destiny" to supersede Native Americans on the North American continent. In the "departure scene" the minister urged the men "to go forward in the great march of civilization," and told them that "thousands yet unborn would bless the hardy pioneers then about to set out upon the exploration of a new and unknown country." The minister assured them that they were engaged in "no idle military conquest . . . but emphatically an enterprise in behalf of their country—of the age—of the world" and finally that they had God's blessing (2:174).

4. For a description of this literary type who had a real-life counterpart, see other fictional representatives in Robert Montgomery Bird's *Nick of the Woods* and Herman Melville's discussion of "Indian Hating" in chapter 26 of *The Confidence Man.*

5. Caruthers's racial views are far more liberal than either Simms's or N. B. Tucker's. In this same conversation he has Frank Lee note that when Jesus appeared, the people in the British Isles "were as great savages as these very red men, against whom you are so prejudiced." Lee notes subsequently, "A red skin and a savage nature are not always inseparable; all the learning and refinement of the world have been transmitted to us through dark skins" (2:83) Nothing like this appears in any of the other writers' novels. Note as well that Caruthers is reflecting the views of Scottish positivist historians discussed in Chapter 3.

6. For a discussion of this tendency toward racist nationalism among nineteenth-century Americans, see George M. Fredrickson, *The Black Image in the White Mind* (New York: Harper and Row, 1972); Frederick Merk, *Manifest Destiny and Mission in American History* (New York: Random House, 1963); Reginald Horsman, *Race and Manifest Destiny: The Origins of American Racial Anglo-Saxonism* (Cambridge: Harvard University Press, 1981); and Robert F. Berkhofer, Jr., *The White Man's Indian: Images of the American Indian from Columbus to the Present* (New York: Knopf, 1978).

7. John Pendleton Kennedy, *Horse-Shoe Robinson: A Tale of the Tory Ascendancy* (1835; reprint, New York: Hurd and Houghton, 1866), 14.

8. The following is a list of Horse-Shoe Robinson's heroic deeds and actions: escapes from Cornwallis's men in Charleston (23–26); when he is captured with Butler by a poor white gang, he manages a clever escape (225–26); outsmarts and captures British officer Ensign St. Jermyn (268–71); leads a patriot attack on British camp holding Butler, frees him, and kills leader of poor-white gang (334–35); accompanies heroine Mildred Lindsey through the enemy lines to her interview with Cornwallis; rescues Butler during the final Battle of King's Mountain, and performs other heroic deeds during the battle (584–94).

9. See for instance Henry Nash Smith, *Democracy and the Novel: Popular Resistance to Classic American Writers* (New York: Oxford University Press, 1978); and Richard Slotkin, *Regeneration Through Violence.* See also Steven Hahn, *The Roots of Southern Populism: Yeoman Farmers and the Transformation of the Georgia Upcountry, 1850–1890* (New York: Oxford University Press, 1983). In part 1, Hahn lays out the social, economic, and political aspects of antebellum yeoman life in upcountry Georgia.

10. Remember that Simms divides the planter between "Loyalists," who are among the wealthiest colonists, and "patriots," who were the first to resist English authority and who recruited yeomen to their cause. "Tories" were native-born "of the very lowest class"; they fought for "love of gain" and "thirst for rapine." According to Simms, having "no sympathy with the more influential classes" (that is, planter patriots), they mingled with the British troops and formed their own gangs, which kidnapped slaves for sale to the British. They scouted out the hiding places of the patriots,

killing them or leading the British to them, and attacked and murdered defenseless women and children. William Gilmore Simms, *The Partisan: A Romance of the Revolution* (1835; reprint, New York: Belford, Clarke, 1885), 94 and 95.

11. "Loyalists" thus described include Sam Peter Adair, a man of fortune in Simms's *Eutaw,* 437–44; Sherrod Nelson and his mother, chap. 50 of *Eutaw;* William Sinclair's father, *The Forayers,* 109, 123, and 124. In this novel, Simms has scout Humphries comment that the richest planters, who are the Loyalists, "have quite too much at stake; they have too much plate; too many negroes, and live too comfortably to be willing to stand a chance of losing all by taking up arms agains' the British" (*The Partisan,* 48).

12. Simms, *Katherine Walton* (1851; reprint, New York: Lovell, Coryell, n.d.), 371.

13. For information about Lance Frampton's family see Simms, *The Partisan,* 69, 52, 53, 78, and 79.

14. Similarly, black men are rarely allowed more than a serving role even when they do go to battle. In *The Forayers,* 'Bram scouts but doesn't fight, and Tom cooks under the direction of Porgy. Only Scipio (*Mellichampe*) kills a British officer, and that is in defense of his mistress's fiancé's life. See discussion of this issue in Chapters 10 and 11 above.

15. Blonay and his mother are discussed in Chapter 8.

16. William Gilmore Simms, *Mellichampe: A Legend of the Santez* (1836; reprint, New York: A. C. Armstrong and Son, 1882), 380.

17. Simms, *The Partisan,* 405 and 406. The spelling of Thumbscrew's proper surname is "Wetherspoon" in *The Partisan* and "Witherspoon" in *Mellichampe.*

18. See discussion of Mellichampe and heroine Janet Berkeley in Chapter 6 above.

19. The portrait of Mellichampe here is Simms at his melodramatic worst.

20. See 31–37, 56–61, 77–82, 133–37 for examples of this common pattern in their relationship.

21. There are five border romances under consideration here: *Guy Rivers: A Tale of Georgia* (1834; reprint, New York: A. C. Armstrong and Son, 1882); *Richard Hurdis: A Tale of Alabama* (1838; reprint, New York: A. C. Armstrong and Son, 1882); *Border Beagles: A Tale of Mississippi* (1840; reprint, New York: A. C. Armstrong and Son, 1882); *Beauchampe; or, the Kentucky Tragedy* (1842; reprint, New York: A. C. Armstrong and Son, 1882); and *Charlemont; or, The Pride of the Village* (1856; reprint, New York: A. C. Armstrong and Son, 1882).

22. Simms's *Border Beagles,* 159; see Chapter 13 above. For similar descriptions see *Guy Rivers,* 13–17, 61–63; *Richard Hurdis,* 13–16, 65, 66, and 144–48; *Charlemont,* 13–16, 17–21, and 24–28.

23. Simms's *Border Beagles,* 170–75, 223–29, 242, and 243; 245–64 on "western justice"; 490–95.

24. See Henry Nash Smith, *The Virgin Land: The American West as Symbol and Myth* (New York: Vintage, 1950); John William Ward, *Andrew Jackson: Symbol for An Age* (New York: Oxford University Press, 1955); Richard Slotkin, *Regeneration Through Violence;* Eric Foner, *Free Soil, Free Labor, Free Men* (London: Oxford University Press, 1970); Marvin Meyers, *The Jacksonian Persuasion: Politics & Belief* (Stanford: Stanford University Press, 1960); 57–100; David W. Noble, *The Eternal Adam and the New World Garden: The Central Myth in the American Novel Since 1830* (New York: George Braziller, 1968), 1–48; and Dixon Wecter, *The Hero in America: A Chronicle of Hero-Worship* (New York: Scribner 1972); see esp. 181–306, 341–63; Stephen B. Oates, *With Malice Toward None: The Life of Abraham Lincoln* (New York: New America Library, 1977).

25. On black men in the American Revolution see Benjamin Quarles, *The Negro in the American Revolution* (1961; reprint, New York: Norton, 1973), and Sidney Kaplan and Emma Nogrady Kaplan, *The Black Presence in the Era of the American Revolution, 1770–1800* (Amherst: University of Massachusetts Press, 1989).

CONCLUSION

1. Gavin Wright, *The Political Economy of the Cotton South* (New York: Norton, 1978), 35.

2. See Theda Perdue, *Slavery and the Evolution of Cherokee Society, 1540–1866* (Knoxville: University of Tennessee Press, 1979); and Daniel F. Littlefield, Jr., *Africans and Creeks from the Colonial Period to the Civil War* (Westport, Conn.: Greenwood, 1976) and *Africans and Seminoles: From Removal to Emancipation* (Westport, Conn.: Greenwood, 1977).

3. Bertram Wyatt-Brown, *Southern Honor: Ethics and Behavior in the Old South* (New York: Oxford University Press, 1982).

4. See Nancy F. Cott, *Bonds of Womanhood: "Woman's Sphere" in New England, 1780–1835* (New Haven: Yale University Press, 1977), 76–83; John D'Emilio and Estelle Freedman, "Seeds of Change," in *Intimate Matters: A History of Sexuality in America* (New York: Harper and Row, 1988), 39–52; Catherine Clinton, *The Plantation Mistress: Woman's World in the Old South* (New York: Pantheon, 1982), 40–44, 59–67.

5. Patrick Gerster and Nicholas Cords, "The Northern Origins of Southern Mythology," *Journal of Southern History* 43, no. 4 (November 1977): 567–82. Another earlier discussion along the lines that Gerster and Cords suggest is Edmund Wilson, "Harriet Beecher Stowe," in *Patriotic Gore: Studies in the Literature of the American Civil War* (New York: Oxford University Press, 1969), 3–58. See as well C. Vann Woodward, "The Search for Southern Identity," in *The Burden of Southern History* (1960; reprint; Baton Rouge: Louisiana State University Press, 1977), 3–25. For a fascinating account of a Northerner's engagement with the South in the 1960s that touches on both the Northerner's "outsiderness" and his fascination with the South, his engagement with it and his distancing from it, see Robert Coles, "The South That is Man's Destiny," in *Black and White in American Culture: An Anthology from "The Massachusetts Review,"* ed. Jules Chametzky and Sidney Kaplan (Amherst: University of Massachusetts Press, 1969), 25–36.

The week I was revising this chapter, the *New York Times* arrived with the front-page announcement that Alexandra Ripley's sequel to Margaret Mitchell's *Gone with the Wind* had outsold all other fiction for 1991 in its first two weeks. Another story describes Northern and Southern building of Tara-like homes to symbolize "style, status and power, of gracious living." See Esther B. Fein, " 'Gone With the Wind' Sequel An Astonishing Best Seller," *New York Times,* 3 October 1991, sec. A, p. 1, col. 5; Patricia Leigh Brown, "Tara, the Myth, Lives on in America's Suburbs," *New York Times,* 3 October 1991, sec. C, p. 1, col. 1.

6. See for instance, Leon Litwack, *North of Slavery: The Negro in the Free States, 1790–1860* (Chicago: University of Chicago Press, 1961).

7. Nathaniel Beverley Tucker, "The Caucasian Master and the African Slave," *Southern Literary Messenger* 10 (1844): 478.

8. Ibid., 480.

9. Ibid.

Bibliography

SOURCES FOR PRE-1900 TEXTS

Bayliss, John F., ed. *Black Slave Narratives.* London: Collier, 1970.

Bontemps, Arna Wendell, comp. *Great Slave Narratives.* Introduction by Arna Wendell Bontemps. Boston: Beacon, 1969.

Brown, William Wells. *Clotel; or, The President's Daughter.* 1853. Reprint, New York: Arno, 1969.

Bryan, George S. "Kennedy's *Swallow Barn.*" *Southern Quarterly Review* 21 (January 1851): 71–86.

Byrd, William, II. *The Westover Manuscripts.* 1841. In *The Prose Works of William Byrd of Westover: Narratives of a Colonial Virginian,* edited by Louis B. Wright. Cambridge: The Belknap Press of Harvard University Press, 1966.

Calhoun, John J. *A Disquisition on Government.* 1854. Reprint, New York: Bobbs-Merrill, 1953.

Caruthers, William Alexander. *The Cavaliers of Virginia; or, The Recluse of Jamestown: An Historical Romance.* 2 vols. New York, Harper, 1835.

———. *The Kentuckians in New York; or, The Adventures of Three Southerners.* 2 vols. New York: Harper, 1834.

———. *The Knights of the Golden Horse-Shoe: A Traditionary Tale of the Cocked Hat Gentry in the Old Dominion.* 1841. Reprint, Chapel Hill: University of North Carolina Press, 1970.

Chesnut, Mary Boykin. *A Diary From Dixie.* Edited by Ben A. Williams. 1905. Reprint, Boston: Houghton Mifflin, 1961.

Delany, Martin R. *Blake; or, The Huts of America.* 1857. Reprint, Boston: Beacon, 1970.

Dew, Thomas R. "On the Characteristic Differences Between the Sexes, and the Position and Influence of Women in Society." *Southern Literary Messenger* 1, nos. 11 and 12 (May–August 1835): 493–512, 621–32, 672–91.

Douglass, Frederick. "*The Heroic Slave.*" In *Violence in the Black Imagination: Essays and Documents,* edited by Ronald T. Takaki, 37–77, New York: Putnam, 1972.

———. *Life and Times of Frederick Douglass.* 1892. Reprint, New York: Macmillan, 1962.

———. *Narrative of the Life of Frederick Douglass: An American Slave.* New York: Doubleday, 1963.

Elliot, E. N., ed. *Cotton Is King and Pro-Slavery Arguments: Comprising the Writings of Hammond, Harper, Christy, String-fellow, Hodge, Bledsoe, and Cartwright on This Important Subject.* 1860. Reprint, New York: Negro Universities Press, 1969.

Everett, Alexander H. "*Swallow Barn.*" *North American Review* 26 (April 1835): 519–44.

Fitzhugh, George. "Cannibals All: or, Slaves Without Masters." In *Ante-Bellum,* edited by Harvey Wish, 99–156. 1857. Reprint, New York: Capricorn Books, 1960.

———. *Sociology for the South; or, The Failure of Free Society.* 1854. Reprint, New York: Burt Franklin, 1964.

Hawthorne, Nathaniel. *The House of the Seven Gables, A Romance.* 1851. Reprint, Boston: Houghton Mifflin, 1960.

Heath, James Ewell. *Edge-Hill; or, The Family of the FitzRoyals. A Novel. By A Virginian.* 2 vols. Richmond, Va.: T. W. White, 1828.

Helper, Hinton Rowan. *The Impending Crisis of the South: How To Meet It.* Edited by Harvey Wish, 159–256. 1857. Reprint, New York: Capricorn Books, 1960.

Hildreth, Richard. *Archy Moore, The White Slave; or, Memoirs of a Fugitive.* 1836. Reprint, New York: Negro Universities Press, 1969.

Holmes, George F. Review of *Uncle Tom's Cabin,* by Harriet Beecher Stowe. *Southern Literary Messenger* 18 (October 1852): 720–31.

Hooper, Johnson Jones. *Adventures of Captain Simon Suggs: Late of the Tallapoosa Volunteers,* with an introduction by Manly Wade Wellman. 1845. Reprint, Chapel Hill: University of North Carolina Press, 1969.

Jacobs, Harriet. *Incidents in the Life of a Slave Girl: Written by Herself.* Edited by Jean Fagan Yellin. Cambridge: Harvard University Press, 1987.

Katz, William Loren, ed. *Five Slave Narratives.* New York: Arno, 1969.

Kennedy, John Pendleton. "Friends of the Union to the Rescue!" *National Intelligencer* 5 (March 5 1850): 2–3.

———. *Horse-Shoe Robinson: A Tale of the Tory Ascendancy.* 1835. Reprint, New York: Hurd and Houghton, 1866.

———. *Rob of the Bowl: A Legend of St. Inigoes.* 1838. Reprint, New Haven: Yale University Press, 1965.

———. *Slavery: Mere Pretext for the Rebellion; Not Its Cause.* Philadelphia: Sherman, 1868.

———. *Swallow Barn; or, A Sojourn in the Old Dominion.* 1832. Reprint, 1853 ed., New York: Hafner, 1971.

Longstreet, Augustus Baldwin. *Georgia Scenes: Characters, Incidents, Etc. in the First Half Century of the Republic.* Introduction by B. R. McElderry, Jr. 1835. Reprint, New York: Sagamore, 1957.

Lowenberg, Bert James, and Ruth Bogin, eds. *Black Women in Nineteenth-Century American Life: Their Words, Their Thoughts, Their Feelings.* University Park: Pennsylvania State University Press, 1976.

McCord, Louisa S. Cheves [L.S.M.]. Review of *Uncle Tom's Cabin,* by Harriet Beecher Stowe. *Southern Quarterly Review* 23 (Janaury 1853): 81–120.

Oliphant, Mary C. Simms, Alfred Taylor O'Dell, and T. C. Duncan Fines, eds. *The Letters of William Gilmore Simms.* 5 vols. Columbia: University of South Carolina Press, 1952–56.

Olmsted, Frederick Law. *The Cotton Kingdom.* Edited by Arthur M. Schlesinger. 1861. Reprint, New York: Modern Library, 1969.

———. *A Journey to the Backcountry.* 1860. Reprint, Williamstown, Mass.: Corner House, 1972.

Osofsky, Gilbert, ed. *Puttin' On Ole Massa.* New York: Harper and Row, 1969.

The Pro-Slavery Argument, As Maintained by the Most Distinguished Writers of the Southern States: Containing the Several Essays, on the Subject, of Chancellor Harper, Governor Hammond, Dr. Simms, and Professor Dew. Philadelphia: Lippincott, Grambo, 1852. Reprint, New York: Negro Universities Press, 1968.

Simms, William Gilmore. *Beauchampe; or, The Kentucky Tragedy.* 1842. Reprint, New York: A. C. Armstrong and Son, 1882.

———. *Border Beagles: A Tale of Mississippi.* 1840. Reprint, New York: A. C. Armstrong and Son, 1882.

———. *Charlemont; or, The Pride of the Village.* 1856. Reprint, New York: A. C. Armstrong and Son, 1882.

———. "Domestic Histories of the South." *Southern Quarterly Review* 21 (April 1852): 507–35.

———. *Eutaw.* 1856. Reprint, New York: A. C. Armstrong and Son, 1882.

——. *The Forayers; or, The Raid of the Dog Days.* 1855. Reprint, New York: A. C. Armstrong and Son, 1882.

——. *Guy Rivers: A Tale of Georgia.* 1834. Reprint, New York: A. C. Armstrong and Son, 1882.

——. *Katherine Walton.* 1851. Reprint, New York: Lovell, Coryell, n.d.

——. *The Loves of the Driver: A Story of the Wigwam. The Magnolia* 3 (May–July 1841): 222–29; 264–73; 317–24.

——. *Mellichampe: A Legend of the Santez.* 1836. Reprint, New York: A. C. Armstrong and Son, 1882.

——. "Modern Prose Fiction." *Southern Quarterly Review* 20 (April 1849): 41–83.

——. "The Morals of Slavery." In *The Proslavery Argument, As Maintained by the Most Distinguished Writers of the Southern States; Containing the Several Essays, on the Subject, of Chancellor Harper, Governor Hammond, Dr. Simms, and Professor Dew.* Philadelphia: Lippincott, Grambo, 1852. Reprint. New York: Negro Universities Press, 1968.

——. *The Partisan: A Romance of the Revolution.* 1835. Reprint, New York: Belford, Clarke, 1885.

——. Preface to "Treatment of Slaves in Southern States." *Southern Quarterly Review* 21 (July 1852): 209–19.

——. Review of *Domestic Manners of the Americans,* by Mrs. Trollope. *Southern Quarterly Review* 3 (September 1832): 109–23.

——. Review of *Society in America,* by H. Martineau. *Southern Literary Messenger* 3 (November 1837): 641–57.

——. *Richard Hurdis: A Tale of Alabama.* 1838. Reprint, New York: A. C. Armstrong and Son, 1882.

——. *The Scout: or, The Black Riders of Congaree.* 1841. Reprint, New York: A. C. Armstrong and Son, 1882.

——. "Stowe's Key to *Uncle Tom's Cabin.*" *Southern Quarterly Review* 24 (July 1853): 214–54.

——. *Views and Reviews in American Literature, History, and Fiction.* Edited by C. Hugh Holman. Cambridge: The Belknap Press of Harvard University Press, 1962.

——. *Woodcraft; or, Hawks About the Dovecote: A Story of the South at the Close of the Revolution.* 1854. Reprint, New York: A. C. Armstrong and Son, 1882.

——. *The Yemassee: A Romance of South Carolina.* 1835. Reprint, Boston: Houghton Mifflin Co., 1961.

Smedes, Susan Dabney. *Memorials of a Southern Planter.* Edited by Fletcher M. Green. 1890. Reprint, New York: Knopf, 1965.

Starobin, Robert S. *Blacks in Bondage: Letters of American Slaves.* New York: New Viewpoints, 1974.

Stowe, Harriet Beecher. *Uncle Tom's Cabin; or, Life Among the Lowly.* 1852. Reprint, New York: Washington Square, 1963.

Tocqueville, Alexis de. *Democracy in America.* 2 vols. 1834. Reprint, New York: Schocken, 1961.

Trollope, Frances. *Domestic Manners of the Americans.* Edited by Donald Smalley. 1832. Reprint, Vintage, 1949.

Tucker, George. *The History of the United States: From Their Colonization to the End of the Twenty-Sixth Congress, in 1841.* Philadelphia: Lippincott, 1856–57.

——. *The Laws of Wages, Profits, and Rents.* 1837. Reprint, New York: Augustus M. Kelley, 1964.

——. *Political Economy for the People.* Philadelphia: C. Sherman and Son, 1859.

——. *The Valley of Shenandoah; or, Memoirs of the Graysons.* 2 vols. 1824. Reprint, Chapel Hill: University of North Carolina Press, 1970.

Tucker, Nathaniel Beverley. "The Caucasian Master and the African Slave." *Southern Literary Messenger* 10 (June 1844): 329–39, 470–80.
——. *George Balcombe. A Novel.* 2 vols. New York: Harper, 1836.
——. *Gertrude: An Original Novel. Southern Literary Messenger* 10 (1844): 513–19, 641–47, 705–13, 11 (1845): 178–86, 219–23, 257–65, 377–82, 434–41, 690–94, 705–12.
——. "Law Lectures at William and Mary." *Southern Literary Messenger* 1 (1834–35): 145–54, 227–31, 266–70, 597–602.
——. "A Lecture on Government." *Southern Literary Messenger* 3 (April 1837): 209–16.
——. *The Partisan Leader: A Tale of the Future.* 1836. Reprint, Chapel Hill: University of North Carolina Press, 1971.
——. "Political Science." *Southern Literary Messenger* 5 (August 1839): 559–66.
——. "Review of President Dew's Address." *Southern Literary Messenger* 3 (April 1837): 268–70.
——. Review of *Slavery in the United States* (1836) by James K. Paulding. *Southern Literary Messenger* 2 (1835–36): 336–38.
Weld, Theodore Dwight. *American Slavery As It Is.* 1839. Reprint, New York: Arno, 1969.
Wright, Frances. *Views of Society and Manners in the United States.* 1821. Cambridge: The Belknap Press of Harvard University Press, 1963.

SECONDARY SOURCES

Albernathy, Thomas P. *The South in the New Nation, 1789–1819.* Baton Rouge: Louisiana State University Press, 1961.
Allen, Jeffrey Brooke. "Were Southern White Critics of Slavery Racists? Kentucky and the Upper South, 1791–1824." *Journal of Southern History* 44 (May 1978): 169–90.
Allport, Gordon. *The Nature o Prejudice.* Cambridge, Mass.: Addison-Wesley, 1954.
Angus, Ian, and Sut Jhally. *Cultural Politics in Contemporary America.* New York: Routledge, Chapman, and Hall, 1989.
Aptheker, Herbert. *American Negro Slave Revolts.* New York: International Publishers, 1969.
Arthur, Marilyn. "'Liberated' Women: The Classical Era." In *Becoming Visible: Women in European History,* edited by Renate Bridenthal and Claudia Koontz, 62–89. Boston: Houghton Mifflin, 1977.
Babbitt, Irving. *Rousseau and Romanticism.* Austin: University of Texas Press, 1977.
Ballagh, James C. *A History of Slavery in Virginia.* Baltimore: Johns Hopkins University Press, 1913.
Bancroft, Frederic. *Slave Trading in the Old South.* New York: Ungar, 1959.
Bank, Stanley. *American Romanticism: A Shape for Fiction.* New York: Putnam, 1969.
Barker-Benfield, G. J. *The Horrors of the Half-Known Life: Male Attitudes Toward Women and Sexuality in Nineteenth Century America.* New York: Harper and Row, 1976.
Barnet, Louise K. *The Ignoble Savage: American Literary Racism, 1790–1890.* Westport, Conn.: Greenwood, 1965.
Bartlett, Irving. *The American Mind in the Mid-Nineteenth Century.* New York: Crowell, 1967.
Baym, Nina. *Women's Fiction: A Guide to Novels By and About Women in America, 1820–1870.* Ithaca: Cornell University Press, 1978.
Beard, Mary R. *Women as Force in History.* New York: Collier, 1973.
Beauvoir, Simone de. *The Second Sex.* New York: Knopf, 1949.
Bell, Roseanne P., Bettye J. Parker, and Beverly Guy-Sheftall, eds. *Sturdy Black Bridges: Visions of Black Women in Literature.* Garden City, N.Y.: Anchor, 1979.
Benjamin, Walter. "The Author as Producer." In *Reflections: Essays, Aphorisms, Auto-*

biographical Writings, edited by Peter Demetz, 220–38. New York: Harcourt Brace Jovanovich, 1978.

Benson, Lee. *The Concept of Jacksonian Democracy.* Princeton: Princeton University Press, 1961.

Benson, Mary Sumner. *Women in Eighteenth-Century America.* Port Washington, N.Y.: Kennikat, 1966.

Berg, Barbara. *The Remembered Gate: Origins of American Feminism-the Woman and the City, 1800–1860.* New York: Oxford University Press, 1978.

Berkhofer, Robert F., Jr. *The White Man's Indian: Images of the American Indian from Columbus to the Present.* New York: Knopf, 1978.

Berlin, Ira. *Slaves Without Masters.* New York: Vintage, 1976.

Bernard, Jessie. "George Tucker: Liberal Southern Social Scientist." *Social Forces* 25 (1946–47): 131–45; 406–16.

Bertelson, David. *The Lazy South.* New York: Oxford University Press, 1967.

Berwanger, Eugene H. *The Frontier Against Slavery.* Urbana: University of Illinois Press, 1975.

Blassingame, John W. *The Slave Community: Plantation Life in the Antebellum South.* New York: Oxford University Press, 1972.

——, ed. *Slave Testimony: Two Centuries of Letters, Speeches, Interviews, and Autobiographies.* Baton Rouge: Louisiana State University Press, 1977.

Bledstein, Burton J. *The Culture of Professionalism: The Middle Class and the development of Higher Education in America.* New York: Norton, 1978.

Bleser, Carol, ed. *The Hammonds of Redcliffe.* New York: Oxford University Press, 1981.

——. *In Joy and in Sorrow: Women, Family, and Marriage in the Victorian South, 1830–1900.* New York: Oxford University Press, 1991.

Boas, Ralph P. "The Romantic Lady." In *Romanticism in America,* edited by George Boas, 62–88. Baltimore: The Johns Hopkins University Press.

Bohner, Charles H. " 'As Much History as Invention': John Pendleton Kennedy's *Rob of the Bowl.*" *William and Mary Quarterly,* 3d ser., 17 (1960): 329–40.

——. *John Pendleton Kennedy: Gentleman from Baltimore.* Baltimore: Johns Hopkins University Press, 1961.

——. "The Poe-Kennedy Friendship." *Pennsylvania Magazine of History and Biography* 82 (April 1958): 220–22.

——. "*Swallow Barn:* John P. Kennedy's Chronicle of Virginia Society." *Virginia Magazine of History and Biography* 68 (July 1960): 317–30.

Boney, F. N. "The Ante-Bellum Elite." In *Red, White and Black,* edited by Charles M. Huson, 76–87. Athens: University of Georgia Press, 1971.

Bonner, James G. "Profile of a Late Antebellum Community." *American Historical Review* 50 (July 1944): 663–809. Reprinted in Elinor Miller and Eugene D. Genovese, eds., *Plantation, Town, and Country.* Urbana: University of Illinois Press, 1974.

Boskin, Joseph. *Sambo: The Rise and Demise of an American Jester.* New York: Oxford University Press, 1986.

Branca, Patricia. *Silent Sisterhood: Middle-class Women in the Victorian Home.* London: Croom Helm, 1975.

Bresnahan, Roger J. "William Gilmore Simms's Revolutionary War Novels: A Romantic View of Southern History." *Studies in Romanticism* 15 (Fall 1976): 573–87.

Bridenthal, Renate, Atina Grossman, and Marion Kaplan, eds. *When Biology Became Destiny: Women and Nazi Germany.* New York: Monthly Review Press, 1984.

Brown, David. *Walter Scott and the Historical Imagination.* London: Routledge and Kegan Paul, 1979.

Brown, Herbert Ross. *The Sentimental Novel in America, 1789–1860.* Durham: Duke University Press, 1940.

Brown, Richard H. "The Missouri Crisis, Slavery, and the Politics of Jacksonianism." *South Atlantic Quarterly* 65 (Winter 1966): 55–72.

Brown, Sterling. *The Negro in American Fiction.* New York: Atheneum, 1972.

Brownmiller, Susan. *Femininity.* New York: Simon and Schuster, 1984.

Bruccoli, Matthew J., ed. *The Profession of Authorship in America, 1800–1870: The Papers of William Charvat.* Columbus: Ohio State University Press, 1968.

Bruchey, Stuart. *The Roots of American Economic Growth, 1607–1861.* New York: Harper and Row, 1968.

Brugger, Robert J. *Beverley Tucker: Heart Over Head in the Old South.* Baltimore: Johns Hopkins University Press, 1978.

Buck, Paul H. "Poor Whites of the Old South." *American Historical Review* 31 (October 1925): 41–54.

Buck, Philip W. *How Conservatives Think.* Harmondsworth, Middlesex, Eng.: Penguin, 1975.

Burton, R. C. "John Pendleton Kennedy and the Civil War." *Journal of Southern History* 29 (August 1963): 373–76.

Butcher, S. H., trans. *Aristotle's Theory of Poetry and Fine Art.* With a new introduction by John Gassner and critical notes by S. H. Butcher. New York: Dover, 1951.

Buton, Michael, and Jonathan Harwood. *The Race Concept.* New York: Praeger, 1975.

Bynum, Victoria E. *The Politics of Social and Sexual Control in the Old South.* Chapel Hill: University of North Carolina Press, 1992.

Calhoun, Richard J. "The Antebellum Literary Twilight: *Russell's Magazine.*" *Southern Literary Journal* 3 (Fall 1970): 89–110.

Campbell, Jane. *Mythic Black Fiction: The Transformation of History.* Knoxville: University of Tennessee Press, 1986.

Carby, Hazel V. *Reconstructing Womanhood: The Emergence of the Afro-American Woman Novelist.* New York: Oxford University Press, 1987.

Cardwell, Guy A. "The Plantation House: An Analogical Image." *Southern Literary Journal* 2 (Fall 1969): 3–21.

Carpenter, Frederick I. "Puritans Prefer Blondes: The Heroines of Melville and Hawthorne." *New England Quarterly* 9 (June 1936): 253–72.

Carroll, Bernice A., ed. *Liberating Women's History: Theoretical and Critical Essays.* Urbana: University of Illinois Press, 1976.

Carsel, Wilfred. "The Slaveholders' Indictment of Northern Wage Slavery." *Journal of Southern History* 6 (November 1940): 504–20.

Cash, Wilbur J. *The Mind of the South.* New York: Knopf, 1941.

Castle, Terry. *Clarissa's Ciphers: Meaning and Disruption in Richardson's Clarissa.* Ithaca: Cornell University Press, 1982.

Chametzky, Jules, and Sidney Kaplan, eds. *Black and White in American Culture: An Anthology from "The Massachusetts Review."* Amherst: University of Massachusetts Press, 1969.

Charvat, William. *Literary Publishing in America, 1790–1850.* 2nd ed. Amherst: University of Massachusetts Press, 1993.

———. *The Origins of American Critical Thought, 1810–1835.* New York: Barnes, 1961.

Chase, Richard. *The American Novel and Its Tradition.* New York: Doubleday, 1957.

Chodorow, Nancy. *The Reproduction of Mothering: Psychoanalysis and the Sociology of Gender.* Berkeley and Los Angeles: University of California Press, 1978.

Christian, Barbara. *Black Feminist Criticism: Perspectives on Black Women Writers.* New York: Pergamon, 1985.

———. *Black Women Novelists: The Development of a Tradition, 1892–1976.* Westport, Conn.: Greenwood, 1980.

Clark, Blanche Henry. *The Tennessee Yeomen, 1840–1860.* New York: Octagon, 1971.

Clinton, Catherine. "The Plantation Mistress: Another Side of Southern Slavery, 1780–1835." Ph.D. diss., Princeton University, 1980.

——. *The Plantation Mistress: Women's World in the Old South.* New York: Pantheon, 1982.

Coles, Harry L., Jr. "Some Notes on Slaveownership and Landownership in Louisiana, 1850–1860." *Journal of Southern History* 9 (August 1943): 381–94.

Commager, Henry Steele. *The American Mind: An Interpretation of American Thought and Character since the 1880s.* New Haven: Yale University Press, 1950.

Conrad, Susan P. *Perish the Thought: Intellectual Women in Romantic America, 1830–1860.* Secaucus, N.J.: Citadel, 1978.

Conway, Jill. "Stereotypes of Femininity in a Theory of Sexual Evolution." *Victorian Studies* 14 (September 1970): 47–62.

Cooper, William J., Jr. *The South and the Politics of Slavery, 1828–1856.* Baton Rouge: Louisiana State University Press, 1978.

Cott, Nancy F. *The Bonds of Womanhood: "Women's Sphere" in New England, 1780–1835.* New Haven: Yale University Press, 1977.

Cowie, Alexander. *The Rise of the American Novel.* New York: American Book, 1948.

Craig, David, ed. *Marxists on Literature.* London: Penguin, 1975.

Craven, Avery O. *The Growth of Southern Nationalism, 1848–1861.* Baton Rouge: Louisiana State University Press, 1953.

——. "Poor Whites and Negros in the Antebellum South." *Journal of Negro History* 15 (January 1930): 14–25.

Crawford, Thomas. *Scott.* Edinburgh: Oliver and Bond, 1965.

Cross, Whitney R. *The Burned-Over District.* New York: Harper, 1950.

Crozier, Alice. *The Novels of Harriet Beecher Stowe.* London: Oxford University Press, 1969.

Current-Garcia, Eugene. "Southern Literary Criticisms and the Sectional Dilemma." *Journal of Southern History* 15 (August 1949): 324–41.

Curti, Merle. *The Growth of American Thought.* New York: Harper and Bros., 1943.

Cusac, Marian H. *Narrative Structure in the Novels of Sir Walter Scott.* Paris: Mouton, 1969.

Dahrendorf, Rolf. *Class and Class Conflict in Industrial Society.* Stanford: Stanford University Press, 1959.

Daiches, David. "Literature and Social Mobility," in *Aspects of History and Class Consciousness,* edited by Istvan Meszavos, 152–72. London: Routledge and Kegan Paul, 1971.

——. "Scott's Achievement As a Novelist." *Literary Essays.* 1956. Reprint, London: Oliver Boyd, 1967.

Dauty, Alan. "Urban Slavery in Pro-Slavery Fiction of the 1850's." *Journal of Southern History* 32 (February 1966): 25–41.

Davidoff, Lenore. "Mastered for Life: Servant and Wife in Victorian and Edwardian England." *Journal of Social History* 7 (Summer 1974): 406–28.

Davidson, Basil. *The African Slave Trade: Precolonial History, 1450–1850.* Boston: Little, Brown, 1961.

Davidson, Cathy N. *Revolution and the Word: The Rise of the Novel in America.* New York: Oxford University Press, 1986.

Davidson, Philip G. "Industrialism in the Antebellum South." *South Atlantic Quarterly* 27 (October 1928): 405–25.

Davis, Angela. "Reflections on the Black Woman's Role in the Community of Slaves." *Black Scholar* 3 (December 1971): 3–15.

——. *Women, Race, and Class.* New York: Vintage, 1981.

Davis, Carroll Curtis. *Chronicler of the Cavaliers.* Richmond, Virginia: Dietz, 1953.

Davis, David Brion. *Antebellum Reform.* New York: Harper and Row, 1967.
——. *The Problem of Slavery in the Age of Revolution, 1770–1823.* Ithaca: Cornell University Press, 1975.
——. *The Problem of Slavery in Western Culture.* Ithaca: Cornell University Press, 1966.
Davis, Elizabeth Gould. *The First Sex.* New York: Putnam, 1971.
Davis, Richard Beale. *Intellectual Life in Jefferson's Virginia, 1798–1860.* Chapel Hill: University of North Carolina Press, 1964.
——. "The 'Virginia Novel' Before *Swallow Barn.*" *Virginia Magazine of History and Biography* 71 (July 1963): 278–93.
Dawley, Alan. *Class and Community: The Industrial Revolution in Lynn.* Cambridge: Harvard University Press, 1976.
Degler, Carl N. *At Odds: Women and the Family in America from the Revolution to the Present.* New York: Oxford University Press, 1980.
——. *Neither Black Nor White.* New York: Macmillan, 1971.
——. *The Other South.* New York: Harper and Row, 1974.
——. "What Ought to Be and What Was: Women's Sexuality in the Nineteenth Century." *American Historical Review* 79 (December 1974): 1467–90.
Dekker, George. *The American Historical Romance.* New York: Cambridge University Press, 1987.
D'Emilio, John, and Estelle Freedman. *Intimate Matters: A History of Sexuality in America.* New York: Harper and Row, 1988.
Devlin, D. D. *The Author of Waverley: A Critical Study of Walter Scott.* London: Macmillan, 1971.
Dinnerstein, Dorothy. *The Mermaid and the Minotaur: Sexual Arrangements and Human Malaise.* New York: Harper and Row, 1976.
Dobb, Maurice. *Studies in the Development of Capitalism.* New York: International Publishers, 1963.
Donald, David Herbert. *Lincoln Reconsidered: Essays on the Civil War Era.* New York: Knopf, 1959; 2d ed., enlarged, 1961.
——. "The Proslavery Argument Reconsidered." *Journal of Southern History* 37 (February 1971): 3–18.
——. "Toward a Reconsideration of Abolitionists." *Journal of Southern History* 25 (August 1959): 356–65.
Doody, Margaret. *A Natural Passion: A Study of the Novels of Samuel Richardson.* Oxford: Clarendon Press, 1974.
Douglas, Ann. *The Feminization of American Culture.* New York: Knopf, 1977.
Duberman, Martin B., ed. *The Antislavery Vanguard: New Essays on the Abolitionists.* Princeton: Princeton University Press, 1965.
——. *The Uncompleted Past.* New York: Dutton, 1971.
DuBois, Ellen C., and Vicki L. Ruiz, eds. *Unequal Sisters: A Multi-Cultural Reader in U.S. Women's History.* New York: Random House, 1990.
DuBois, W. E. B. *Darkwater: Voices from Within the Veil.* 1920. Reprint, New York: AMS, 1969.
——. *The Suppression of the African Slave Trade.* Baton Rouge: Louisiana State University Press, 1969.
Dumond, Dwight Lowell. *Antislavery.* New York: Norton, 1961.
Dunn, Richard S. *Sugar and Slaves: The Rise of the Planter Class in the English West Indies, 1624–1713.* New York: Norton, 1972.
DuVall, S. P. C. "W. G. Simms's Review of Mrs. Stowe." *American Literature* 30 (March 1958): 107–17.
Eagleton, Terry. "Ideology and Literary Form." *New Left Review* 90 (March–April 1975): 81–109.

———. *Marxism and Literary Criticism.* Berkeley and Los Angeles: University of California Press, 1976.

———. *The Rape of Clarissa: Writing, Sexuality, and Class Struggle in Samuel Richardson.* Minneapolis: University of Minnesota Press, 1982.

Earnest, Ernest. *The American Eve in Fact and Fiction, 1775–1914.* Urbana: University of Illinois Press, 1974.

Eaton, Clement. "Class Differences in the Old South." *Virginia Quarterly Review* 33 (1957): 357–70.

———. *The Freedom of Thought Struggle in the Old South.* Durham: Duke University Press, 1940.

———. *The Growth of Southern Civilization.* New York: Harper and Row, 1961.

———. *A History of the Old South.* New York: Collier, 1966.

———. *The Mind of the Old South.* Baton Rouge: Louisiana State University Press, 1964.

Ehle, John. *Trail of Tears: The Rise and Fall of the Cherokee Nation.* New York: Doubleday, 1988.

Eisenstein, Zillah, ed. *Capitalist Patriarchy and the Case for Socialist Feminism.* New York: Monthly Review, 1979.

Elkins, Stanley M. *Slavery: A Problem in American Institutional and Intellectual Life.* New York: Grosset and Dunlap, 1963.

Ellison, Ralph, William Styron, Robert Penn Warren, and C. Vann Woodward. "The Uses of History in Fiction." *Southern Literary Journal* 1 (Spring 1969): 58–90.

Ellison, Rhoda C. "An Interview with Horse-Shoe Robinson." *American Literature* 31 (November 1959): 329–32.

Engels, Frederick. *The Family, Private Property and the State.* Edited by Eleanor Leacock. New York: International Publishers, 1972.

Erskine, John. *Leading American Novelists.* New York: Henry Holt, 1910.

Evans, Mari, ed. *Black Women Writers (1950–1980): A Cultural Evaluation.* Garden City, N.Y.: Anchor, 1984.

Evans, Sara. *Born for Liberty: A History of Women in America.* New York: Free Press, 1989.

Faderman, Lillian. *Surpassing the Love of Men: Romantic Friendship and Love Between Women from the Renaissance to the Present.* New York: William Morrow, 1981.

Falk, Robert. *The Victorian Mode in American Fiction.* East Lansing: Michigan State University Press, 1965.

Fanon, Frantz. *Black Skins, White Masks.* New York: Grove, 1967.

Faust, Drew Gilpin. "Culture, Conflict and Community: The Meaning of Power on an Antebellum Plantation." *Journal of Social History* 14 (Fall 1980): 83–97.

———. *James Henry Hammond and the Old South: A Design for Mastery.* Baton Rouge: Louisiana State University Press, 1982.

———. *A Sacred Circle: The Dilemma of the Intellectual in the Old South, 1840–1860.* Baltimore: Johns Hopkins University Press, 1977.

———. "A Southern Stewardship: The Intellectual and the Proslavery Argument." *American Quarterly* 31 (Spring 1979): 63–80.

Feidelson, Charles, Jr. *Symbolism and American Literature.* Chicago: University of Chicago Press, 1953.

Fiedler, Leslie A. "Come Back to the Raft Ag'in, Huck Honey." In *An End to Innocence: Essays on Culture and Politics,* 142–51. Boston: Beacon, 1955.

———. *Love and Death in the American Novel.* Revised ed. New York: Stein and Day, 1966.

Figes, Eva. *Patriarchal Attitudes.* Greenwich, Conn.: Fawcett, 1970.

Filler, Louis. *The Crusade Against Slavery, 1830–1860.* New York: Harper and Row, 1960.

Finley, Moses I. *The Ancient Greeks.* London: Penguin, 1963.

Firestone, Shulamith. *The Dialectics of Sex.* New York: Bantam, 1972.

Fischer, David Hackett. *The Revolution of American Conservatism: The Federalist Party in the Era of Jeffersonian Democracy.* New York: Harper and Row, 1965.

Fisher, Philip. *Hard Facts: Setting and Form in the American Novel.* New York: Oxford University Press, 1985.

Fisher, Philip, ed. *The New American Studies: Essays from "Representations."* Berkeley and Los Angeles: University of California Press, 1991.

Fladeland, Betty. "Who Were the Abolitionists?" *Journal of Southern History* 30 (April 1964): 99–115.

Fleishman, Avrom. *The English Historical Novel: Walter Scott to Virginia Woolf.* Baltimore: Johns Hopkins University Press, 1971.

Flexner, Eleanor. *A Century of Struggle: The Woman's Rights Movement in the United States.* New York: Atheneum, 1973.

Folsom, B. W., II. "Party Formation and Development in Jacksonian America: The Old South." *Journal of American Studies* 7 (1973): 217–29.

Foner, Eric. *Free Soil, Free Labor, Free Men.* London: Oxford University Press, 1970.

Foner, Laura, and Genovese, Eugene D. *Slavery in the New World: A Reader in Comparative History.* Englewood Cliffs, N.J.: Prentice-Hall, 1969.

Forbes, Duncan. "The Rationalism of Sir Walter Scott." *Cambridge Journal* 7 (1953), 20–35.

———. " 'Scientific' Whiggism: Adam Smith and John Millar." *Cambridge Journal* 7 (August 1954): 643–70.

Formisano, Ronald P. "Toward a Reorientation of Jacksonian Politics: A Review of the Literature, 1959–1975." *Journal of American History* 63 (1976): 42–65.

Fossett, Thomas F. *"Uncle Tom's Cabin" and American Culture.* Dallas: Southern Methodist University Press, 1985.

Fowler, David H. "Northern Attitudes Towards Interracial Marriage: A Study of Legislation and Public Opinion in the Middle Atlantic States of the Old Northwest." Ph.D. diss., Yale University, 1963.

Fox-Genovese, Elizabeth. *Within the Plantation Household: Black and White Women of the Old South.* Chapel Hill: University of North Carolina Press, 1988.

Franklin, H. Bruce. *The Victim As Criminal and Artist: Literature from the American Prison.* New York: Oxford University Press, 1978.

Franklin, John Hope. *From Slavery to Freedom: A History of Negro Americans.* New York: Vintage, 1969.

Fredrickson, George M. *The Black Image in the White Mind.* New York: Harper and Row, 1971.

———. *White Supremacy: A Comparative Study in American and South African History.* New York: Oxford University Press, 1981.

Freehling, William W. *Prelude to Civil War: The Nullification Controversy in South Carolina, 1816–1836.* New York: Harper and Row, 1968.

Fryer, Judith. *The Faces of Eve: Women in the Nineteenth-Century American Novel.* New York: Oxford University Press, 1976.

Gabriel, Ralph. *The Course of American Democratic Thought.* New York: Ronald, 1956.

Gaines, Francis Pendleton. *The Southern Plantation: A Study in the Development and the Accuracy of a Tradition.* New York: Columbia University Press, 1924.

Gallman, Robert E. "Self-Sufficiency in the Cotton Economy of the Antebellum South." *Agricultural History* 44 (January 1970): 5–24.

Gara, Larry. "Who Were the Abolitionists?" In *The Antislavery Vanguard: New Essays on the Abolitionists,* edited by Martin B. Duberman, 32–51. Princeton: Princeton University Press, 1965.

Garside, Peter D. "Scott and the 'Philosophical' Historians." *Journal of the History of Ideas* 36, no. 3 (1975): 497–512.

Gates, W. B. "William Gilmore Simms and The Kentucky Tragedy." *American Literature* 32 (May 1960): 158–66.

Genovese, Eugene D. *The Political Economy of Slavery: Studies in the Economy and Society of the Slave South.* New York: Vintage, 1965.

——. "Race and Class in Southern History: An Appraisal of the Work of Ulrich Bonnell Phillips." *Agricultural History* 41 (October 1967): 345–58.

——. "Rebelliousness and Docility in the Negro Slave: A Critique of the Elkins Thesis." *Civil War History* 13 (December 1967): 293–314.

——. *Roll, Jordan, Roll: The World the Slaves Made.* New York: Pantheon, 1974.

——. *The World the Slaveholders Made.* New York: Vintage, 1971.

——. "Yeoman Farmers in a Slaveholders' Democracy." *Agricultural History* 49 (April 1975): 331–42.

Gerster, Patrick, and Nicholas Cords. "The Northern Origins of Southern Mythology." *Journal of Southern History* 43, no. 4 (November 1977): 567–82.

Gilman, Sander L. *Difference and Pathology: Stereotypes of Sexuality, Race, and Madness.* Ithaca: Cornell University Press, 1985.

Gilman, William H. "The Hero and the Heroic in American Literature: An Essay in Definition." In *Patterns of Commitment in American Literature,* edited by Marston LaFrance, 3–18. Toronto: University of Toronto Press, 1967.

Gilmore, Al-Tony, ed. *Revisiting Blassingame's The Slave Community: The Scholars Respond.* Westport: Greenwood Press, 1978.

Goldberg, Rita. *Sex and the Enlightenment: Women in Richardson and Diderot.* Cambridge University Press, 1984.

Goldmann, Lucien. *The Hidden God: A Study of Tragic Vision in the "Pensées" of Pascal and the Tragedies of Racine.* 1964. Reprint, London: Routledge and Kegan Paul, 1976.

Gossett, Thomas F. *Race: The History of an Idea in America.* New York: Schocken, 1965.

Grahn, Judy. "VII. Vera, from My Childhood." In *The Work of a Common Woman: The Collected Poetry of Judy Grahn, 1964–1967,* with an introduction by Adrienne Rich, 59–73. Trumansburg, N.Y.: Crossing, 1978.

Gramsci, Antonio. *Selections from the Prison Notebooks.* Edited by Quintin Hoare and Geoffrey Nowell Smith. New York: International Publishers, 1973.

Grantham, Dewey W. "History, Mythology and the Southern Lady." *Southern Literary Journal* 3 (Spring 1973): 98–108.

Gray, Virginia Gearhart. "Activities of Southern Women: 1840–1860." *South Atlantic Quarterly* 27 (July 1928): 264–79.

Green, Fletcher Melvin. "Democracy in the Old South." In *Democracy in the Old South, and Other Essays,* edited by J. Isaac Copeland, 65–86. Nashville: Vanderbilt University Press, 1969.

Greenberg, Kenneth S. "Revolutionary Ideology and the Proslavery Argument: The Abolition of Slavery in Antebellum South Carolina." *Journal of Southern History* 42 (August 1976): 365–84.

Greene, Lorenzo Johnston. *The Negro in Colonial New England.* New York: Atheneum, 1971.

Greven, Philip. *The Protestant Temperament: Patterns of Child-Rearing, Religious Experience, and the Self in Early America.* New York: Knopf, 1977.

Gross, Seymour L., and John Edward Hardy, eds. *Images of the Negro in American Literature.* Chicago: University of Chicago Press, 1966.

Gross, Theodore L. *The Heroic Ideal in American Literature.* New York: Free Press, 1971.

Grossberg, Lawrence, et al. *Cultural Studies.* New York: Routledge, Chapman, and Hall, 1992.

Guilds, John Caldwell. *"Long Years of Neglect": The Work and Reputation of William Gilmore Simms.* Fayetteville: University of Arkansas Press, 1988.
——. *Simms: A Literary Life.* Fayetteville: University of Arkansas Press, 1992.
Gutman, Herbert G. *The Black Family in Slavery and Freedom, 1750–1925.* New York: Vintage, 1977.
——. "Persistent Myths About the Afro-American Family." *Journal of Interdisciplinary History* 6 (Autumn 1975): 181–210.
——. *Work, Culture and Society in Industrializing America.* New York: Vintage, 1977.
Gwathmey, Edward M. *John Pendleton Kennedy.* New York: Thomas Nelson and Sons, 1931.
Gwin, Minrose C. *Black and White Women of the Old South: The Peculiar Sisterhood in American Literature.* Knoxville: University of Tennessee Press, 1985.
Hagler, D. Harland. "The Ideal Woman in the Antebellum South: Lady or Farmwife?" *Journal of Southern History* 46 (August 1980): 405–18.
Hahn, Steven. *The Roots of Southern Populism: Yeoman Farmers and the Transformation of the Georgia Upcountry, 1850–1890.* New York: Oxford University Press, 1983.
Hall, Stuart, Bob Lumley, and Gregor McLennon. "Politics and Ideology in Antonio Gramsci." In *Working Papers in Cultural Studies* 10: 45–76. London: Centre for Contemporary Cultural Studies, 1978.
Hardwick, Elizabeth. *Seduction and Betrayal: Women and Literature.* New York: Vintage, 1975.
Harper, C. W. "House Servants and Field Hands: Fragmentation in the Antebellum Slave Community." *North Carolina Historical Review* 55 (January 1978): 42–59.
Hartman, Mary S., and Lois Banner, eds. *Clio's Consciousness Raised.* New York: Harper and Row, 1974.
Hartz, Louis. *The Liberal Tradition in America: An Interpretation of American Political Thought Since the Revolution.* New York: Harcourt, Brace, and World, 1955.
Hauser, Arnold. "The l'art pour l'art Problem." *Critical Theory* 5 (Spring 1979): 425–40.
——. *The Social History of Art.* Vol. 3. New York: Pocket Book, 1972.
Hays, H. R. *The Dangerous Sex: The Myth of Feminine Evil.* New York: Pocket Book, 1972.
Hazard, Lucy Lockwood. *The Frontier in American Literature.* New York: Ungar, 1961.
Helderman, Leonard C. "A Satirist in Old Virginia." *American Scholar* 6 (1937): 481–97.
——. "A Social Scientist of the Old South." *Journal of Southern History* 2 (1936): 148–74.
Henderson, Harry B. *Versions of the Past: The Historical Imagination in American Fiction.* New York: Oxford University Press, 1974.
Hernton, Calvin. *Sex and Racism.* New York: Crane, 1965.
Hesseltine, William B. "Some New Aspects of the Pro-Slavery Argument." *Journal of Negro History* 21 (January 1936): 1–14.
——. *The South in American History.* New York: Prentice-Hall, 1943.
Hetherington, Hugh. *Cavalier of Old South Carolina: William Gilmore Simms's Captain Porgy.* Chapel Hill: University of North Carolina Press, 1966.
Hickin, Patricia. "Gentle Agitator: Samuel Janney and the Anti-Slavery Movement in Virginia, 1842–1851." *Journal of Southern History* 37 (May 1971): 159–90.
Hillhouse, James T. *The Waverley Novels and Their Critics.* New York: Octagon, 1968.
Hoagland, Ronald. "The 'Female Appendage': Feminine Life Styles in America, 1820–1960." *Civil War History* 17 (June 1971): 101–14.
Hobson, Fred. "The Poor White in Transition." *Southern Literary Journal* 9 (Fall 1976): 166–74.
Hoffman, Daniel. *Form and Fable in American Fiction.* New York: Oxford University Press, 1965.
Hoffman, Ronald. "The 'Disaffected' in the Revolutionary South." In *The American Revolution: Explorations in the History of American Radicalism,* edited by Alfred F. Young, 275–316. DeKalb: Northern Illinois University Press, 1976.

Hollander, A. N. J. "The Tradition of 'Poor Whites.'" In *Culture in the South* edited by W. T. Couch, 403–31. 1934. Reprint, Westport, Conn.: Negro Universities Press, 1970.

Holman, C. Hugh. *The Immoderate Past: The Southern Writer and History.* Athens: University of Georgia Press, 1977.

———. "The Influence of Scott and Cooper on Simms." *American Literature* 23 (May 1951): 203–18.

———. *The Roots of Southern Writing.* Athens: University of Georgia Press, 1972.

———. "Simms's Changing View of the Loyalists During the Revolution." *Mississippi Quarterly* 29 (Fall 1976): 500–13.

———. "The Southerner as American Writer." In *The Southerner as American,* edited by Charles G. Sellers, Jr., 181–99. Chapel Hill: University of North Carolina Press, 1960.

———. "The Status of Simms." *American Quarterly* 10 (July 1958): 181–85.

———. "William Gilmore Simms's Picture of the Revolutionary War as a Civil War." *Journal of Southern History* 15 (November 1949): 441–62.

hooks, bell. *Ain't I a Woman: Black Women and Feminism.* Boston: South End Press, 1981.

Horsman, Reginald. *Race and Manifest Destiny: The Origins of American Racial Anglo-Saxonism.* Cambridge: Harvard University Press, 1981.

Houghton, Walter E. *The Victorian Frame of Mind, 1830–1870.* New Haven: Yale University Press, 1957.

Howell, Elmo. "The Concept of Character in Simms's Border Romances." *Mississippi Quarterly* 22 (Fall 1969): 303–12.

———. "William Gilmore Simms and the American Indian." *South Carolina Review* 5 (June 1973): 57–64.

Hubbell, Jay B. "Cavalier and Indentured Servant in Virginia Fiction." *South Atlantic Quarterly* 26 (January 1927): 22–39.

———. *The South and the Southwest.* Durham: Duke University Press, 1965.

———. *Southern Life in Fiction.* Athens: University of Georgia Press, 1960.

———. *The South in American Literature.* Durham: Duke University Press, 1954.

———. *Who Are the Major American Writers?* Durham: Duke University Press, 1972.

Hugins, Walter. *Jacksonian Democracy and the Working Class.* Stanford: Stanford University Press, 1960.

Hymowitz, Carol, and Michaele Weissman. *A History of Women in America.* New York: Bantam, 1978.

Jackson, Blyden. *A History of Afro-American Literature.* Baton Rouge: Louisiana State University Press, 1989.

Jacobs, Robert D. "Campaign for a Southern Literature." *Southern Literary Journal* 2 (Fall 1969): 66–98.

Jenkins, William Sumner. *Pro-Slavery Thought in the Old South.* Gloucester, Mass.: Peter Smith, 1960.

Jennings, Francis. *The Invasion of America: Indians, Colonialism, and the Cant of Conquest.* New York: Norton, 1976.

Johnston, James Hugo. *Race Relations in Virginia and Miscegenation in the South, 1776–1860.* Amherst: University of Massachusetts Press, 1970.

Jones, Bobby. "A Cultural Middle Passage: Slave Marriage and Family in the Ante-Bellum South." Ph.D. diss., University of North Carolina at Chapel Hill, 1965.

Jones, Howard Mumford. "The Nature of Literary History." *Journal of the History of Ideas* 28 (April–June 1967): 147–60.

———. *O Strange New World, American Culture: The Formative Years.* New York: Viking, 1967.

———. *The Theory of American Literature.* Ithaca: Cornell University Press, 1948.

Jones, Jacqueline. *Labor of Love, Labor of Sorrow.* New York: Basic Books, 1985.

Jordan, Winthrop. *White Over Black: American Attitudes Toward the Negro, 1550–1812.* Baltimore: Penguin, 1968.

Josephy, Alvin. *The Indian Heritage of America.* New York: Knopf, 1968.

Kallsen, Loren J. *The Kentucky Tragedy: A Problem in Romantic Attitudes.* New York: Bobbs-Merrill, 1963.

Kanowitz, Leo. *Woman and the Law: The Unfinished Revolution.* Albuquerque: University of New Mexico Press, 1969.

Kaplan, Sidney. *The Black Presence in the Era of the American Revolution, 1700–1800.* New York: New York Graphic Society with the Smithsonian Institution Press, 1973.

——. "The Miscegenation Issue in the Election of 1864." *Journal of Negro History* 34 (July 1949): 274–343. Reprinted in his *American Studies in Black and White: Selected Essays, 1949–1989,* edited by Allan D. Austin, 47–100. Amherst: University of Massachusetts Press, 1991.

Kaplan, Sidney, and Emma Nogrady Kaplan. *The Black Presence in the Era of the American Revolution.* Amherst: University of Massachusetts Press, 1989.

Kartigan, Donald M., and Malcolm A. Griffith. *Theories of American Literature.* New York: Macmillan, 1972.

Kaul, A. N. *The American Vision: Actual and Ideal Society in Nineteenth Century Fiction.* New Haven: Yale University Press, 1963.

Kelly, Joan. *Women, History, and Theory: The Essays of Joan Kelly.* Chicago: University of Chicago Press, 1984.

Kerber, Linda. *Women of the Republic: Intellect and Ideology in Revolutionary America.* Chapel Hill: University of North Carolina Press, 1980.

Kibler, James E. "Simms's Indebtedness to Folk Tradition in 'Sharp Snaffles.'" *Southern Literary Journal* 4 (Spring 1972): 55–68.

Kilian, Martin A., and E. Lynn Tatom. "Marx, Hegel, and the Marxian of the Master Class: Eugene D. Genovese on Slavery." *Journal of Negro History* 66 (Fall 1981): 189–208.

Kinkead-Weekes, Mark. *Samuel Richardson: Dramatic Novelist.* London: Methuen, 1972.

Kirk, Russell. *The Conservative Mind.* New York: Avon, 1960.

Klein, Melanie. *Contributions to Psycho-Analysis, 1921–1945.* London: Hogarth, 1948.

Knox, Bernard. *Oedipus at Thebes.* New York: Norton, 1971.

Koch, Adrienne. "The Versatile George Tucker." *Journal of Southern History* 29 (November 1963): 502–12.

Kolodny, Annette. *The Lay of the Land: Metaphor as Experience and History in American Life and Letters.* Chapel Hill: University of North Carolina Press, 1975.

——. "The Unchanging Landscape: The Pastoral Impulse in Simms's Revolutionary War Romances." *Southern Literary Journal* 5 (Fall 1972): 46–67.

Koonz, Claudia. *Mothers in the Fatherland: Women, the Family, and Nazi Politics.* New York: St. Martins, 1987.

Kovel, Joel. *White Racism: A Psychohistory.* New York: Pantheon, 1970.

Kreyling, Michael. *Figures of the Hero in Southern Narrative.* Baton Rouge: Louisiana State University Press, 1987.

Krieger, Murray. "Fiction, History and Empirical Reality." *Critical Inquiry* 1 (December 1971): 335–60.

Kuhn, Annette, and Ann Marie Wolpe, eds. *Feminism and Materialism.* London: Routledge and Kegan Paul, 1979.

Landes, Joan B. *Women and the Public Sphere in the Age of the French Revolution.* Ithaca: Cornell University Press, 1988.

Landrum, Grace Warren. "Sir Walter Scott and His Literary Rivals in the Old South." *American Literature* 2 (November 1930): 256–76.

Lapansky, Emma Jones. "'Since They Got Those Separate Churches': Afro-Americans and Racism in Jacksonian Philadelphia." *American Quarterly* 32 (Spring 1980): 54–78.

Lasch, Christopher, and William R. Taylor. "Two Kindred Spirits: Sorority and Family in New England, 1839–1846." *New England Quarterly* 36 (March 1963): 23–41.

Laslett, Peter. *The World We Have Lost.* New York: Scribner's, 1965.

Laurie, Bruce. *Working People of Philadelphia, 1800–1850.* Philadelphia: Temple University Press, 1980.

Lawrence, D. H. *Studies in Classic American Literature.* New York: Viking, 1972. (Originally published 1923)

Lebsock, Suzanne. *The Free Women of Petersburg: Status and Culture in a Southern Town, 1784–1860.* New York: Norton, 1984.

Legman, Gershon. *Love and Death: A Study in Censorship.* New York: Harcher Art Books, 1963.

Lehmann-Haupt, Helmut. *The Book in America: A History of the Making and Selling of Books in the United States.* New York: Bowker, 1952.

Lentricchia, Frank, and Thomas McLaughlin, eds. *Critical Terms for Literary Study.* Chicago: University of Chicago Press, 1990.

Lerner, Gerda. *The Grimké Sisters from South Carolina.* New York: Schocken, 1971.

——. *The Majority Finds Its Past: Placing Women in History.* New York: Oxford University Press, 1979.

——. *The Origins of Patriarchy.* New York: Oxford University Press, 1986.

Levin, Harry. *The Power of Blackness: Hawthorne, Poe, Melville.* New York: Knopf, 1958.

Levine, George, ed. *Realism and Representation: Essays on the Problem of Realism in Relation to Science, Literature, and Culture.* Madison: University of Wisconsin Press, 1993.

Levine, Lawrence W. *Black Culture and Black Consciousness: Afro-American Folk Thought from Slavery to Freedom.* New York: Oxford University Press, 1977.

Lewis, R. W. B. *The American Adam: Innocence, Tragedy, and Tradition in the Nineteenth Century.* Chicago: University of Chicago Press, 1955.

Lewis, Ronald. "Slave Families at Early Chesapeake Ironworks." *Virginia Magazine of History and Biography* 86 (April 1978): 169–79.

Lichtman, Richard. "Marx and Freud, Part Three: Marx's Theory of Human Nature." *Socialist Revolution* 7 (November–December 1977): 37–78.

Liedel, D. "The Anti-Slavery Novel, 1836–1861." Ph.D. diss., University of Michigan, 1961.

Lippmann, Walter, *Public Opinion.* New York: Free Press, 1922.

Littlefield, Daniel F., Jr. *Africans and Creeks from the Colonial Period to the Civil War.* Westport, Conn.: Greenwood, 1976.

——. *Africans and Seminoles: From Removal to Emancipation.* Westport, Conn.: Greenwood, 1977.

Linden, Fabian. "Economic Democracy in the Slave South: An Appraisal of Some Recent Views." *Journal of Negro History* 31 (April 1946): 140–89.

Litwack, Leon. *Been in the Storm So Long: The Aftermath of Slavery.* New York: Vintage, 1980.

——. *North of Slavery: The Negro in the Free States, 1790–1860.* Chicago: University of Chicago Press, 1961.

Loehr, Rodney C. "Self-Sufficiency on the Farm." *Agricultural History* 26 (January 1952): 37–41.

Loggins, Vernon. *The Negro Author: His Development in America to 1900.* Port Washington, N.Y.: Kennicut, 1964.

Lorde, Audre. "Age, Race, Class and Sex: Women Redefining Difference." In *Sister Outsider.* 114–23, Trumansburg, N.Y.: Crossing Press, 1967.

Lovell, Terry. *Consuming Fiction.* London: Vergo, 1987.

Lowenthal, Leo. *Literature, Popular Culture, and Society.* Palo Alto, Calif.: Pacific Books, 1961.

Lukács, Georg. *The Historical Novel.* Translated by Hannah Mitchell and Stanley Mitchell. Boston: Beacon, 1962.

———. *The Theory of the Novel: A Historic-Philosophical Essay on the Forms of Great Epic Literature.* Translated by Anna Bostock. 1920. Reprint, Cambridge: MIT Press, 1971.

Luraghi, Raimondo. *The Rise and Fall of the Plantation South.* New York: New Viewpoints, 1978.

McColley, Robert. *Slavery and Jeffersonian Virginia.* Urbana: University of Illinois Press, 1973.

McCormick, Richard. *The Second American Party System.* Chapel Hill: University of North Carolina Press, 1966.

MacDonald, Dwight. "Masscult and Midcult." In his *Against the American Grain,* 3–75. New York: Vintage, 1962.

McDowell, Tremaine. "The Negro in the Southern Novel Prior to 1850." *Journal of English and German Philogy* 25 (October 1926): 455–73.

Macherey, Pierre. *A Theory of Literary Production.* London: Routledge and Kegan Paul, 1978.

McIlwaine, Shields. *The Southern Poor-White From Lubberland to Tobacco Road.* Norman: University of Oklahoma Press, 1939.

McKitrick, Eric L., ed. *Slavery Defended: The Views of the Old South.* Englewood Cliffs, N.J.: Prentice-Hall, 1963.

McLean, Robert Colin. *George Tucker: Moral Philosopher and Man of Letters.* Chapel Hill: University of North Carolina Press, 1961.

McMaster, Graham. *Scott and Society.* Cambridge: Cambridge University Press, 1981.

MacPherson, C. B. *The Political Theory of Possessive Individualism: Hobbes to Locke.* New York: Oxford University Press, 1962.

McPherson, James M. "Slavery and Race." *Perspectives in American History* 3 (1969): 460–73.

Maddox, Jack P., Jr. "Proslavery Millennium: Social Eschatology in Antebellum Southern Calvinism." *American Quarterly* 21 (Spring 1979): 47–62.

Madison, Charles A. *Book Publishing in America.* New York: McGraw-Hill Book Co., 1966.

Main, Jackson Turner. "The Distribution of Property in Post-Revolutionary Virginia." *Mississippi Valley Historical Review* 41 (1954): 241–58.

Mandle, Jay R. *The Roots of Black Poverty.* Durham, N.C.: Duke University Press, 1978.

Mannoni, O. *Prospero and Caliban: The Psychology of Colonization.* London: Methuen, 1956.

Marshall, Lynn. "The Strange Stillbirth of the Whig Party." *American Historical Review* 72 (1967): 445–68.

Martinez-Alier, Verena. *Marriage, Class, and Colour in Nineteenth-Century Cuba.* Cambridge: Cambridge University Press, 1974.

Marx, Karl. *The German Ideology.* New York: International Publishers, 1965.

Marx, Leo. *The Machine in the Garden: Technology and the Pastoral Ideal in America.* New York: Oxford University Press, 1964.

Matthiessen, F. O. *American Renaissance: Art and Expression in the Age of Emerson and Whitman.* New York: Oxford University Press, 1964.

May, Henry F. *The Enlightenment in America.* New York: Oxford University Press, 1976.

Meltzer, Milton, Patricia G. Holland, eds. Francine Krazno, assoc. ed. *Lydia Maria Child: Selected Letters, 1817–1880.* Amherst: University of Massachusetts Press, 1982.

Merk, Frederick. *Manifest Destiny and Mission in American History.* New York: Random House, 1963.

Meyers, Marvin. *The Jacksonian Persuasion: Politics and Belief.* 1957. Reprint, Stanford: Stanford University Press, 1960.

Miller, Elinor, and Eugene D. Genovese, eds. *Plantation, Town and Country.* Urbana: University of Illinois Press, 1974.

Miller, Nancy K. *The Heroine's Text.* New York: Columbia University Press, 1980.

Miller, Perry. *Nature's Nation.* Cambridge, Mass.: The Belknap Press of Harvard University Press, 1967.

———. *The Raven and The Whale: The War of Words and Wits in the Era of Poe and Melville.* New York: Harcourt Brace Jovanovich, 1956.

Millet, Kate. *Sexual Politics.* New York: Avon, 1969.

Mitchell, Betty L. *Edmund Ruffin. A Biography.* Bloomington: Indiana University Press, 1981.

Mitchell, Juliet. *Psycho-Analysis and Feminism: Freud, Reich, Lang, and Weiner.* New York: Vintage, 1975.

———. "Women: The Longest Revolution." *New Left Review* 40 (November–December 1966): 11–37.

———. *Women's Estate.* New York: Random House, 1971.

Mittleman, Amy. "A Perceptual Study of the Ante-Bellum Yeomanry, 1820–1860." M.A. thesis, Columbia University, 1978.

Moers, Ellen. *Literary Women.* Garden City, N.Y.: Anchor, 1977.

Montagu, Ashley. *The Concept of Race.* 1964. Reprint, New York: Collier, 1972.

———. *Man's Most Dangerous Myth: The Fallacy of Race.* 1942. Reprint, New York: World Publishing, 1965.

Mooney, Chase C. "Some Industrial and Statistical Aspects of Slavery in Tennessee." *Tennessee Historical Quarterly* 1 (1942): 195–228.

Moore, John R. "Kennedy's *Horse-Shoe Robinson:* Fact or Fiction?" *American Literature* 4 (May 1932): 160–66.

Morgan, Edmund S. *American Slavery, American Freedom: The Ordeal of Colonial Virginia.* New York: Norton, 1975.

Morris, Richard B. "Labor Controls in Maryland in the Nineteenth Century." *Journal of Southern History* 14 (August 1948): 385–400.

———. "The Measure of Bondage in the Slave States." *Mississippi Valley Historical Review* 41 (1954): 219–40.

Morrow, Ralph E. "The Pro-Slavery Argument Revisited." *Mississippi Valley Historical Review* 48 (June 1961): 79–94.

Mott, Frank Luther. *A History of American Magazines.* 5 vols. Cambridge: Harvard University Press, 1938–68.

Mukerji, Chandra, and Michael Schudson. *Rethinking Popular Culture: Contemporary Perspectives in Cultural Studies.* Berkeley and Los Angeles: University of California Press, 1991.

Mullin, Gerald W. *Flight and Rebellion: Slave Resistance in Eighteenth-Century Virginia.* New York: Oxford University Press, 1972.

Mumford, Lewis. *The Golden Day.* New York: Horace Liveright, 1926.

Nash, Gary B. *Red, White, and Black: The Peoples of Early America.* Englewood Cliffs, N.J.: Prentice-Hall, 1974.

Nash, Roderick. *Wilderness and the American Mind.* New Haven: Yale University Press, 1973.

Neale, R. S. *Class and Ideology in the Nineteenth Century.* London: Routledge and Kegan Paul, 1972.

Noble, David W. *The Eternal Adam and the New World Garden: The Central Myth in the American Novel Since 1830.* New York: George Braziller, 1968.

Norton, Mary Beth. *Liberty's Daughters: The Revolutionary Experience of Women, 1750–1800.* Boston: Little, Brown, 1980.

———. *Major Problems in American Women's History: Documents and Essays.* Lexington, Mass.: Heath, 1989.

———, et al. *A People and a Nation: A History of the United States.* 3d ed. Boston: Houghton Mifflin, 1991.

Oakes, James. *The Ruling Race: A History of American Slaveholders.* New York: Knopf, 1982; 2d ed., New York: Vintage, 1983.

O'Brien, John. "Factory, Church and Community: Blacks in Antebellum Richmond." *Journal of Southern History* 44 (November 1978): 509–36.

O'Faolain Sean. *The Vanishing Hero.* Boston: Little, Brown, 1957.

Okin, Susan Moller. *Women in Western Political Thought.* Princeton: Princeton University Press, 1979.

Orions, G. Harrison. "The Romance Ferment After *Waverley.*" *American Literature* 3 (January 1932): 408–31.

Osborne, William S. "Kennedy's *Horse-Shoe Robinson:* A Novel with 'the Utmost Historical Accuracy.'" *Maryland Historical Magazine* 59 (September 1964): 286–96.

Ostendorf, Berndt. *Black Literature in White America.* Sussex, Eng.: Harvester, 1982.

Osterweis, Rollin G. *The Myth of the Lost Cause, 1865–1900.* Hamden, Conn.: Archon, 1973.

———. *Romanticism and Nationalism in the Old South.* Gloucester, Mass.: Peter Smith, 1964.

Owens, Leslie Howard. *This Species of Property: Slave Life and Culture in the Old South.* New York: Oxford University Press, 1976.

Owsley, Frank L. *Plain Folk of the Old South.* Baton Rouge: Louisiana State University Press, 1949.

Owsley, Frank L. and Harriet C. Owsley. "The Economic Basis of Society in the Late Antebellum South." *Journal of Southern History* 6 (1940): 24–45.

———. "The Economic Structure of Rural Tennessee, 1850–1860." *Journal of Southern History* 8 (1942): 161–82.

Parker, Andrew, et al. *Nationalisms and Sexualities.* New York: Routledge, Chapman, and Hall, 1992.

Parker, William N., ed. *The Structure of the Cotton Economy of the Antebellum South.* Washington, D.C.: Agricultural Historical Society, 1970.

Parkhurst, Jesse W. "The Black Mammy in the Plantation Household." *Journal of Negro History* 23 (July 1938): 349–69.

Parks, Edd Winfield. *The Antebellum Southern Literary Critics.* Athens: University of Georgia Press, 1962.

———. *William Gilmore Simms as Literary Critic.* Athens: University of Georgia Press, 1961.

Parrington, Vernon L. *Main Currents in American Thought,* Vol. 2, 1800–1860: *The Romantic Revolution in America.* 1927. Reprint, New York: Harcourt, Brace, and World, 1954.

Pattee, Frederick Lewis. *The Feminine Fifties.* New York: Appleton-Century, 1940.

Patterson, Tim. "Notes on the Historical Application of Marxist Cultural Theory." *Science and Society* 39 (Fall 1975): 257–89.

Pearce, Roy Harvey. *Historicism Once More.* Princeton: Princeton University Press, 1969.

———. *Savagism and Civilization: A Study of the Indian and the American Mind.* Baltimore: Johns Hopkins University Press, 1965.

Peckham, Morse, ed. *Romanticism: The Culture of the Nineteenth Century.* New York: George Braziller, 1965.

Perdue, Theda. *Slavery and the Evolution of Cherokee Society, 1540–1866.* Knoxville: University of Tennessee Press, 1979.

Pessen, Edward. *Jacksonian America: Society, Personality, and Politics.* Homewood, Ill.: Dorsey, 1969.

——. *Riches, Class, and Power Before the Civil War.* Lexington, Mass.: Heath, 1973.

Petter, Henry. *The Early American Novel.* Columbus: Ohio State University Press, 1971.

Phillips, Ulrich Bonnell. *American Negro Slavery: A Survey of the Supply, Employment, and Control of Negro Labor As Determined by the Plantation Regime.* Baton Rouge: Louisiana State University Press, 1966.

——. "The Central Theme of Southern History." *American Historical Review* 34 (October 1928): 30–43.

——. *Life and Labor in the Old South.* Boston: Little, Brown, 1929.

Porte, Joel. *The Romance in America: Studies in Cooper, Poe, Hawthorne, Melville, and Jones.* Middletown, Conn.: Wesleyan University Press, 1969.

Pryse, Marjorie, and Hortense Spillers, eds. *Conjuring: Blacks, Women, Fiction, and Literary Tradition.* Bloomington: Indiana University Press, 1985.

Quarles, Benjamin. *The Negro in the American Revolution.* Chapel Hill: University of North Carolina Press, 1961. Reprint, New York: Norton, 1973.

——. *The Negro in the Civil War.* Boston: Little, Brown, 1953.

Quinn, Arthur Hobson. *American Fiction: An Historical and Critical Survey.* New York: Appleton-Century, 1962.

Raboteau, Albert J. *Slave Religion: The "Invisible Institution" in the Antebellum South.* New York: Oxford University Press, 1978.

Rawick, George P. *From Sundown to Sunup: The Making of the Black Community.* Westport, Conn.: Greenwood, 1972.

Reiter, Rayna R., ed. *Toward an Anthropology of Women.* New York: Monthly Review Press, 1975.

Reuter, Edward B. *The Mulatto in the United States.* New York: Negro Universities Press, 1969.

Rich, Adrienne. "Disloyal to Civilization: Feminism, Racism and Gynephobia." In her *On Lies, Secrets and Silences,* 275–310. New York: Norton, 1979.

——. "Husband Right and Father Right." In her *On Lies, Secrets and Silences,* 215–22. New York: Norton, 1979.

——. *Of Women Born: Motherhood as Experience and Institution.* New York: Bantam, 1977.

Richards, Leonard. *The Advent of American Democracy, 1815–1848.* Glenview, Ill.: Scott, Foresman, 1977.

——. *Gentlemen of Property and Standing: Anti-Abolition Mobs in Jacksonian America.* New York: Oxford University Press, 1970.

Ridgely, J. V. *John Pendleton Kennedy.* New York: Twayne, 1966.

——. *Nineteenth-Century Southern Literature.* Lexington: University Press of Kentucky, 1980.

——. *William Gilmore Simms.* New York: Twayne, 1962.

——. "*Woodcraft:* Simms's First Answer to *Uncle Tom's Cabin.*" *American Literature* 31 (January 1960): 420–33.

Ringe, Donald A. "The American Revolution in American Romance." *American Literature* 49 (November 1977): 352–65.

Roark, James L. *Masters Without Slaves: Southern Planters in the Civil War and Reconstruction.* New York: Norton, 1977.

Robinson, Lillian. "Dwelling in Decencies: Radical Criticism and the Feminist Perspective." *College English* 32 (May 1971): 879–89.

Rogers, Katharine M. *The Troublesome Helpmate: A History of Misogyny in Literature.* Seattle: University of Washington Press, 1966.

Rose, Alan Henry. "The Image of the Negro in the Pre-Civil War Novels of John Pendleton Kennedy and William Gilmore Simms." *Journal of American Studies* 4 (1970): 217–26.

Rosenberg, Charles E. "Sexuality, Class and Role in Nineteenth Century America." *American Quarterly* 25 (May 1973): 131–54.

Rourke, Constance. *American Humor: A Study of the National Character.* 1931. Reprint, New York: Harcourt Brace Jovanovich, 1959.

Rowbotham, Sheila. *Hidden From History: Rediscovering Women in History From the 17th Century to the Present.* New York: Vintage, 1976.

——. *Woman's Consciousness, Man's World.* London: Penguin, 1976.

——. *Women, Resistance and Revolution.* New York: Vintage, 1972.

Rubin, Louis Decimus, Jr. *The Edge of the Swamp: A Study in the Literature and Society of the Old South.* Baton Rouge: Louisiana State University Press, 1989.

——. *The Writer in the South.* Athens: University of Georgia Press, 1972.

——, ed. *The Comic Imagination in American Literature.* New Brunswick: Rutgers University Press, 1973.

Rubin, Louis Decimus, Jr., and C. Hugh Holman, eds. *Southern Literary Study: Problems and Possibilities.* Chapel Hill: University of North Carolina Press, 1975.

Rudich, Norman. *Weapons of Criticism: Marxism and the American Literary Tradition.* Palo Alto, Calif.: Ramparts, 1976.

Ruoff, John C. "Frivolity to Consumption: Or, Southern Womanhood in Antebellum Literature." *Civil War History* 18 (September 1972): 214–25.

Russell, Robert R. "The Effects of Slavery Upon Nonslaveholders in the Antebellum South." *Agricultural History* 15 (April 1941): 112–26.

Ryan, Mary P. *Cradle of the Middle Class: The Family in Oneida County, New York, 1790–1865.* New York: Cambridge University Press, 1981.

——. *Womanhood in America: From Colonial Times to the Present.* New York: New Viewpoints, 1975.

Salley, A. S. "William Gilmore Simms." In *The Letters of William Gilmore Simms,* edited by Mary C. Simms Oliphant, Alfred Taylor O'Dell, and T. C. Duncan Fines, vol. 1 lix–lxxix. Columbia: University of South Carolina Press, 1952.

Samuels, Shirley, ed. *The Culture of Sentiment: Race, Gender, and Sentimentality in Nineteenth Century America.* New York: Oxford University Press, 1992.

Sargent, Lydia. *Women and Revolution: A Discussion of the Unhappy Marriage of Marxism and Feminism.* Boston: South End, 1981.

Schlesinger, Arthur M., Jr. *The Age of Jackson.* Boston: Little, Brown, 1945.

Schluter, Herman. *Lincoln, Labor and Slavery.* New York: Russell and Russell, 1965.

Schochet, Gordon J. *Patriarchalism in Political Thought: The Authoritarian Family and Political Speculation and Attitudes Especially in Seventeenth-Century England.* Oxford, Basil Blackwell, 1975.

Scholes, Robert E. *Semiotics and Interpretation.* New Haven: Yale University Press, 1982.

Scott, Anne Firor. *The Southern Lady.* Chicago: University of Chicago Press, 1970.

Sedgwick, Eve Kosofsky. *Between Men: English Literature and Male Homosocial Desire.* New York: Columbia University Press, 1985.

Sellers, Charles Grier, Jr. *The Southerner as American.* Chapel Hill: University of North Carolina Press, 1960.

——. "Who Were the Southern Whigs?" *American Historical Review* 59 (1954): 335–46.

Shalhope, Robert E. "Race, Class, Slavery, and the Antebellum Southern Mind." *Journal of Southern History* 37 (November 1971): 557–74.

Shaw, Harry E. *The Forms of Historical Fiction: Sir Walter Scott and His Successors.* Ithaca: Cornell University Press, 1983.

Shillingsburg, Miriam J. "The Influence of Sectionalism on the Revision in Simms's Revolutionary Romances." *Mississippi Quarterly* 29 (Fall 1976): 526–38.

Shugg, Roger Wallace. *Origins of Class Struggle in Louisiana.* Baton Rouge: Louisiana State University Press, 1939.

Simonini, R. C., Jr. *Southern Writers: Appraisals in Our Time.* New York: Freeport, 1958.

Simpson, Lewis P. *The Dispossessed Garden: Pastoral and History in Southern Literature.* Athens: University of Georgia Press, 1975.

——. *The Man of Letters in New England and the South: Essays in the History of the Literary Vocation in America.* Baton Rouge: Louisiana State University Press, 1973.

Skaggs, Merrill Maguire. *The Folk of Southern Fiction.* Athens: University of Georgia Press, 1972.

Slater, Philip E. *The Glory of Hera: Greek Mythology and the Greek Family.* Boston: Beacon, 1968.

Slotkin, Richard. "Dreams and Genocide: The American Myth of Regeneration Through Violence." *Journal of Popular Culture* 5 (Summer 1971): 38–59.

——. *Regeneration Through Violence: The Mythology of the American Frontier, 1600–1860.* Middletown: Wesleyan University Press, 1973.

Smith, Barbara. *Home Girls: A Black Feminist Anthology.* New York: Kitchen Table, Women of Color Press, 1983.

Smith, C. A. *Southern Literary Studies.* Port Washington, N.Y.: Kennikat, 1927.

Smith, Henry Nash. *Democracy and the Novel: Popular Resistance to Classic American Writers.* New York: Oxford University Press, 1978.

——. "The Scribbling Woman and the Cosmic Success Story." *Critical Inquiry* 1 (September 1974): 47–70.

——. *The Virgin Land: The American West as Symbol and Myth.* New York: Vintage, 1950.

Smith, Lillian. *Killers of the Dream.* New York: Norton, 1949.

Smith-Rosenberg, Carroll. "Beauty, the Beast, and the Militant Woman: A Case Study in Sex Roles and Social Stress in Jacksonian America." *American Quarterly* 33 (October 1971): 562–84.

——. "The Female World of Love and Ritual: Relations Between Women in Nineteenth-Century America." *Signs* 1 (Autumn 1975): 1–29. Reprinted in her *Disorderly Conduct: Visions of Gender in Victorian America* (New York: Knopf, 1985), 53–76.

——. "The Hysterical Woman: Sex Roles and Role Conflict in Nineteenth-Century America." *Social Research* 39 (1972): 652–78.

Smith-Rosenberg, Carroll, and Charles Rosenberg. "The Female Animal: Medical and Biological Views of Woman and Her Role in Nineteenth-Century America." *Journal of American History* 9 (September 1973): 332–56.

Snavely, Tipton R. *George Tucker as Political Economist.* Charlottesville: University of Virginia Press, 1964.

Sobel, Mechal. *Trabelin' On: The Slave Journey to an Afro-Baptist Faith.* Princeton: Princeton University Press, 1979.

Sontag, Susan. *Under the Sign of Saturn.* New York: Farrar, Straus, and Giroux, 1980.

Spender, Dale. *Mothers of the Novel.* London: Pandora, 1986.

Spruill, Julia Cherry. *Woman's Life and Work in the Southern Colonies.* New York: Norton, 1972.

Stampp, Kenneth. "An Analysis of T. R. Dew's Review of the Debates in the Virginia Legislature." *Journal of Negro History* 27 (October 1942): 380–87.

——. *The Peculiar Institution: Slavery in the Ante-Bellum South.* New York: Vintage, 1956.

——. "Rebels and Sambos: The Search for the Negro's Personality in Slavery." *Journal of Southern History* 37 (August 1971): 367–92.

Starke, Catherine. *Black Portraiture in American Fiction: Stock Characters, Archetypes, and Individuals.* New York: Basic Books, 1971.

Starobin, Robert S. *Industrial Slavery in the Old South.* New York: Oxford University Press, 1970.

Stavenhagen, Rodolfo. *Social Classes in Agrarian Societies.* New York: Anchor, 1975.

Stuckey, Sterling. *Slave Culture: Nationalist Theory and the Foundations of Black America.* New York: Oxford University Press, 1987.

Stubbs, Patricia. *Women and Fiction: Feminism and the Novel, 1880–1920.* New York: Barnes and Noble, 1979.

Sydnor, Charles S. *The Development of Southern Sectionalism, 1819–1848.* Baton Rouge: Louisiana State University Press, 1948.

Takaki, Ronald T. *Iron Cages: Race and Culture in Nineteenth-Century America.* Seattle: University of Washington Press, 1979.

——. *A Proslavery Crusade: The Agitation to Reopen the African Slave Trade.* New York: Collier, Macmillan, 1971.

——. *Violence in the Black Imagination: Essays and Documents.* New York: Putnam, 1972.

Tandy, Jeanette Reid. "Pro-Slavery Propaganda in American Fiction of the Fifties." *South Atlantic Quarterly* 21 (January 1922): 41–50, 170–78.

Taylor, William Rogers. *Cavalier and Yankee: The Old South and the American Natural Character.* New York: Harper and Row, 1961.

Tebbel, John. *Between Covers: The Rise and Transformation of Book Publishing in America.* New York: Oxford University Press, 1987.

——. *A History of Book Publishing in the United States.* Vol. 1, *The Creation of an Industry, 1630–1865.* New York: Bowker, 1972.

Thomas, Keith. "The Double Standard," *Journal of the History of Ideas* 20 (1959): 195–216.

Thompson, E. P. "Eighteenth-Century English Society: Class Struggle Without Class?" *Social History* 3 (May 1978): 133–65.

——. "Time, Work-Discipline and Industrial Capitalism." *Past and Present* 38 (December 1967): 56–97.

Thorpe, Earl E. *Eros and Freedom in Southern Life and Thought.* Durham: Seeman Printery, 1967.

——. *The Mind of the Negro: An Intellectual History of Afro-Americans.* Westport, Conn.: Greenwood, 1970.

Tischler, Nancy M. *Black Masks: Negro Characters in Modern Southern Fiction.* University Park: The Pennsylvania State University Press, 1969.

Tise, Larry E. *Proslavery: A History of the Defense of Slavery in America, 1701–1840.* Athens: University of Georgia Press, 1987.

Toll, Robert C. *Blacking Up: The Minstrel Show in Nineteenth-Century America.* New York: Oxford University Press, 1974.

Tompkins, Jane. *Sensational Designs: The Cultural Work of American Fiction, 1790–1860.* New York: Oxford University Press, 1985.

Trent, William P. *William Gilmore Simms.* New York: Greenwood, 1892.

Trilling, Diana. "The Image of Women in Contemporary Literature." In *The Woman in America,* edited by Robert J. Lifton, 52–71. Boston: Beacon, 1964.

Tucker, Beverley D., and Percy Winfield Turrentine. *Nathaniel Beverley Tucker: Prophet of the Confederacy, 1784–1851.* Tokyo, Japan: Nan'Un-do, 1979.

Tuckerman, Henry. *The Life of John Pendleton Kennedy.* New York: Putnam, 1871.

Turner, Frederick Jackson. *Rise of the New West, 1819–1829.* New York: Collier, 1962.

Van Doren, Carl. *The American Novel.* New York: Macmillan, 1931.

Vauthier, Simone. "Of Time and the South: The Fiction of William Gilmore Simms." *Southern Literary Journal* 5 (Fall 1972): 3–45.

Veblen, Thorstein, "The Barbarian Status of Women." In *Essays on the Changing Order,* edited by Leon Ardgrooni, 50–64. New York: Viking, 1934.

Violette, Augusta Genevieve. *Economic Feminism in American Literature Prior to 1848.* Orono, Maine: University Press, 1925.

Wade, Richard C. *Slavery in the Cities: The South, 1820–1860.* New York: Oxford University Press, 1964.

Wakelyn, Jon L. *The Politics of a Literary Man: William Gilmore Simms.* Westport, Conn.: Greenwood, 1973.

Walker, Alice. *In Search of Our Mothers' Gardens.* New York: Harcourt Brace Jovanovich, 1983.

Wallace, Anthony F. C. *Rockdale: The Growth of an American Village in the Early Industrial Revolution.* New York: Knopf, 1978.

Wallace, Michael. "Changing Concepts of Party in the United States: New York, 1815–1828." *American Historical Review* 74 (1968): 453–91.

——. "Paternalism and Violence." *Violence and Aggression in the History of Ideas,* edited by Philip P. Wiener and John Fisher, 203–20. New Brunswick: Rutgers University Press, 1972.

Ward, John William. *Andrew Jackson: Symbol for an Age.* New York: Oxford University Press, 1955.

Ware, Caroline F. *The Early New England Cotton Manufacture.* Boston: Houghton Mifflin Co., 1931.

Warner, William Beatty. *Reading Clarissa: The Struggle of Interpretation.* New Haven: Yale University Press, 1979.

Wasson, Richard. "New Marxist Criticism: Introduction." *College English* 34 (November 1972): 169–73.

Waters, Ronald G. "The Erotic South: Civilization and Sexuality in American Abolitionism." *American Quarterly* 25 (May 1973): 177–201.

Watson, Charles S. "Simms and the American Revolution." *Mississippi Quarterly* 29 (Fall 1976): 498–500.

——. "Simms's Answer to *Uncle Tom's Cabin:* Criticism of the South in *Woodcraft.*" *Southern Literary Journal* 9 (Fall 1976): 78–90.

——. "Simms's Review of *Uncle Tom's Cabin.*" *American Literature* 48 (1976): 365–68.

Watt, Ian. *The Rise of the Novel: Studies in Defoe, Richardson, and Fielding.* Berkeley and Los Angeles: University of California Press, 1974.

Weaver, Herbert. *Mississippi Farmers, 1850–1860.* Nashville: Vanderbilt University Press, 1945.

Weaver, Richard M. *The Southern Tradition at Bay: A History of Postbellum Thought.* New Rochelle, N.Y.: Arlington House, 1968.

Wecter, Dixon. *The Hero in America: A Chronicle of Hero-Worship.* New York: Scribner, 1969.

Weidman, Bette S. "White Man's Red Man: A Penitential Reading of Four American Novels." *Modern Language Studies* 4 (Fall 1974): 14–26.

Weinstein, Allen, and Frank Otto Gatell. *American Negro Slavery: A Modern Reader.* New York: Oxford University Press, 1973.

Welsh, John R. "William Gilmore Simms, Critic of the South." *Journal of Southern History* 26 (May 1960): 201–14.

Welter, Barbara. "The Cult of True Womanhood, 1820–1860." *American Quarterly* 18 (Summer 1966): 151–74.

——. *Dimity Convictions: The American Woman in the Nineteenth Century.* Athens: Ohio University Press, 1976.

Welter, Rush. *The Mind of America, 1820–1860.* New York: Columbia University Press, 1975.

White, Deborah Gray. *Ar'n't I a Woman? Female Slaves in the Plantation South*. New York: Norton, 1985.

Whitlaw, Roger. *Black American Literature: A Critical Inquiry*. Chicago: Nelson Hall, 1973.

Wiener, Jonathan M. "Female Planters and Planters' Wives in the Civil War and Reconstruction: Alabama, 1850–1870." *Alabama Review* 30 (April 1977): 135–49.

——. *Social Origins of the New South: Alabama, 1860–1885*. Baton Rouge: Louisiana State University Press, 1978.

Wilentz, Sean. *Chants Democratic: New York City and the Rise of the American Working Class, 1788–1850*. New York: Oxford University Press, 1984.

——. "On Class and Politics in Jacksonian America." *Reviews in American History* 10 (December 1982): 45–63.

Williams, Eric. *Capitalism and Slavery*. New York: Capricorn, 1966.

Williams, Raymond. "Base and Superstructure in Marxist Cultural Theory." *New Left Review* 82 (November–December 1973): 3–16.

——. *The Country and the City*. New York: Oxford University Press, 1973.

——. *Culture and Society, 1780–1950*. New York: Anchor, 1960.

——. *Keywords: A Vocabulary of Culture and Society*. New York: Oxford University Press, 1976.

——. *Marxism and Literature*. London: Oxford University Press, 1977.

——. *The Sociology of Culture*. New York: Schocken, 1982.

Wilson, Edmund. *Patriotic Gore: Studies in the Literature of the American Civil War*. New York: Oxford University Press, 1969.

Wimsatt, Mary Ann. *The Major Fiction of William Gilmore Simms: Cultural Traditions and Literary Form*. Baton Rouge: Louisiana State University Press, 1989.

——. "Simms and Irving." *Mississippi Quarterly* 20 (Winter 1965–66): 25–37.

——. "Simms as a Novelist of Manners: *Katherine Walton*." *Southern Literary Journal* 5 (Fall 1972): 68–88.

Wolfe, Margaret Ripley. "The Southern Lady: Long-Suffering Counterpart of the 'Good Ole Boy.'" *Journal of Popular Culture* 11 (Summer 1977): 18–27.

Wolff, Cynthia Griffen. "A Mirror for Men: Stereotypes of Women in Literature." In *Woman: An Issue,* edited by Lee Edwards, Mary Heath, and Lsa Baskin, 205–18. Special issue of *Massachusetts Review* 13 (Winter–Spring 1972).

Woloch, Nancy. *Women and the American Experience*. 2d ed. New York: McGraw-Hill, 1994.

Wood, Gordon S. *The Creation of the American Republic, 1776–1787*. Chapel Hill: University of North Carolina Press, 1969, and New York: Norton, 1972.

Wood, Peter H. *Black Majority: Negroes in South Carolina from 1670 through the Stono Rebellion*. New York: Knopf, 1971.

Woodward, C. Vann. *The Burden of Southern History*. Baton Rouge: Louisiana State University Press, 1960; 3d ed., 1993.

Wright, Gavin. *The Political Economy of the Cotton South*. New York: Norton, 1978.

Wrobel, Arthur. "'Romantic Realism': Nathaniel Beverley Tucker." *American Literature* 43 (November 1970): 325–35.

Wyatt-Brown, Bertram. *Southern Honor: Ethics and Behavior in the Old South*. New York: Oxford University Press, 1982.

Yellin, Jean Fagan. *The Intricate Knot: Black Figures in American Literature, 1776–1863*. New York: New York University Press, 1972.

Young, Alfred F., ed. *The American Revolution: Explorations in the History of American Radicalism*. DeKalb: Northern Illinois University Press, 1976.

Zaretsky, Eli. *Capitalism, The Family, and Personal Life*. New York: Harper, 1976.

Zimbalist, Michele, and Louise Lamphere, eds. *Women, Culture, and Society*. Stanford: Stanford University Press, 1974.

Index

Abolitionist fiction, 142–43, 174
Abolitionists, 29–31, 249n. 5. *See also*
  Slavery, institution of
African Americans. *See also* Black men;
  Black women; Master-slave relationship; Slavery, institution of
  in American Revolution, 174, 212, 259n.
    20, 270n. 14
  culture of resistance and, 74, 174
  depiction of black children, 145, 148
  families of, 104, 114, 115–17, 174
  Jacksonian politics and, 27–28
  in Northern *vs.* Southern antebellum
    novels, 215
  rebellion by, 146–47, 174, 215, 259n. 19
  relations between poor whites and,
    167–68
  representation of lives as slaves, 143,
    144–50
  representation of views of, 56, 145–47,
    160
  stereotyping of, 42–43, 59, 60–61, 90,
    147, 149–50, 215, 248n. 30, 259n. 20
Allport, Gordon, 44
American cultural identity, 33
American politics, in antebellum period,
  27–29, 31–32
American Revolution
  African Americans in, 174, 212, 259n. 20,
    270n. 14
  generational differences over, 183,
    188–89
  non-plantation whites in, 187, 197–99,
    203
  planter hero in, 9, 18, 39, 40, 155, 183,
    197, 203, 205–6
Antislavery activism. *See* Abolitionists
Audience, 21–22, 26

Bacon, Nathaniel, 247n. 16
Beauvoir, Simone de, 3, 73
Behn, Aphra, 34
Belle, the, 75–90
  passive heroine stereotype and, 76–82
  personality characteristics of, 75–76
  strong women characters and, 82–90
Bernier, François, 152
Bibb, Henry, 140
Black men
  attempted emasculation of, 17–18, 147,
    155–56, 172, 212
  sexuality of, 18–19, 58, 72, 143–44, 162–
    64, 242n. 24
Black women
  as "good" mothers, 105–6, 115–17
  "Jezebel" stereotype and, 72, 90, 103,
    248n. 30
  "mammy" figure and, 61, 115, 144
  representation of, 56, 59, 61, 70, 72, 90,
    103, 117
  sexual abuse of, 14, 70, 72, 90, 174
Blassingame, John, 3, 147, 151, 259n. 20
Bledstein, Burton J., 229n. 2
Blumenbach, Johann Friedrich, 152
Bohner, Charles H., 25, 230n. 13
Bonner, James G., 177
Border Beagles (Simms), 176
  belle characters in, 76, 81–82
  fallen women in, 95–97
  hero in, 254n. 18
  major figures in, 221
  poor whites in, 194–95
  yeoman farmer in, 210–11
Border romance
  American themes in, 113–15
  female nurture and, 106
  frontier whites and, 194–96

major figures in works by, 220

master-slave relationship and, 156–58, 168, 169

motherhood and, 109–11, 117–18

personal politics *vs.* proslavery writing of, 213

plantation mistress in, 104, 105, 107, 108, 109

political beliefs of, 267n. 8

poor whites and, 117–18, 186–88, 267n. 2

quoted on slavery, 140

rebellious blacks and, 146–47

Rob of the Bowl, 220

spinsters in, 92, 93–94

standard of living problem and, 147

works by, 220

yeoman farmer and, 200–203

Kerber, Linda, 12

Knights of the Golden Horse-Shoe (Caruthers)

belle characters in, 88

fallen women in, 95, 97–98, 100, 103

issue of sexuality and, 143

major figures in, 220

mistress-slave relationship and, 259n. 21

rebellious blacks and, 146

spinsters in, 92–93

yeoman farmer in, 197–200

Lafayette, James Armistead, 241n. 22

LeClear, Thomas, 42

Leclerc, Georges Louis, comte de Buffon, 152

Levine, George, 45–46, 239n. 39

Levine, Lawrence, 3, 151

Liberalism

antebellum Southern opposition to, 217

James Ewell Heath and, 4, 49, 50, 56, 64–65

Northern society and, 10, 13, 196

pre-1830s plantation novels and, 48, 49, 50, 56, 64–65

Liberation movements, 217, 234n. 46

Lippmann, Walter, 43–44

Locke, John, 11, 15

Longstreet, Augustus Baldwin, *Georgia Scenes,* 177, 264n. 2

Lukács, Georg, 39

Macherey, Pierre, *A Theory of Literary Production,* 257n. 4

"Mammy" figure, 61, 115, 144

"Manifest destiny," 41, 153, 196, 269n. 3

Marriage, institution of. *See also* Unmarried women

paternalism and, 17

reproduction of class relations and, 50–54, 181–83

women's freedom and, 54, 55–56

Martineau, Harriet, 14

Society in America, 153, 154, 262n. 32

Marx, Karl, 1–2, 231n. 23

Masculinity

black masculinity and, 17–18, 147, 155–56, 215, 259n. 20

cult of, 17, 111, 183–84

female nurture and, 106, 109–11, 113

in Northern *vs.* Southern antebellum novels, 214–15

passive femininity and, 82

planter-class superiority and, 155–56, 197, 209–10, 211–12, 214

sentimental novel and, 230n. 11

Master-slave relationship, 151–74, 228n. 27. *See also* Mistress-slave relationship

character of, 16, 58, 149

in pre-1830s plantation novels, 64

in proslavery *vs.* abolitionist fiction, 142–43

relationships among slaves and, 169–70

romantic attachments and, 103

social relationships of production and, 144–45

Mellichampe (Simms), 270n. 17

belle characters of, 84–86

black men in battle roles and, 270n. 14

class relations in, 168, 259n. 21

major figures in, 221

yeoman farmer in, 203, 206, 207, 208–10

Melville, Herman, 22, 41

"Benito Cereno," 215

proslavery argument and, 29–32
role of women in class relations and,
50–54, 75
sexual abuse of lower classes by, 256n.
33
slaveholding in definition of, 263n. 1
social relations with subordinate
groups and, 16–17, 117
Southern novel as cultural artifact of,
5, 217–18
stratification within, 63–64
Planter hero
in American Revolution, 9, 18, 39, 40,
155, 183, 197, 203, 205–6
domination of the Other and, 4–5
freedom of, 55–56
masculinity and, 155–56, 210, 214–15
role in Southern literature, 35–36, 39–
41
Poor-white class. *See also* Yeoman class
"bad" mothers and, 122–24
crime and, 186–88, 189
degraded condition of, 178, 189
"good" mothers and, 105–6, 117–20,
192
origins of, 177–78
planter-class relations with, 17, 178–
80, 205–6
relations with black slaves, 168
representation of, 185–96
symbolic role in Southern literature,
35–36
Power
institutionalization of, 1–2
paternalism as mask for, 16–17, 90,
173
Projection theory, and stereotyping, 42–
46
Prostitution, 92
Public-private dichotomy, 106, 268n. 1
Publishing houses in antebellum period,
20–22

Race, concept of, 152, 260n. 4
Racism
black internalization of, 58
class conflict and, 31, 234n. 48
interracial friendships and, 238n. 27

Northern *vs.* Southern antebellum
novels and, 215
plantation mythology and, 216
Rape of white women, 13, 123. *See also*
Miscegenation
Rawick, George, 3, 151
Rebellious blacks, 146–47, 174, 259n. 19
Religion. *See also* Christianity
African Americans and, 146
poor whites and, 191–93
in Southern society, 145–46, 194
Representation, concept of, 45–46, 239n.
39
Republican motherhood, 12
Republican virtue, ideal of, 10–12, 27
Rich, Adrienne, 3, 106
Richard Hurdis (Simms), 255n. 25. *See also*
Border Beagles
hero in, 254n. 18
major figures in, 221
master-slave relationship in, 159
mothers in, 110, 112–14, 119–20, 254n. 20
poor whites in, 119–20, 186, 194–95
Richardson, Samuel, 9, 33
Clarissa, 34, 35, 71, 235n. 8
Pamela, 34, 35, 71
Ripley, Alexandra, 271n. 5
Roark, James L., 179, 265n. 10
Rogers, Katherine, 72
Romantic form, conservatism of, 4–5,
215–16. *See also* Historical novel;
Southern historical romance
Rowbotham, Sheila, 3, 68
Rowson, Susannah, 34
Ruffin, Edmund, 30
Ruling class, 1–2, 27. *See also* Planter
class

"Sambo" stereotype, 78–79, 144, 154–56,
261n. 9
Scott, Anne Firor, 3, 245n. 18
Scott, Sir Walter, 9, 34
family background of, 38
Rob Roy, 39
romantic tradition and, 3, 36–39
social philosophy of, 38, 236n. 18
Southern writers and, 37–39
Waverley, 38